SOLARO

STUDY GUIDE

Mathematics 9 Applied

Foundations of Mathematics (MFM1P)

SOLARO Study Guide is designed to help students achieve success in school. The content in each study guide is 100% curriculum aligned and serves as an excellent source of material for review and practice. To create this book, teachers, curriculum specialists, and assessment experts have worked closely to develop the instructional pieces that explain each of the key concepts for the course. The practice questions and sample tests have detailed solutions that show problem-solving methods, highlight concepts that are likely to be tested, and point out potential sources of errors. ***SOLARO Study Guide*** is a complete guide to be used by students throughout the school year for reviewing and understanding course content, and to prepare for assessments.

Rao, Gautam, 1961 –
THE KEY – Math 9 Applied Ontario (MFM1P)

1. Mathematics – Juvenile Literature. I. Title

Castle Rock Research Corp.
2410 Manulife Place
10180 – 101 Street
Edmonton, AB T5J 3S4

4 5 6 FP 13 12 11

Publisher
Gautam Rao

Contributors
Monica Dhamrait
Bill Glover
Alan Jones
Betty Morris
Ron Zukowsky

CASTLE ROCK
RESEARCH CORP

Dedicated to the memory of Dr. V. S. Rao

SOLARO STUDY GUIDE—Mathematics 9 Applied Foundations of Mathematics (MFM1P)

SOLARO STUDY GUIDE consists of the following sections:

Key Tips for Being Successful at School gives examples of study and review strategies. It includes information about learning styles, study schedules, and note taking for test preparation.

Class Focus includes a unit on each area of the curriculum. Units are divided into sections, each focusing on one of the specific expectations, or main ideas, that students must learn about in that unit. Examples, definitions, and visuals help to explain each main idea. Practice questions on the main ideas are also included. At the end of each unit is a test on the important ideas covered. The practice questions and unit tests help students identify areas they know and those they need to study more. They can also be used as preparation for tests and quizzes. Most questions are of average difficulty, though some are easy and some are hard—the harder questions are called *Challenger Questions*. Each unit is prefaced by a ***Table of Correlations***, which correlates questions in the unit (and in the practice tests at the end of the book) to the specific curriculum expectations. Answers and solutions are found at the end of each unit.

Key Strategies for Success on Tests helps students get ready for tests. It shows students different types of questions they might see, word clues to look for when reading them, and hints for answering them.

Practice Tests includes one to three tests based on the entire course. They are very similar to the format and level of difficulty that students may encounter on final tests. In some regions, these tests may be reprinted versions of official tests, or reflect the same difficulty levels and formats as official versions. This gives students the chance to practice using real-world examples. Answers and complete solutions are provided at the end of the section.

For the complete curriculum document (including specific expectations along with examples and sample problems), visit http://www.edu.gov.on.ca/eng/curriculum/

SOLARO STUDY GUIDE *Study Guides* are available for many courses. Check www.castlerockresearch.com for a complete listing of books available for your area.

For information about any of our resources or services, please call Castle Rock Research at 1.800.840.6224 or visit our website at http://www.castlerockresearch.com.

At Castle Rock Research, we strive to produce an error-free resource. If you should find an error, please contact us so that future editions can be corrected.

TABLE OF CONTENTS

Key Tips for being Successful at School

KEY TIPS FOR BEING SUCCESSFUL AT SCHOOL

KEY FACTORS CONTRIBUTING TO SCHOOL SUCCESS

In addition to learning the content of your courses, there are some other things that you can do to help you do your best at school. You can try some of the following strategies:

- **Keep a positive attitude:** Always reflect on what you can already do and what you already know.
- **Be prepared to learn:** Have the necessary pencils, pens, notebooks, and other required materials for participating in class ready.
- **Complete all of your assignments:** Do your best to finish all of your assignments. Even if you know the material well, practice will reinforce your knowledge. If an assignment or question is difficult for you, work through it as far as you can so that your teacher can see exactly where you are having difficulty.
- **Set small goals for yourself when you are learning new material:** For example, when learning the parts of speech, do not try to learn everything in one night. Work on only one part or section each study session. When you have memorized one particular part of speech and understand it, move on to another one. Continue this process until you have memorized and learned all the parts of speech.
- **Review your classroom work regularly at home:** Review to make sure you understand the material you learned in class.

- **Ask your teacher for help:** Your teacher will help you if you do not understand something or if you are having a difficult time completing your assignments.
- **Get plenty of rest and exercise:** Concentrating in class is hard work. It is important to be well-rested and have time to relax and socialize with your friends. This helps you keep a positive attitude about your schoolwork.
- **Eat healthy meals:** A balanced diet keeps you healthy and gives you the energy you need for studying at school and at home.

How to Find Your Learning Style

Every student learns differently. The manner in which you learn best is called your learning style. By knowing your learning style, you can increase your success at school. Most students use a combination of learning styles. Do you know what type of learner you are? Read the following descriptions. Which of these common learning styles do you use most often?

- **Linguistic Learner:** You may learn best by saying, hearing, and seeing words. You are probably really good at memorizing things such as dates, places, names, and facts. You may need to write down the steps in a process, a formula, or the actions that lead up to a significant event, and then say them out loud.
- **Spatial Learner:** You may learn best by looking at and working with pictures. You are probably really good at puzzles, imagining things, and reading maps and charts. You may need to use strategies like mind mapping and webbing to organize your information and study notes.
- **Kinesthetic Learner:** You may learn best by touching, moving, and figuring things out using manipulatives. You are probably really good at physical activities and learning through movement. You may need to draw your finger over a diagram to remember it, tap out the steps needed to solve a problem, or feel yourself writing or typing a formula.

SCHEDULING STUDY TIME

You should review your class notes regularly to ensure that you have a clear understanding of all the new material you learned. Reviewing your lessons on a regular basis helps you to learn and remember ideas and concepts. It also reduces the quantity of material that you need to study prior to a test. Establishing a study schedule will help you to make the best use of your time.

Regardless of the type of study schedule you use, you may want to consider the following suggestions to maximize your study time and effort:

- Organize your work so that you begin with the most challenging material first.
- Divide the subject's content into small, manageable chunks.
- Alternate regularly between your different subjects and types of study activities in order to maintain your interest and motivation.
- Make a daily list with headings like "Must Do," "Should Do," and "Could Do."
- Begin each study session by quickly reviewing what you studied the day before.
- Maintain your usual routine of eating, sleeping, and exercising to help you concentrate better for extended periods of time.

Creating Study Notes

Mind-Mapping or Webbing

Use the key words, ideas, or concepts from your reading or class notes to create a mind map or web (a diagram or visual representation of the given information). A mind map or web is sometimes referred to as a knowledge map. Use the following steps to create a mind map or web:

1. Write the key word, concept, theory, or formula in the centre of your page.
2. Write down related facts, ideas, events, and information, and link them to the central concept with lines.
3. Use coloured markers, underlining, or symbols to emphasize things such as relationships, timelines, and important information.

The following examples of a Frayer Model illustrate how this technique can be used to study vocabulary.

Perimeter

Definition	Notes
• Perimeter is the distance around the outside of a polygon.	• Perimeter is measured in linear units (e.g., metres, centimetres, and so on).
Examples	**Non-Examples**
• The length of a fence around a yard • The distance around a circle (circumference)	• The area of grass covering a lawn • The size of a rug lying on a floor

Cube

Definition	Notes
• A cube is a solid 3-D object with six faces.	• A cube is different from other shapes because it has six equally-sized square faces, eight vertices, and twelve equal edges.
Examples	**Non-Examples**
	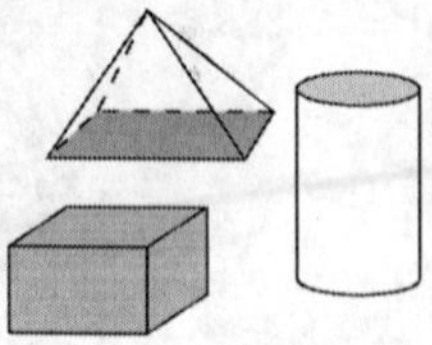

INDEX CARDS

To use index cards while studying, follow these steps:

1. Write a key word or question on one side of an index card.
2. On the reverse side, write the definition of the word, answer to the question, or any other important information that you want to remember.

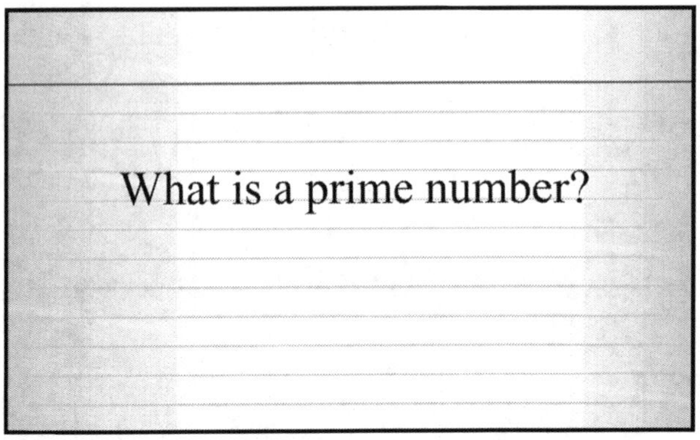

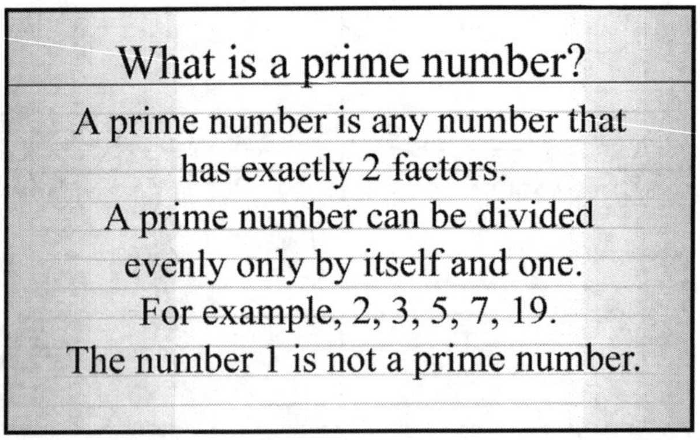

SYMBOLS AND STICKY NOTES—IDENTIFYING IMPORTANT INFORMATION

Use symbols to mark your class notes. The following are some examples:

- An exclamation mark (!) might be used to point out something that must be learned well because it is a very important idea.
- A question mark (?) may highlight something you are not certain about
- A diamond (◊) or asterisk (*) could highlight interesting information that you want to remember.

Sticky notes are useful in the following situations:

- Use sticky notes when you are not allowed to put marks in books.
- Use sticky notes to mark a page in a book that contains an important diagram, formula, explanation, or other information.
- Use sticky notes to mark important facts in research books.

MEMORIZATION TECHNIQUES

- **Association** relates new learning to something you already know. For example, to remember the spelling difference between dessert and desert, recall that the word *sand* has only one *s*. So, because there is sand in a desert, the word *desert* has only one *s*.
- **Mnemonic** devices are sentences that you create to remember a list or group of items. For example, the first letter of each word in the phrase "Every Good Boy Deserves Fudge" helps you to remember the names of the lines on the treble-clef staff (E, G, B, D, and F) in music.

- **Acronyms** are words that are formed from the first letters or parts of the words in a group. For example, RADAR is actually an acronym for Radio Detecting and Ranging, and MASH is an acronym for Mobile Army Surgical Hospital. HOMES helps you to remember the names of the five Great Lakes (Huron, Ontario, Michigan, Erie, and Superior).
- **Visualizing** requires you to use your mind's eye to "see" a chart, list, map, diagram, or sentence as it is in your textbook or notes, on the chalkboard or computer screen, or in a display.
- **Initialisms** are abbreviations that are formed from the first letters or parts of the words in a group. Unlike acronyms, an initialism cannot be pronounced as a word itself. For example, GCF is an initialism for **G**reatest **C**ommon **F**actor.

KEY STRATEGIES FOR REVIEWING

Reviewing textbook material, class notes, and handouts should be an ongoing activity. Spending time reviewing becomes more critical when you are preparing for a test. You may find some of the following review strategies useful when studying during your scheduled study time:

- Before reading a selection, preview it by noting the headings, charts, graphs, and chapter questions.
- Before reviewing a unit, note the headings, charts, graphs, and chapter questions.
- Highlight key concepts, vocabulary, definitions, and formulas.
- Skim the paragraph, and note the key words, phrases, and information.
- Carefully read over each step in a procedure.
- Draw a picture or diagram to help make the concept clearer.

KEY STRATEGIES FOR SUCCESS: A CHECKLIST

Reviewing is a huge part of doing well at school and preparing for tests. Here is a checklist for you to keep track of how many suggested strategies for success you are using. Read each question, and put a check mark (✓) in the correct column. Look at the questions where you have checked the "No" column. Think about how you might try using some of these strategies to help you do your best at school.

Key Strategies for Success	Yes	No
Do you attend school regularly?		
Do you know your personal learning style—how you learn best?		
Do you spend 15 to 30 minutes a day reviewing your notes?		
Do you study in a quiet place at home?		
Do you clearly mark the most important ideas in your study notes?		
Do you use sticky notes to mark texts and research books?		
Do you practise answering multiple-choice and written-response questions?		
Do you ask your teacher for help when you need it?		
Are you maintaining a healthy diet and sleep routine?		
Are you participating in regular physical activity?		

and Algebra

NUMBER SENSE AND ALGEBRA

Table of Correlations				
	Specific Expectation	**Practice Questions**	**Unit Test Questions**	
NA1.01	*illustrate equivalent ratios, using a variety of tools*	1, 2, 3, 4	1, 2	
NA1.02	*represent, using equivalent ratios and proportions, directly proportional relationships arising from realistic situations*	5, 6, 7, 8	3, 4	
NA1.03	*solve for the unknown value in a proportion, using a variety of methods*	9, NR 1, NR 2, 10	NR1	
NA1.04	*make comparisons using unit rates*	11, 12, 13, 14	5, 6, 7	
NA1.05	*solve problems involving ratios, rates, and directly proportional relationships in various contexts using a variety of methods*	15, 16, NR 3, 17	NR2, OR1	
NA1.06	*solve problems requiring the expression of percents, fractions, and decimals in their equivalent forms*	18, 19, 20, NR 4, OR 1	9, 10, OR1	
NA2.01	*simplify numerical expressions involving integers and rational numbers, with and without the use of technology*	NR 5, 21, 22	11, 12	
NA2.02	*relate their understanding of inverse operations to squaring and taking the square root, and apply inverse operations to simplify expressions and solve equations*	NR 6, 23, 24, 25	13, 14	
NA2.03	*describe the relationship between the algebraic and geometric representations of a single-variable term up to degree three [i.e., length, which is one dimensional, can be represented by x; area, which is two dimensional, can be represented by (x)(x) or x^2; volume, which is three dimensional, can be represented by (x)(x)(x), (x^2)(x), or x^3]*	26, 27, 28, 29	15, 16	
NA2.04	*substitute into and evaluate algebraic expressions involving exponents (i.e., evaluate expressions involving natural-number exponents with rational-number bases)*	30, 31, 32, 33	17, 18	
NA2.05	*add and subtract polynomials involving the same variable up to degree three, using a variety of tools*	34, 35, 36, 37	19, 20	
NA2.06	*multiply a polynomial by a monomial involving the same variable to give results up to degree three, using a variety of tools*	38, 39, 40, 41	21, 22	
NA2.07	*solve first-degree equations with non-fractional coefficients, using a variety of tools and strategies*	42, 43, 44, 45	23, 24	
NA2.08	*substitute into algebraic equations and solve for one variable in the first degree*	NR 7, 46, 47, 48, OR 2	NR3, 25, OR2	

NUMBER SENSE AND ALGEBRA

NA1.01 illustrate equivalent ratios, using a variety of tools

EQUIVALENT RATIOS

A **ratio** is a comparison of two or more numbers with the same units. Two-term ratios can be presented in several different forms; for example, 3:5, 3 to 5, or $\frac{3}{5}$. These ratios are called two-term ratios because they contain two numbers.
The order of the terms in a ratio is important. Terms in a ratio are written in the order in which they are presented in a question.

Example

Using ratio form, write a ratio that compares the number of shaded circles to the number of unshaded circles.

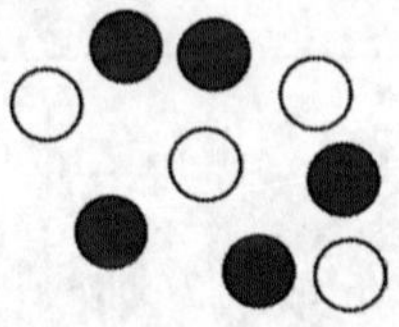

There are five shaded circles and four unshaded circles. Since the question mentions shaded circles first, the number of shaded circles will be the first term in the ratio. Therefore, the ratio of shaded circles to unshaded circles is 5:4.

A ratio may also consist of more than two terms. In the above example, if you compare the number of shaded circles to the number of unshaded circles to the total number of circles, you get a ratio of 5:4:9.

All terms in a ratio must be expressed using the same unit of measurement.

Example

Express the times 30 minutes and 2 hours as a ratio.

The times must be converted to the same unit of measurement before they can be compared in a ratio. Since $1 \text{ h} = 60 \text{ min} \Rightarrow 2 \text{ h} = 120 \text{ min}$. Remove the units from the terms, and write the ratio in minutes as 30:120.

Equivalent ratios are ratios that express the same comparison using different terms. When they are written as being equal, the two ratios are called **proportions**.

Example

Show that 2:3 is equivalent to 4:6 and 6:9, and then write the ratios as proportions.

This could be shown pictorially as follows:

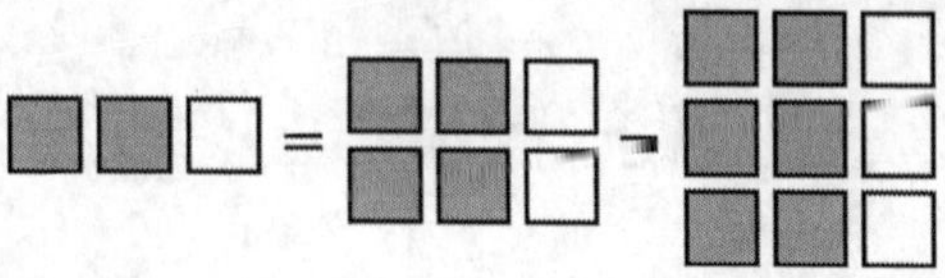

2:3 = 4:6 = 6:9

(two out of 3) = (four out of 6) = (six out of 9)

$$\frac{2}{3}=\frac{4}{6}=\frac{6}{9}$$

Each diagram contains one more row of squares than the previous diagram.
This could also be shown algebraically by multiplying each term of the first ratio by the same number.

$$2:3 = 2\times2:3\times2 = 4:6$$
$$2:3 = 2\times3:3\times3 = 6:9$$

Sometimes, it is difficult to determine if ratios are equivalent, but it becomes clear when each ratio is written in lowest terms.

Example

Does $\frac{3}{15} = \frac{5}{25}$?

Compare the two fractions by reducing each fraction to lowest terms. If the two fractions are the same when they are written in lowest terms, they are equivalent. If the two fractions are different when written in lowest terms, they are not equivalent.

$\frac{3}{15} = \frac{3 \div 3}{15 \div 3} = \frac{1}{5}$ and $\frac{5}{25} = \frac{5 \div 5}{25 \div 5} = \frac{1}{5}$

Since $\frac{1}{5} = \frac{1}{5}$, then $\frac{3}{15} = \frac{5}{25}$.

PRACTICE QUESTIONS

Use the following information to answer the next 2 questions.

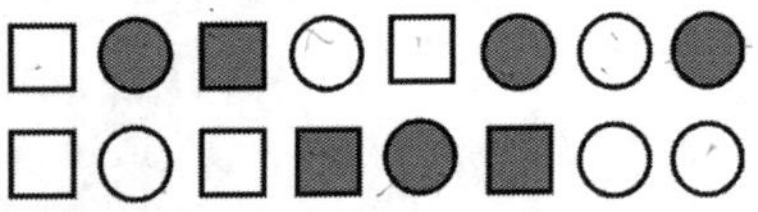

1. The ratio of shaded squares to shaded circles in the diagram is

A. 4:3

B. 3:4

C. 4:4

D. 3:5

2. Which of the following ratios is equivalent to the ratio of unshaded circles to the total number of shapes?

A. $\frac{1}{4}$

B. $\frac{8}{32}$

C. $\frac{15}{48}$

D. $\frac{32}{10}$

Use the following information to answer the next question.

> The largest planet in the solar system is Jupiter, and the second largest planet is Saturn. Compared to these planets, Earth is quite small.

3. A three-term ratio comparing the size of Jupiter to the size of Earth to the size of Saturn is 33:3:30. Expressed in its simplest form, this ratio is

A. 11:1:10

B. 11:3:10

C. 10:1:11

D. 13:1:3

CHALLENGER QUESTION

4. In which of the following proportions are the ratios equivalent?

A. $\frac{2}{3} = \frac{10}{25}$

B. $\frac{3}{8} = \frac{18}{42}$

C. $\frac{75}{60} = \frac{36}{24}$

D. $\frac{9}{15} = \frac{21}{35}$

NA1.02 represent, using equivalent ratios and proportions, directly proportional relationships arising from realistic situations

PROPORTIONAL RELATIONSHIPS

When working with proportions, given one complete ratio and a part or portion of another ratio, the goal is to make two equivalent ratios.

Example

The ratio of height to base of a skateboard ramp is 2:3. If the height of the ramp is changed to 4.5 m, what proportion could be used to determine the base?

To write this proportion, use the symbol b to represent the base of the new ramp.

$2:3 = 4.5:b$ **or** $\frac{2}{3} = \frac{4.5}{b}$

Sometimes, it is useful to convert the given ratio so that one term is equal to 1.
For example, in the above problem, this directly related proportion would be easier to understand if the top term in the first ratio was converted to 1. This could be accomplished by dividing each of the two terms in the first ratio by 2.

$$\frac{2}{3} = \frac{2 \div 2}{3 \div 2} = \frac{1}{1.5}$$

Now, align the two ratios to solve for the value of b (the base).

$$\frac{1}{1.5} = \frac{4.5}{b}$$

To go from the first ratio of the proportion to the next, multiply both terms of the first ratio by 4.5.

$$\frac{1 \times 4.5}{1.5 \times 4.5} = \frac{4.5}{b}$$

Therefore, $b = 6.75$

PRACTICE QUESTIONS

Use the following information to answer the next 2 questions.

Jake wanted to cut a triangular piece of wood. The sides of his triangular piece of wood must have the same ratios as between the sides of the triangle shown. The height of the triangle shown is 3, the base is 4, and the hypotenuse is 5.

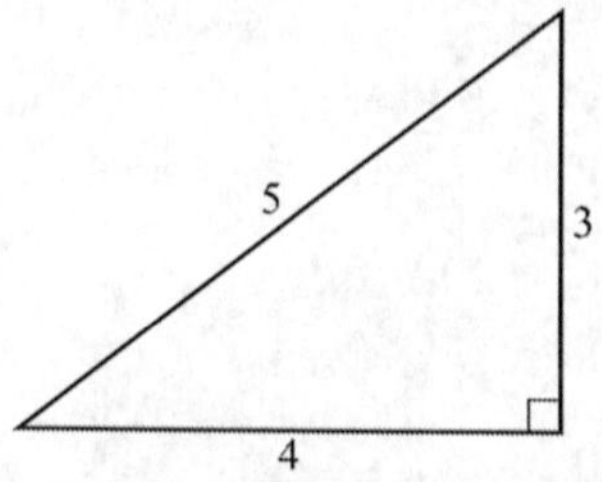

5. If the height of Jake's piece of wood is 45 cm, then the proportion that could be used to determine his base length, b, is

A. $\frac{3}{45} = \frac{b}{4}$

B. $\frac{3}{4} = \frac{45}{b}$

C. $\frac{3}{4} = \frac{b}{45}$

D. $\frac{3}{5} = \frac{45}{b}$

6. Jake also wanted to cut a smaller triangular piece of wood in the same shape as the triangle shown. If the hypotenuse of this new piece is 24 cm, then which of the following proportions could be used to determine the height, h, of his second triangular piece of wood?

A. $\frac{3}{5} = \frac{24}{h}$

B. $\frac{5}{4} = \frac{24}{h}$

C. $\frac{5}{3} = \frac{24}{h}$

D. $\frac{4}{3} = \frac{24}{h}$

CHALLENGER QUESTION

7. A rectangle has a length of 20 cm and an area of 600 cm^2. Another smaller rectangle has an area of 300 cm^2 and is directly proportional to the dimensions of the larger rectangle. The proportion that could be used to determine the width, w, of the smaller rectangle is

A. $\frac{20}{600}=\frac{w}{300}$

B. $\frac{20}{600}=\frac{300}{w}$

C. $\frac{30}{600}=\frac{300}{w}$

D. $\frac{30}{600}=\frac{w}{300}$

8. Karim wrote the proportion $\frac{10}{15}=\frac{32}{x}$ to represent the ratio between the number of red marbles to blue marbles in bag 1 and the ratio between the number of red marbles to blue marbles in bag 2. In this proportion, x represents the number of

A. red marbles in bag 1

B. red marbles in bag 2

C. blue marbles in bag 1

D. blue marbles in bag 2

NA1.03 solve for the unknown value in a proportion, using a variety of methods

SOLVING UNKNOWN PROPORTIONS

To solve proportions, change any ratios in word or ratio form to fraction form, and set the fractions equal to each other.

$$3:4=x:8 \Rightarrow \frac{3}{4}=\frac{x}{8}$$

There are several methods of solving an unknown value in a proportion.

Example

Solve $\frac{2}{3}=\frac{x}{6}$

Method 1: Using Concrete Diagrams or Logical Reasoning

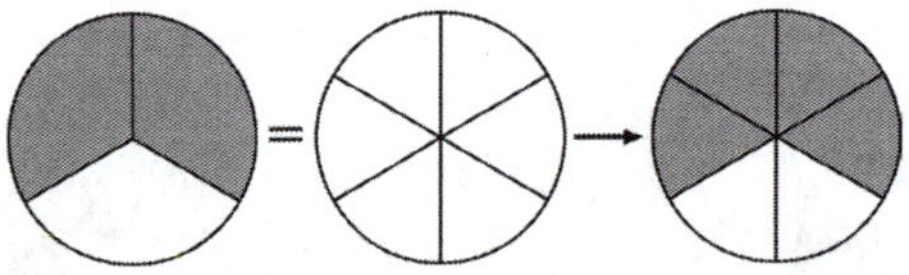

In the diagram on the left, the ratio $\frac{2}{3}$ is expressed as two shaded pieces out of three. Therefore, if two out of three pieces are shaded in the first diagram, when the same proportion of pieces is shaded in a diagram containing six pieces, four pieces must be shaded. In other words, x is equal to 4.

Method 2: Using Equivalent Ratios

Make the known terms of each ratio equal by multiplying or dividing by an appropriate number.

$$\frac{2\times 2}{3\times 2}=\frac{x}{6}$$
$$\frac{4}{6}=\frac{x}{6}$$

Since the ratios are equal, the unknown term, x, must be 4.

Method 3: Using the Cross-Product Rule

If the ratios $\frac{a}{b}=\frac{c}{d}$ are equal and b and d are not equal to zero, then the cross products $(a\times d)=(b\times c)$ are equal.

$$\frac{2}{3}=\frac{x}{6}$$
$$(2)(6)=(3)(x)$$
$$12=3x$$
$$\frac{12}{3}=\frac{3x}{3}$$
$$4=x$$

Method 4: Using the Unit Ratio

The final method was used in lesson 1.02, where the given ratio was reduced to make one term equal to 1. This ratio is called the unit rate or constant of proportionality.

$$\frac{2}{3}=\frac{x}{6}$$
$$\frac{2\div 3}{3\div 3}=\frac{x}{6}$$
$$\frac{\frac{2}{3}}{1}=\frac{x}{6}$$

To solve for x, multiply the numerator of the known ratio by 6, since the denominators of both ratios portray that relationship.

$$x=\frac{2}{3}\times 6$$
$$x=\frac{12}{3}$$
$$x=4$$

PRACTICE QUESTIONS

9. Kerri earned \$146.25 for 15 h of babysitting. Lan earned \$194.40 for 18 h of yard work. Which of the following statements about Kerri's and Lan's rate of pay is **true**?

A. Lan earned \$1.05/h more than Kerri.

B. Kerri earned \$1.05/h more than Lan.

C. Kerri earned \$4.83/h more than Lan.

D. Lan earned \$4.83/h more than Kerri.

Use the following information to answer the next question.

The ratio between shaded and total squares in the diagrams shown can be represented by the proportion $\frac{6}{10}=\frac{x}{25}$.

Diagram I

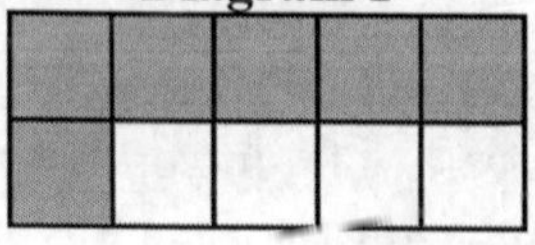

Diagram II

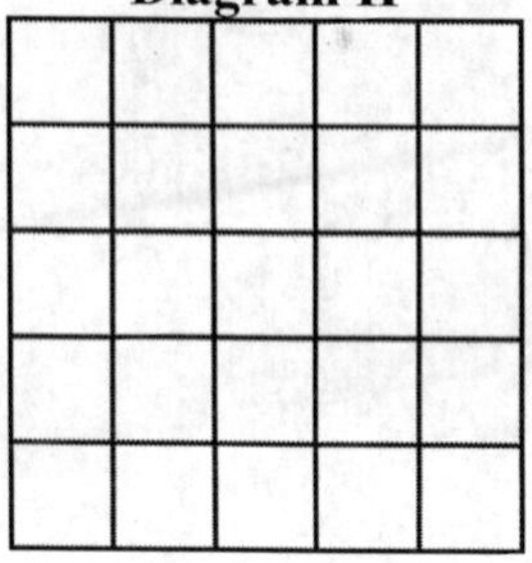

Numerical Response

1. If x represents the number of squares that should be shaded in Diagram II, then the value of x in the proportion $\frac{6}{10}=\frac{x}{25}$ is __________.

2. Bobby is driving on the highway at a constant speed of 96 km/h. The distance he will drive in $6\frac{1}{2}$ h is ___________ km.

CHALLENGER QUESTION

10. The ratio of width to length of a picture frame is 3:5. If the actual width of the picture frame is 12 cm, then the perimeter of the picture frame is

A. 20 cm
B. 32 cm
C. 64 cm
D. 240 cm

NA1.04 make comparisons using unit rates

Comparing Unit Rates

A **rate** is a comparison of two or more quantities with different units. A **unit rate** is a rate where the second term is 1.

Example

If Pierre is paid $48 for working four hours at a music store, what is his hourly wage, or unit rate of pay?

$$\frac{48}{4} = \frac{x}{1}$$

Divide each term of the first ratio by 4 to create equivalent ratios.

$$\frac{48 \div 4}{4 \div 4} = \frac{x}{1}$$
$$\frac{12}{1} = \frac{x}{1}$$

His hourly wage or unit rate of pay is $12.

Unit rates can also be used to compare similar scenarios and decide which is better.

Example

A box of 12 chocolate bars costs $5.25, while a box of 20 chocolate bars costs $7.50. Which box is the better buy and by how much?

$$\frac{5.25}{12} = \frac{x}{1} \Rightarrow x = \frac{5.25(1)}{12} = \$0.44\text{/bar}$$
$$\frac{7.50}{20} = \frac{x}{1} \Rightarrow x = \frac{7.50(1)}{20} = \$0.38\text{/bar}$$

The box of 20 chocolate bars is a better buy by $\$0.44 - \$0.38 = \$0.06$ per bar.

Practice Questions

11. Laundry soap comes in either a 1.7 L box or a 0.8 L box. The 1.7 L box sells for $3.27, and the 0.8 L box sells for $1.49. Which of the following statements regarding the unit price of each box of laundry soap is **true**?

A. The unit price of the 1.7 L box is $0.06/L more than the unit price of the 0.8 L box.

B. The unit price of the 0.8 L box is $0.06/L more than the unit price of the 1.7 L box.

C. The unit price of the 1.7 L box is $0.05/L more than the unit price of the 0.8 L box.

D. The unit price of the 0.8 L box is $0.05/L more than the unit price of the 1.7 L box.

Use the following information to answer the next question.

A 56 g container of potato chips costs 85¢, and a 190 g container costs $1.89.

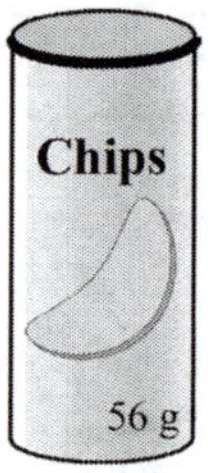

12. How much money per gram is saved if the larger container is purchased?

A. 2¢

B. 134¢

C. 1.14¢

D. 0.523¢

CHALLENGER QUESTION

13. For three cases of pop (each case containing 10 bottles), the price is \$9.99 per case plus an additional environmental fee of \$0.60 per case. For two cases of pop (each case containing 12 bottles), the price is \$11.28 per case plus an additional environmental fee of \$0.60 per case. Which of the following statements about these cases of pop is **true**?

A. The better buy is two cases because the average cost per bottle is \$0.930.

B. The better buy is two cases because the average cost per bottle is \$0.990.

C. The better buy is three cases because the average cost per bottle is \$0.999.

D. The better buy is three cases because the average cost per bottle is \$1.059.

14. Dalia biked 42 km in $1\frac{3}{4}$ hours, and Janet biked 18 km in 50 minutes. Which of the following statements is **true**?

A. Dalia biked 0.04 km/min faster than Janet.

B. Janet biked 0.04 km/min faster than Dalia.

C. Dalia biked 0.05 km/min faster than Janet.

D. Janet biked 0.05 km/min faster than Dalia.

NA1.05 solve problems involving ratios, rates, and directly proportional relationships in various contexts, using a variety of methods

Ratios, Rates, and Direct Proportions

Problems involving ratios, rates, and directly proportional relationships can be solved using the methods shown in lesson 1.03.

Example

The length of a particular rectangle varies in direct proportion to the width. The ratio 5:3 illustrates this relationship. John is constructing a rectangular cement pad in terms of the given ratio. If the length of the pad is 18 m, what is its area?

Since the length varies in direct proportion to the width, *w*, set up the following proportion:

$$\frac{5}{3}=\frac{18}{w}$$

Now, solve for *w* using the cross-product rule.

$$(5)(w)=(18)(3)$$
$$5w=54$$
$$w=10.8 \text{ m}$$

The area of the cement pad can now be found using the formula $A=(l)(w)$.

The area of the cement pad $=(18 \text{ m})(10.8 \text{ m})$
$=194.4 \text{ m}^2$

Example

Maura wishes to convert 180 Canadian dollars (CAD) into Japanese yen (JPY).
The exchange rate is 104 JPY:1 CAD. How much money will she receive in Japanese yen?

To solve this problem, set up a proportion where x is the amount of Japanese yen Maura will receive.

$$\frac{104\text{ JPY}}{1\text{ CAD}}=\frac{x\text{ JPY}}{180\text{ CAD}}$$

Create equivalent ratios.

$$\frac{104\times 180}{1\times 180}=\frac{x}{180}$$
$$\frac{18\ 720}{180}=\frac{x}{180}$$

Since the ratios are equal, the unknown term, x, must be 18 720. Maura will receive 18 720 yen in this exchange.

You can also use proportions to solve problems involving scale diagrams. A map is an example of a scale diagram where the scale factor of the map is the ratio of the distance on the map to the actual distance.

Example

A distance of 2 cm on a map represents an actual distance of 70 km. Given an actual distance of 220 km, determine the scale factor and the distance on the map.

Convert 70 km into centimetres.
Since $1\text{ km}=100\ 000\text{ cm}$,
$70\text{ km}=7\ 000\ 000\text{ cm}$.

The scale factor of the map is 2:7 000 000.

Now, set up a proportion where x is the distance on the map and
$220\text{ km}=22\ 000\ 000\text{ cm}$.

$$\frac{2\text{ cm}}{7\ 000\ 000\text{ cm}}=\frac{x\text{ cm}}{22\ 000\ 000\text{ cm}}$$
$$(2)(22\ 000\ 000)=(7\ 000\ 000)(x)$$
$$44\ 000\ 000=7\ 000\ 000x$$
$$\frac{44\ 000\ 000}{7\ 000\ 000}=\frac{7\ 000\ 000x}{7\ 000\ 000}$$
$$x\approx 6.286$$

The distance on the map is approximately 6.29 cm.

PRACTICE QUESTIONS

CHALLENGER QUESTION

15. If the temperature at 3:00 A.M. was −12°C and the temperature rose 2°C/h over the next 12 h, at what time was the temperature 3°C?

A. 10:30 A.M. **B.** 11:00 A.M.

C. 12:30 P.M. **D.** 2:30 P.M.

16. The scale factor of an illustration of a bicycle is 1 mm:20 cm. If the length of the bicycle in the illustration is 15 mm, what is the actual length of the bicycle in metres?

A. 0.15 m

B. 0.30 m

C. 1.50 m

D. 3.00 m

Numerical Response

3. Luke invested a sum of money.
The interest earned on his investment was directly proportional to the amount of money he invested. For every $2 000 invested, the interest earned was $160.
If Luke earned $400 in interest, then the amount he invested is $__________.

17. Ravi flew from Thunder Bay, Ontario, to Munich, Germany. Upon his arrival, Ravi used $1 900 CAD to purchase euros at an exchange rate of 1.4947 CAD:1 EUR. To the nearest whole number, how many euros did Ravi purchase?

A. 1 183 EUR

B. 1 271 EUR

C. 2 321 EUR

D. 2 840 EUR

NA1.06 solve problems requiring the expression of percents, fractions, and decimals in their equivalent forms

SOLVING PROBLEMS WITH PERCENTAGES, FRACTIONS, AND DECIMALS

A number written as a percentage can be expressed as a fraction with a denominator of 100 or as a decimal (by dividing the percentage by 100). The word **percent** describes how much out of 100 is represented. A percentage can also be expressed in decimal terms as a certain amount out of 1.

Example

$73\% = \frac{73}{100}$ represents 73 out of 100.

$73\% = 73 \div 100 = 0.73$ represents 0.73 out of 1.

To find a certain percentage of a number, convert the percentage to a decimal number or fraction, and then multiply that value by the given number.

Example

Find 25% of 800 g.

Using Fractions

Step 1: Convert the percentage to a fraction.

$$25\% \rightarrow 25 \div 100 = \frac{1}{4}$$

Step 2: Multiply the fraction $\left(\frac{1}{4}\right)$ by the given number (800).

$$\frac{1}{4} \times \frac{800}{1} = \frac{800}{4} = 200 \text{ g}$$

Using Decimals

Step 1: Convert the percentage to a decimal
$25\% \rightarrow 25 \div 100 = 0.25$

Step 2: Multiply the decimal (0.25) by the given number (800).
$0.25 \times 800 = 200 \text{ g}$

Questions involving sales tax, GST/PST, simple interest, commissions, or the analysis of data require the use of percentages.

Example

In a Grade 9 classroom made up of 32 students, 15 students are taking Grade 9 Science this semester. Given that this class is representative of the 240 students in Grade 9, estimate and then calculate the percentage and total number of Grade 9 students that are taking Grade 9 Science this semester.

In the given class, 15 of 32 students are taking Grade 9 Science this semester.

This represents almost $\frac{1}{2}$ or 0.50 of the class and thus of all Grade 9 students at the school. To convert either $\frac{1}{2}$ or 0.50 to a percentage, multiply by 100.

$\frac{1}{2} \times 100 = \frac{100}{2} = 50\%$ **or** $0.50 \times 100 = 50\%$

Approximately 50% of all Grade 9 students are taking science this semester. You can estimate the number of Grade 9 students taking science this semester by multiplying $\frac{1}{2}$ by 240 or multiplying 0.5 by 240.

$\frac{1}{2} \times 240 = 120$ **or** $0.50 \times 240 = 120$

To calculate the actual number of Grade 9 students taking science this semester, follow the same steps with the actual fraction $\left(\frac{15}{32}\right)$.

$\frac{15}{32} \times 100 = \frac{15 \times 100}{32} = \frac{1\,500}{32} \approx 46.9\%$

Thus, 46.9% of all Grade 9 students are taking science this semester.

$\frac{15}{32} \times 240 = \frac{15 \times 240}{32} = 112.5$

or

$0.469 \times 240 = 112.5$

There are 112 students in Grade 9 taking science this semester.

Sales tax questions can involve Provincial Sales Tax (**PST**) and the Goods and Services Tax (**GST**).

Example

Milo purchased a guitar priced at $600 in a music store in Ontario. The PST on the purchase was $48. What is Ontario's PST as a percentage, and how much PST would Milo's friend Candice pay on the purchase of a $1 280 guitar?

Convert $\frac{48}{600}$ to a percentage.

$$\frac{48}{600}\times 100=\frac{48\times 100}{600}=8\%$$

Ontario's provincial sales tax is 8%.

Calculate Candice's PST.

8% of $1 280

$$=\left(\frac{8}{100}\right)\$1\ 280$$
$$=(0.08)(\$1\ 280)$$
$$=\$102.40$$

The amount of PST Candice pays is $102.40.

When making an investment, the amount of money invested, *P*, is directly proportional to the simple interest earned.

Example

Luis invests $200 in an account that earns a simple interest rate of 9.25% annually.
How much interest does Luis' investment earn after one year?

9.25% of 200

$$=\frac{9.25}{100}\times 200$$
$$=0.0925\times 200$$
$$=\$18.50$$

After one year, Luis' investment has earned $18.50 in interest.

Practice Questions

18. Kenji wrote an 80 question multiple-choice exam and got 72 questions correct. The next day, he wrote another test consisting of 120 multiple-choice questions. If Kenji got the same percentage of questions correct on both tests, how many questions did he get **incorrect** on the second test?

A. 10 **B.** 12

C. 30 **D.** 48

CHALLENGER QUESTION

19. Alexandra knows that the PST in Ontario is 8% and the GST is 5%. If she buys a pair of $95 running shoes, what will be the total cost including both taxes?

A. $12.35 **B.** $102.98

C. $107.35 **D.** $107.73

Use the following information to answer the next question.

Commission is a percentage of money earned by a salesperson based on his or her total sales. The given and unknown values in the table shown indicate the amount of money earned by two different salespeople based on their total sales and rates of commission.

	Total Sales	**Amount Earned**	**Commission**
Zoe	\$2 400	x	8%
Luke	\$4 200	\$651	y

20. Which of the following tables shows the correct values for x and y?

A.

x	y
\$192	15.5%

B.

x	y
\$192	6.4%

C.

x	y
\$300	15.5%

D.

x	y
\$300	6.4%

Numerical Response

4. Petra and Stephen invested money in savings accounts paying the same amount of simple interest. Petra invested \$2 400, and Stephen invested \$10 000. If Petra's investment earned \$168 interest after one year, how much interest did Stephen's investment earn in the same amount of time?

\$__________

Open Response

1. Simple interest is directly proportional to the amount of money invested.

Two banks advertise the simple interest earned in a year on a \$1 000 investment.

Bank I:
The simple interest earned on \$1 000 is \$55.

Bank II:
The simple interest earned on \$1 000 is \$65.

a) What is the annual simple interest rate, as a percentage, at each bank? Show your work.

b) If Lin invested \$2 400 at each bank, what would be the total simple interest she would earn from her two investments after one year? Show your work.

NA2.01 simplify numerical expressions involving integers and rational numbers, with and without the use of technology

Numerical Expressions with Integers and Rational Numbers

When solving questions involving integers and rational numbers, you must perform the operations in the proper order to get the correct answer. Use the acronym **BEDMAS** to remember the order. **BEDMAS** stands for:

B – brackets first

E – exponents second

D – division
M – multiplication } in the order they appear

A – addition
S – subtraction } in the order they appear

Example

Evaluate

$7^2+6-8(5-3)\div 2+2$

$=7^2+6-8(2)\div 2+2=49+6-8(2)\div 2+2$

$=49+6-16\div 2+2$

$=49+6-8+2$

$=55-8+2$

$=47+2$

$=49$

Example

Evaluate $12.35\div 1.3\times(-2.6)+(1.2-6.8)$

$=12.35\div 1.3\times(-2.6)+(-5.6)$

$=9.5\times(-2.6)+(-5.6)$

$=-24.7+(-5.6)$

$=-30.3$

Operations with Fractions

Adding and Subtracting Fractions

To add or subtract fractions with the same denominators, the numerators are added or subtracted and placed over the value of the denominator. If possible, the resulting fraction is reduced to lowest terms.

Example

$\frac{1}{4}+\frac{1}{4}=?$

$\frac{1}{4}+\frac{1}{4}=\frac{1+1}{4}=\frac{2}{4}\xrightarrow{\text{reduce}}\frac{2\div 2}{4\div 2}=\frac{1}{2}$

Therefore, $\frac{1}{4}+\frac{1}{4}=\frac{1}{2}$.

When adding or subtracting fractions with different denominators, find the lowest common denominator (LCD) of the given fractions. Create new equivalent fractions of the original fractions using the LCD, then add or subtract the numerators and place the result over the LCD. If possible, reduce the resulting fraction to lowest terms.

Example

$\frac{2}{3}-\frac{1}{4}=?$

Express each fraction in terms of the lowest common denominator. Write the multiples of each denominator until a common multiple appears.

Multiples of 3: 3, 6, 9, 12, 15

Multiples of 4: 4, 8, 12, 16, 20

The lowest common denominator of 3 and 4 is 12. Create two new equivalent fractions from the original fractions using the denominator of 12.

$\frac{2\times 4}{3\times 4}-\frac{1\times 3}{4\times 3}$

$\downarrow \quad \downarrow$

$\frac{8}{12}-\frac{3}{12}$

Subtract the numerators, and keep the same denominator.

$\frac{8-3}{12}=\frac{5}{12}$

Therefore, $\frac{2}{3}-\frac{1}{4}=\frac{5}{12}$

When adding or subtracting fractions that involve mixed numbers in the form $a\frac{b}{c}$, follow the steps outlined below.

Example

$$2\frac{1}{4}+1\frac{2}{3}=?$$

Step 1:
Convert mixed numbers to improper fractions.

$2\times4+1=9\rightarrow\frac{9}{4}$ and $1\times3+2=5\rightarrow\frac{5}{3}$

Step 2:
Create equivalent fractions with the same denominator.

$$\frac{9\times3}{4\times3}+\frac{5\times4}{3\times4}$$

$$\downarrow\qquad\downarrow$$

$$\frac{27}{12}+\frac{20}{12}$$

Step 3:
Add or subtract the numerators, and keep the same denominator.

$$\frac{27+20}{12}=\frac{47}{12}$$

Note: $\frac{47}{12}$ could be written as $3\frac{11}{12}$.

Therefore, $2\frac{1}{4}+1\frac{2}{3}=3\frac{11}{12}$

MULTIPLYING FRACTIONS

When multiplying fractions, start by converting any mixed numbers to improper fractions. Then multiply the numerators together to give a new numerator. Next, multiply the denominators together to give a new denominator. Finally, reduce the resulting fraction to lowest terms.

Example

$$3\frac{2}{5}\times1\frac{3}{4}=?$$

$$3\frac{2}{5}\times1\frac{3}{4}\rightarrow\frac{17}{5}\times\frac{7}{4}$$

$$\frac{17}{5}\times\frac{7}{4}=\frac{17\times7}{5\times4}=\frac{119}{20}$$

Note: $\frac{119}{20}=5\frac{19}{20}$

Therefore, $3\frac{2}{5}\times1\frac{3}{4}=5\frac{19}{20}$

DIVIDING FRACTIONS

When dividing two fractions, convert the division question to a multiplication question by multiplying the first fraction by the reciprocal of the second fraction.

Example

$$\frac{8}{15}\div\frac{2}{7}=?$$

$$\frac{8}{15}\div\frac{7}{2}=\frac{8\times7}{15\times2}=\frac{56}{30}$$

In lowest terms, $\frac{56}{30}=\frac{28}{15}$.

Written as a mixed number, $\frac{28}{15}$ is $1\frac{13}{15}$.

Therefore, $\frac{8}{15}\div\frac{2}{7}=1\frac{13}{15}$

Practice Questions

Numerical Response

5. The value of $6^2 - 8 \div (3-1) + 3 \times 2$ is ____________.

21. To divide $2\frac{3}{4}$ by $\frac{2}{3}$, the correct sequence of steps is

A. $\frac{4}{11} \div \frac{2}{3} = \frac{4}{11} \times \frac{2}{3} = \frac{8}{33}$

B. $\frac{11}{4} \div \frac{2}{3} = \frac{11}{4} \times \frac{2}{3} = \frac{11}{6} = 1\frac{5}{6}$

C. $\frac{4}{11} \div \frac{2}{3} = \frac{4}{11} \times \frac{3}{2} = \frac{12}{22} = \frac{6}{11}$

D. $\frac{11}{4} \div \frac{2}{3} = \frac{11}{4} \times \frac{3}{2} = \frac{33}{8} = 4\frac{1}{8}$

Use the following image to answer the next question.

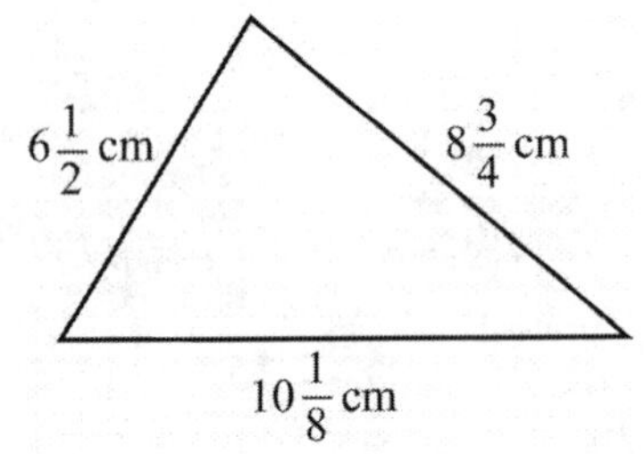

22. What is the perimeter of the triangle shown?

A. $25\frac{3}{8}$ cm

B. $25\frac{1}{4}$ cm

C. $24\frac{7}{8}$ cm

D. $24\frac{5}{8}$ cm

NA2.02 relate their understanding of inverse operations to squaring and taking the square root, and apply inverse operations to simplify expressions and solve equations

Inverse Operations of Squaring and Taking the Square Root

Squaring and taking the square root are inverse operations. **Squaring a number** is expressed by writing the number with an exponent of two. For example, squaring the number 5 is expressed as 5^2. The expression 5^2 has a value of 25 since $(5)(5) = 25$.

To do the inverse operation of squaring a number, take the **square root** of the number. For example, to take the square root of 9, called the **radicand**, find the number that when multiplied by itself is equal to the radicand 9. The square root of 9 is written as $\sqrt{9}$. Since $3 \times 3 = 9$, it follows that $\sqrt{9} = \sqrt{3 \times 3} = 3$. Notice that only the positive square root is given when the radical sign is by itself like this: $\sqrt{\ }$

When evaluating a square root such as $\pm\sqrt{25}$, however, there are two square root values: 5, because $(5)^2 = 25$, and –5, because $(-5)^2 = 25$. Since both values equal 25 when squared, you must write ±5 as your answer.

To eliminate the square root sign in $\sqrt{25}$, perform the opposite operation, which is squaring the radical $\left(\sqrt{25}\right)^2 = 25$.

Some equations can be solved by squaring both sides of the equation. Other equations can be solved by taking the square root of both sides of the equation.

Example

Solve the equation $\sqrt{k} = 7$.

The inverse of taking the square root of a number is squaring a number, so square both sides of the equation to eliminate the radical sign.

$$\left(\sqrt{k}\right)^2 = 7^2$$
$$k = 49$$

Example

Solve the equation $p^2 = 36$.

The inverse of squaring a number is taking the square root, so take the square root of both sides of the equation.

$$p^2 = 36$$
$$\sqrt{p^2} = \pm\sqrt{36}$$
$$\sqrt{p \times p} = \sqrt{6 \times 6}$$
$$p = \pm 6$$

Example

If the area of a square is 64 cm^2, what is the length of each side?

The area of a square can be determined using the formula $A = s^2$, where A represents the area of the square and s represents the length of a side of the square.

Substitute 64 for A in the formula, and solve for s.

$$A = s^2$$
$$64 = s^2$$
$$\sqrt{64} = \sqrt{s^2}$$
$$8 = s$$

The length of each side of the square is 8 cm.

Note: Do not write $\pm\sqrt{64}$, because the length of a side of a square cannot be a negative value.

PRACTICE QUESTIONS

Numerical Response

6. If $\sqrt{x} = 9$, then the value of x is ___________.

23. Which of the following statements about square roots is **true**?

A. The value of $\sqrt{16}$ equals 4.

B. The value of $\sqrt{16}$ equals ± 4.

C. The value of $\sqrt{16}$ equals 256.

D. The value of $\sqrt{16}$ equals ± 256.

Use the following information to answer the next question.

CHALLENGER QUESTION

The pyramids are ancient Egyptian tombs built by the pharaohs 4 000 years ago. The pharaohs built these tombs to protect their bodies as they prepared for the afterlife. The pyramids were built with amazing precision.

Their bases were perfect squares, and the limestone blocks that make up many pyramids fit together so well that in many places, a piece of paper cannot slide between them.

24. If the base of a pyramid covers an area of 10 000 m^2 and x represents the length of each side of the base, then which of the following pairs of equations correctly solve for x?

A. $x^2 = 10\ 000\ m^2$
$x = 500$ m

B. $x^2 = 10\ 000\ m^2$
$x = 400$ m

C. $x^2 = 10\ 000\ m^2$
$x = 200$ m

D. $x^2 = 10\ 000\ m^2$
$x = 100$ m

25. Which of the following diagrams of square tiles can be used to find the square root of 64?

A.

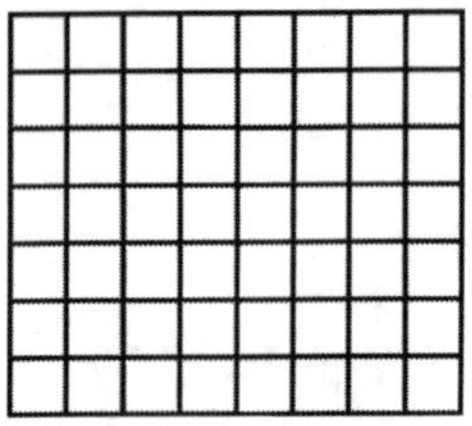

B.

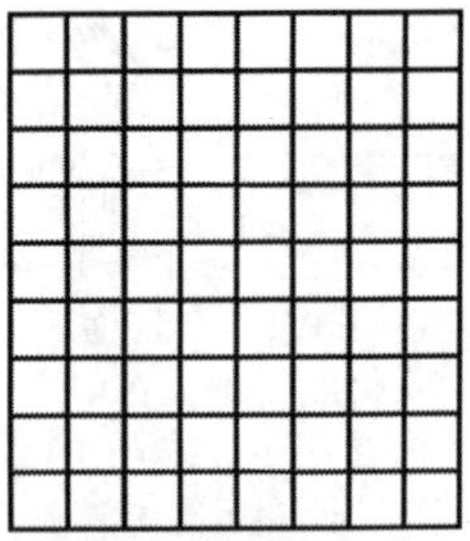

C.

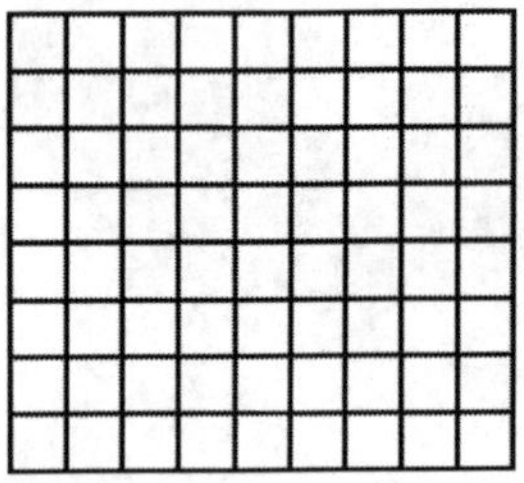

D.

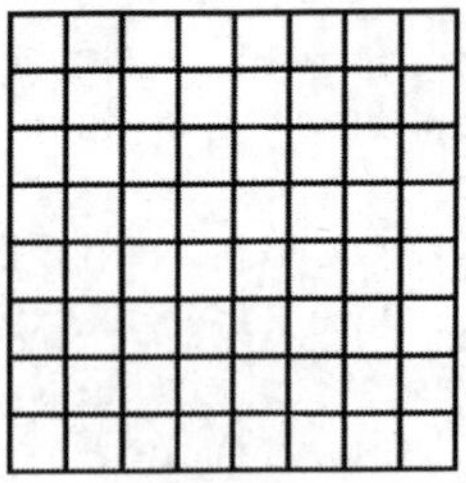

NA2.03 describe the relationship between the algebraic and geometric representations of a single-variable term up to degree three [i.e., length, which is one dimensional, can be represented by x; area, which is two dimensional, can be represented by (x) (x) or x^2; volume, which is three dimensional, can be represented by (x) (x) (x), (x^2) (x), or x^3]

FIRST-, SECOND-, AND THIRD-DEGREE TERMS

A **variable** is any letter that represents a value that can change or vary in an expression.

A term can be either of the following:

- a constant $\rightarrow 2, -3, 4$
- a numerical coefficient with one or more variables having one or more exponents $\rightarrow 2x, 3x^2y, -5x^3, \pi r^2h$

Terms can be classified by degree. The degree of a term is the sum of the exponents of its variables. If there is no exponent, it is understood that the exponent is one.

first-degree term

$$\rightarrow 2x, x$$

second-degree term

$$\rightarrow x^2, 2x(x), 2xy$$

third-degree term

$$\rightarrow x^3, x(x^2), (x)(4x)(2x)$$

ONE-DIMENSIONAL

A single variable can be used to represent the unknown length of a line segment.
The length of the line segment shown below is x cm. The power x, or x^1, is used to represent length, which is a one-dimensional quantity and a first-degree term.

x cm

TWO-DIMENSIONAL

When finding the area of a rectangle, multiply the length by the width. Notice that the units are also multiplied and the result is cm^2 a second-degree term. Area is two-dimensional.

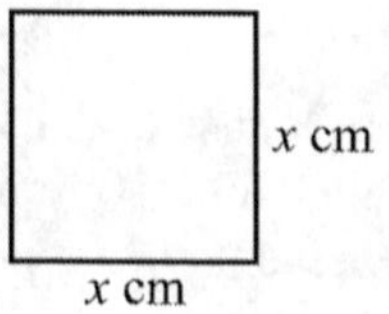

$$\text{Area} = (\text{length})(\text{width})$$
$$A = (x\text{ cm})(x\text{ cm})$$
$$A = x^2\text{ cm}^2$$

THREE-DIMENSIONAL

Find the volume of a rectangular prism by multiplying length × width × height.

Notice that the units are also multiplied to get cm^3 a third-degree term. Volume is three-dimensional.

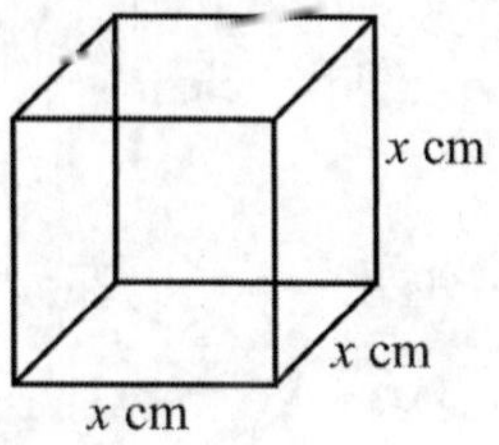

$$\text{Volume} = (\text{length})(\text{width})(\text{height})$$
$$V = (x\text{ cm})(x\text{ cm})(x\text{ cm})$$
$$= (x^2\text{ cm}^2)(x\text{ cm})$$
$$V = x^3\text{ cm}^3$$

PRACTICE QUESTIONS

Use the following information to answer the next question.

A cube is shown with labelled sides.

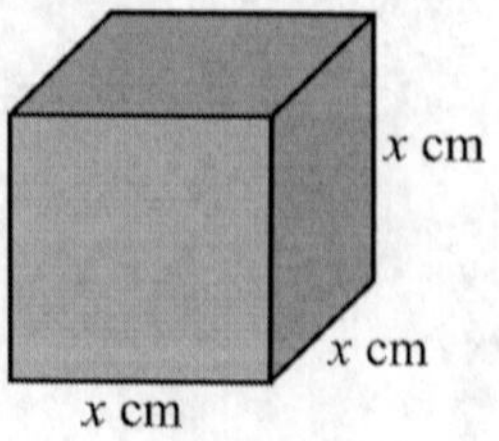

26. If x represents the length of an edge of the cube, then which of the following expressions does **not** represent the volume of the cube?

A. $(x)(x)(x)$

B. $(x^2)(x)$

C. x^2

D. x^3

Use the following diagram to answer the next question.

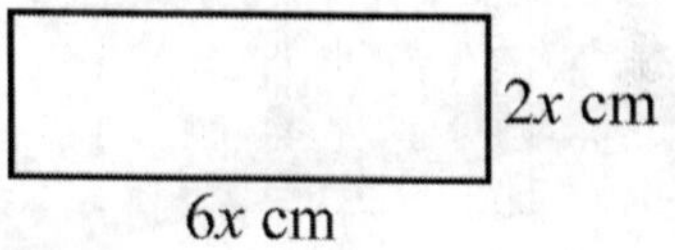

27. The area of the rectangle shown can be represented as

A. $12x^2\text{ cm}^2$

B. $12x\text{ cm}^2$

C. $8x^2\text{ cm}^2$

D. $8x\text{ cm}^2$

Use the following diagram to answer the next question.

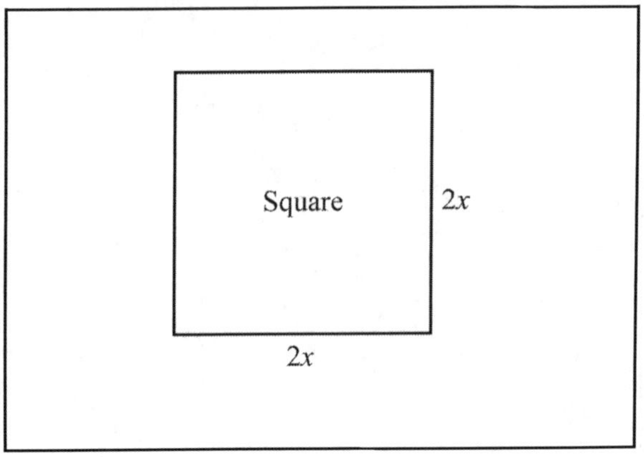

28. The perimeter of the square shown can be represented as

A. $4x$ **B.** $4x^2$

C. $8x$ **D.** $8x^3$

CHALLENGER QUESTION

The area of the shape shown can be represented as: $A = 7x^2$

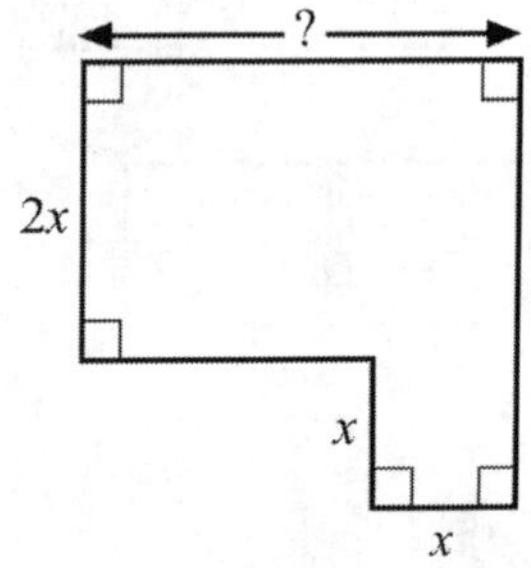

29. The missing expression at the top of the shape is

A. $3x$ **B.** $4x$

C. $6x$ **D.** $7x$

NA2.04 substitute into and evaluate algebraic expressions involving exponents (i.e., evaluate expressions involving natural-number exponents with rational-number bases)

EXPONENTS AND ALGEBRAIC EXPRESSIONS

A power consists of a base and an exponent. In the power 10^3, the value 10 represents the base, and the value 3 represents the exponent.

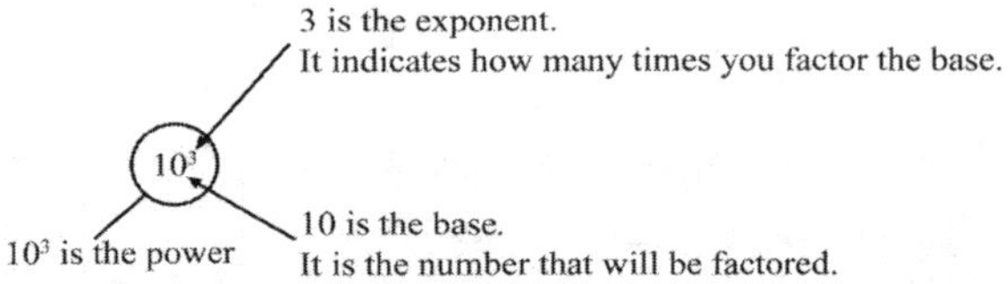

To evaluate a power, factor the base the number of times the exponent indicates, and then do the necessary multiplication.

$$10^3 = (10)\,(10)\,(10) = 1\ 000$$

A variable may be used as the base with or without a leading numerical coefficient.

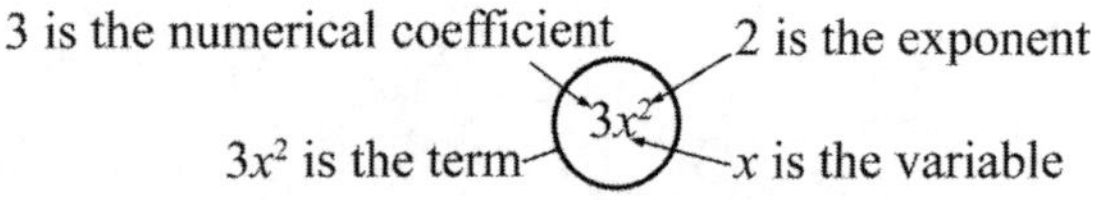

A variable can have a numerical coefficient of 1. For example, in the power x^3, x is the base, 3 is the exponent, and the numerical coefficient is 1.

$$x^3 = 1\ x\ x\ x$$

In the power $-x^2$, x is the base, 2 is the exponent, and the coefficient is -1.

$$-x^2 = -1\ x\ x$$

SUBSTITUTION AND EVALUATION OF EXPRESSIONS

Algebraic expressions can be evaluated by substituting any value into the variable.

Example

If $y = -2$, determine the value of $y^3 + y^2$.

Substitute the value –2 for the variable y.

$$(-2)^3 + (-2)^2$$

Evaluate each power.

$$= (-2)(-2)(-2) + (-2)(-2)$$
$$= (-8) + 4$$
$$= -4$$

Note: On your calculator, you can use the keystroke [^][3] and [^][2] to calculate each power: $(-2)\text{^}3 + (-2)\text{^}2 = -4$

PRACTICE QUESTIONS

30. When $x = -2$, the value of the expression $8x^3$ is

A. – 4 096

B. – 64

C. 64

D. 4 096

CHALLENGER QUESTION

A candy company called Bits & Bites wants to compare the volumes of two containers, a cube and a cylinder, to determine which container has a greater volume.

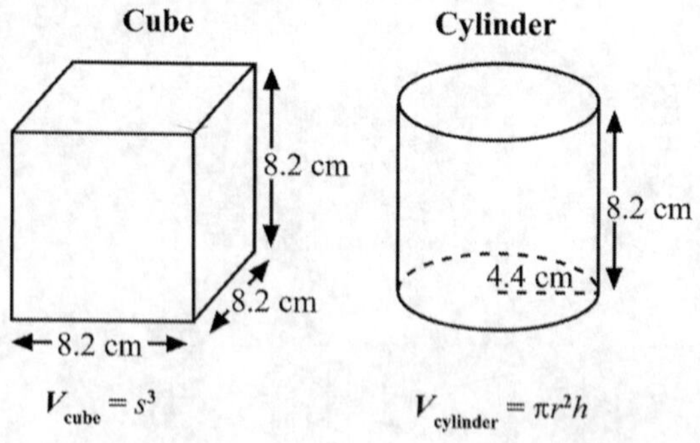

31. Which of the following statements about the volumes of the containers is **true**?

A. The volume of the cylinder is approximately 15.5 cm^3 more than the volume of the cube.

B. The volume of the cylinder is approximately 52.6 cm^3 more than the volume of the cube.

C. The volume of the cube is approximately 15.5 cm^3 more than the volume of the cylinder.

D. The volume of the cube is approximately 52.6 cm^3 more than the volume of the cylinder.

32. Which of the following expressions is equivalent to $3\left(-\frac{3}{2}\right)\left(-\frac{3}{2}\right)\left(-\frac{3}{2}\right)+2\left(\frac{1}{2}\right)\left(\frac{1}{2}\right)$?

A. $3\left(-\frac{3}{2}\right)^3+2\left(\frac{1}{2}\right)^2$

B. $-9\left(-\frac{3}{2}\right)^2+\frac{1}{2}$

C. $3\left(\frac{3}{2}\right)^3+2\left(\frac{1}{2}\right)^2$

D. $\left(-\frac{9}{2}\right)^3+2\left(\frac{1}{2}\right)^2$

Use the following shapes to answer the next question.

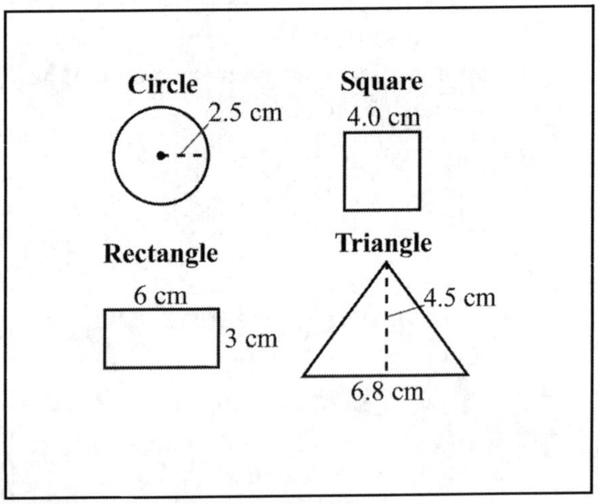

33. Which of the illustrated shapes covers the greatest area?

A. Circle

B. Square

C. Rectangle

D. Triangle

NA2.05 add and subtract polynomials involving the same variable up to degree three, using a variety of tools

Adding and Subtracting Polynomials

Poly means "many," and **nomial** means "term." A polynomial is an algebraic expression consisting of one or more terms that are connected with addition or subtraction signs. For example, in the polynomial $5x^2 + 4x + 6$, there are three terms: $5x^2$, $4x$, and 6.

To add or subtract polynomials, gather like terms. Like terms are terms that have the exact same variables with identical exponents. $2x^2$ and $5x^2$ are like terms because they both involve the variable x and each x is squared.

$2x$ and $5x^2$ are not like terms and cannot be combined, since their variables have different exponents. $2y$ and $2x$ are also not like terms, since their variables are different.

To add polynomials, gather like terms in descending order of degree, and perform the necessary operations on the coefficients.

$$\left(3x^2+5x+5\right)+\left(-2x+4x^2-11\right)$$
$$=\left(3x^2+4x^2\right)+\left(5x-2x\right)+\left(5-11\right)$$
$$=7x^2+3x-6$$

or

$$\begin{array}{r} 3x^2+5x+5 \\ +\underline{4x^2-2x-11} \\ 7x^2+3x-6 \end{array}$$

To subtract polynomials, use the integer rule of adding the opposite. Change the subtraction sign between the brackets to addition, and then change every sign inside the brackets to its opposite sign.

$(2y^3 + 3y - y^2 - 12) - (5y + 3y^3 - y^2 + 6)$
$= (2y^3 + 3y - y^2 - 12) + (-5y - 3y^3 + y^2 - 6)$

Gather like terms in descending order of degree, and perform the operations on the coefficients.

$= (2y^3 - 3y^3) + (-y^2 + y^2) + (3y - 5y) + (-12 - 6)$
$= -y^3 + 0y^2 - 2y - 18$
$= -y^3 - 2y - 18$

Algebra tiles can be used to add and subtract polynomials.

This legend shows the tiles and what they represent.

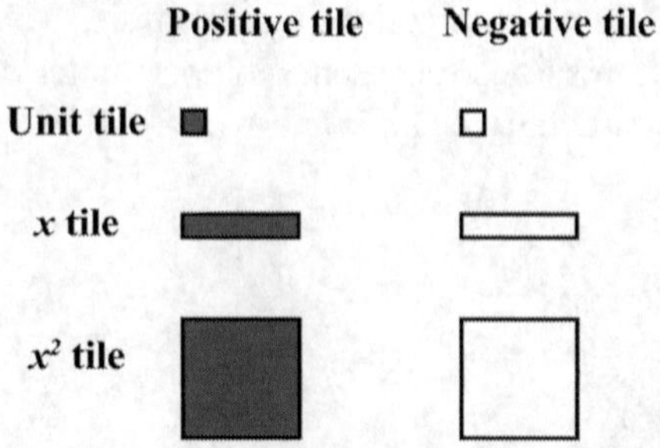

Example

The polynomial $2x^2 - 3x + 3$ is represented as follows:

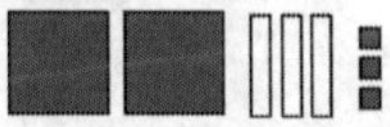

The expression $(2x^2 - 3x + 4) + (x^2 + 5x - 6)$ is represented as follows:

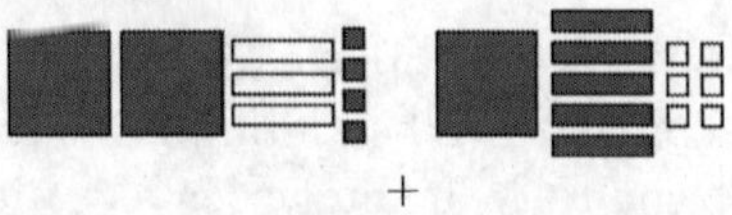

Positive and negative tiles of the same size cancel each other out.

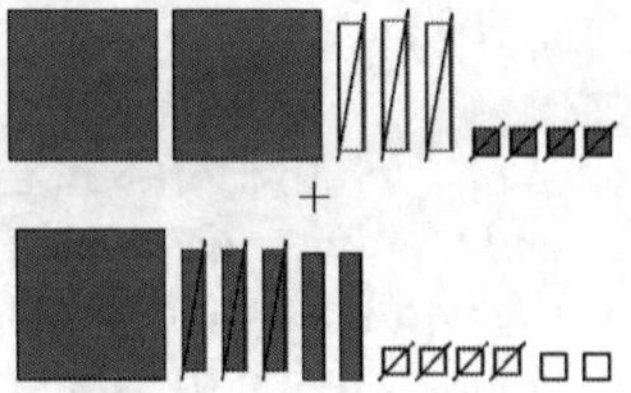

The answer is $3x^2 + 2x - 2$

The expression $(2x^2 - 3x + 4) - (x^2 + 5x - 6)$ is represented as:

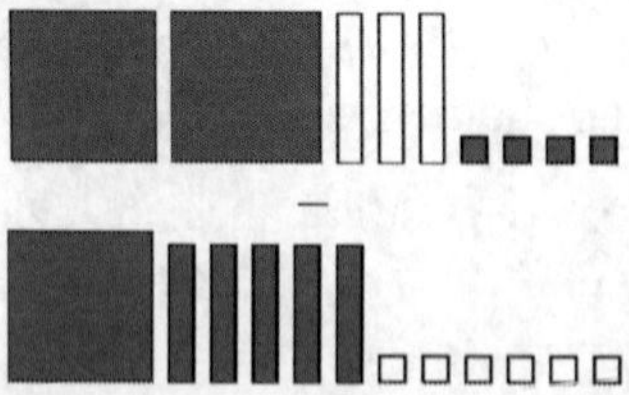

Remember, when subtracting polynomials, add their opposites (change the tiles of the second polynomial to the opposite colour).

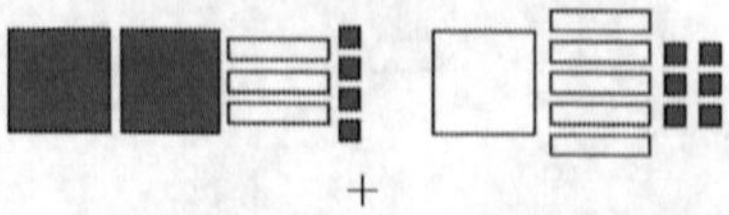

A positive tile cancels out a negative tile of the same size.

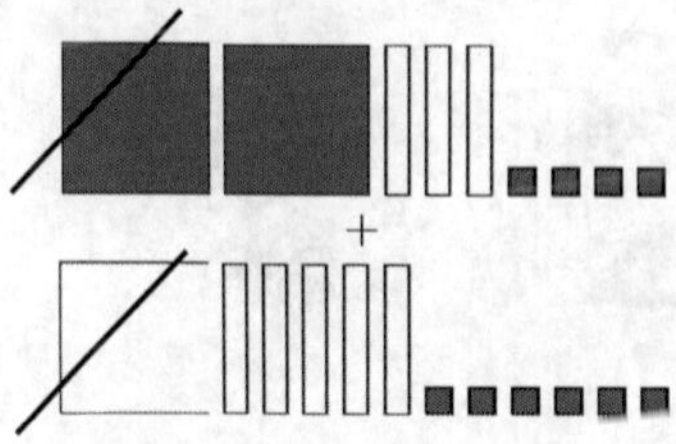

The answer is $x^2 - 8x + 10$

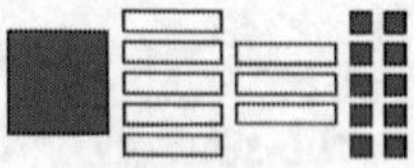

Practice Questions

34. When the expression $(6x^2 + 4x - 7) + (2x^2 - 4x - 3)$ is simplified, it is equivalent to

A. $8x^2 + 8x - 10$

B. $8x^2 + 8x - 4$

C. $8x^2 - 10$

D. $8x^2 - 4$

Use the following information to answer the next question.

The algebra tiles shown represent an algebraic expression or numerical value.

Shaded tiles are positive, and unshaded tiles are negative.

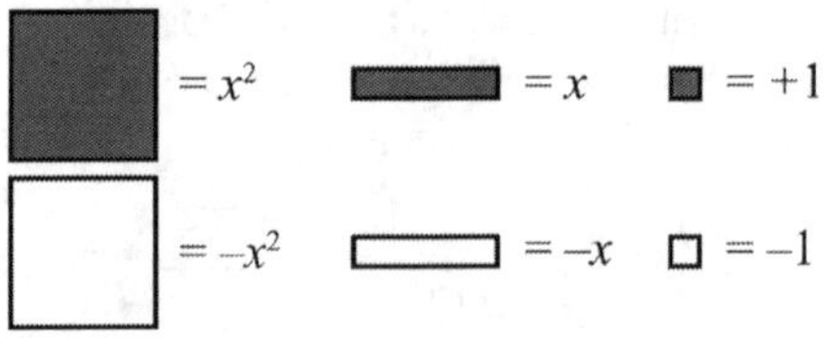

The algebra-tile model shown represents the addition of two polynomials.

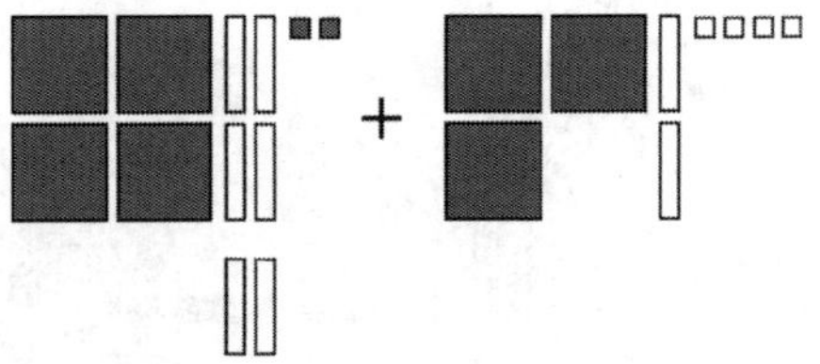

35. The solution to the sum of the two polynomials represented by the algebra-tile model is represented by which of the following algebraic expressions?

A. $7x^2 - 8x + 2$

B. $7x^2 + 8x + 6$

C. $7x^2 - 4x + 2$

D. $7x^2 - 8x - 2$

36. An algebraic expression equivalent to $\left(4x^2+3x-9\right)-\left(3x+2-6x^2+x^3\right)$ is

A. $x^3 - 2x^2 - 7$

B. $-x^3 + 10x^2 - 11$

C. $x^3 - 2x^2 + 6x - 7$

D. $-x^3 + 10x^2 + 6x - 11$

Use the following information to answer the next question.

CHALLENGER QUESTION

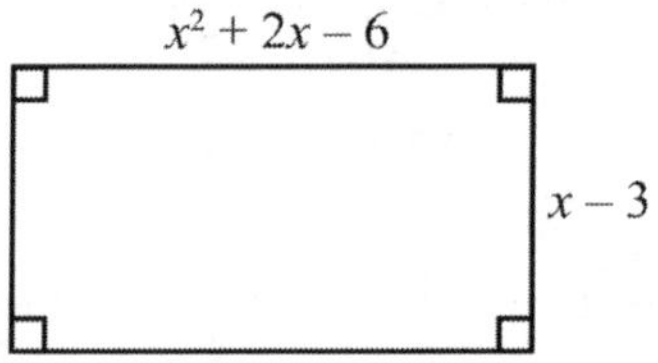

37. Which of the following algebraic expressions represents the perimeter of the rectangle shown above?

A. $6x - 18$

B. $x^2 + 3x - 9$

C. $x^2 + 6x - 18$

D. $2x^2 + 6x - 18$

NA2.06 multiply a polynomial by a monomial involving the same variable to give results up to degree three, using a variety of tools

Multiplying Polynomials by Monomials

A **monomial** is an algebraic expression that consists of one term. When multiplying two monomials, multiply the numerical coefficients together, and combine like variables by adding their respective exponents.

$$(6x)\left(3x^2\right)=(6)(3)(x)\left(x^2\right)=18x^{1+2}=18x^3$$

Algebra tiles can be used to represent the product of a monomial and a polynomial. Each term is represented by the width and length of a rectangle. The terms are then multiplied by filling in the middle to create the area of a rectangle. The area represents the solution.

$(2x)$ (3) is represented as follows:

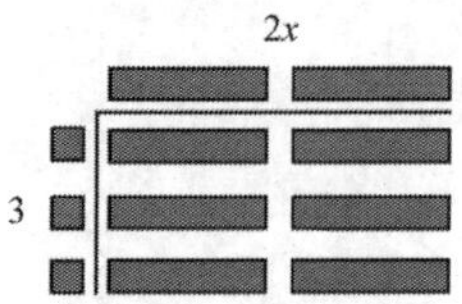

Multiply 1 times x and 1 times x again to get the answer for the first row. Repeat this process for the second and third rows. This results in the following rectangular area:

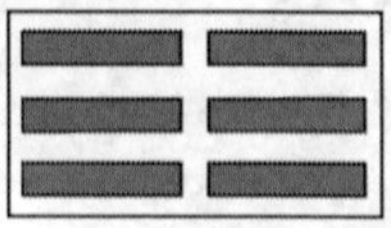

When multiplication is complete, add like terms to identify the solution as $6x$.

The multiplication of $2(x + 2)$ can be represented as follows:

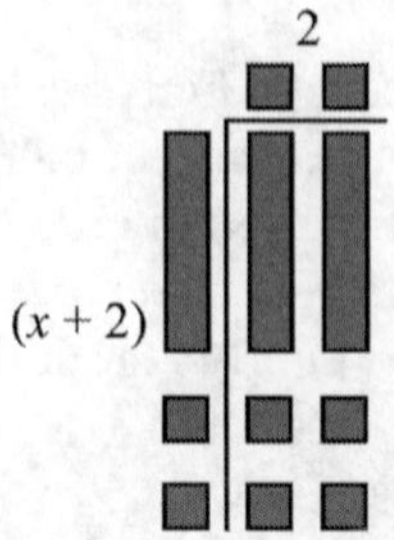

When multiplication is complete, the answer is $2x + 4$.

The product of a monomial and a polynomial can also be determined using a procedure similar to the multiplication of two integers.

For example, the product of $3x$ and $4x + 5$ can be determined as follows:

$$\begin{array}{r} 4x+5 \\ \nwarrow\ \uparrow \\ \times\ \ 3x \\ \hline 12x^2+15x \\ \downarrow\qquad\downarrow \\ (3x\times 4x)\ (3x\times 5) \end{array}$$

When determining the product of a monomial and a polynomial that is within brackets, the monomial must be multiplied by each term of the polynomial in the brackets. This process is referred to as the **distributive property**.

$$3x\left(2x^2-6x+4\right)$$
$$=(3x)\left(2x^2\right)+(3x)(-6x)+(3x)(4)$$
$$=(3)(2)(x)\left(x^2\right)+(3)(-6)(x)(x)+(3)(4)(x)$$
$$=6x^{1+2}-18x^{1+1}+12x$$
$$=6x^3-18x^2+12x$$

Practice Questions

38. When the algebraic expression $3(4y+7)-21$ is expanded and simplified, the resulting expression is

A. 12 **B.** $12y$

C. $12y-14$ **D.** $33y-21$

39. When the monomial $7x$ and the polynomial $5x^2 - 3x + 14$ are multiplied, the resulting expression is

A. $35x^3-21x^2+98x$

B. $35x^2+21x+14$

C. $5x^2+10x+14$

D. $35x^2+119x$

CHALLENGER QUESTION

40. When the monomial $2x$ and the polynomial x^2+4x+7 are multiplied, the product is a polynomial expression of the form $ax^p+bx^q+cx^r$, where a, b, and c as well as p, q, and r are real numbers. The value of the expression $p+q+r$ is

A. 3 **B.** 4

C. 6 **D.** 7

Use the following information to answer the next question.

The following algebra tiles represent an algebraic expression or numerical value.

Shaded tiles are positive, and unshaded tiles are negative.

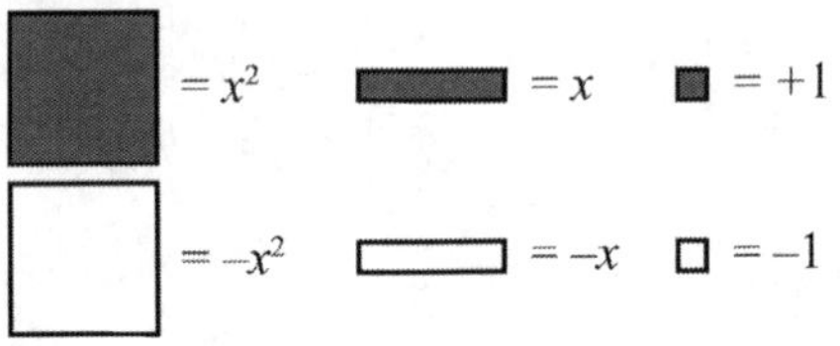

The algebra-tile model shown represents the product of the multiplication of two polynomials.

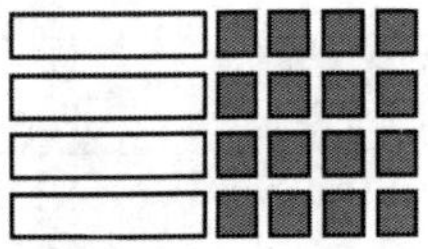

41. The product of which of the following two polynomials could result in the algebra-tile model shown?

A. $4(x-4)$

B. $2(2x-4)$

C. $4(-x+4)$

D. $2(-2x+4)$

NA2.07 solve first-degree equations with non-fractional coefficients, using a variety of tools and strategies

SOLVING FIRST-DEGREE EQUATIONS

A **first-degree equation** in one variable is a mathematical statement containing an equal sign between two polynomials, where each term cannot have a degree greater than 1. The exponent of the variable is always 1.

An example of a first degree equation is $2x+7=6(x-1)+15$.

Simple first-degree equations are solved by adding or subtracting a particular real number value from both sides of the equation in order to isolate the variable, or by dividing each term on both sides of the equation by the coefficient of the variable.

Example

1. The equation $x + 5 = 13$ is solved by subtracting 5 from both sides of the equation.
   $x + 5 - 5 = 13 - 5$
   $x = 8$

2. The equation $-2y = 10$ is solved by dividing each term on both sides of the equation by −2.
   $\frac{-2y}{-2}=\frac{10}{-2}$
   $y = -5$

More complicated equations involve a number of steps.

Example

The equation $2(3x-4)+7=5-4(6-2x)$ is solved by performing the following steps:

Eliminate brackets by multiplying each term in the brackets by the numerical value in front of the given bracket.

$6x-8+7=5-24+8x$

Collect like terms on both sides of the equation.

$6x-1=8x-19$

Subtract $6x$ from both sides of the equation.

$$6x-6x-1=8x-6x-19$$
$$-1=2x-19$$

Realign the equation with the x term on the left side of the equal sign.

$$2x-19=-1$$

Add 19 to both sides of the equation.

$$2x-19+19=-1+19$$
$$2x=18$$

Divide each term on both sides of the equation by 2.

$$\frac{2x}{2}=\frac{18}{2}$$
$$x=9$$

The solution to the equation can be verified by substituting the value of x into the original equation and showing that the left and right sides of the equation have equal values.

You can also use the balance model to portray the solution process of an equation.
Like algebra tiles, the shaded objects are positive, and the white objects are negative.

	Positive	**Negative**
x		
1		

To solve the equation using this model, add squares and circles to both sides until a shaded square  ends up on one side and the equivalent number of circles  or  end up on the other side.

Example

$$2x+5=4x-1$$

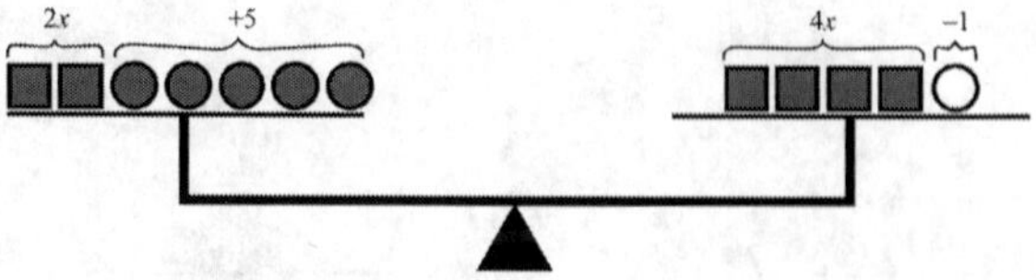

Add +1 to both sides by adding one shaded circle to both sides.

$$2x+5+1=4x-1+1$$

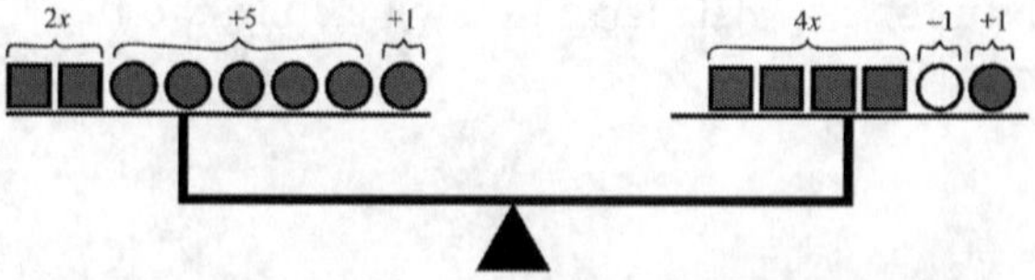

Cancel the values on the right side by taking away the white circle and shaded circle.

$$2x+6=4x$$

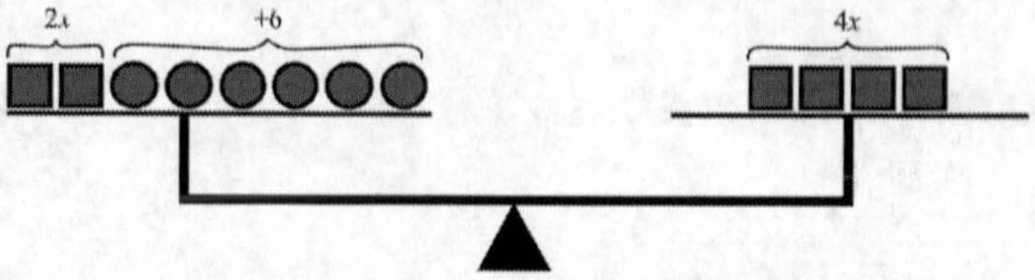

Add $-2x$ to both sides by adding two white squares to both sides.

$$2x-2x+6=4x-2x$$

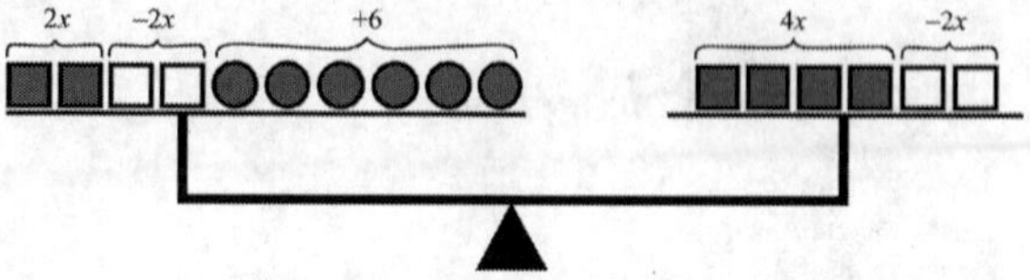

Subtract $-2x$ from both sides by taking away two white and two shaded squares.

$$6=2x$$

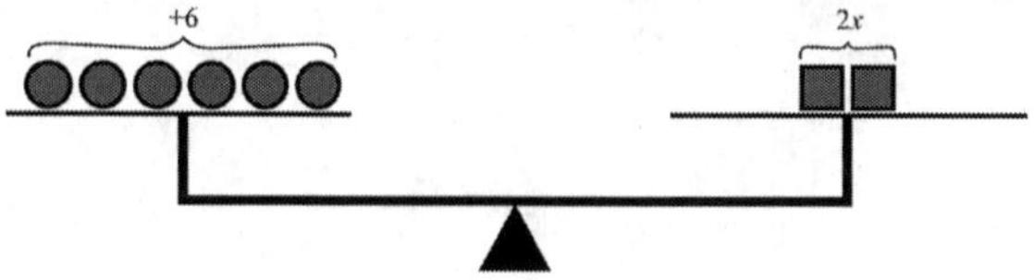

Divide both sides by 2.

Determine how many circles represent each box using a dotted line.

$$\frac{6}{2}=\frac{2x}{2}$$

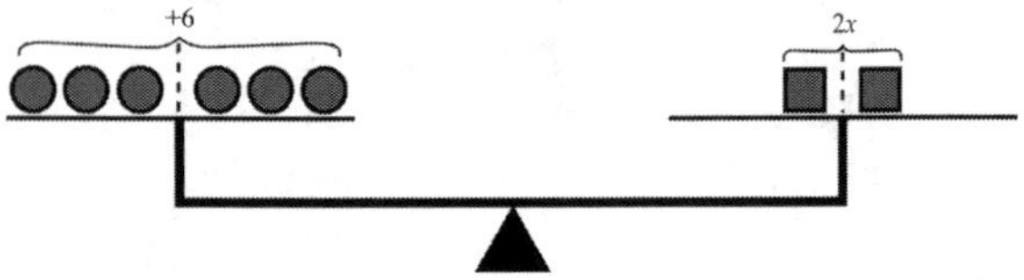

Isolate for x by balancing the single square to the number of circles.

$$3=x$$

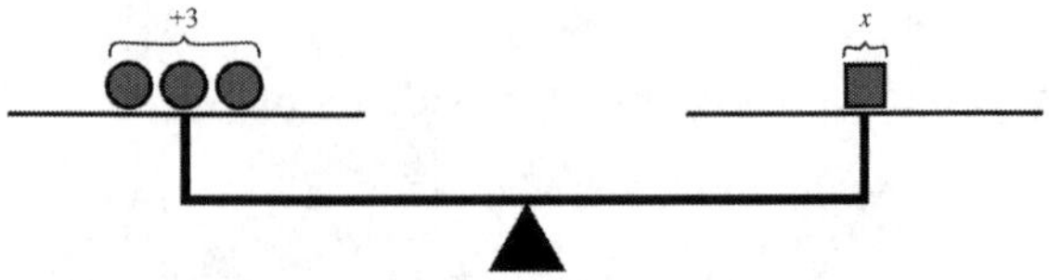

This balance portrays the final solution: $x = 3$.

PRACTICE QUESTIONS

42. The solution to the equation $3x-5=7$ is

A. $x = 12$

B. $x = 4$

C. $x = 2$

D. $x = -4$

43. The solution to the equation $4(2x-1)=20-2(6-x)$ is

A. $x=-2$

B. $x=1$

C. $x=2$

D. $x=12$

CHALLENGER QUESTION

The following scale is balanced.
Each shaded square represents x, and each shaded circle represents 1.

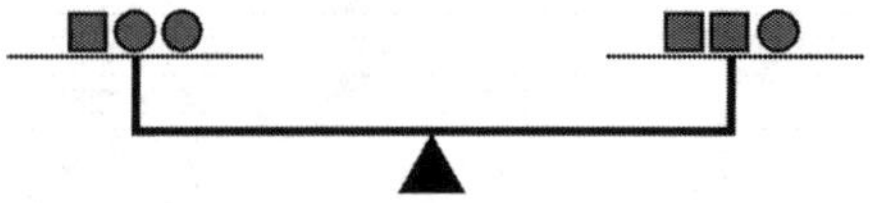

44. Which of the following scales is also balanced?

A.

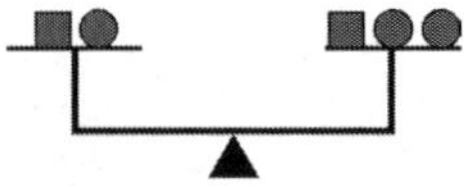

B.

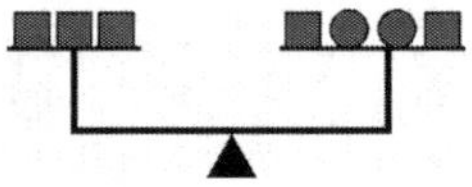

C.

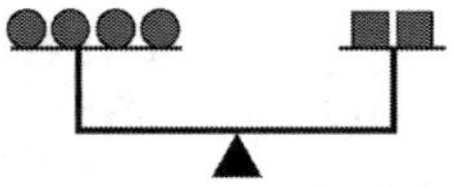

D.

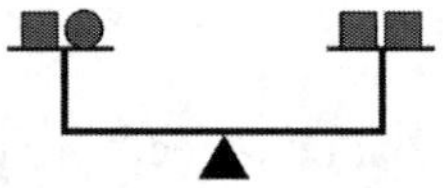

45. Which of the following scales is a balanced representation of the solution to the equation $2(x-3)+1=3x-2$, where each shaded square represents x, each shaded circle represents 1, and each unshaded circle represents –1?

A.

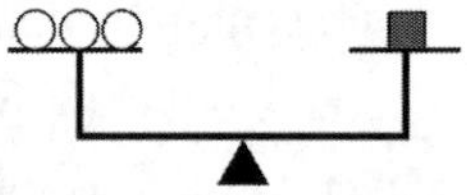

B.

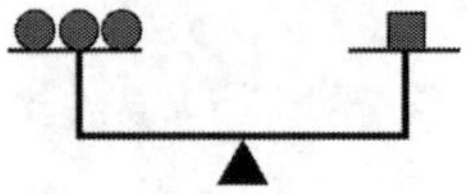

C.

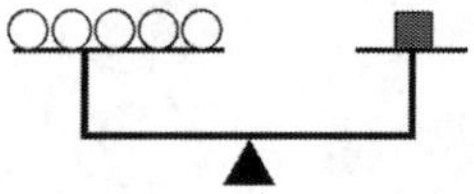

D.

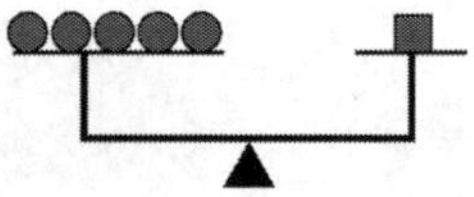

NA2.08 substitute into algebraic equations and solve for one variable in the first degree

SUBSTITUTING VALUES INTO ALGEBRAIC EQUATIONS

Algebraic equations involving several variables in the first degree can be solved by substituting stated values into the given equation.

Example

If $y = 6$ and $t = 4$, solve for x in the equation $2y - 3 = 2x + 1 + t$.

Substitute 6 for y and 4 for t in the given equation.

$2(6) - 3 = 2x + 1 + (4)$

Multiply where necessary, and then collect like terms on each side of the equation.

$12 - 3 = 2x + 1 + 4$

$9 = 2x + 5$

Subtract 5 from each side of the equation.

$9 - 5 = 2x + 5 - 5$

$4 = 2x$

Divide both sides of the equation by 2.

$\frac{4}{2} = \frac{2x}{2}$

$2 = x$

Realign the equation.

$x = 2$

This process of substitution and then solving the equation is useful in practical problems where more than one variable is present.

Example

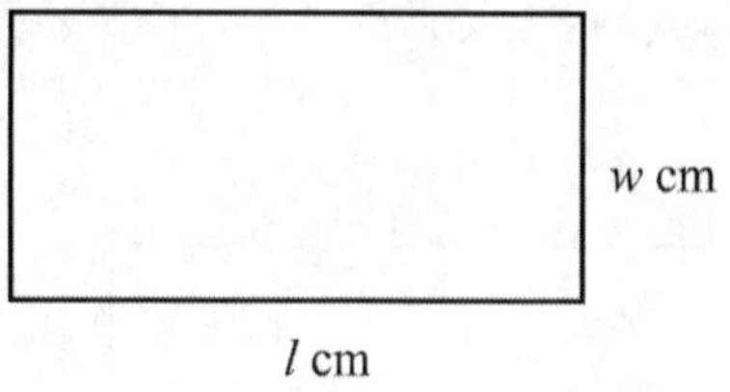

The perimeter, P, of a rectangle is $P = 2(w + l) = 2w + 2l$. If the perimeter is 83 cm and the width is 12 cm, what is the length?

Substitute 83 for P and 12 for w in the equation $P = 2w + 2l$.

$83 = 2(12) + 2l$

$83 = 24 + 2l$

Subtract 24 from both sides of the equation.

$83 - 24 = 24 - 24 + 2l$

$59 = 2l$

Divide both sides by 2.

$\frac{59}{2} = \frac{2l}{2}$

$29.5 = l$

$l = 29.5$

The length of the rectangle is 29.5 cm.

PRACTICE QUESTIONS

Numerical Response

7. The cost, C, in dollars, to rent a hall and provide a meal for each person attending a wedding reception is modelled by the equation $C = 52n + 800$, where n is the number of people attending the reception. If the total cost of the wedding was \$10 264, then the number of people that attended the wedding was ____________.

Use the following information to answer the next question.

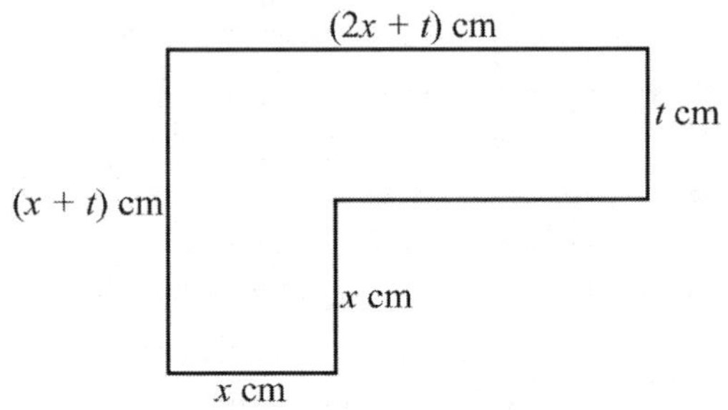

The perimeter of this shape, P, is represented by the equation $P = (6x + 4t)$ cm.

46. If the perimeter is 122 cm and x is 16 cm, then what is the value of t?

A. 6.5 cm

B. 14.0 cm

C. 14.8 cm

D. 42.0 cm

CHALLENGER QUESTION

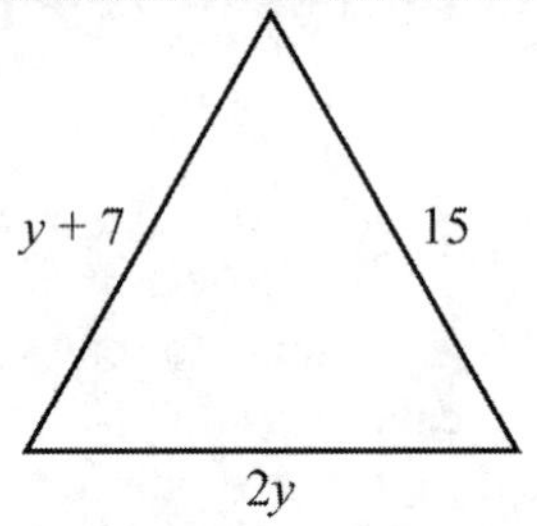

47. The lengths in centimetres representing the sides of the triangle are shown.
If the perimeter of the triangle is 37 cm, then what is the value of y?

A. 15.0 cm

B. 8.5 cm

C. 8.0 cm

D. 5.0 cm

Use the following information to answer the next question.

The total cost, C, in dollars of renting a facility for adults, a, and children, c, is given by the equation $C = 12a + 4(2c + 300)$.

48. If the total cost of renting the facility was \$3 208 and 86 adults attended, then how many children attended?

A. 272

B. 235

C. 165

D. 122

Open Response

2. An artist designed a rectangular frame for each of two different children's murals that are to be displayed on the wall of an art gallery. The murals, with their respective frames and labelled dimensions, are shown.

Mural I

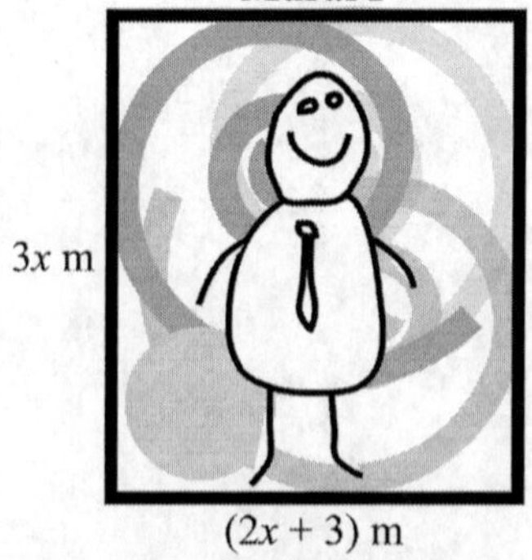

Mural II

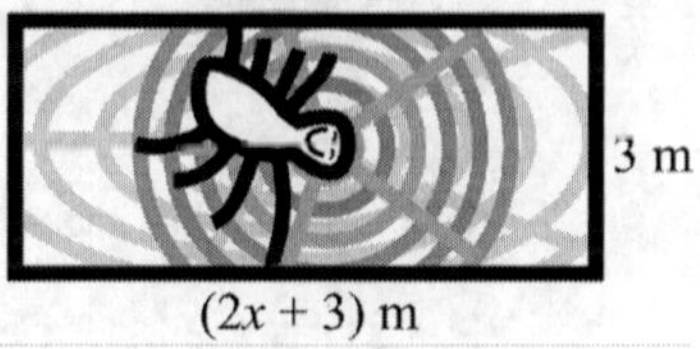

The total area, A, in square metres of the two framed murals is represented by the equation $A = 3x(2x+3)+3(2x+3)$.

a) Simplify the algebraic expression on the right side of the above equation using the operations of multiplication and addition.

b) If $x = 2.5$ m, determine the total area of the two framed murals.

ANSWERS AND SOLUTIONS—PRACTICE QUESTIONS

1. B	NR2. 624	18. B	24. D	34. C	44. D
2. C	10. C	19. C	25. D	35. D	45. A
3. A	11. A	20. A	26. C	36. B	NR7. 182
4. D	12. D	NR4. 700	27. A	37. D	46. A
5. B	13. B	OR1. **	28. C	38. B	47. D
6. C	14. A	NR5. 38	29. A	39. A	48. D
7. D	15. A	21. D	30. B	40. C	OR2. **
8. D	16. D	22. A	31. D	41. C	
9. A	NR3. 5 000	NR6. 81	32. A	42. B	
NR1. 15	17. B	23. A	33. A	43. C	

****SEE SOLUTION**

1. B

There are 3 shaded squares and 4 shaded circles; therefore, the ratio is 3:4.

2. C

There are 5 unshaded circles and a total of 16 shapes, producing a ratio of $\frac{5}{16}$.

This ratio is equivalent to $\frac{15}{48}$, since it is formed by multiplying the numerator and denominator of $\frac{5}{16}$ by 3.

$$\frac{5}{16}=\frac{5\times3}{16\times3}=\frac{15}{48}$$

3. A

To solve this problem, reduce each term of the given ratio by dividing out the greatest common factor of 3.

$33 \div 3 = 11$
$3 \div 3 \;\; = 1$
$30 \div 3 = 10$

Therefore, the reduced ratio is 11:1:10.

4. D

Reduce each fraction to lowest terms.

$$\frac{9}{15}\xrightarrow[\div 3]{\div 3}\frac{3}{5} \text{ and } \frac{21}{35}\xrightarrow[\div 7]{\div 7}\frac{3}{5} \quad \frac{3}{5}=\frac{3}{5}$$

Since these two fractions are equivalent, the proportion $\frac{9}{15}=\frac{21}{35}$ has equivalent ratios.

5. B

The ratio of the height to base of the illustrated triangle is 3:4. Jake's triangular piece of wood has a height-to-base ratio that could be represented as 45:b. The proportion between these two triangles is shown as: $\frac{3}{4}=\frac{45}{b}$

6. C

The ratios of the hypotenuse to the height for each triangle are as follows:

Triangle in diagram $\Rightarrow$ 5:3

New triangular wood piece $\Rightarrow$ 24:h

Therefore, the correct proportion representing this relationship is

$\frac{5}{3}=\frac{24}{h}$.

7. **D**

First, find the width of the original rectangle by applying the formula $A = lw$ as follows:

$A = lw$

Substitute 600 for A and 20 for l.

$600 = 20w$

Divide both sides by 20.

$\frac{600}{20} = \frac{20w}{20}$

$30 = w$

The correct proportion showing the ratios between the width and area of the two rectangles is $\frac{30}{600} = \frac{w}{300}$.

8. **D**

The ratio of red marbles to blue marbles in each bag is written as follows:

Bag 1: 10:15

Bag 2: 32:x

Since x is written as the second term in the second ratio, it represents the number of blue marbles in bag 2.

9. **A**

Determine the unit rates for Kerri and Lan.

Kerri:

Use the cross-product rule: $\frac{\$146.25}{15} = \frac{x}{1}$

$15x = \$146.25$

Divide each side of the equation by 15

$\frac{15x}{15} = \frac{\$146.25}{15}$

$x = \$9.75$

Lan:

Use the cross-product rule: $\frac{\$194.40}{18} = \frac{x}{1}$

$18x = \$194.40$

Divide both sides by 18

$\frac{18x}{18} = \frac{\$194.40}{18}$

$x = \$10.80$

Therefore, Lan earned $\$10.80 - \$9.75 = \$1.05/\text{h}$ more than Kerri.

NR 1 **15**

Six out of 10 squares in Diagram I are shaded. In lowest terms, three out of five squares are shaded.

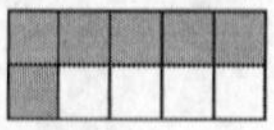

When the same proportion is applied to Diagram II, which is made up of 25 squares, $5 \times 3 = 15$ squares are shaded.

Therefore, $x = 15$.

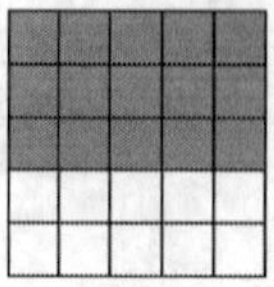

or

Set up the proportion of shaded to total squares for both diagrams.

$\frac{6}{10} = \frac{x}{25}$

Use the cross-product rule.

$(10)(x) = (6)(25)$

$10x = 150$

Divide both sides by 10.

$\frac{10x}{10} = \frac{150}{10}$

$x = 15$

NR 2 **624**

Using the method of equivalent ratios works well in solving this question.

$$\frac{96}{1}=\frac{x}{6.5}$$

Multiply each term in the left ratio by 6.5

$$\frac{96\times 6.5}{1\times 6.5}=\frac{x}{6.5}$$
$$\frac{624}{6.5}=\frac{x}{6.5}$$

Therefore, $x=624$ km

10. C

Begin by determining the actual length of the picture frame. Set up and solve the following proportion, where l represents length.

$$\frac{3}{5}=\frac{12}{l}$$

Use the cross-product rule.

$$(3)(l)=(12)(5)$$
$$3l=60$$

Divide both sides by 3.

$$\frac{3l}{3}=\frac{60}{3}$$
$$l=20$$

Now, to find the perimeter, apply the formula $P=2(l+w)$ as follows:

$P=2(\,l+w\,)$

Substitute 20 for l and 12 for w

$P=2\,(20+12\,)$

$P=2\,(32)$

$P=64$

The perimeter of the picture frame is 64 cm.

11. A

To solve this problem, determine the unit price for each box of laundry soap.

1.7 L box

$$\frac{3.27}{1.7}=\frac{x}{1}\Rightarrow\frac{(3.27)(1)}{(1.7)}=x$$
$$x=\$1.92/\text{L}$$

0.8 L box

$$\frac{1.49}{0.8}=\frac{x}{1}\Rightarrow\frac{(1.49)(1)}{0.8}=x$$
$$x=\$1.86/\text{L}$$

The unit price of the 1.7 L box is $\$1.92-\$1.86=\$0.06\,/\,\text{L}$ more than the unit price of the 0.8 L box.

12. D

A 56 g container of potato chips costs 85¢, and a 190 g container costs $1.89. The cost of 1 g of chips in each of the containers is shown as:

56-g container at 85¢:

$$\text{cost of 1 g}=\frac{85¢}{56\text{ g}}=1.518¢$$

190-g container at $1.89:

$$\text{cost of 1 g}=\frac{189¢}{190\text{ g}}=0.995¢$$

If the larger container is purchased, the amount saved per gram is $1.518¢-0.995¢=0.523¢$

13. B

First, calculate the total price of the three cases and the total price of the two cases, including the environmental fees:

Three cases
$(\$9.99+\$0.60)\times 3=\$10.59\times 3=\$31.77$

Two cases
$(\$11.28+\$0.60)\times 2=\$11.88\times 2=\$23.76$ Now, find the unit cost per bottle:

Three cases (30 bottles)
$\$31.77\div 30=\$1.059\,/\,\text{bottle}$

Two cases (24 bottles)
$\$23.76\div 24=\$0.990\,/\,\text{bottle}$

The better buy is two cases at an average cost of $0.990/bottle.

14. **A**

First, convert Dalia's time into minutes:

$1\text{ h} = 60\text{ min}$ and $\frac{3}{4}\text{ h} = 45\text{ min}$

Therefore, $1\frac{3}{4}\text{ h} = 60 + 45 = 105\text{ min}$

Now, find the unit rate of each biker:

Dalia

$\frac{42}{105} = 0.40\text{ km/min}$

Janet

$\frac{18}{50} = 0.36\text{ km/min}$

Dalia biked faster than Janet by $0.40 - 0.36 = 0.04\text{ km/min}$.

15. **A**

First, find the temperature change from –12°C to 3°C.

Temperature change $= 3 - (-12) = 15°\text{C}$

Now, set up the proportion to find the number of hours, x, it took to reach a temperature of 3°C.

$\frac{2°\text{C}}{1\text{h}} = \frac{15°\text{C}}{x}$

Use the cross-product rule.

$(2)(x) = (1)(15)$

$2x = 15$

Divide both sides by 2

$\frac{2x}{2} = \frac{15}{2}$

$x = 7.5\text{ h}$

7.5 hours after 3:00 A.M. is $3 + 7.5 = 10.5$ or 10:30 A.M.

The temperature was 3°C at 10:30 A.M.

16. **D**

Recall that $1\text{ cm} = 10\text{ mm}$; therefore, $20\text{ cm} = 200\text{ mm}$. Now, set up a proportion where x is the actual length of the bicycle.

$\frac{1}{200} = \frac{15}{x}$

Multiply each term in the first ratio by 15 to create equivalent ratios

$\frac{1 \times 15}{200 \times 15} = \frac{15}{x}$

$\frac{15}{3\ 000} = \frac{15}{x}$

Since the ratios are equivalent, $x = 3\ 000\text{ mm}$.

There are 1 000 mm in 1 m, so $x = \frac{3\ 000}{1\ 000} = 3$

The length of the bicycle is 3.00 m.

NR 3 **5 000**

Determine the proportionality for an investment of \$2 000 that earns \$160 in interest by setting up a proportion where x is the amount of money Luke invested.

$\frac{2\ 000}{160} = \frac{x}{400}$

Use the cross-product rule

$(160)(x) = (2000)(400)$

$160x = 800\ 000$

Divide both sides by 160

$\frac{160x}{160} = \frac{800\ 000}{160}$

$x = 5\ 000$

Luke invested \$5 000 in order to earn \$400 interest.

17. B

Set up the proportion between CAD and EUR.

$$\frac{1.494\,7\ \text{CAD}}{1\ \text{EUR}}=\frac{1\,900\ \text{CAD}}{x}$$

Use the cross-product rule.

$$\begin{aligned}(1.494\,7)(x)&=(1)(1\,900)\\ 1.494\,7x&=1\,900\end{aligned}$$

Divide both sides by 1 4947.

$$\frac{1.494\,7x}{1.494\,7}=\frac{1\,900}{1.494\,7}$$

$$x\approx 1\,271$$

Ravi purchased 1 271 euros.

18. B

Determine Kenji's percentage on the first test.

$$\begin{aligned}P&=\frac{72}{80}\times 100=\frac{72}{80}\times\frac{100}{1}=\frac{7\,200}{80}\\ P&=90\%\end{aligned}$$

Determine the number of questions, n, Kenji got correct on the second test.

$$\begin{aligned}n&=90\%\text{ of }120\\ &=\left(\frac{90}{100}\right)(120)\\ &=(0.90)(120)\\ &=108\end{aligned}$$

If Kenji got 108 questions correct on the second test, then the number of questions that were incorrect was $120-108=12$.

19. C

Determine the PST and GST on the shoes.

$$\begin{aligned}8\%\text{ of }\$95&=0.08\times\$95=\$7.60\\ 5\%\text{ of }\$95&=0.05\times\$95=\$4.75\end{aligned}$$

Now, add these taxes to the original price.

$$\$95+\$7.60+\$4.75=\$107.35$$

The total cost of the running shoes is $107.35

20. A

Determine the amount, x, earned.

$$\begin{aligned}x&=8\%\text{ of }\$2\,400\\ x&=\left(\frac{8}{100}\right)\$2\,400\\ x&=(0.08)\$2\,400\\ x&=\$192\end{aligned}$$

Find the rate of commission, y, as follows:

$$y=\frac{\$651}{\$4\,200}\times 100=\frac{(\$651)(100)}{(\$4\,200)}=15.5\%$$

The correct values for x and y are $192 and 15.5%, respectively.

NR 4 700

Calculate the interest rate of Petra's investment, I.

$$\begin{aligned}I&=\frac{\$168}{\$2\,400}\times 100\\ &=\frac{\$16\,800}{\$2\,400}\\ &=7\%\end{aligned}$$

Now, determine 7% of Stephen's investment of $10 000.

$$\frac{7}{100}\times\$10\,000=0.07\times\$10\,000=\$700$$

or

Set up a proportion where the unknown interest earned is x.

$$\frac{\$168}{\$2\,400}=\frac{x}{\$10\,000}$$

Use the cross-product rule

$$\begin{aligned}(2\,400)(x)&=(168)(10\,000)\\ 2\,400x&=1\,680\,000\end{aligned}$$

Divide both sides by 2 400

$$\frac{2\,400x}{2400}=\frac{1\,680\,00}{2\,400}$$

$$x=700$$

After one year, Stephen's investment of $10 000 would have earned $700 interest.

OR1

Determine the annual simple interest rate, I, at each bank.

Bank I

$I_1 = \frac{\$55}{\$1\,000} \times 100 = \frac{\$5\,500}{\$1\,000} = 5.5\%$

Bank II:

$I_2 = \frac{\$65}{\$1\,000} \times 100 = \frac{\$6\,500}{1\,000} = 6.5\%$

Determine the simple interest, S, earned at each bank on an investment of $2 400.

Bank I:

$S_2 = \frac{5.5}{100} \times \$2\,400 = \frac{\$13\,200}{100} = \$132$

Bank II:

$S_2 = \frac{6.5}{100} \times \$2\,400 = \frac{\$15\,600}{100} = \$156$

The total simple interest Lin would earn on her two investments is $S_1 + S_2 = \$132 + \$156 = \$288$

NR 5 **38**

Follow the order of operations of BEDMAS.

$6^2 - 8 \div (3-1) + 3 \times 2$	
$= 6^2 - 8 \div (2) + 3 \times 2$	Brackets first.
$= 36 - 8 \div (2) + 3 \times 2$	Exponent next.
$= 36 - 4 + 3 \times 2$	Multiply/divide in order
$= 36 - 4 + 6$	
$= 32 + 6$	Add/subtract in order.
$= 38$	

21. **D**

Begin by writing $2\frac{3}{4}$ as an improper fraction, and then convert the operation from division to multiplication by taking the reciprocal of the second fraction. Multiply the numerators and denominators. Finally, write the resulting fraction in mixed form.

These steps are shown as:

$$\begin{aligned}\frac{11}{4} \div \frac{2}{3} &= \frac{11}{4} \times \frac{3}{2}\\ &= \frac{33}{8}\\ &= 4\frac{1}{8}\end{aligned}$$

22. **A**

The perimeter of the given triangle can be found by finding the sum of the lengths of the sides of the triangle. Begin by converting the fractions so that they all have a common denominator of 8.

$6\frac{1}{2} = 6\frac{4}{8}$ $\quad 8\frac{3}{4} = 8\frac{6}{8}$ $\quad 10\frac{1}{8} = 10\frac{1}{8}$

Now add the three resulting fractions.

$$\begin{aligned}6\frac{4}{8} + 8\frac{6}{8} + 10\frac{1}{8} &= (6+8+10) + (\frac{4}{8} + \frac{6}{8} + \frac{1}{8})\\ &= 24\frac{11}{8}\end{aligned}$$

Simplify $24\frac{11}{8}$ to

$24 + \frac{11}{8} = 24 + 1\frac{3}{8} = 25\frac{3}{8}$

or

Write each fraction as an improper fraction. $6\frac{1}{2} = \frac{13}{2}$ $\quad 8\frac{3}{4} = \frac{35}{4}$ $\quad 10\frac{1}{8} = \frac{81}{8}$

Convert each fraction so they all have a common denominator of 8.

$\frac{13}{2} = \frac{52}{8}$ $\quad \frac{35}{4} = \frac{70}{8}$

Now, add the three improper fractions, and convert the resulting fraction to mixed form.

$$\frac{52}{8}+\frac{70}{8}+\frac{81}{8}$$
$$=\frac{203}{8}$$
$$=25\frac{3}{8}$$

The perimeter of the triangle is $25\frac{3}{8}$ cm.

NR 6 **81**

$\sqrt{x}=9$

Square both sides of the equation to eliminate the radical sign.

$$\left(\sqrt{x}\right)^2=(9)^2$$
$$x=81$$

23. **A**

$\sqrt{16}$ means the positive square root of 16, which is 4, because $(4)(4)=16$.

24. **D**

The area of a square is $A=(x)(x)$ or $A=x^2$. The area of the base of the pyramid is given as 10 000 m^2.

$x^2=10\ 000\text{m}^2$

Take the square root of each side of the equation.

$$\sqrt{x^2}=\sqrt{10\ 000\text{m}^2}$$
$$x=\pm\sqrt{10\ 000\text{m}^2}$$
$$x=\pm100\text{ m}$$

The length of a side of a square cannot be negative, so the value of x is 100 m.

25. **D**

To find the square root of 64, use a square with an area of 64 square units. The length of each side of the square is the square root of the number.

Since each side of a square with an area of 64 square units is 8 units long, the square root of 64 is 8. Diagram D is a square with an area of 64 square units.

26. **C**

The volume of the cube is a three-dimensional quantity.

$$V=(x\text{ cm})(x\text{ cm})(x\text{ cm})$$
$$V=(x^2\text{ cm}^2)(x\text{ cm})$$
$$V=x^3\text{ cm}^3$$

Therefore, the expression that does not represent the volume of the cube is x^2.

27. **A**

The area of the rectangle is a two-dimensional quantity.

Use the formula $A=lw$ to determine the area of the given rectangle as follows:

$$A=(6x\text{ cm})(2x\text{ cm})$$
$$A=(6)(2)(x\text{ cm})(x\text{ cm})$$
$$A=12x^2\text{ cm}^2$$

Therefore, the area of the rectangle can be represented as $12x^2$ cm^2.

28. **C**

The perimeter of a square is the distance around the square and is a one-dimensional quantity.

Use the formula $P=4s$ to determine the perimeter of the given square as follows:

$$P=4(2x)$$
$$P=8x$$

The perimeter of the square can be represented as $8x$.

29. **A**

The area of this shape is determined by calculating the sum of the area of the bottom square and the area of the upper rectangle.

$$A=A_{\text{square}}+A_{\text{rectangle}}$$
$$A=lw+lw$$
$$A=(x)(x)+\boxed{?}(2x)$$
$$7x^2=x^2+\boxed{?}(2x)$$

The area of the rectangle must be $6x^2$ so that when added to the area of the square x^2, it will produce the total area of $7x^2$.

$$6x^2=\boxed{?}(2x)$$

Divide both sides by $2x$

$$\frac{6x^2}{2x}=\frac{\boxed{?}(2x)}{2x}$$

$3x=\boxed{?}$, since $(3x)(2x)=6x^2$

Therefore, the missing expression is $3x$.

30. **B**

Substitute the value of –2 in for x, and then evaluate the resulting expression as follows:

$$8x^3=8(-2)^3=8(-2)(-2)(-2)=-64$$

31. **D**

Substitute the given values into each appropriate expression of volume.

$V_{\text{cube}}=s^2=(8.2)^3=8.2^3=551.368\text{ cm}^3$ **or** $(8.2)(8.2)(8.2)=551.368\text{ cm}^3$

$$\begin{aligned}V_{\text{cylinder}}&=\pi r^2h=\pi(4.4\text{ cm})^2(8.2\text{ cm})\\&=\pi(4.4\text{ cm})(4.4\text{ cm})(8.2\text{ cm})\\&\approx 498.734\text{ cm}^3\end{aligned}$$

The volume of the cubic container is approximately $551.368\text{ cm}^3-498.734\text{ cm}^3=52.6\text{ cm}^3$ more than the volume of the cylindrical container.

32. **A**

Each part of the expression defines a particular power.

$$3\left(-\frac{3}{2}\right)\left(-\frac{3}{2}\right)\left(-\frac{3}{2}\right)=3\left(-\frac{3}{2}\right)^3$$

$$2\left(\frac{1}{2}\right)\left(\frac{1}{2}\right)=2\left(\frac{1}{2}\right)^2$$

The expression $3\left(-\frac{3}{2}\right)^3+2\left(\frac{1}{2}\right)^2$

is equivalent to

$$3\left(-\frac{3}{2}\right)\left(-\frac{3}{2}\right)\left(-\frac{3}{2}\right)+2\left(\frac{1}{2}\right)\left(\frac{1}{2}\right).$$

33. **A**

Calculate the area of each shape.

$$\begin{aligned}A_{\text{circle}}&=\pi r^2=\pi(2.5\text{ cm})^2\\&=\pi(2.5\text{ cm})(2.5\text{ cm})\\&=19.6\text{ cm}^2\\A_{\text{square}}&=s^2=(4.0\text{ cm})^2=16.0\text{ cm}^2\\A_{\text{triangle}}&=\frac{1}{2}bh\\&=\frac{1}{2}(4.5\text{ cm})(6.8\text{ cm})\\&=15.3\text{ cm}^2\\A_{\text{rectangle}}&=lw=(6\text{ cm})(3\text{ cm})=18\text{ cm}^2\end{aligned}$$

The circle with an area of 19.6 cm^2 covers the greatest area.

34. **C**

Simplify by collecting like terms.

$$\begin{aligned}&(6x^2+4x-7)+(2x^2-4x-3)\\&=(6x^2+2x^2)+(4x-4x)+(-7-3)\\&=8x^2+0x-10\\&=8x^2-10\end{aligned}$$

or

$$\begin{array}{r}6x^2+4x-7\\ \underline{+2x^2-4x-3}\\ 8x^2-0x-10\\ =8x^2-10\end{array}$$

When the expression $(6x^2+4x-7)+(2x^2-4x-3)$ is simplified, it is equivalent to $8x^2-10$.

35. **D**

To translate the arrangement of algebra tiles into algebraic form, use the following legend:

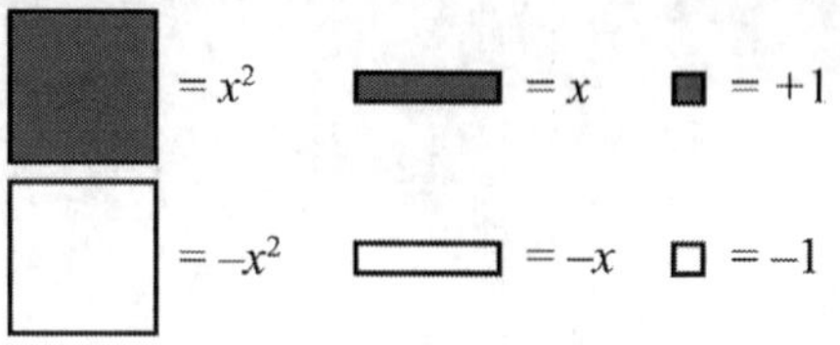

Written algebraically, the arrangement of algebra tiles is $(4x^2-6x+2)+(3x^2-2x-4)$

By collecting like terms, the expression simplifies to

$$\begin{aligned}&(4x^2+3x^2)+(-6x-2x)+(2-4)\\&=7x^2-8x-2\end{aligned}$$

36. B

Change every sign of each term in the second polynomial to switch the problem to an addition question.

$$(4x^2+3x-9)-(3x+2-6x^2+x^3)$$
$$=(4x^2+3x-9)+(-3x-2+6x^2-x^3)$$

Simplify by collecting like terms.

$$(-x^3)+(4x^2+6x^2)+(3x-3x)+(-9-2)$$
$$=-x^3+10x^2+0x-11$$
$$=-x^3+10x^2-11$$

or

Set up the problem vertically by aligning common terms between the two polynomials.

$$\begin{array}{rr} & 4x^2+3x-9 \\ - & \underline{x^3-6x^2+3x+2} \end{array}$$

Change to addition by reversing the signs of the bottom polynomial.

$$\begin{array}{rr} & 4x^2+3x-9 \\ + & \underline{-x^3+6x^2-3x-2} \\ & -x^3+10x^2+0x-11 \\ = & -x^3+10x^2-11 \end{array}$$

37. D

The perimeter of a rectangle is the distance around the outside, which can be found using the formula $P=l+w+l+w$:

$$P=\left(x^2+2x-6\right)+\left(x-3\right)+\left(x^2+2x-6\right)+\left(x-3\right)$$

Collect like terms, and simplify the expression.

$$P=\left(x^2+x^2\right)+\left(2x+x+2x+x\right)+(-6-3-6-3)$$

$$P=2x^2+6x-18$$

38. B

Multiply each term in the brackets by 3.

$$3(4y+7)-21$$
$$=(3)(4y)+(3)(7)-21$$

or

$$\begin{array}{r} 4y+7 \\ \times\quad 3 \\ \hline 12y+21 \end{array}$$

Simplify each term, and then collect like terms.

$$=12y+21-21$$
$$=12y$$

39. A

Multiply the monomial $7x$ by each term of the polynomial $5x^2+3x+14$

$$7x(5x^2+3x+14)$$
$$=(7x)(5x^2)+(7x)(3x)+(7x)(14)$$

or

$$\begin{array}{r} 5x^2+3x+14 \\ \times \qquad\quad 7x \\ \hline (7x)(5x^2)+(7x)(3x)+(7x)(14) \end{array}$$

Multiply the numerical coefficients together and add the exponents of the variable, *x*, in each term.

$$(7)(5)(x)(x^2)+(7)(3)(x)(x)+(7)(14)(x)$$
$$=35x^{1+2}+21x^{1+1}+98x$$
$$=35x^3+21x^2+98x$$

40. C

Multiply the monomial 2*x* by each term of the polynomial x^2+4x+7.

$$2x(x^2+4x+7)$$
$$=(2x)(x^2)+(2x)(4x)+(2x)(7)$$

Multiply the numerical coefficients together, and add the exponents of the variable, *x*, in each term.

$$=2x^3+8x^2+14x^1$$
$$=2x^{1+2}+8x^{1+1}+14x^1$$

or

$$\begin{array}{r} x^2+4x+7 \\ \times \qquad 2x \\ \hline (2x)(x^2)+2x(4x)+(2x)(7) \end{array}$$

The value of $p = 3$, $q = 2$, and $r = 1$.

$p+q+r=3+2+1=6.$

41. C

In the given algebra-tile model, there are four identical rows of algebra tiles. Each row contains one unshaded x-tile and four shaded 1-tiles. This represents 4 times $(-x + 4)$ or $4(-x + 4)$.
The product of 4 and $-x + 4$ represents the algebra-tile model.

42. B

$3x - 5 = 7$

Add 5 to both sides.

$$\begin{aligned} 3x-5+5&=7+5 \\ 3x&=12 \end{aligned}$$

Divide both sides by 3.

$$\begin{aligned} \frac{3x}{3}&=\frac{12}{3} \\ x&=4 \end{aligned}$$

43. C

$$\begin{aligned} 4(2x-1)&=20-2(6-x) \\ 4(2x)+4(-1)&=20-2(6)-2(-x) \\ 8x-4&=20-12+2x \end{aligned}$$

Collect like terms.

$8x-4=8+2x$

Subtract $2x$ from both sides.

$$\begin{aligned} 8x-2x-4&=8+2x-2x \\ 6x-4&=8 \end{aligned}$$

Add 4 to both sides

$$\begin{aligned} 6x-4+4&=8+4 \\ 6x&=12 \end{aligned}$$

Divide both sides by 6.

$$\begin{aligned} \frac{6x}{6}&=\frac{12}{6} \\ x&=2 \end{aligned}$$

44. D

The original scale represents the algebraic equation $x+2=2x+1$.

Solve for x as follows:

$x+2=2x+1$

Subtract 1 from both sides.

$x+2-1=2x+1-1$

$x+1=2x$

Subtract x from both sides.

$x-x+1=2x-x$

$1=x$

Realign the equation

$x=1$

The scale illustrated in alternative **D** represents the equation $x+1=2x$.

Solve for x as follows:

$x+1=2x$

$x-x+1=2x-x$

Subtract x from both sides.

$1=x$

Realign the equation.

$x=1$

Since the solution to both equations is $x=1$, the scale shown in alternative **D** is balanced.

45. A

Solve for x in the equation $2(x-3)+1=3x-2$ as follows:

$2(x-3)+1=3x-2$

Multiply each term in the brackets by 2.

$2x-6+1=3x-2$

Collect like terms

$2x-5=3x-2$

Add 2 to both sides.

$2x-5+2=3x-2+2$

$2x-3=3x$

Subtract $2x$ from both sides.

$$2x - 2x - 3 = 3x - 2x$$
$$-3 = x$$

Realign the equation

$x = -3$

The balanced scale that models this solution is the scale illustrated in choice A.

NR 7: 182

Substitute 10 264 for C in the equation $C = 52n + 800$. Now, solve the equation $10\ 264 = 52n + 800$ as follows:

$10\ 264 = 52n + 800$

Subtract 800 from both sides

$10\ 264 - 800 = 52n + 800 - 800$

$9\ 464 = 52n$

Divide both sides by 52

$$\frac{9\ 464}{52} = \frac{52n}{52}$$
$$182 = n$$

Realign the equation

$n = 182$

There were 182 people at the reception.

46. A

Begin by substituting 122 for P and 16 for x in the equation $P = 6x + 4t$. $122 = 6(16) + 4t$ or $122 = 96 + 4t$.
Solve the equation $122 = 96 + 4t$ as follows:

$122 = 96 + 4t$

Subtract 96 from both sides.

$122 - 96 = 96 - 96 + 4t$

$26 = 4t$

Divide both sides by 4.

$$\frac{26}{4} = \frac{4t}{4}$$

$6.5 = t$

Realign the equation

$t = 6.5$

The value of side t is 6.5 cm.

47. D

The perimeter, P, of the triangle can be described by the equation

$P = 2y + y + 7 + 15$.

When like terms are collected, the equation becomes $P = 3y + 22$.

Substitute 37 for P in the equation $P = 3y + 22$, and solve for y as follows:

$37 = 3y + 22$

Subtract 22 from both sides.

$37 - 22 = 3y + 22 - 22$

$15 = 3y$

Divide both sides by 3.

$$\frac{15}{3} = \frac{3y}{3}$$

$5 = y$

Realign the equation.

$y = 5$

The value of y is 5.0 cm.

48. D

Substitute 3 208 for C and 86 for a in the equation $C = 12a + 4(2c + 300)$,
and then solve for c as follows:

$$C = 12a + 4(2c + 300)$$
$$3\ 208 = 12(86) + 4(2c + 300)$$
$$3\ 208 = 1\ 032 + 4(2c + 300)$$

Multiply each term in the brackets by 4

$3\ 208 = 1\ 032 + 4(2c) + 4(300)$

Simplify

$3\ 208 = 1\ 032 + 8c + 1\ 200$

Collect like terms:

$3\ 208 = 8c + 2\ 232$

Subtract 2 232 from both sides:

$3\ 208 - 2\ 232 = 8c + 2\ 232 - 2\ 232$

$976 = 8c$

Divide both sides by 8

$$\frac{976}{8} = \frac{8c}{8}$$

$122 = c$

Realign the equation

$c = 122$

The number of children that attended the facility was 122.

OR2

Multiply each term in front of the brackets by each term inside the brackets as follows:

$$A = 3x(2x+3)+3(2x+3)$$
$$A = 3x(2x)+3x(3)+3(2x)+3(3)$$

Multiply the numerical coefficients together and add the exponents of the variable, x, in each term

$$A = (3)(2)(x)(x)+(3)(3)(x)+3(2)(x)+9$$
$$A = 6x^{1+1}+9x+6x+9$$

Collect like terms

$$A = 6x^2+15x+9$$

Substitute $x = 2.5$ into the original equation or into the simplified equation for area, A.

$$A = 3(2.5)[2(2.5)+3]+3[2(2.5)+3]$$

Calculate the values in the nested brackets first, following the rules of BEDMAS (multiply first then add).

$$A = 3(2.5)[5.0+3]+3[5.0+3]$$

$$A = 3(2.5)(8.0)+3(8.0)$$

Multiply and then add the terms.

$A = 60 + 24$

$A = 84\text{ m}^2$

or

Substitute $x = 2.5$ in the simplified equation in part (a).

$$A = 6(2.5)+15(2.5)+9$$

Following BEDMAS, do exponents first, then multiply, and finally add.

$$A = 6(2.5)(2.5)+1.5(2.5)+9$$
$$A = 37.5+37.5+9$$
$$A = 84\text{ m}^2$$

The total area of the two framed murals is 84 m^2.

UNIT TEST—NUMBER SENSE AND ALGEBRA

1. Tom has 10 green marbles and 7 blue marbles. Which of the following ratios is equivalent to the ratio of blue marbles to the total number of marbles?

   A. 20:34

   B. 21:30

   C. 21:51

   D. 68:28

2. There are 20 girls, 16 boys, and 8 adults at a birthday party. The three-term ratio of girls to boys to adults in lowest terms is

   A. 20:16:8

   B. 10:8:4

   C. 10:8:1

   D. 5:4:2

3. The sail of a small sailboat has a height-to-width ratio of 5 m to 8 m. The sail of a large sailboat, with the same ratio of dimensions as the sail of the small sailboat, has a width of 8 m. The proportion that could be used to determine the height, h, of the sail of the larger sailboat is

   A. $\frac{5}{8} = \frac{h}{8}$

   B. $\frac{5}{8} = \frac{8}{h}$

   C. $\frac{8}{8} = \frac{h}{5}$

   D. $\frac{8}{8} = \frac{5}{h}$

4. Marcus wanted to cut a piece of wood with a length of 48 cm and a width of w cm. If the wood is to be cut in a length-to-width ratio of 5:2, then the simplified proportion Marcus could write to help him determine his width is

   A. $\frac{1}{0.4} = \frac{48}{w}$

   B. $\frac{1}{0.4} = \frac{w}{48}$

   C. $\frac{1}{2.5} = \frac{48}{w}$

   D. $\frac{2}{5} = \frac{48}{w}$

Numerical Response

1. The ratio of DVDs to VHS tapes at a movie store is 13:2. If there are 650 DVDs in the store, then the number of VHS tapes is

____________.

Use the following information to answer the next question.

The local supermarket sells a 6-kg bag of oranges for $7.50.

5. What is the unit price for 1 kg of oranges?

   A. $0.67

   B. $0.80

   C. $1.25

   D. $1.43

Use the following information to answer the next question.

Michael Johnson set a world record of 19.32 seconds in the 200-m race at the 1996 Summer Olympic Games.	Donovan Bailey set a world record of 9.84 seconds in the 100-m race at the same Games.

6. Which of the following statements about the runners' average speeds is **true**?
   A. Donovan Bailey's average speed was 0.19 m/s faster than Michael Johnson's average speed.
   B. Michael Johnson's average speed was 0.19 m/s faster than Donovan Bailey's average speed.
   C. Donovan Bailey's average speed was 1.9 m/s faster than Michael Johnson's average speed.
   D. Michael Johnson's average speed was 1.9 m/s faster than Donovan Bailey's average speed.

Use the following information to answer the next question.

Ketchup comes in four sizes at a supermarket. The price of each size is shown.

200 mL = $1.24

500 mL = $2.50

1 000 mL = $4.98

2 200 mL = $13.20

7. Which ketchup size is the best buy?
   A. 200 mL
   B. 500 mL
   C. 1 000 mL
   D. 2 200 mL

Use the following information to answer the next question.

A cheetah is the fastest land animal and can maintain a steady speed over a certain distance. The table shows the distance, *d*, in meters, travelled by a cheetah for different times, *t*, in seconds.

***t* (s)**	2	3	5	8	10	14
***d* (m)**	56	84	140	224	280	392

8. If the distance is directly proportional to the time, then how far would the cheetah travel in 1 min?
   A. 1 680 m
   B. 2 520 m
   D. 3 360 m
   C. 5 040 m

Numeric Response

2. Renée is travelling from Toronto, Canada to Acapulco, Mexico. If the exchange rate is 9.77 Mexican pesos (MXN) to 1 Canadian dollar (CAD), then the number of Mexican pesos she would receive for 200 Canadian dollars is __________(MXN).

9. People purchasing products in Alberta only pay 5% GST, while people purchasing products in Ontario pay 8% PST and 5% GST. How much more tax does a person in Ontario pay on a $1 200 purchase than a person in Alberta?
   A. $72
   B. $96
   C. $100
   D. $168

Use the following information to answer the next question.

Jacques made four investments at four different banks. The table shows the interest earned on each investment after one year.

Bank	Investment	Interest Earned
1	$2 000	$180
2	$800	$68
3	$1500	$117
4	$1 600	$128

10. Which bank provided the lowest interest rate?

A. Bank 1

B. Bank 2

C. Bank 3

D. Bank 4

Use the following diagram to answer the next question.

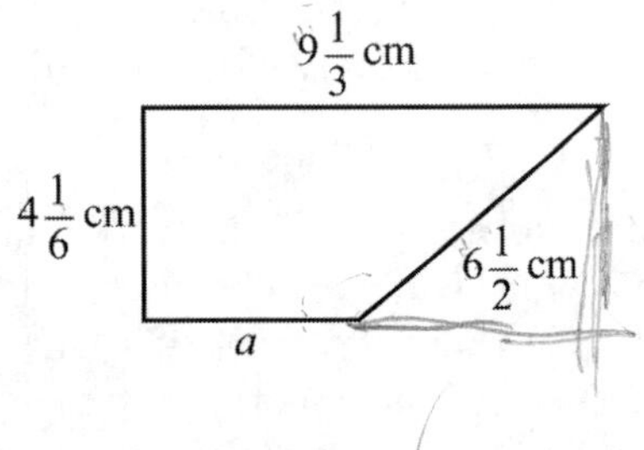

11. The perimeter of the illustrated shape is $22\frac{2}{3}$ cm. What is the measure of the missing side, a?

A. $19\frac{5}{6}$ cm

B. $3\frac{4}{6}$ cm

C. $3\frac{1}{3}$ cm

D. $2\frac{2}{3}$ cm

Use the following diagram to answer the next question.

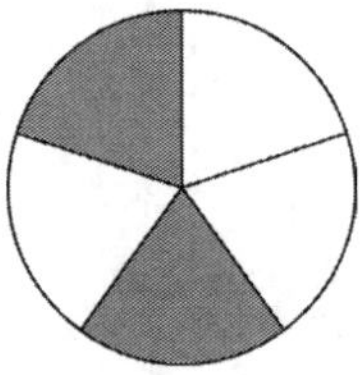

12. The number of shaded sections in relation to the total number of sections in the given diagram can be represented as a fraction. What is the reciprocal of this fraction?

A. $\frac{5}{2}$

B. $\frac{7}{5}$

C. $\frac{5}{7}$

D. $\frac{3}{5}$

13. The number of solutions to the equation $x^2 = 12$ is

A. zero

B. one

C. two

D. four

Use the following information to answer the next question.

Derek stated that $\sqrt{9} = \pm 3$.

Emily stated that $(-4)^2 = -16$.

Jeremy stated that in $x^2 = 25$, x is only equal to 5.

Charissa stated that in $\sqrt{x} = 10$, x is only equal to 100.

14. The person that made a correct statement is

A. Derek

B. Emily

C. Jeremy

D. Charissa

Use the following information to answer the next question.

A structure is formed by stacking seven identically sized cubes.

15. If the sides of the cubes are x cm long, what is the volume of the entire structure?

A. $6x$ cm^3

B. $7x$ cm^3

C. $6x^3$ cm^3

D. $7x^3$ cm^3

16. If the area of a square can be represented as $16x^2$ cm^2, then what is the representation of the length of each side of the square?

A. $16x$ cm

B. $8x$ cm

C. $4x$ cm

D. $2x$ cm

Use the following information to answer the next question.

Four different students evaluated the expression $2p^3 - p^2$, where $p = -2.2$. Their answers are shown.

Paula: 16.456

Dahlia: 90.024

James: 26.136

Landon: 16.456

17. Which student evaluated the expression correctly?

A. Paula

B. Dahlia

C. James

D. Landon

Use the following information to answer the next question.

A company was designing a cup. Two different possible cup shapes are shown

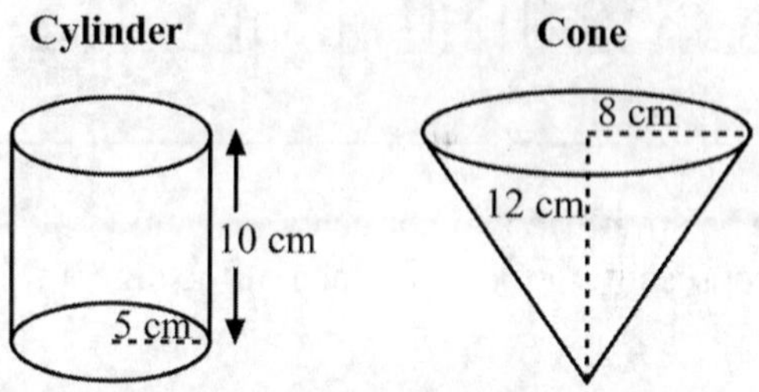

$V_{cylinder} = \pi r^2 h$ $V_{cone} = \frac{1}{3}\pi r^2 h$

18. With respect to the volume of each cup, the volume of the cylinder is

A. 18.8 cm^3 more than the volume of the cone

B. 18.8 cm^3 less than the volume of the cone

C. 6.0 cm^3 more than the volume of the cone

D. 6.0 cm^3 less than the volume of the cone

19. Which of the following expressions is equivalent to $(4x^2 + 3x - 9) + (2x + 2 + 6x^2)$?

A. 6x2 + 5x – 77

B. 10x2 + 5x –7

C. 10x2 + 5x –11

D. 24x2 + 6x –18

Use the following information to answer the next question.

The algebra tiles below represent an algebraic term or numerical value. Shaded tiles are positive, and unshaded tiles are negative.

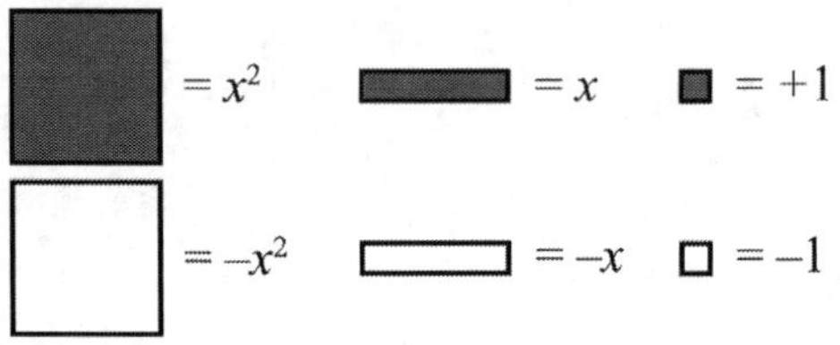

The diagram below represents the subtraction of two polynomials.

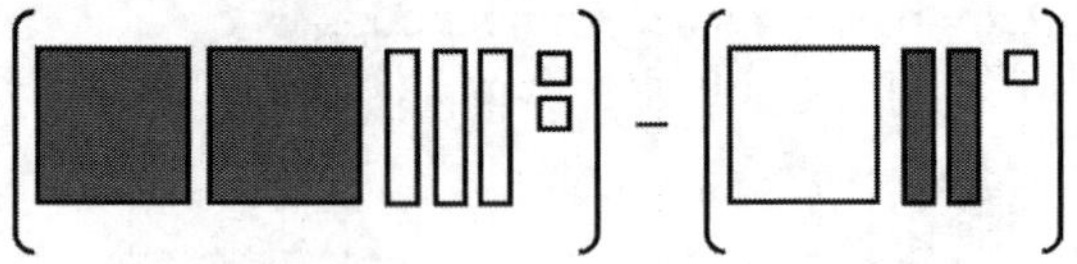

20. The simplified algebraic expression representing the difference of the algebra tiles is

A. $3x^2 - 5x - 1$

B. $3x^2 - 5x - 3$

C. $x^2 - 5x - 3$

D. $x^2 - x - 1$

21. The expression $2x^2(-3x+2)$ is equivalent to

A. $-12x^3$

B. $6x^3 + 4x$

C. $-6x^3 + 4x$

D. $-6x^3 + 4x^2$

Use the following information to answer the next question.

Craig attempted to solve the expression $4x(-x^2 + 2x - 3)$ using the following four steps:

Step 1

$(4x)(-x^2)+(4x)(2x)+(4x)(-3)$

Step 2:

$(4)(-1)(x)(x^2)+(4)(2)(x)(x)+(4)(-3)(x)$

Step 3:

$-4x^2 + 8x^2 - 12x$

Step 4:

$4x^2 - 12x$

22. In which step did Craig's first error in multiplication occur?

A. Step 1

B. Step 2

C. Step 3

D. Step 4

Use the following information to answer the next question.

Four students were given four different equations to solve. Their work in finding the solutions is shown.

Chantelle
$$2(x+3)=4x$$
$$2x+6=4x$$
$$x=6$$

Karim
$$4(x-1)=3x+2$$
$$4x-1=3x+2$$
$$x=3$$

Stephanie
$$6x-4=2(2x-1)$$
$$6x-4=4x-2$$
$$x=1$$

Tristan
$$5x+2=3(x-4)$$
$$5x+2=3x-4$$
$$x=3$$

23. The student that has the correct solution is

A. Chantelle

B. Karim

C. Stephanie

D. Tristan

24. Which of the following equations has the same solution as the equation $2(x-3)=5x+3$?

A. $3x=x+6$

B. $2x+3=5x-6$

C. $2x+1=4x-7$

D. $7x-3=3x-15$

Numerical Response

3. Stefan works part-time in a shoe store. His monthly wage is calculated according to the equation $W=12t+\frac{2d}{7}$, where W represents his wages, t is the number of hours worked, and d is the dollar value of the shoes he sells in a month. One month, Stefan sold $1 470 worth of shoes and received a wage of $1 044. For that given month, the number of hours Stefan worked was ________hours.

Use the following information to answer the next question.

Shawn was building a web, with the dimensions shown.

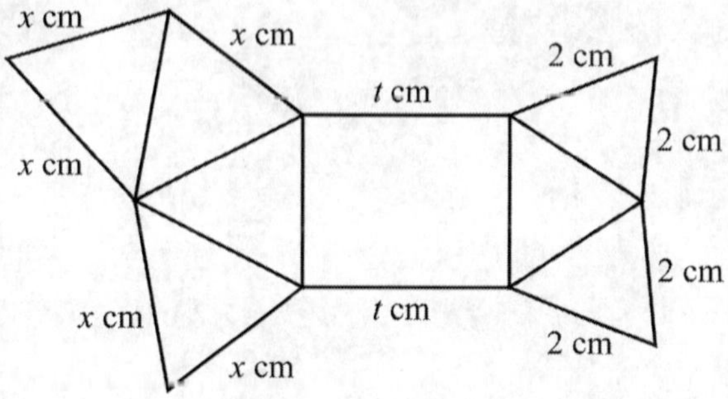

The equation describing the perimeter, *P*, of this web is $P=5x+2(t+4)$.

25. If the perimeter of this web is 26 cm and the length of *x* is 2.4 cm, then what is the value of *t*?

A. 2.0

B. 3.0

C. 4.0

D. 5.0

Open Response

1. Jessica, Katie, and Hannah are all forwards on the same hockey team. In a tournament, Jessica took 16 shots and scored 3 goals. Katie took 11 shots and scored 2 goals. Hannah took 19 shots and scored 4 goals. Which player had the highest scoring rate of goals per shot, and which player had the lowest scoring rate of goals per shot? Justify your answer.

Open Response

2. David needed to do two questions for homework. In each question, he needed to solve for x, in centimeters. Show your steps in solving each equation for both questions.

a) Question 1 area of a square is $A = s^2$ Determine the length of each side, x, to the nearest 0.1 centimetre if the area of the square is 22 cm^3.

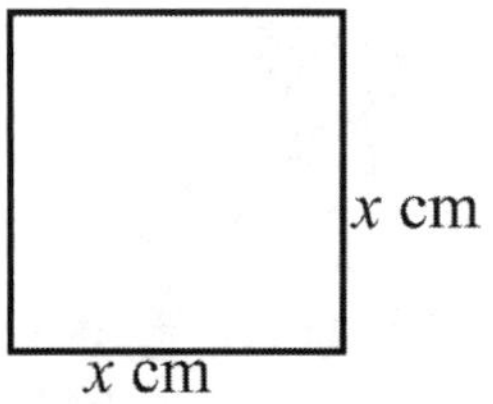

b) **Question II**: The perimeter of a rectangle e is $P = 2(w + l)$. If the perimeter is 36 cm, then determine the value of x to the nearest whole centimeter.

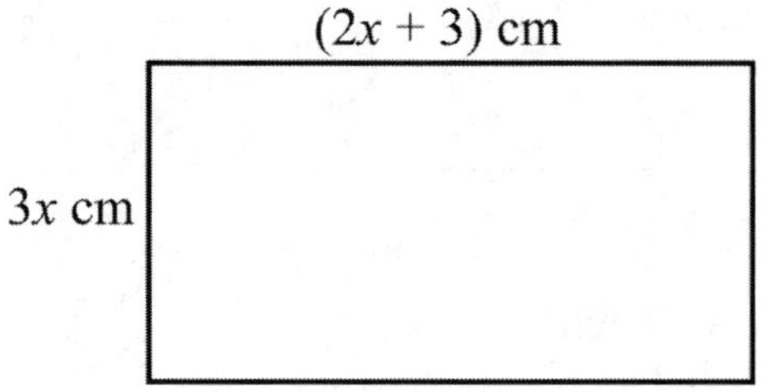

ANSWERS AND SOLUTIONS—UNIT TEST

1. C	**5. C**	**9. B**	**14. D**	**19. B**	**24. D**
2. D	**6. B**	**10. C**	**15. D**	**20. A**	**NR3. 52**
3. B	**7. C**	**11 D**	**16. C**	**21. D**	**25. B**
4. A	**8. A**	**12. A**	**17. C**	**22. C**	**OR1. ****
NR1. 100	**NR2. 1 954**	**13. C**	**18. B**	**23. C**	**OR2. ****

****SEE SOLUTION**

1. **C**

The ratio of blue marbles to the total number of marbles is 7:17. An equivalent ratio is 21:51, which is formed by multiplying each term in the original ratio by 3. $7 \times 3 : 17 \Rightarrow 21:51$

2. **D**

The original three-term ratio of girls to boys to adults is 20:16:8. This ratio can be reduced to lowest terms by dividing each term by 4.

$$\frac{20}{4}:\frac{16}{4}:\frac{8}{4}=5:4:2$$

The simplified ratio is 5:4:2.

3. **B**

The ratio of height to width of both sails can be written as:

Sail of smaller boat: 5:8
Sail of larger boat: 8:*w*

These two ratios can be written as the proportion:

$$\frac{5}{8}=\frac{8}{w}$$

4. **A**

The unsimplified proportion that could be written to solve for *w* is $\frac{5}{2}=\frac{48}{w}$.

To simplify this proportion and make it easier to determine the value of *w*, divide each term in the first ratio by 5.

$$\frac{5}{2}\xrightarrow[\div 5]{\div 5}\frac{1}{\frac{2}{5}} \text{ or } \frac{1}{0.4}$$

The simplified proportion would be $\frac{1}{0.4}=\frac{48}{w}$.

NR1 **100**

Set up the proportion of DVDs to VHS tapes, where x represents the number of VHS tapes in the store. Use the cross-product rule.

$$\frac{13}{2}=\frac{650}{x}$$

$$(13)(x)=(650)(2)$$

Divide both sides by 3.

$$\frac{(13)(x)}{13}=\frac{1300}{13}$$

$$x=100$$

There are 100 VHS tapes in the store.

5. **C**

$$\frac{7.50}{6}=\frac{x}{1}$$

$6 \div 6 = 1$, so the unit price is

$7.50 \div 6 = 1.25$.

or

Use the cross-product rule

$(7.50)(1)=(6)(x)$

Divide both sides by 6

$$\frac{7.50}{6}=\frac{6x}{6}$$

$1.25 = x$

Realign the equation

$x = 1.25$

The unit price for 1 kg of oranges is $1.25.

6. **B**

Michael Johnson ran at a unit rate (average speed) of $200 \text{ m} \div 19.32 \text{ s} = 10.35 \text{ m/s}$.
Donovan Bailey ran at a unit rate (average speed) of $100 \text{ m} \div 9.84 \text{ s} = 10.16 \text{ m/s}$.

Michael Johnson's average speed was 10.36 m/s −10.16 m/s = 0.19 m/s faster than Donovan Bailey's average speed.

7. **C**

The unit price of each size of ketchup will determine which size is the best buy.

$$\begin{aligned}200 \text{ mL} &\rightarrow \$1.24 \div 200 = \$0.0062/\text{mL}\\ 500 \text{ mL} &\rightarrow \$2.50 \div 500 = \$0.0050/\text{mL}\\ 1\,000 \text{ mL} &\rightarrow \$4.98 \div 1\,000 = \$0.00498/\text{mL}\\ 2\,200 \text{ mL} &\rightarrow \$13.20 \div 2\,200 = \$0.0060/\text{mL}\end{aligned}$$

The best buy is the 1 000 mL size, since it has the lowest unit price.

8. **A**

To find the constant of proportionality (speed), take any two vertically aligned values in the table, and convert them to a distance-per-time unit ratio.

$$\frac{84 \text{ m}}{3 \text{ s}} = \frac{(84 \div 3) \text{ m}}{(3 \div 3) \text{ s}} = 28 \text{ m/s}$$

To find the distance travelled by the cheetah in 1 minute, convert 1 minute to 60 seconds.
Set up the proportion between the unit rate and the distance, d, travelled by the cheetah in 60 s.

$$\frac{28 \text{ m}}{1 \text{ s}} = \frac{d \text{ m}}{60 \text{ s}}$$

Create equivalent ratios by multiplying each term in the first ratio by 60.

$$\frac{(28 \times 60) \text{ m}}{(1 \times 60) \text{ s}} = \frac{d \text{ m}}{60 \text{ s}}$$
$$\frac{1\,680 \text{ m}}{60 \text{ s}} = \frac{d \text{ m}}{60 \text{ s}}$$

The cheetah covered 1 680 m in 1 min.

NR2 1 954

The proportion between CAD and MXN currencies can be set up as shown below, where x is the number of Mexican pesos Renée will receive in exchange for 200 Canadian dollars.

$$\frac{9.77 \text{ MXN}}{1 \text{ CAD}} = \frac{x \text{ MXN}}{200 \text{ CAD}}$$

To find the number of pesos she will receive for 200 Canadian dollars, multiply the ratio on the left by 200.

$$\frac{9.77 \text{ MXN}}{1 \text{ CAD}} \xrightarrow{\times 200} \frac{x \text{ MXN}}{200 \text{ CAD}}$$

$$x = (9.77 \times 200)\text{MXN}$$

$$x = 1\,954\text{MXN}$$

Renée will receive 1 954 Mexican pesos.

9. **B**

Calculate the total tax on a $1 200 purchase in each province.

Alberta:
$$\begin{aligned}\text{Tax} &= 5\% \times \$1\,200\\ &= \left(\frac{5}{100}\right)\$1\,200\\ &= 0.05 \times \$1\,200\\ &= \$60\end{aligned}$$

Ontario:
$$\begin{aligned}\text{Tax} &= (5\% + 8\%) \times \$1\,200\\ &= \left(\frac{13}{100}\right)\$1\,200\\ &= 0.13 \times \$1\,200\\ &= \$156\end{aligned}$$

The person in Ontario will pay $156 - $60 = $96 more than the person in Alberta.

10. **C**

Calculate the interest rate as a percentage, P, for each bank, and choose the lowest rate.

Bank 1:
$$P = \left(\frac{180}{2\,000}\right) \times 100 = \frac{18\,000}{2\,000} = 9\%$$

Bank 2:
$$P = \left(\frac{68}{800}\right) \times 100 = \frac{6\,800}{800} = 8.5\%$$

Bank 3:

$$P=\left(\frac{117}{1\,500}\right)\times 100=\frac{11\,700}{1\,500}=7.8\%$$

Bank 4:

$$P=\left(\frac{128}{1\,600}\right)\times 100=\frac{12\,800}{1\,600}=8\%$$

Bank 3 provided the lowest interest rate.

11. D

Begin by converting each of the given fractions into improper fractions.

$$9\frac{1}{3}=\frac{28}{3},6\frac{1}{2}=\frac{13}{2},4\frac{1}{6}=\frac{25}{6}$$

Convert each fraction so that it has the same lowest common denominator of 6.

$$\frac{28\times 2}{3\times 2}=\frac{56}{6} \quad \frac{13\times 3}{2\times 3}=\frac{39}{6} \quad \frac{25}{6}=\frac{25}{6}$$

Find the sum of these fractions as follows:

$$\frac{56}{6}+\frac{39}{6}+\frac{25}{6}$$

$$=\frac{120}{6}$$
$$=20$$

Finally, subtract this sum from the perimeter to find the measure of side a

$$a=22\frac{2}{3}-20=2\frac{2}{3}$$

The measure of the missing side is $2\frac{2}{3}$cm

12. A

The fraction representing the number of shaded sections in relation to the total number of sections in the diagram is $\frac{2}{5}$.

The reciprocal of this fraction is $\frac{5}{2}$.

13. C

Take the square root of each side of the equation.

$$x^2=12$$
$$\sqrt{x^2}=\pm\sqrt{12}$$
$$x=\pm\sqrt{12}$$

The square root of any natural number will have exactly one positive and one negative solution.

Therefore, there are two solutions.

14. D

Enzo should have stated: $\sqrt{9}=3$

Eva should have stated: $(-4)^2=16$

Jeremy should have stated that if $x^2=25$, then $x=\pm 5$

Charissa correctly stated that if $\sqrt{x}=10$ then $x=100$, since $\sqrt{100}=10$.

15. D

The volume of each box can be represented as a three-dimensional figure.

$$V=(x\text{ cm})(x\text{ cm})(x\text{ cm})$$
$$V=x^3\text{cm}^3$$

Since there are seven cubes in the structure, the total volume is $7\times x^3=7x^3$ cm.

16. C

The area of a square is a two-dimensional representation given by the formula A=s^2; therefore, $16x^2\text{cm}^2=s^2$

Take the square root of each side of the equation.

$$\sqrt{16x^2\text{ cm}^2}=\sqrt{s^2}$$
$$\sqrt{4x\times 4x\text{ cm}^2}=\sqrt{s^2}$$
$$4x\text{ cm}=\text{s}$$

Since $A=(4x)(4x)=16x^2$, the length of each side of the square is $4x$ cm.

17. C

The correct process of the substitution of $p=-2.2$ into the given expression $2p^3-p^2$ is

$$2(-2.2)^3-(-2.2)^2=-26.136$$

or

$= 2(-2.2)(-2.2)(-2.2) - (-2.2)(-2.2) = -26$ Jame s evaluated the expression correctly.

18. B

Determine the volume of each shape:

$$\begin{aligned} V_{\text{cylinder}} &= \pi r^2 h \\ &= \pi(5\text{ cm})^2(10\text{ cm}) \\ &= \pi(5\text{ cm})(5\text{ cm})(10\text{ cm}) = 785.4\text{ cm}^3 \end{aligned}$$

$$\begin{aligned} V_{\text{cone}} &= \frac{1}{3}\pi r^2 h \\ &= \left(\frac{1}{3}\right)(\pi)(8\text{ cm})^2(12\text{ cm}) \\ &= 804.2\text{ cm}^3 \end{aligned}$$

Find the difference between the two volumes $804.2\text{ cm}^3 - 785.4\text{ cm}^3 = 18.8\text{ cm}^3$

The volume of the cylinder is 18.8 cm^3 less than the volume of the cone.

19. B

To add the polynomials, collect like terms, and then add the numerical coefficients of the like terms.

$$\begin{aligned} &(4x^2+3x-9)+(6x^2+2x+2) \\ &= (4x^2+6x^2)+(3x+2x)+(-9+2) \\ &= 10x^2+5x-7 \end{aligned}$$

or

$$\begin{array}{r} 4x^2+3x-9 \\ +\ \underline{6x^2+2x+2} \\ 10x^2+5x-7 \end{array}$$

20. A

Convert the subtraction process to an addition process. This is done by switching all the tiles from shaded to unshaded and from unshaded to shaded in the second set of bracketed tiles.

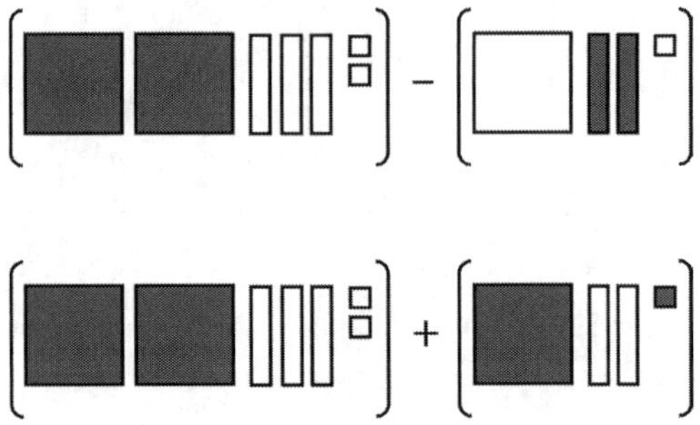

Next, combine tiles representing like terms, and cancel negative ones with positive ones.

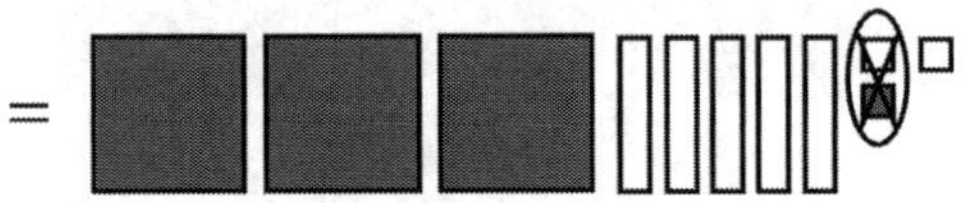

The simplified algebraic expression representing the difference of the algebra tiles is $3x^2 - 5x - 1$.

21. D

Multiply the monomial to each term of the polynomial, and simplify each resulting term.

$$\begin{aligned} &2x^2(-3x+2) \\ &= (2x^2)(-3x)+(2x^2)(2) \\ &= (2x)(-3)(x^2)+(2)(2)(x^2) \\ &= -6x^{2+1}+4x^2 \\ &= -6x^3+4x^2 \end{aligned}$$

or

$$\begin{array}{r} -3+2 \\ \nwarrow\uparrow \\ \times\ 2x^2 \\ \hline -6x^3+4x^2 \end{array}$$

22. C

From step 2 to step 3, the correct process should have been:

Step 2:

$$(4)(-1)(x)(x^2)+(4)(2)(x)(x)+(4)(-3)(x)$$

Step 3:

$$-4x^{1+2}+8x^{1+1}-12x^1$$

$$-4x^3+8x^2-12x$$

Therefore, Hana's first error occurred in Step 3.

23. **C**

Stephanie's solution and process is correct.

$$6x-4=2(2x-1)$$

Eliminate the brackets by multiplying each term in the brackets by 2.

$$6x-4=2(2x)+2(-1)$$
$$6x-4=4x-2$$

Add 4 to both sides.

$$6x-4+4=4x-2+4$$
$$6x=4x+2$$

Subtract $4x$ from both sides.

$$6x-4-4x=4x-4x+2$$
$$2x=2$$

Divide both sides by 2.

$$\frac{2x}{2}=\frac{2}{2}$$
$$x=1$$

24. **D**

The solution to the original equation is found as follows:

Eliminate the brackets by multiplying each term in the brackets by 2.

$$2(x-3)=5x+3$$
$$2x-6=5x+3$$

Subtract 3 from both sides.

$$2x-6-3=5x+3-3$$
$$2x-9=5x$$

Subtract $2x$ from both sides.

$$2x-2x-9=5x-2x$$
$$-9=3x$$

Divide both sides by 3.

$$\frac{-9}{3}=\frac{3x}{3}$$
$$-3=x$$

Realign the equation.

$$x=-3$$

The solution to the equation in choice **D** has the same solution.

$$7x-3=3x-15$$

Add 3 to both sides.

$$7x-3+3=3x-15+3$$
$$7x=3x-12$$

Subtract $3x$ from both sides.

$$7x-3x=3x-3x-12$$
$$4x=-12$$

Divide both sides by 4.

$$\frac{4x}{4}=\frac{-12}{4}$$
$$x=-3$$

NR3. 52

Substitute \$1 044 for W and \$1 470 for d in the equation

$$W=12t+\frac{2d}{7}$$

in order to solve for t, the total number of hours worked.

$$W=12t+\frac{2(1\,470)}{7}$$
$$1\,044=12t+420$$

Subtract 420 from both sides.

$$1\,044-420=12t+420-420$$
$$624=12t$$

Divide both sides by 12.

$$\frac{624}{12}=\frac{12t}{12}$$
$$52=t$$

Realign the equation.

$$t=52$$

Stefan worked 52 hours that month.

25. **B**

To solve for the value of *t*, substitute 26 for *P* and 2.4 for *x* in the equation

$$P=5x+2(t+4)$$
$$26=5(2.4)+2(t+4)$$
$$26=12+2(t+4)$$

Eliminate the brackets by multiplying each term in the brackets by 2.

$$26=12+2t+8$$

Collect like terms.

$26 = 20 + 2t$

Subtract 20 from both sides.

$26 - 20 = 20 - 20 + 2t$

$6 = 2t$

Divide both sides by 2.

$\frac{6}{2} = \frac{2t}{2}$

$3 = t$

Realign the equation.

$t = 3$

The value of t is 3.0.

OR 1.

One method is to write each ratio of shots and goals and then find the unit rate.

Jessica: $\frac{3}{16} = 0.1875$ goals/shot

Chloe: $\frac{2}{11} \approx 0.1818$ goals/shot

Hannah: $\frac{4}{19} \approx 0.2105$ goals/shot

Hannah had the highest scoring rate of 0.2105 goals/shot, and Chloe had the lowest scoring rate of 0.1818 goals/shot.

Another method is to write each ratio of shots and goals and make equivalent ratios out of all three.

The lowest common multiple of 16, 11, and 19 is $16 \times 11 \times 19 = 3\,344$

Jessica: $\frac{3}{16} = \frac{3 \times 11 \times 19}{16 \times 11 \times 19} = \frac{627}{3\,344}$

Chloe: $\frac{2}{11} = \frac{2 \times 16 \times 19}{11 \times 16 \times 19} = \frac{608}{3\,344}$

Hannah: $\frac{4}{19} = \frac{4 \times 11 \times 16}{19 \times 11 \times 16} = \frac{704}{3\,344}$

When the three ratios have equivalent denominators, it is easier to see that Hannah had the highest scoring rate $\left(\frac{704}{3\,344}\right)$ and

Chloe had the lowest scoring rate $\left(\frac{608}{3\,344}\right)$.

OR 2.

a)

To solve question I, substitute 22 cm^2 for A, and solve for x.

$A = x^2$
$22 \text{ cm}^2 = x^2$

Take the square root of both sides

$\sqrt{22 \text{ cm}^2} = \sqrt{x^2}$

The square root of x^2 is x.

$\sqrt{22 \text{ cm}^2} = x$

Using your calculator, solve for x to the nearest 0.1 cm.

$x = \sqrt{22 \text{ cm}^2} = 4.69041576$

The length of each side of the square is 4.7 cm.

b)

To solve question II, substitute 36 for P, substitute $3x$ for w, and substitute $(2x+3)$ for l.

$P = 2(w + l)$
$36 = 2[(3x) + (2x + 3)]$

Collect like terms in the bracket.

$36 = 2[5x + 3]$

Eliminate the brackets by multiplying each term in the brackets by 2.

$36 = 2(5x) + 2(3)$
$36 = 10x + 6$

Subtract 6 from both sides.

$36 - 6 = 10x + 6 - 6$
$30 = 10x$

Divide both sides by 10.

$\frac{30}{10} = \frac{10x}{10}$
$3 = x$

Realign the equation.

$x = 3$

To the nearest whole centimetre, the value of x is 3 cm.

Linear Relations

LINEAR RELATIONS

Table of Correlations			
	Specific Expectation	**Practice Questions**	**Unit Test Questions**
LR1.01	*interpret the meanings of points on scatter plots or graphs that represent linear relations, including scatter plots or graphs in more than one quadrant*	1, NR1, 2, 3	1, 2
LR1.02	*pose problems, identify variables, and formulate hypotheses associated with relationships between two variables*	4, 5	3
LR1.03	*carry out an investigation or experiment involving relationships between two variables, including the collection and organization of data, using appropriate methods, equipment, and/or technology and techniques*	6, 7, 8	4
LR1.04	*describe trends and relationships observed in data, make inferences from data, compare the inferences with hypotheses about the data, and explain any differences between the inferences and the hypotheses*	9, 10, 11, 12	5, 6, 7
LR2.01	*construct tables of values and graphs, using a variety of tools, to represent linear relations derived from descriptions of realistic situations*	13, 14, 15, 16	8, 9
LR2.02	*construct tables of values, scatter plots, and lines or curves of best fit as appropriate, using a variety of tools, for linearly related and non-linearly related data collected from a variety of sources*	17, 18, 19, 20, 21, 22, 23, OR1	10, 11, 12
LR2.03	*identify, through investigation, some properties of linear relations (i.e., numerically, the first difference is a constant, which represents a constant rate of change; graphically, a straight line represents the relation), and apply these properties to determine whether a relation is linear or non-linear*	24	13, 14, 18
LR3.01	*determine, through investigation, that the rate of change of a linear relation can be found by choosing any two points on the line that represents the relation, finding the vertical change between the points (i.e., the rise) and the horizontal change between the points (i.e., the run), and writing the ratio* $\frac{rise}{run}$ *(i.e., rate of change =* $\frac{rise}{run}$*)*	25, 26, 27, 28	15
LR3.02	*determine, through investigation, connections among the representations of a constant rate of change of a linear relation*	29, 30, 31, 32	17
LR3.03	*compare the properties of direct variation and partial variation in applications, and identify the initial value*	33, 34, 35	19, OR2
LR3.04	*express a linear relation as an equation in two variables, using the rate of change and the initial value*	36, 37, 38, 39, 40, 41, 42, 43	16, 20, 21, 28, 29, OR2
LR3.05	*describe the meaning of the rate of change and the initial value for a linear relation arising from a realistic situation, and describe a situation that could be modelled by a given linear equation*	44, 45, 46, OR 2	22, 23

LR4.01	*determine values of a linear relation by using a table of values, by using the equation of the relation, and by interpolating or extrapolating from the graph of the relation*	47, 48, 49, 50, OR3	24, 25
LR4.02	*describe a situation that would explain the events illustrated by a given graph of a relationship between two variables*	51, 52	26, 27, OR3
LR4.03	*determine other representations of a linear relation arising from a realistic situation, given one representation*	53, 54	
LR4.04	*solve problems that can be modelled with first-degree equations, and compare the algebraic method to other solution methods*	55, 56	30, 1
LR4.05	*describe the effects on a linear graph and make the corresponding changes to the linear equation when the conditions of the situation they represent are varied*	57, 58	32, 33
LR4.06	determine *graphically the point of intersection of two linear relations, and interpret the intersection point in the context of an application*	59, 60	34, 35
LR4.07	*select a topic involving a two-variable relationship, pose a question on the topic, collect data to answer the question, and present its solution using appropriate representations of the data*	61	

LINEAR RELATIONS

LR1.01 interpret the meanings of points on scatter plots or graphs that represent linear relations, including scatter plots or graphs in more than one quadrant

INTERPRETING SCATTER PLOTS AND LINEAR RELATIONS

INTERPRETING SCATTER PLOTS

A **scatter plot** is a graph of points displaying the data of two variables. Points are plotted as ordered pairs on a **coordinate plane**.

Consider the following scatter plot:

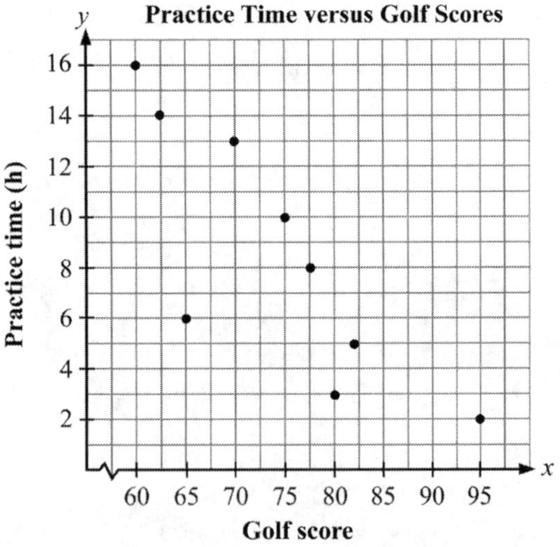

The **ordered pair** (70, 13) represents a golf score of 70 when the practice time is 13 hours. Similarly, the ordered pair (95, 2) represents a golf score of 95 when the practice time is 2 hours.

INTERPRETING LINEAR RELATIONS

A **linear relation** is a relation that has a constant rate of change. The graph of a linear relation will always be a straight line.

Consider the following linear relation:

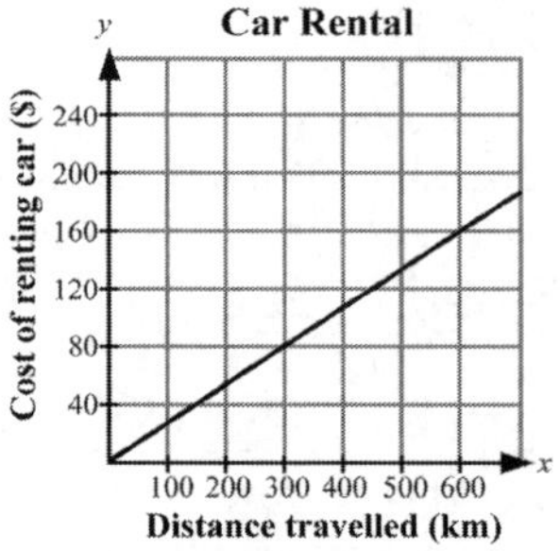

The ordered pair (300, 80) indicates that if a rental car is driven 300 km, the cost will be $80. Similarly, the ordered pair (600, 160) indicates that if a rental car is driven 600 km, the cost will be $160.

PRACTICE QUESTIONS

Use the following information to answer the next two questions.

The scatter plot represents the outside temperature in a town in Ontario at various times on a February day.

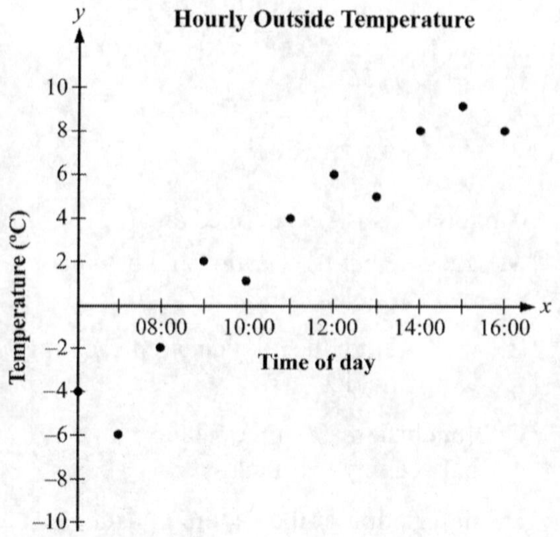

1. At what time of day was the outside temperature the lowest?

   A. 06:00

   B. 07:00

   C. 08:00

   D. 10:00

Numerical Response

1. How many points on the graph show an outside temperature that is **lower** than the outside temperature one hour earlier?

____________________________.

CHALLENGER QUESTION

The shaft speed of a jet engine determines the amount of power generated. The partial graph shows the relationship between shaft speed measured in revolutions per minute (rpm) and power output measured in watts (W) for a jet engine.

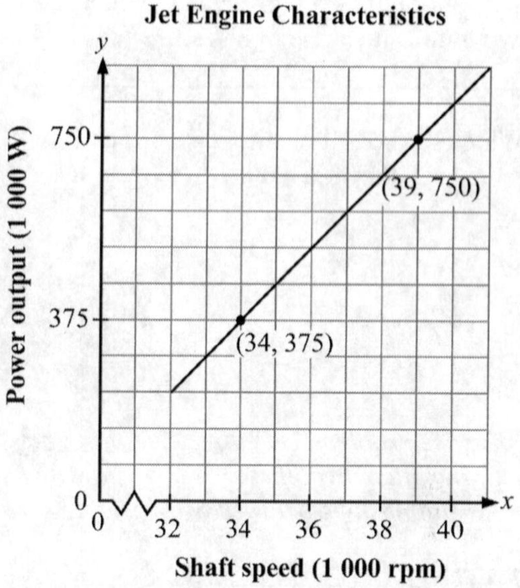

2. The point (34, 375) represents a shaft speed of

   A. 34 rpm and a power output of 375 W

   B. 375 W and a power output of 34 rpm

   C. 3 400 rpm and a power output of 37 500 W

   D. 34 000 rpm and a power output of 375 000 W

Use the following information for the next question.

Clarissa analyzed a graph of points representing the outside temperature at different times on a particular day. She noticed that the point (2, –6) represented the outside temperature at 2:00 P.M., and the point to the right of (2, –6) represented an increase of two hours and a rise of 3°C.

3. Which of the following points correctly represents this new point?

A. (2, 3)

B. (2, –3)

C. (4, –3)

D. (4, –9)

LR1.02 pose problems, identify variables, and formulate hypotheses associated with relationships between two variables

RELATING TWO VARIABLES

To understand the relationship between two variables, you need to pose a question, identify the variables, and then formulate one or more hypotheses. A **hypothesis** is an educated guess or statement about the relationship between the two variables.

Example

Scenario: A ball is dropped onto a concrete pad. The height the ball is dropped from and the height to which it rebounds is recorded.

Question: Does the rebound height of a ball depend upon the height from which it was dropped?

Variables:
a) The height the ball is dropped from
b) The height the ball rebounds to

Hypotheses: The rebound height of a ball increases as the height from which it was dropped increases.

The rebound height of a ball is directly proportional to the height from which it was dropped. As one variable increases, the other variable increases by a related amount.

The rebound height of a ball decreases as the height from which it was dropped increases.

Note: All three statements are hypotheses; however, the third hypothesis seems highly unlikely and would be considered a poor hypothesis.

PRACTICE QUESTIONS

4. A hypothesis is best defined as a

A. guess about the relationship between two variables

B. method of collecting data representing two variables

C. conclusion about the relationship between two variables

D. description of the pattern of data representing two variables

5. Which of the following statements best describes the relationship between attendance and a student's final mark in a Grade 9 Math class?

A. A student with very good attendance will never get a low final mark.

B. A student with very poor attendance will most likely get a low final mark.

C. A student with very poor attendance will most likely get a high final mark.

D. A student with very good attendance will always get a very high final mark.

LR1.03 carry out an investigation or experiment involving relationships between two variables, including the collection and organization of data, using appropriate methods, equipment, and/or technology and techniques

INVESTIGATING RELATIONSHIPS BETWEEN VARIABLES

To carry out an experiment involving the relationship between two variables, you must decide on the two variables you are going to examine, the method you will use to measure the data, and how best to organize and present your collected data.

Example

Investigate the relationship between the height from which a ball is dropped and its rebound height.

You need a ball and a tape measure. Drop a ball from various heights, and record its rebound height.

The table below shows possible data from this experiment.

Height the Ball is Dropped from (cm)	Rebound Height of the Ball (cm)
100	25
200	52
300	77
400	110
500	123
600	147
700	179
800	210
900	222
1 000	257

The information in this table can be displayed in a scatter plot. A scatter plot makes it easier to examine the relationship between the two variables (the height the ball is dropped from and rebound height).

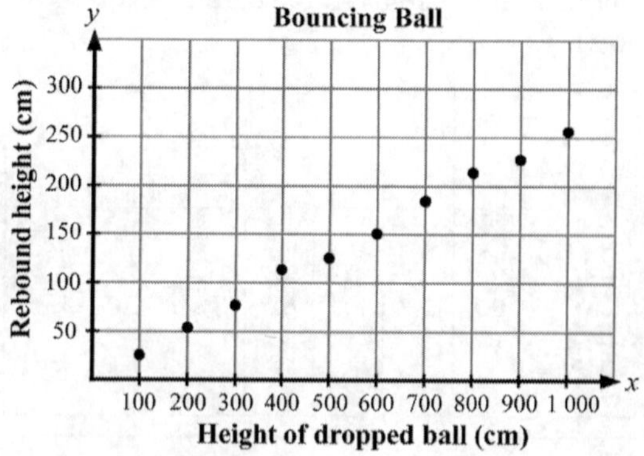

PRACTICE QUESTIONS

Use the following information to answer the next question.

> Josette wanted to analyze the temperature change of ice water in a plastic cup with respect to time. To perform the experiment, Josette needed to choose the correct measuring items, collect data in a table, and then graph the results.

6. In addition to a plastic cup and ice water, which of the following items does Josette need in order to carry out this experiment?

A. Scale and thermometer

B. Clock and thermometer

C. Metre stick, clock, and thermometer

D. Scale, metre stick, and thermometer

Use the following information to answer the next two questions.

Josette collected 500 mL of ice water and took the temperature of the water every four minutes. She displayed the data in the table shown.

Time (min)	0	4	8	12	16	20	24
Temperature of water (°C)	0.5	2.0	4.0	6.5	8.5	11.0	13.5

7. Which of the following scatter plots represents the information given in the table?

A.

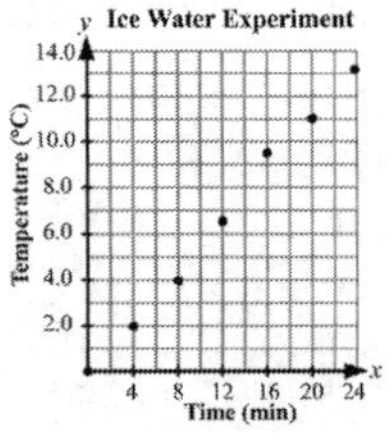

B.

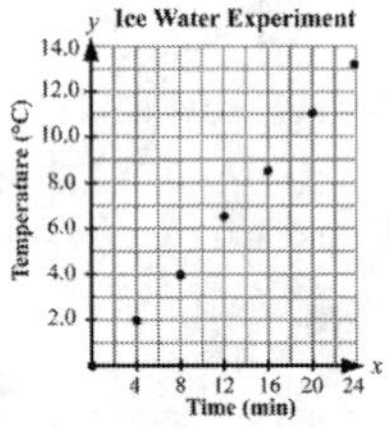

C.

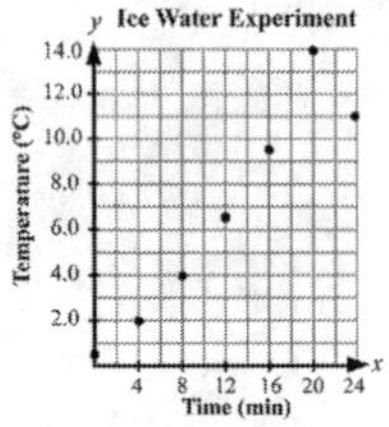

D.

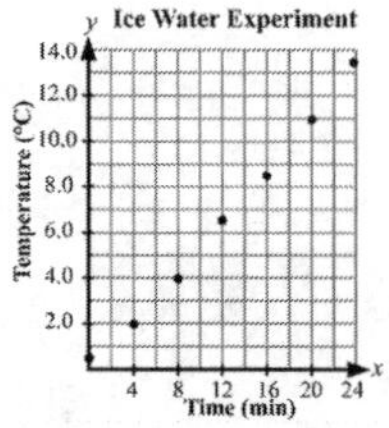

CHALLENGER QUESTION

8. Josette then performed the same experiment using a thermal mug instead of a plastic cup. Which of the following tables most likely represents the data collected?

A.

Temperature (°C)	Time (min)
0.5	0
–1.0	4
–2.0	8
–3.0	12
–4.0	16
–4.0	20

B.

Temperature (°C)	Time (min)
0.5	0
2.5	4
4.5	8
7.0	12
9.5	16
13.0	20
15.0	24

C.

Temperature (°C)	Time (min)
0.5	0
0.5	4
0.5	8
0.5	12
0.5	16
0.5	20

D.

Temperature (°C)	Time (min)
0.5	0
1.0	4
1.5	8
2.5	12
4.0	16
5.0	20

LR1.04 describe trends and relationships observed in data, make inferences from data, compare the inferences with hypotheses about the data, and explain any differences between the inferences and the hypotheses

TRENDS AND RELATIONSHIPS BETWEEN TWO VARIABLES

After collecting data and graphing it on a scatter plot, you can describe trends and relationships between the two variables. If one set of data consistently increases or decreases in a linear pattern when the other set of data increases or decreases in a similar linear pattern, you can describe it as a **proportional relationship**.
If there is a proportional relationship between the two variables, you can infer the rate at which this relationship increases or decreases.
This **inference** could be compared to the original hypothesis made about the relationship.

Example

Look again at the scatter plot from lesson 1.03.

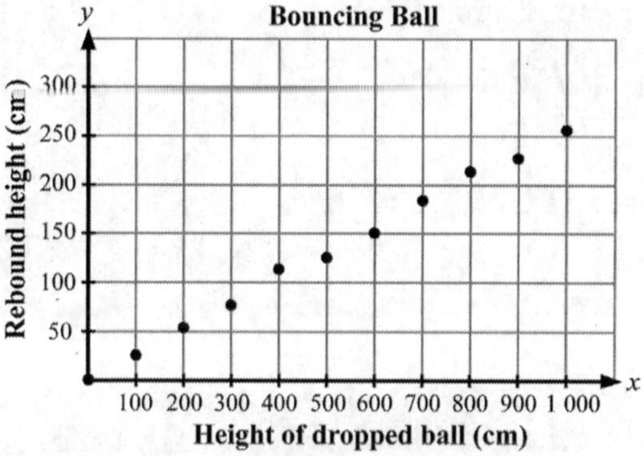

You can see that as the height the ball is dropped from increases, the height of the rebound also increases. Since the points seem to follow a linear pattern that passes through the **origin** (0, 0), the relationship is described as a **direct proportion**.

The pattern of the points can also be described as a **rate**. For every increase of about 200 cm in the height from which the ball is dropped, there is an increase of about 50 cm in the ball's rebound height. In simplified terms, for every increase of 4 cm in the height from which the ball is dropped, there is a corresponding increase of 1 cm in the ball's rebound height.

This inference confirms the first two stated hypotheses from lesson 1.02.

PRACTICE QUESTIONS

Use the following information to answer the next two questions.

Tina collected data pertaining to the age in years and the height in centimetres of seven students at her school. She entered the data into lists L_1 and L_2 of a graphing calculator, as shown.

L1	L2	L3 2
13	155	------
14	163	
15	171	
16	180	
16	145	
17	187	
18	195	
L2(1)=155		

9. Which of the following statements best describes the relationship between the ages and heights of the students?

A. As age increases, height increases at a rate of about 8 cm per year.

B. As age increases, height increases at a rate of about 4 cm per year.

C. As age increases, height decreases at a rate of about 8 cm per year.

D. As age increases, height decreases at a rate of about 4 cm per year.

10. Which of the following statements with regard to the height and age of a student is most likely correct?

A. The point (16, 145) describes a student who is shorter than most other students his or her age.

B. The point (13, 155) describes a student who is shorter than most other students his or her age.

C. The point (16, 145) describes a student who is taller than most other students his or her age.

D. The point (13, 155) describes a student who is taller than must other students his or her age.

Use the following information to answer the next question.

The table shows percentages of rural and non-farm-based Canadians.

Percentage of Rural and Non-Farm-Based Canadians

Year	Percentage
1951	16%
1956	17%
1961	18%
1966	17%
1971	19%
1976	20%
1981	20%
1986	20%

11. Which of the following statements regarding the trend in the data is true?

A. The percentage stayed constant from 1956 to 1966.

B. The percentage stayed constant from 1966 to 1986.

C. The percentage increased slightly from 1951 to 1986.

D. The percentage increased at a constant rate from 1951 to 1986.

Use the following information for the next question.

Four students made inferences about data collected for the amount of daily sunlight from Dec. 21, 2007 to Dec. 21, 2008.

Dante: The amount of daily sunlight increases over this time period.

Tammy: The amount of daily sunlight
decreases over this time period.

Ramsay: The amount of daily sunlight
increases and then decreases over this time period.

Keri: The amount of daily sunlight decreases and increases over this time period.

12. The student that made the correct inference is

A. Dante

B. Tammy

C. Ramsay

D. Keri

LR2.01 construct tables of values and graphs, using a variety of tools, to represent linear relations derived from descriptions of realistic situations

CONSTRUCTING TABLES AND GRAPHS TO REPRESENT A LINEAR RELATION

A **relation** is any set of ordered pairs. A relation is a **linear relation** if its scatter plot forms a line.

Example

A telephone company has a monthly cellphone plan that costs $25 a month plus $0.10 per minute of airtime.

The following table of values can be constructed to represent the given information.

Airtime (minutes)	Total Monthly Cost ($)
0	25 + 0(0.10) = 25.00
5	25 + 5(0.10) = 25.50
10	25 + 10(0.10) = 26.00
15	25 + 15(0.10) = 26.50
20	25 + 20(0.10) = 27.00
25	25 + 25(0.10) = 27.50
30	25 + 30(0.10) = 28.00
35	25 + 35(0.10) = 28.50
40	25 + 40(0.10) = 29.00
45	*25 + 45(0.10) = 29.50*

A scatter plot can be drawn to represent the data in the table.

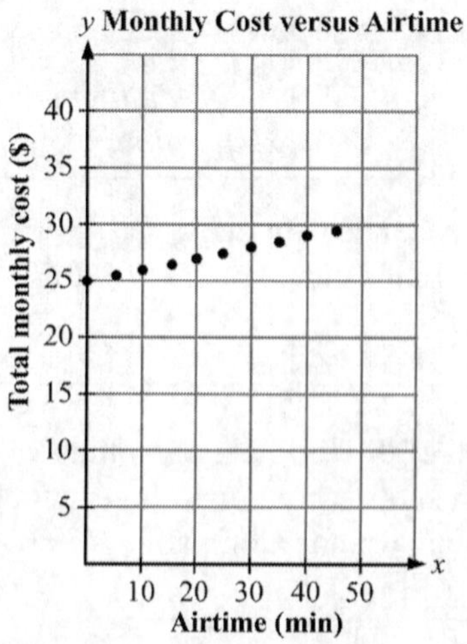

You could also use your graphing calculator to create the scatter plot. Select the **STAT EDIT** feature, and enter the values for the airtime in L_1 and the values for the total monthly cost in L_2. Choose an appropriate window setting.
One possible window setting is shown below.
Next, select the $y =$ key, and highlight plot 1.
Finally, press the Graph Key to display the scatter plot.

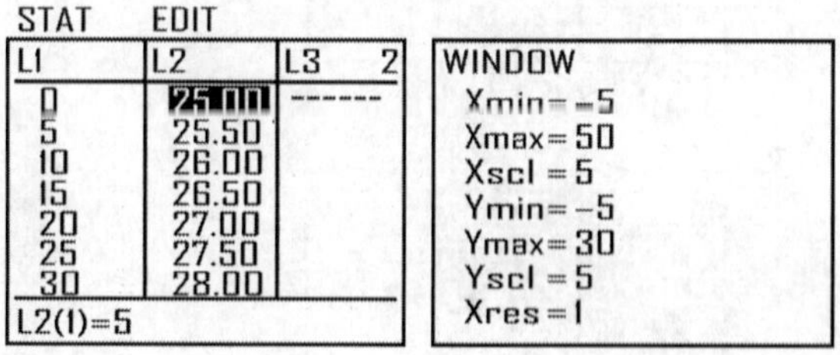

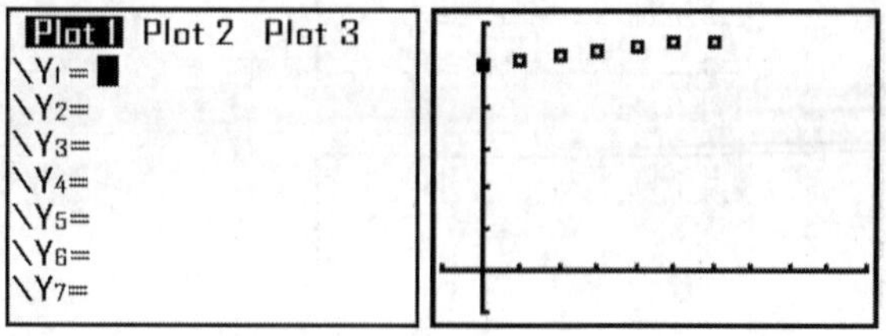

Both scatter plots show that this relationship is linear, since the graphed points form a line.
If the points from the scatter plot are connected, a line will result; therefore, the relationship between airtime and total monthly cost is linear.

PRACTICE QUESTIONS

Use the following information to answer the next question.

> Carmen's Canoe Company charges a flat fee of $20 to rent a canoe plus $1.20 for every 30 min of use.

13. Which of the following graphing calculator screen shots correctly portrays data from Carmen's Canoe Company?

A.

L1	L2	L3 2
0	20.00	------
10	21.20	
20	22.40	
30	23.60	
40	24.80	
50	26.00	
60	27.20	

L2(1)=20.00

B.

L1	L2	L3 2
0	20.00	------
10	20.60	
20	21.20	
30	21.80	
40	22.40	
50	23.00	
60	23.60	

L2(1)=20.00

C.

L1	L2	L3 2
0	20.00	------
10	20.40	
20	20.80	
30	21.20	
40	21.60	
50	22.00	
60	22.40	

L2(1)=20.00

D.

L1	L2	L3 2
0	20.00	------
10	20.30	
20	20.60	
30	20.90	
40	21.20	
50	21.50	
60	21.80	

L2(1)=20.00

Use the following information to answer the next question.

> Stephan was selling tickets to a concert. After selling most of his tickets, he graphed a scatter plot to illustrate the relationship between the numbers of tickets left to sell, y, and the amount of time, x, in minutes, it takes to sell them.

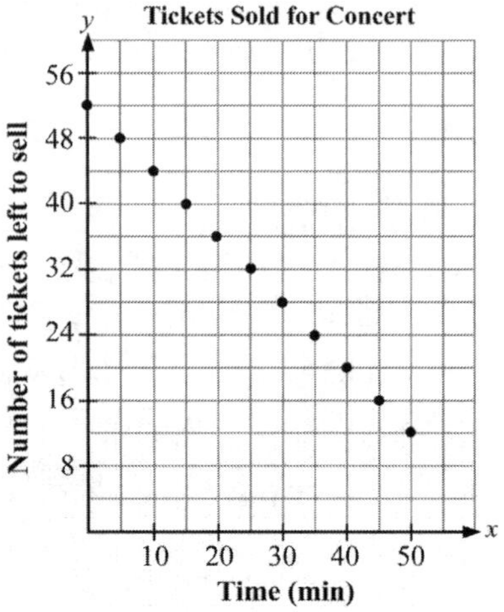

14. Which of the following statements best describes the information given in the scatter plot?

A. Stephan started with 50 tickets and sold 4 tickets every 5 minutes.

B. Stephan started with 50 tickets and sold 2 tickets every 5 minutes.

C. Stephan started with 52 tickets and sold 4 tickets every 5 minutes.

D. Stephan started with 52 tickets and sold 2 tickets every 5 minutes.

15. A snail moves at a constant rate of 4 cm every minute. If it starts from a point 40 cm from the edge of the sidewalk, which of the following tables correctly represents the snail's distance from the edge of the sidewalk over time?

A.

Time (min)	0	2	4	6	8
Distance (cm)	40	36	32	28	24

B.

Time (min)	0	2	4	6	8
Distance (cm)	40	32	24	16	8

C.

Time (min)	0	2	4	6	8
Distance (cm)	0	8	16	24	32

D.

Time (min)	0	2	4	6	8
Distance (cm)	0	4	8	12	11

Use the following information to answer the next question.

A typist earns $10 for the first 400 lines and an additional $0.10 per line after that.

16. Which of the following tables correctly represents the given situation?

A.

Number of extra lines	0	10	20	30	40
Earnings ($)	400	410	420	430	440

B.

Number of extra lines	0	10	20	30	40
Earnings ($)	400	401	402	403	404

C.

Number of extra lines	0	10	20	30	40
Earnings ($)	10	11	12	13	14

D.

Number of extra lines	0	10	20	30	40
Earnings ($)	20	21	22	23	24

LR2.02 construct tables of values, scatter plots, and lines or curves of best fit as appropriate, using a variety of tools, for linearly related and non-linearly related data collected from a variety of sources

LINEAR AND NON-LINEAR RELATIONS

When data is collected and a scatter plot is created, a linear or a non-linear relationship will be observed.

LINEAR RELATIONS

For linear scatter plots, you can draw a **line of best fit** to represent the data. When drawing a line of best fit, use a ruler and line it up so that it goes through the middle of the pattern formed by the points on your scatter plot. Keep approximately the same number of points above the line as below the line.

Example

Use the following data about the population of Canada to create a scatter plot, and then draw the line of best fit for the data.

Year	Population (millions)
1950	*13.8*
1960	*18*
1970	24
1980	27
1985	*29.5*
1990	*31*
1995	32
2005	35

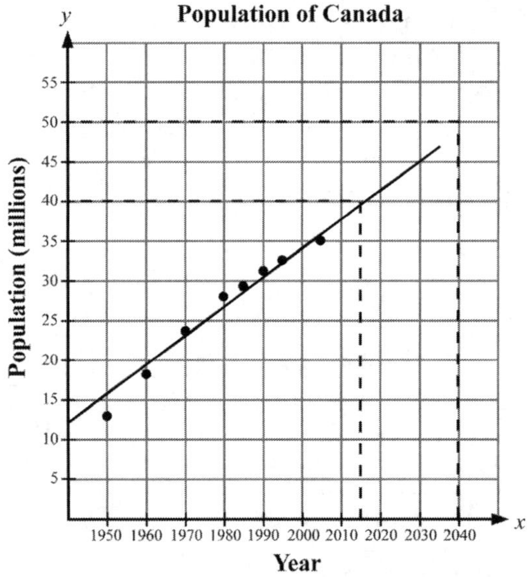

After the line of best fit is drawn, you can make predictions about other points. For example, you can predict that in 2040 the population will be a little less than 50 million. You can also predict that a population of 40 million will occur around the year 2013. These points can be traced by following the dotted lines shown on the graph.

NON-LINEAR RELATIONS

Non-linear data is data that does not form a line but is best represented by a **curve of best fit**.

Example

Rebecca conducted an experiment to study the relationship between the temperature, T, of water in a glass, and the time, t, in minutes after placing an ice cube into the glass.

Rebecca's data is given in the following table of values and graph:

Elapsed time (min)	Water temperature (°C)
0	23
2	17
4	13
6	12
8	12.5
10	14
12	15
14	18
16	22

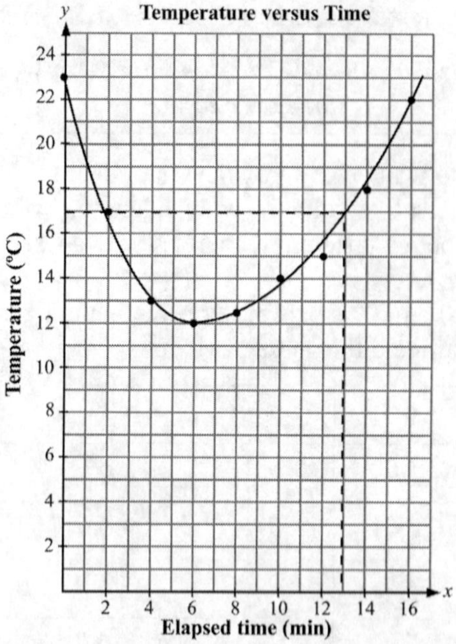

By looking at the curve of best fit, you can predict that when the elapsed time is 13 min, the temperature of the water will be about 17°C. This point can be traced by following the dotted lines.

PRACTICE QUESTIONS

Use the following information to answer the next question.

Bindu wanted to study the relationship between the width, w, and the length, l, of a number of different rectangles with a fixed area, A,
of 6.0 cm². As part of her investigation, she constructed this table of values.

w (cm)	*l (cm)*	*A = lw cm2*
1.0	*6.0*	*6.0*
2.0	*3.0*	*6.0*
3.0	*2.0*	*6.0*
4.0	*1.5*	*6.0*
5.0	*1.2*	*6.0*
6.0	*1.0*	*6.0*

17. Which of the following graphs best represents the data in Bindu's table?

A.

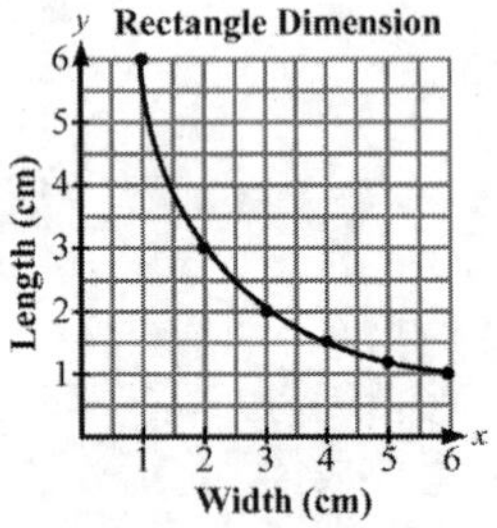

B.

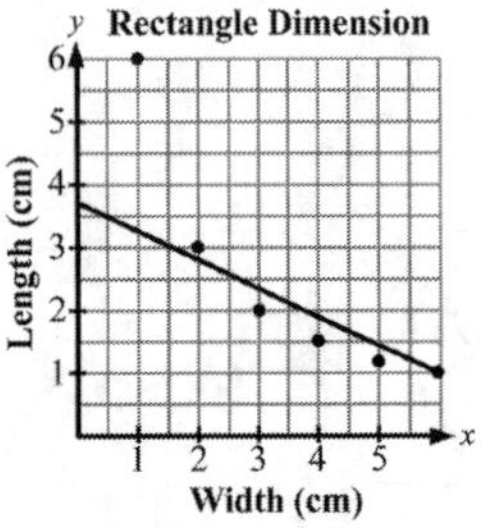

C.

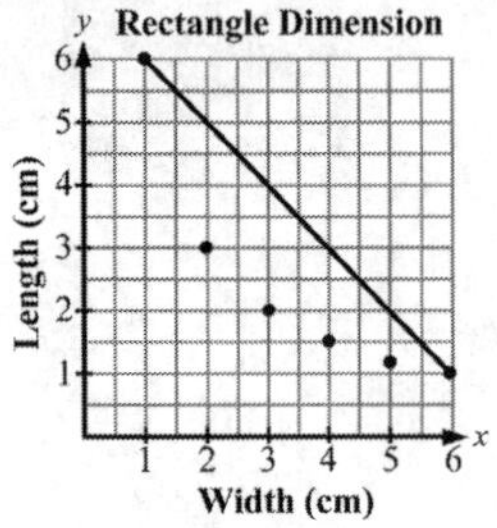

D.

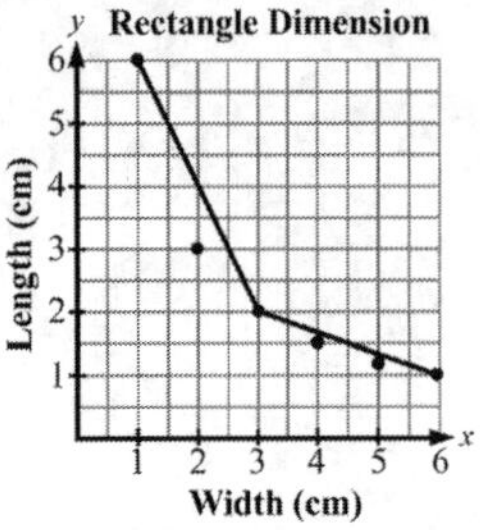

CHALLENGER QUESTION

The scatter plot shown illustrates the relationship between the size of a house and the cost to build the house.

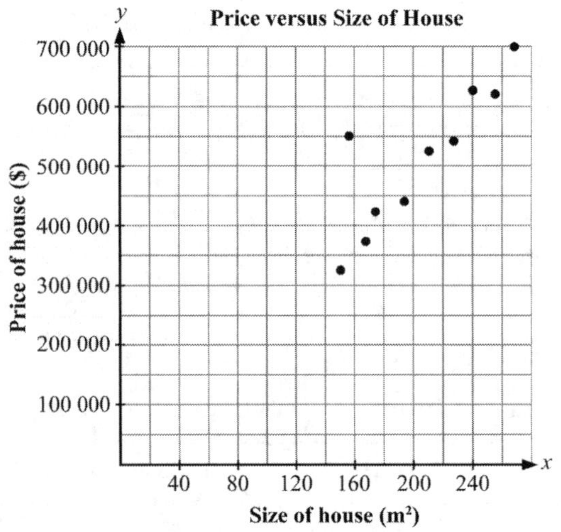

18. A line of best fit is drawn and then used to estimate the size of a house that costs \$200 000 to build. The estimate for the size of the house is

A. 120 m²

B. 110 m²

C. 100 m²

D. 90 m²

19. For every increase of 10 m² in the size of a house, the total cost of the house increases by approximately

A. \$20 000

B. \$60 000

C. \$120 000

D. \$200 000

Use the following information to answer the next question.

A student determined the volume, V, in cubic centimetres of various cubes where the length, l, in centimetres of each side of the cube was given. The student's data is shown in the following table.

Volume of Cube Related to Length of its Sides						
l (cm)	*2*	*3*	*4*	*5*	*6*	*7*
V (cm³)	*8*	*27*	*64*	*125*	*216*	*343*

20. The relationship between the length of a side, l, and the volume, V, of the cubes is a

A. linear relationship, since as l increases, V increases by a constant amount

B. linear relationship, since as l increases, V decreases by a constant amount

C. non-linear relationship, since as l increases, V decreases by a constant amount

D. non-linear relationship, since as l increases, V does not increase by a constant amount

21. In a Canadian city, gas prices fell at a constant rate from the spring to the fall of a particular year. Which of the following graphs portrays this relationship if spring starts at the orgin along the x-axis?

A.

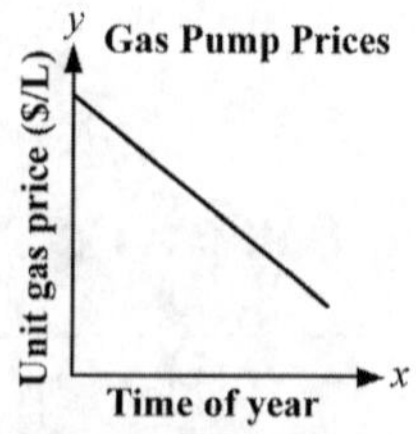

B.

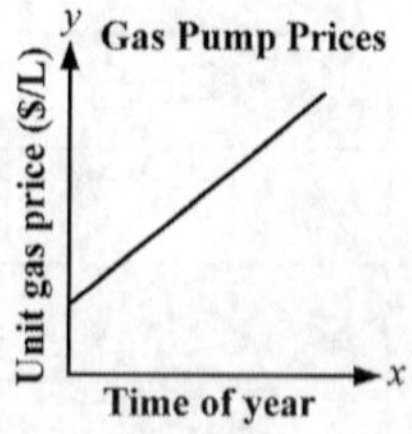

C.

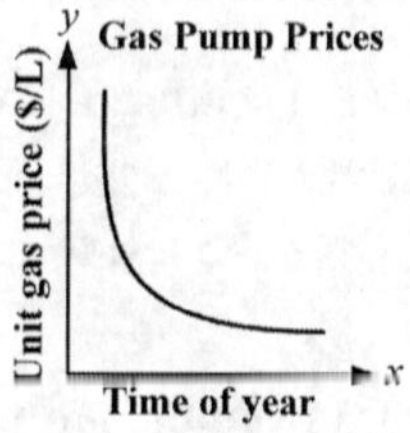

D.

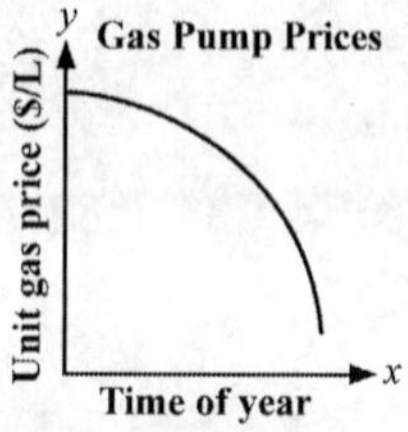

Use the following information to answer the next question.

Gary collected data describing the relationship between the unit price of a T-shirt, *C*, and the total number ordered at one time, *n*. His data is recorded in the following table of values.

Number ordered	**Unit price ($)**
200	20.00
400	19.00
600	17.50
800	15.50
1 000	13.00
1 200	10.00

22. If this data is plotted as a scatter plot with points (*n*, *C*), the points move

A. linearly upward from the left to the right of the graph

B. linearly downward from the left to the right of the graph

C. in an upward curve from the left to the right of the graph

D. in a downward curve from the left to the right of the graph

23. The cost of fencing a field is $0.25/m. Which of the following tables correctly represents the given situation regarding the cost of fencing?

A.

Fencing (m)	**0**	**25**	**50**	**75**	**100**
Cost ($)	**0**	**6.00**	**12.25**	**18.50**	**25.00**

B.

Fencing (m)	**0**	**25**	**50**	**75**	**100**
Cost ($)	**0**	**6.00**	**12.25**	**18.50**	**25.50**

C.

Fencing (m)	**0**	**25**	**50**	**75**	**100**
Cost ($)	**0**	**6.25**	**12.50**	**18.75**	**25.00**

D.

Fencing (m)	**0**	**25**	**50**	**75**	**100**
Cost ($)	**0**	**6.25**	**12.25**	**18.75**	**25.75**

Open Response

1. Roller Coaster Ride

In one year, Cheyenne visited 16 different amusement parks. At each amusement park, she went on one roller coaster ride. The distance, *d*, in metres travelled from start to finish on each roller coaster with respect to the maximum height, *h*, in metres of the roller coaster above the ground during the ride is shown in the scatter plot.

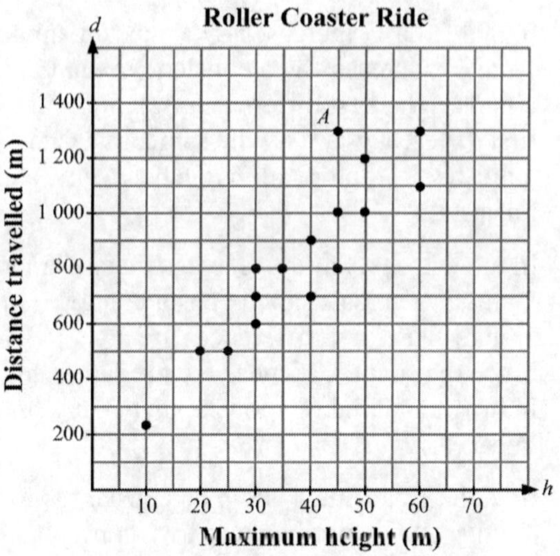

a) Draw a line of best fit to represent the data. Assume that the maximum height is 0 m when the distance is 0 m.

b) Based on your line of best fit, what would be the distance travelled by a roller coaster that reaches a maximum height of 55 m? Show your work.

c) Cheyenne stated that point *A* on the graph represents a roller coaster ride that reaches a high maximum height but travels a short distance. Do you agree or disagree with Cheyenne's interpretation of point *A*? Explain your answer.

LR2.03 identify, through investigation, some properties of linear relations, (i.e., numerically, the first difference is a constant, which represents a constant rate of change; graphically, a straight line represents the relation), and apply these properties to determine whether a relation is linear or non-linear

PROPERTIES OF LINEAR RELATIONS

Data in tables of values is linear if the first differences are equal. **First differences** describe the difference between consecutive y-values with evenly-spaced x-values. If the first differences between consecutive y-values are all the same, the relation is **linear.** If they are not the same, the relation is **non-linear**.

Example

Examine the following three tables of values.

Table 1		
x	y	First Differences
0	32	
1	38	$38 - 32 = 6$
2	44	$44 - 38 = 6$
3	50	$50 - 44 = 6$
4	56	$56 - 50 = 6$

Table 2		
x	y	First Differences
0	18	
2	15	$15 - 18 = -3$
4	12	$12 - 15 = -3$
6	9	$9 - 12 = -3$
8	6	$6 - 9 = -3$

Table 3		
x	y	First Differences
0	10	
4	12	$12 - 10 = 2$
8	17	$17 - 12 = 5$
12	25	$25 - 17 = 8$
16	37	$37 - 25 = 12$

In table 1, as x increases by a constant amount of 1 unit, y increases by a constant amount of 6 units. The first differences are all 6. Since the first differences are all the same, this data indicates that the relationship between x and y is linear.

In table 2, as x increases by a constant amount of 2 units, y decreases by a constant amount of 3 units. The first differences are all -3. Since the first differences are the same, this data indicates that the relationship between x and y is linear.

In table 3, as x increases by a constant amount of 4 units, y does **not** increase by a constant amount; the first differences are **not** the same. Since the first differences are not all the same, the relationship between x and y is non-linear.

Table 1 **Table 2** **Table 3**

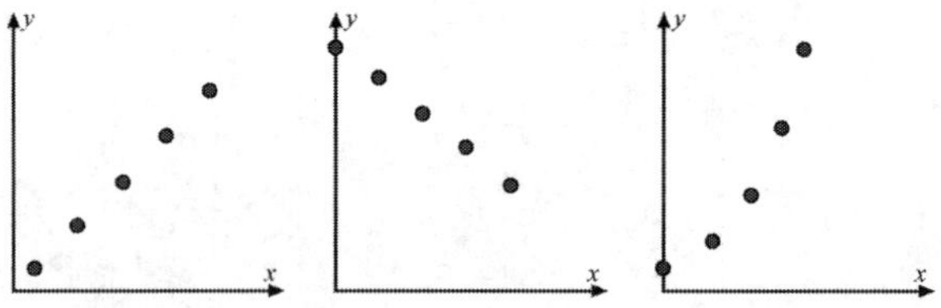

The graphs of tables 1 and 2 show points that form a line, while the graph of table 3 portrays points forming a curve, which is a non-linear pattern.

PRACTICE QUESTIONS

Use the following information to answer the next question.

The given scatter plot shows the relationship between the Celsius and Kelvin temperature scales.

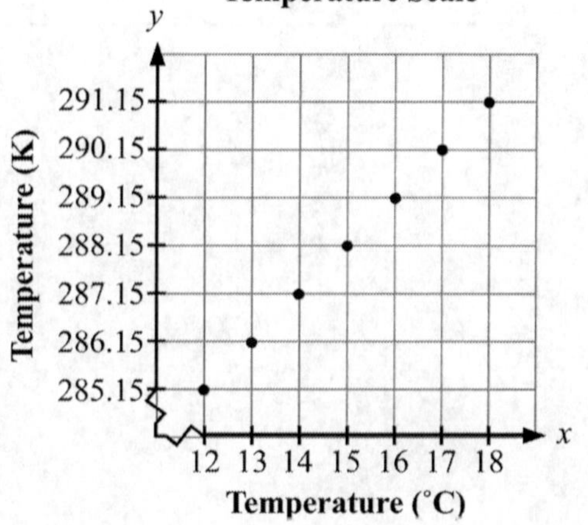

24. If this pattern between the temperature scales continues, what is the expected temperature in Celsius for 304.15 K?

A. 28°C

B. 29°C

C. 30°

D. 31°C

LR3.01 determine, through investigation, that the rate of change of a linear relation can be found by choosing any two points on the line that represents the relation, finding the vertical change between the points (i.e., the rise) and the horizontal change between the points (i.e., the run), and writing the ratio $\frac{rise}{run}$ (i.e., rate of change $= \frac{rise}{run}$)

RATE OF CHANGE

To find the **rate of change** of a linear relation, you need to find the rise and run between two points on the line. The formula is as shown:

$$\textit{Rate of change} = \frac{\text{rise}}{\text{run}}$$

The **rise** is the vertical change between two points, and the **run** is the horizontal change between the same two points.

Example

You can examine the graphs of two linear relations with five labelled points and find their corresponding rates of change.

Line 1

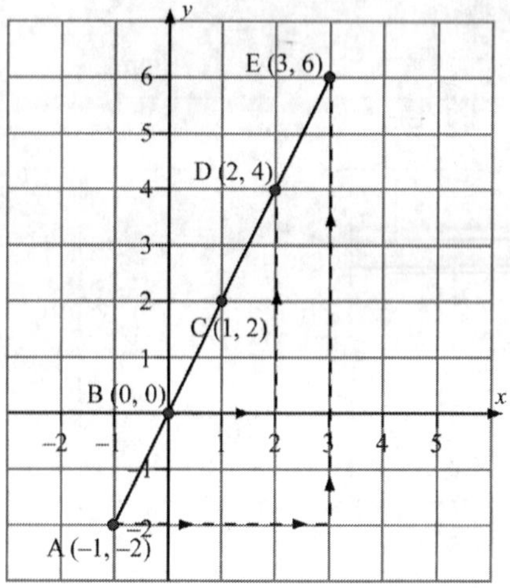

Line 1		
Run $(A \rightarrow B)$	Run $(B \rightarrow D)$	Run $(A \rightarrow E)$
$0-(-1)=1$	$2-0=2$	$3-(-1)=4$
Rise $(A \rightarrow B)$	Rise $(B \rightarrow D)$	Rise $(A \rightarrow E)$
$0-(-2)=2$	$4-0=4$	$6-(-2)=8$
Rate $(A \rightarrow B)$	Rate $(B \rightarrow D)$	Rate $(A \rightarrow E)$
$\frac{\text{rise}}{\text{run}}=\frac{2}{1}=2$	$\frac{\text{rise}}{\text{run}}=\frac{4}{2}=2$	$\frac{\text{rise}}{\text{run}}=\frac{8}{4}=2$

Line 2

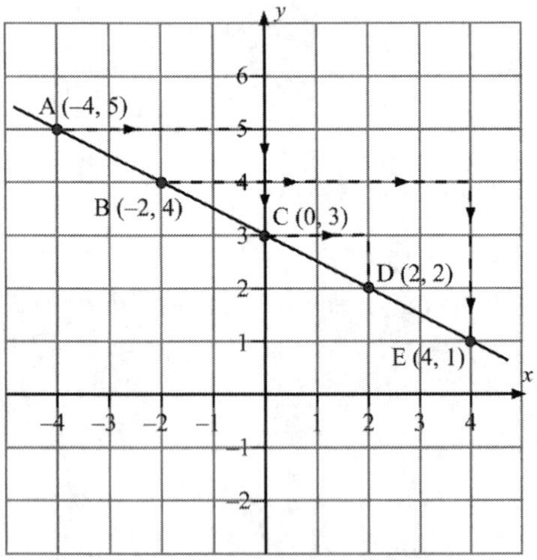

Line 2		
Run $(A \rightarrow C)$	Run $(B \rightarrow E)$	Run $(C \rightarrow D)$
$0-(-4)=4$	$4-(-2)=6$	$2-0=2$
Rise $(A \rightarrow C)$	Rise $(B \rightarrow E)$	Rise $(C \rightarrow D)$
$3-5=-2$	$1-4=-3$	$2-3=-1$
Rate $(A \rightarrow C)$	Rate $(B \rightarrow E)$	Rate $(C \rightarrow D)$
$\frac{-2}{4}=\frac{-1}{2}$ or -0.5	$\frac{-3}{6}=\frac{-1}{2}$ or -0.5	$\frac{-1}{2}$ or -0.5

Note: The rate of change between any two points of a line is **always** the same, or constant:

Rate of change (line 1) = 2
Rate of change (line 2) = –0.5

PRACTICE QUESTIONS

Use the following graph to answer the next question.

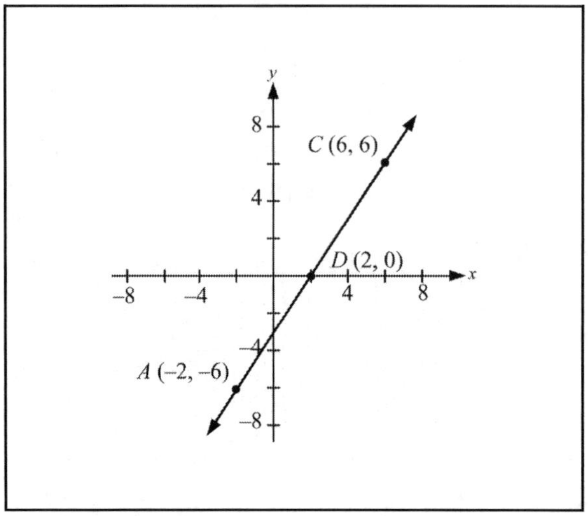

25. What is the rate of change for the line shown?

A. $\frac{3}{2}$

B. $\frac{5}{2}$

C. $-\frac{3}{2}$

D. $-\frac{5}{2}$

26. Which of the following lines has a rate of change of –3?

A.

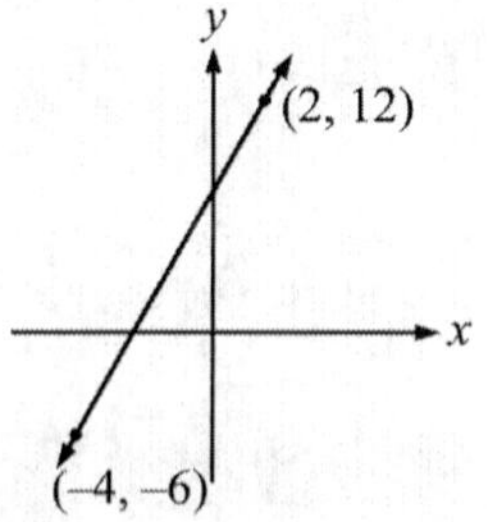

B.

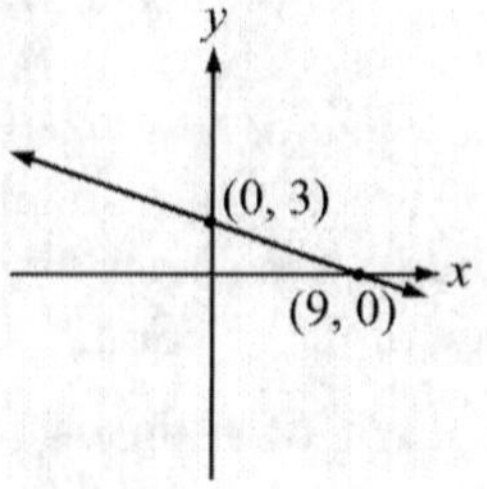

C.

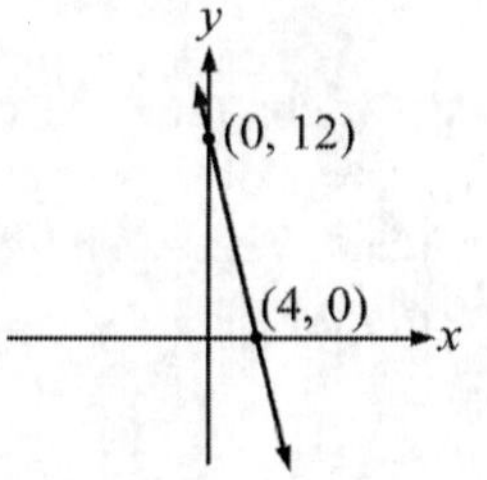

D.

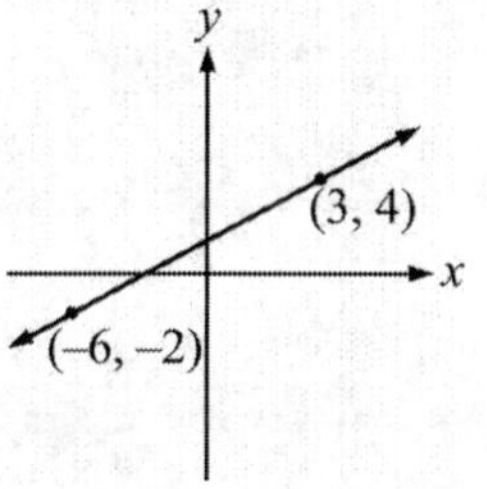

27. The constant rate of change between points P(3, –2) and Q(5, –8) on a linear graph is

A. $\frac{\text{rise}}{\text{run}} = \frac{6}{2} = 3$

B. $\frac{\text{rise}}{\text{run}} = \frac{2}{6} = \frac{1}{3}$

C. $\frac{\text{rise}}{\text{run}} = \frac{-6}{2} = -3$

D. $\frac{\text{rise}}{\text{run}} = \frac{2}{-6} = \frac{-1}{3}$

Use the following information to answer the next question.

The given graph shows the linear relationship between the variables x and y.

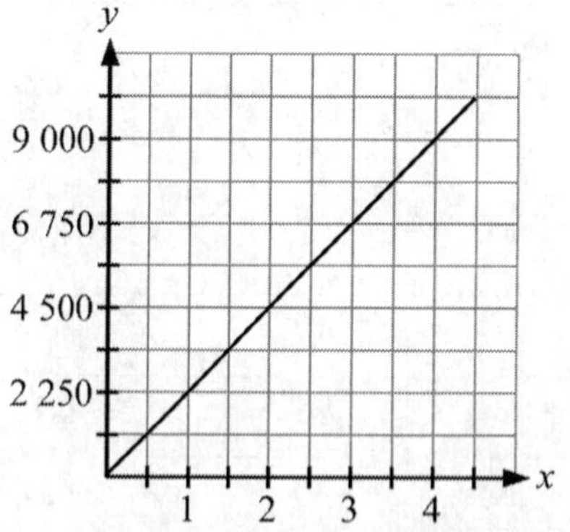

28. What is the constant rate of change of the line on the graph?

A. 9 000

B. 2 250

C. 4

D. 1

LR3.02 determine, through investigation, connections among the representations of a constant rate of change of a linear relation

CONSTANT RATE OF CHANGE

To evaluate the constant rate of change of a linear relation, you could use the following methods:

- Make a table of values where the x-values increase by one unit, and then find the first differences.
- Draw a graph of the relation, and determine the rise and run between several points.
- Write an algebraic equation that relates the two variables.

Example

The cost of producing a book of photographs is \$50 plus \$5 per book. Determine the constant rate of change for this scenario.

Number of Books	Cost (\$)	First Differences
0	*50*	
1	*55*	*55 − 50 = 5*
2	*60*	*60 − 55 = 5*
3	*65*	*65 − 60 = 5*
4	*70*	*70 − 65 = 5*

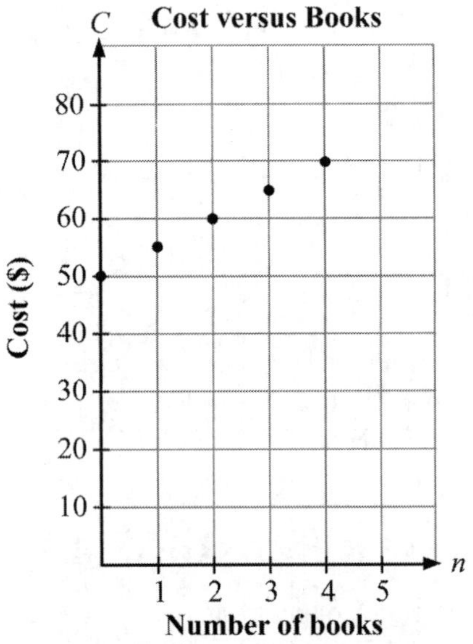

The table of values shows that the first differences are all equal to 5, which means that the constant rate of change is 5 or \$5/book. For every increase of 1 in the number of books, the cost increases by 5.

Also, if you picked any two points from the graph, you would see that the rate of change is as follows:

$$=\frac{\text{rise}}{\text{run}}=\frac{5}{1}=5$$

For every 1 unit to the right (run) in the x-direction, move up 5 units (rise) in the y-direction.

Therefore, the rate of change is 5 or \$5/book.

To write an algebraic equation relating the two variables in this example, let the cost of the book be C and the number of books be n. In this scenario, the algebraic equation is $C=50+5n$. The coefficient of the independent variable, which in this example is n, represents the constant rate of change of the relation.

Therefore, the constant rate of change is 5 or \$5/book.

Note: The constant rate of change is described in word problems using some of these phrases: *so much per, changes by, decreases or increases by, so much for each, rate of.*

PRACTICE QUESTIONS

Use the following information to answer the next question.

Tina and Andro each examined two different tables of values depicting linear relations. In each table, the value of n was unknown.

Table 1

x	0	1	2
y	–3	n	–13

Table 2

x	–2	1	4
y	–1	n	7

Tina and Andro realize that in order for each table to represent a linear relation, n has to be a value such that the first differences of all y-values in each table are the same.

29. Which of the following statements is true?

A. In table 2, $n = 4$, and the first differences are all 3.

B. In table 1, $n = –8$, and the first differences are all 5.

C. In table 2, $n = 3$, and the first differences are all –4.

D. In table 1, $n = –8$, and the first differences are all –5.

CHALLENGER QUESTION

30. On a warm April day, the height of a snow bank was decreasing at a constant rate of change of 2 cm/h. Which of the following graphs correctly illustrates the relationship between the height of the snow bank and the time?

A.

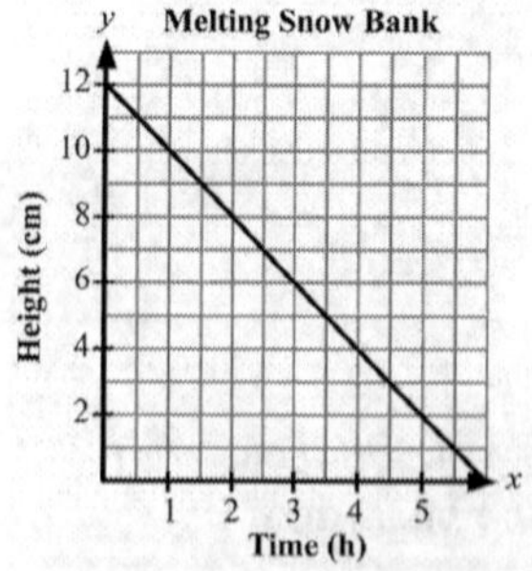

B.

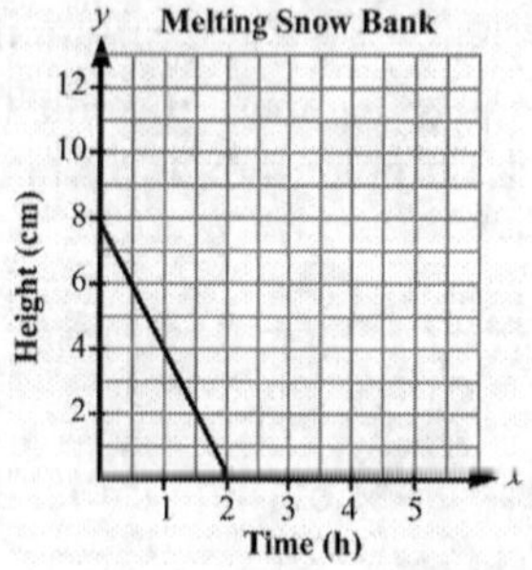

C.

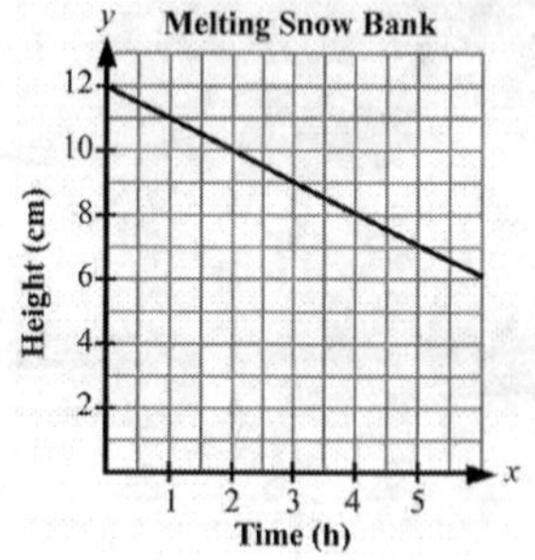

D.

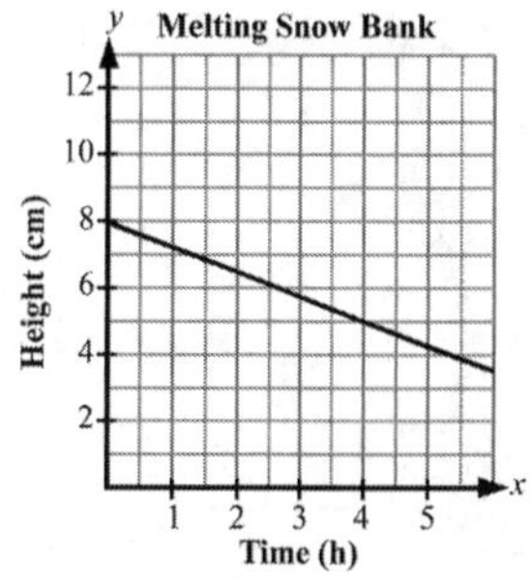

CHALLENGER QUESTION

To rent a cab, Carla has to pay a fixed charge and an additional constant rate for every kilometre driven.

31. If the cab driver charges \$23 for 10 km and \$33 for 15 km, then what is the fixed charge to rent this cab?

A. \$1

B. \$2

C. \$3

D. \$4

Use the following information to answer the next question.

At an initial distance of 120 m from his house, Aidan began biking at a constant speed of 5 m/s. If Aidan's distance from his house, d, is related to the time, t, then the equation is $d = 5t + 120$.

32. How long will it take Aidan to be at a position that is two times the initial distance from his house?

A. 14 s

B. 17 s

C. 21 s

D. 24 s

LR3.03 compare the properties of direct variation and partial variation in applications, and identify the initial value

Properties of Direct Variation and Partial Variation

There are two types of linear relations: direct variation and partial variation.

In a **direct variation**, the linear relation has a constant rate of change between the variables x and y, and the graph of this relation passes through the origin.

In a **partial variation**, the linear relation also has a constant rate of change between the variables x and y; however, the graph of this relation does **not** pass through the origin.

The **initial value** or **vertical intercept** is the value of the dependent variable, y, when the value of the independent variable, x, is zero. If the initial value is zero, then the linear relation is a direct variation. If the initial value is a value other than zero, then the linear relation is a partial variation.

Examples of different presentations of direct and partial variations are given below.

Direct Variation

Example

Yoga costs \$14 per class.
⇒Constant rate of change is 14, with a starting value of 0.

$y = -4x$

⇒Constant rate of change is −4, with a starting value of 0.

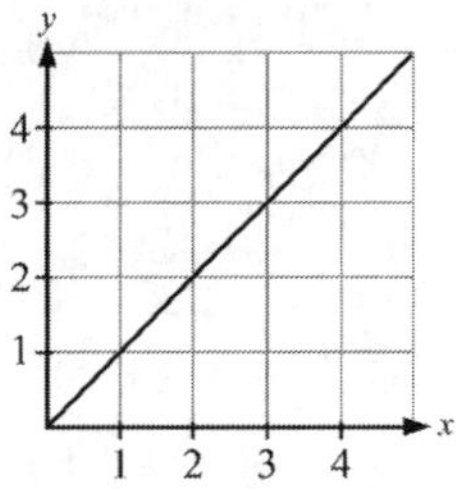

⇒Constant rate of change is 1, with a starting value of 0 (passing through the origin).

PARTIAL VARIATION

Example

Kung fu costs $30 for registration plus $10 per class.
$\Rightarrow$Constant rate of change is 10, with an initial value of 30.

$y = 2x + 9$

$\Rightarrow$Constant rate of change is 2, with an initial value of 9.

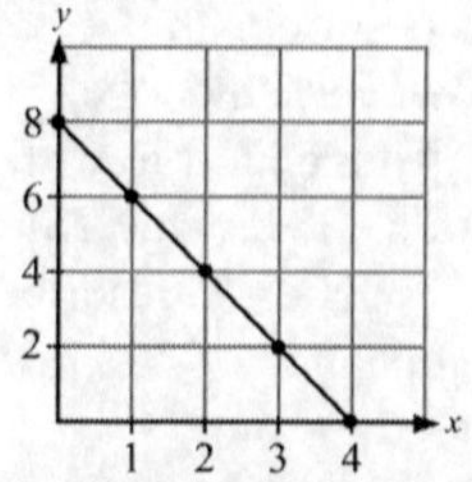

$\Rightarrow$Constant rate of change is -2, with an initial value of 8.

PRACTICE QUESTIONS

Use the following information to answer the next question.

> Four different equations describing the linear relationship between the velocity (V) of a particle in metres per second and the time (t) in seconds are shown below.
>
> **I** $V = 4t$
> **II** $V = 30 - 2t$
> **III** $V = 6t + 13$
> **IV** $V = 14t - 3t$

33. A partial variation between the velocity of the particle and the time is represented by

A. equation I only

B. equation III only

C. equations II and III

D. equations II, III, and IV

34. Which of the following graphs shows a direct variation between the cost of renting a car and the distance travelled?

A.

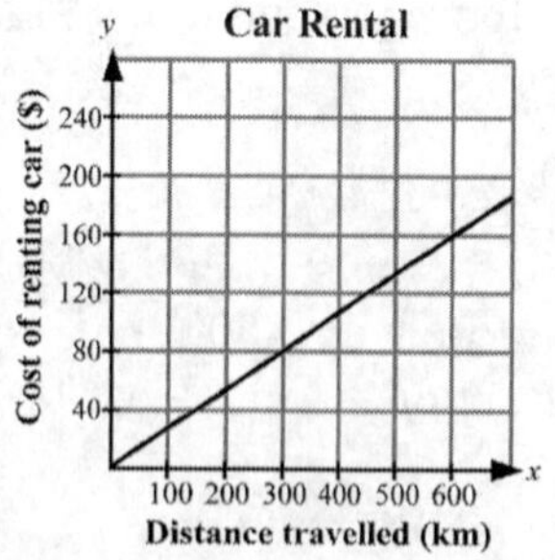

B.

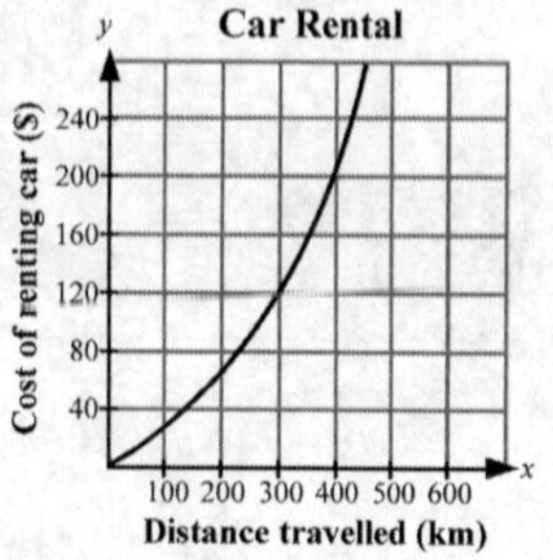

C.

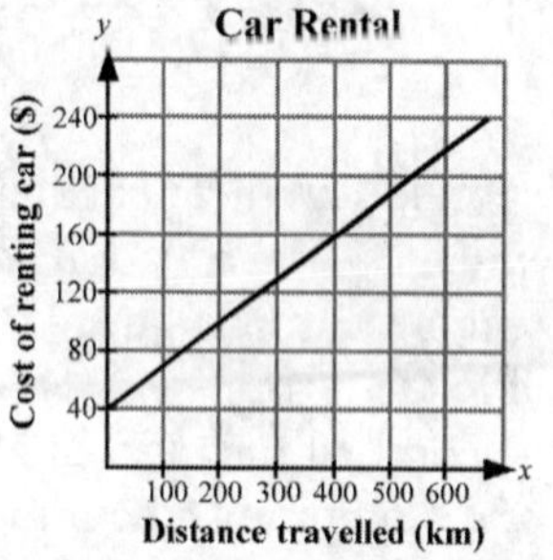

D.

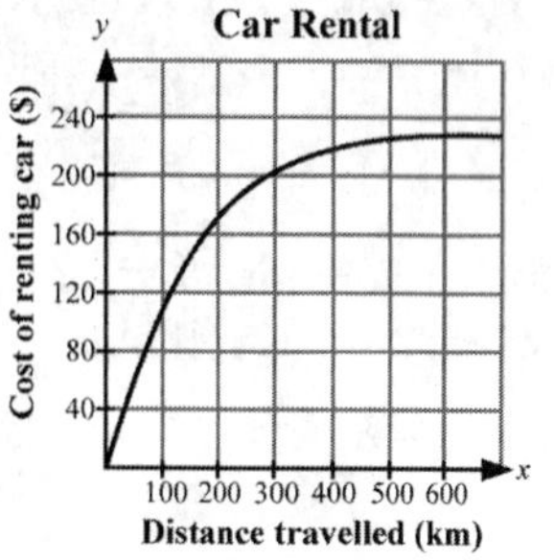

CHALLENGER QUESTION

Three different yoga instructors charge the following fees for their respective programs:

Instructor I: \$45 for registration plus \$12 per class

Instructor II: \$20 per class

Instructor III: \$160 for registration, \$25 for a uniform, and \$80 for instruction

35. Partial variations result from the instruction fees of

A. Instructor I only

B. Instructor II only

C. Instructors I and III

D. Instructors II and III

LR3.04 express a linear relation as an equation in two variables, using the rate of change and the initial value

EXPRESSING LINEAR RELATIONS AS EQUATIONS

An **equation** is an algebraic statement equating two or more related variables. An equation with two variables, *x* and *y*, representing a linear relation can be written in the form $y = mx + b$, where *m* represents the constant rate of change of the linear relation and *b* represents the initial value of the relation.

In a direct variation, where the initial value is 0, write the equation as follows:

$$y = mx + 0 \quad or \quad y = mx$$

In a partial variation, where the initial value is other than 0, write the equation as follows:

$$y = mx + b$$

Example

Dylan is participating in a walkathon. The total course is 25 km, and he walks at a steady pace of 5 km/h. If *d* represents the distance left to walk and *t* represents the number of hours walked, then the equation representing this relation is $d = 25 - 5t$.

Compare this equation to $y = mx + b$, where *t* represents the variable *x*, and the numerical coefficient *m* is −5. Since Dylan is walking at a steady pace of 5 km/h, this describes the constant rate of change; however, since the question is in terms of the distance left to walk, it actually represents −5 km/h. The value 25 in the equation, representing the letter *b*, describes the initial value or starting distance of 25 km.

PRACTICE QUESTIONS

Use the following information to answer the next question.

Meg leaves from work on a holiday. The graph shows the distance of Meg's car from her house.

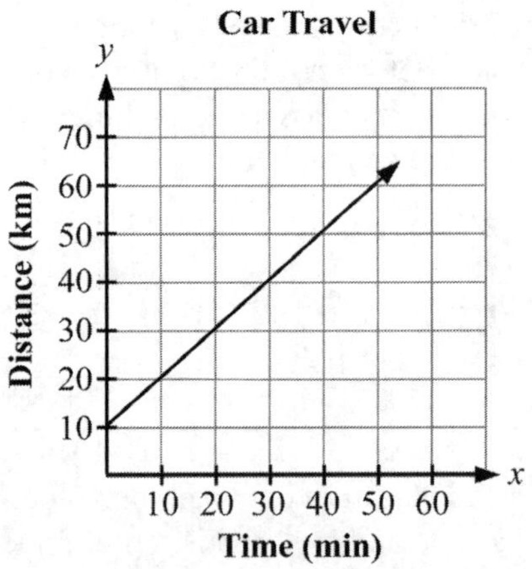

36. If the origin represents Meg's house, then how far is her place of work from her house?

A. 10 km

B. 20 km

C. 30 km

D. 40 km

37. The cost to place an advertisement in a local paper is $35 plus 39¢ per letter. If an advertisement consists of n letters, which of the following equations represents the cost, C, of placing the advertisement in the paper?

A. $C=(35+0.39)n$

B. $C=(35-0.39)n$

C. $C=35n+0.39$

D. $C=35+0.39n$

CHALLENGER QUESTION

38. Which of the following tables of values represents the equation $C = 20 + 2n$?

A.

n	C
0	20
2	21
4	22
6	23

B.

n	C
0	20
2	24
4	28
6	32

C.

n	C
0	20
2	22
4	24
6	26

D.

n	C
0	20
2	18
4	16
6	14

CHALLENGER QUESTION

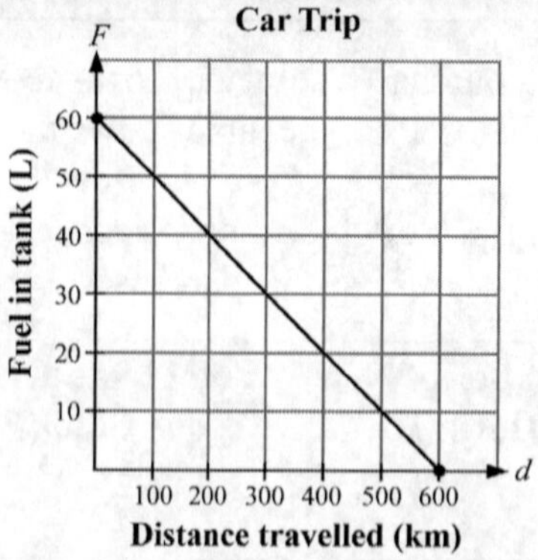

39. Which of the following equations defines the given line segment?

A. $F=60-10d$

B. $F=60-\frac{1}{10}d$

C. $F=60+10d$

D. $F=60+\frac{1}{10}d$

Use the following information to answer the next question.

A farmer purchases some new hens to add to his existing flock. The table shows the total number of eggs laid (E) in one week by the farmer's flock of chickens with respect to the number of new hens (H) purchased.

Number of New Hens (H)	Total Number of Eggs Laid (E)
0	75
1	82
2	89
3	96
4	103

40. The equation that represents the relationship between the total number of eggs laid in one week and the number of new hens purchased is

A. $E = 7H$

B. $E = 75H$

C. $E = 75H + 7$

D. $E = 75 + 7H$

CHALLENGER QUESTION

Pamela's Printing Shop prints yearbooks for schools. Schools that purchase their yearbooks from Pamela's Printing Shop are charged as follows:

- A fixed cost of \$700
- A cost of \$0.50 per yearbook cover
- A cost of \$3.50 per yearbook (not including the cover cost)

41. Which of the following equations represents the total cost, C, for the purchase of n yearbooks from Pamela's Printing Shop?

A. $C = 700 + 0.50n$

B. $C = 700 + 3.50n$

C. $C = 700 + 4.00n$

D. $C = 700n + 4.00n$

Use the following information to answer the next question.

Dirk is a contestant on a quiz show. He will be asked 12 questions, getting a maximum of 2 points for each correct answer and 0 points for each incorrect answer. This is illustrated by line of best fit.

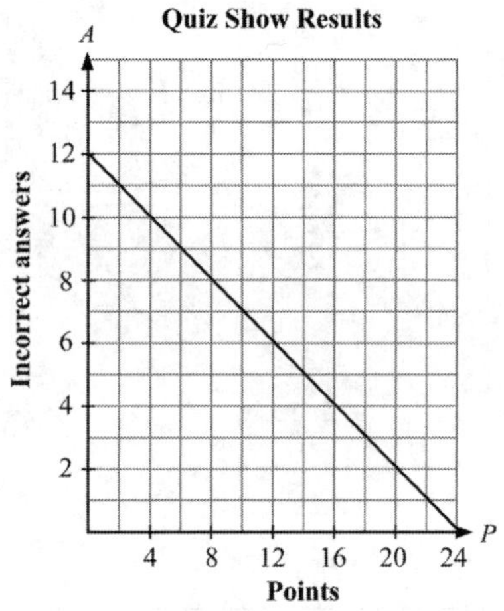

42. The equation of the line of best fit that represents the relationship between the number of incorrect answers and the number of points Dirk scored is

A. $A = 24 - 2P$

B. $A = 24 - 0.5P$

C. $A = 12 - 2P$

D. $A = 12 - 0.5P$

Use the following information to answer the next question.

Geoff decided to go for a Sunday drive. At the start of his drive, he had 60 L of fuel in his truck's gas tank. As he drove, the fuel, F, in the tank decreased at a rate of 1 L/10 km.

43. Which of the following graphs and equations could Geoff use to determine the number of kilometres, d, he could drive on 60 L of fuel?

A.

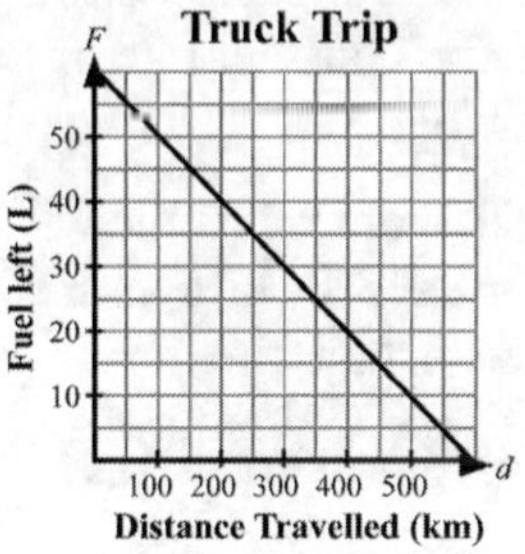

$F = 60 - 0.1d$

B.

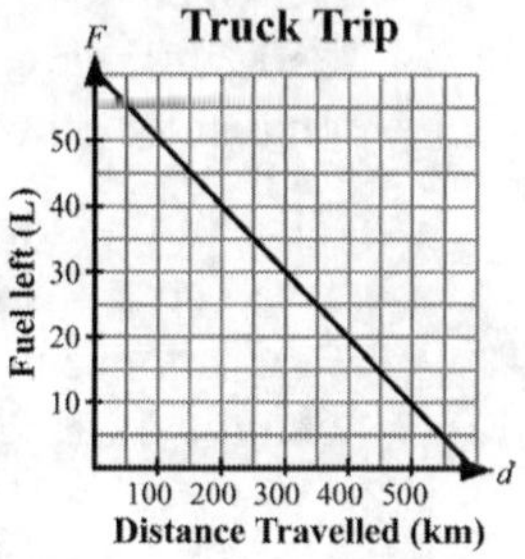

$F = 60 + 0.1d$

C.

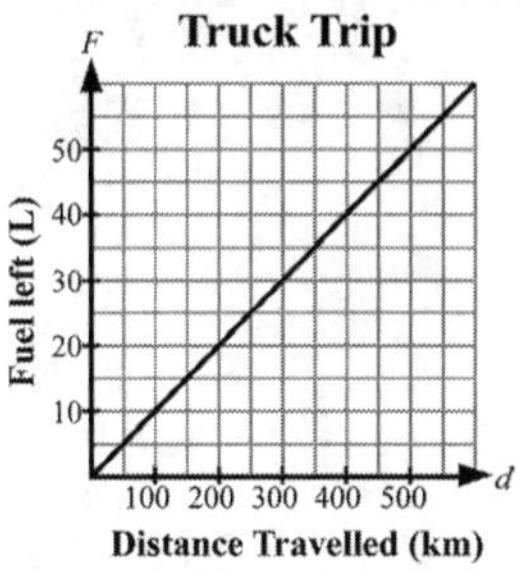

$F = 60 - 0.1d$

D.

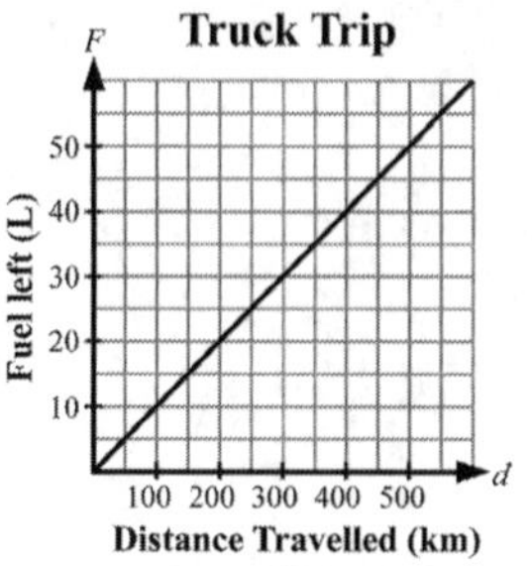

$F = 60 + 0.1d$

LR3.05 describe the meaning of the rate of change and the initial value for a linear relation arising from a realistic situation, and describe a situation that could be modelled by a given linear equation

DESCRIBING RATES OF CHANGE

To describe the meaning of the rate of change and initial value described in a realistic situation, the initial value is described as a **fixed value**, while the **constant rate of change** is described by the amount the y-variable changes with respect to a change in the x-variable of the relation.

Example

The cost to rent a community hall is $100 plus $3 per person attending. There is also a $50 fee for the janitorial service.

The vertical intercept or initial value of 150 represents the fixed values of $100 and $50 for renting the hall, while 3 represents the constant rate of change of $3 per person.

Similarly, you can describe a realistic situation that can be modelled by a given linear equation.

Example

A box of books has a mass of 60 g. There is an added mass of 15 g per additional book added to the box.

Using the initial equation $y = mx + b$, the mass of the box can be modelled by the equation $M = 15x + 60$. The value 60 represents an initial mass of 60 g. The value of m is 15, since it represents a constant rate of change of 15. The value of x represents the number of books.

Practice Questions

Use the following information to answer the next question.

Shaun created this table of values to show the temperature change in degrees Celsius with respect to the time in hours.

Time (h)	Temperature (°C)
0	–8
1	–2
2	4
3	10
4	16

44. Which of the following statements represents the data given in the table of values?

A. The temperature rose 6°C every hour.

B. The temperature rose 8°C every hour.

C. The temperature dropped 6°C every hour.

D. The temperature dropped 10°C every hour.

Use the following information to answer the next question.

Mun wishes to buy a T-shirt with a logo on the front from T&S Sportswear. T&S Sportswear charges $15 for a T-shirt, $2 for a logo on the front, and $0.25 for each letter placed on the back of the T-shirt.

45. If Mun decides to place the name of one of his favourite sports teams on the back of his T-shirt, then which of the following statements with respect to the total coat of his T-shirt is **true**?

A. The initial value of 17 represents the fixed cost of $17 for each T-shirt, and 0.25 represents the constant rate of change of $0.25 per letter.

B. The initial value of $17.25 represents the fixed cost of $17.25 for each T-shirt, and 2.00 represents the constant rate of change $2.00 per logo.

C. The initial value of $15.25 represents the fixed cost of $15.25 for each T-shirt, and 2.00 represents the constant rate of change of $2.00 per logo.

D. The initial value of 15 represents the fixed cost of $15 for each T-shirt, and 2.25 represents the constant rate of change of $2.25 per logo and letter.

46. Which of the following scenarios is modelled by the equation $C = 20 + 13n$?

A. The total cost, C, of boarding a dog at a kennel, where an initial rate of \$13 is charged plus \$20 per day, n, that the dog is at the kennel

B. The total cost, C, of boarding a dog at a kennel, where an initial rate of \$20 is charged plus \$13 per day, n, that the dog is at the kennel

C. The total wage, C, of paying a student to work in a warehouse, where \$13 is the cost for coveralls and 20 is the number of days, n, worked

D. The total wage, C, of paying a student to work in a warehouse, where 20 represents the number of hours, n, worked and 13 is the hourly wage

Open Response

Warehouse Work

Jasmine works at a warehouse where she packs large crates with fresh produce. She gets paid a fixed amount per day as well as an amount based on the number of crates she packs per day. Her daily wage, W, in dollars related to the number of crates, n, that she packs is shown in the graph.

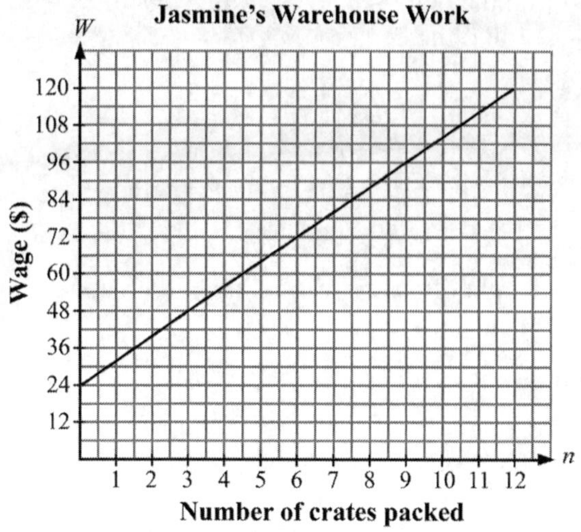

2.

a) What is the fixed amount Jasmine is paid daily?

b) Choose two points from the graph, and use them to determine the constant rate of pay per crate packed. Show your work.

c) Write an equation that describes the linear relationship between Jasmine's daily wage and the number of crates that she packs per day. Show your work.

LR4.01 determine values of a linear relation by using a table of values, by using the equation of the relation, and by interpolating or extrapolating from the graph of the relation

DETERMINING VALUES OF LINEAR RELATIONS

For a linear relation, values in the table can be found using the following three methods:

Find the constant rate of change exhibited in a table of values, and then follow this pattern to find other values.

Substitute the x- or y-value into the equation representing the linear relation, and then use algebra to solve for the other value.

Interpolate and extrapolate other values from the graph representing the linear relation.

USING CONSTANT RATE OF CHANGE

Example

Analyze the height of a hot air balloon, h, in metres to the time of its descent, t, in minutes.

This relation can be portrayed by the following table of values:

Time (min)	Height (m)
0	320
1	280
2	240
3	200
4	160

To find other values of the linear relation, you must understand the pattern or constant rate of change. The initial height is 320 m, and the height decreases by 40 m for every 1 minute (first differences are 40); therefore, the rate of change is constant at −40 m/min.

To find the height of the balloon at 5 min, subtract 40 m from the height at 4 min, or continue with the constant rate of change at −40 m/min after 4 min.

The height of the hot air balloon at 5 min is $160-40=120$ m.

You could also predict how long it would take for the balloon to touch the ground (h = 0 m). To determine this, continue the pattern in the table using the constant rate of change until you reach a height, h, of 0 m. This process is shown in the table below.

Time (min)	Height (m)
5	120
6	120 – 40 = 80
7	80 – 40 = 40
8	40 – 40 = 0

It would take 8 min for the hot air balloon to touch the ground (h = 0).

SUBSTITUTING THE X- OR Y-VALUE

This relation can be portrayed by the equation $h = 320 - 40t$, where 320 is the initial value representing the height of the balloon of 320 m at t = 0, and −40 represents the constant rate of change of −40 m/min.

To find the missing values, substitute the given value into the appropriate variable and determine the value of the missing variable.

To find the height, h, at 5.5 min, substitute t = 5.5 into the equation.

$$h=320-40t$$
$$h=320-40(5.5)$$
$$h=320-220$$
$$h=100$$

The height of the hot-air balloon at 5.5 min is 100 m.

Similarly, to find the time, t, when the height is 0 m, substitute $h = 0$ into the equation.

$$h = 320 - 40t$$
$$0 = 320 - 40t$$

Subtract 320 from both sides of the equation.

$$0 - 320 = 320 - 320 - 40t$$
$$-320 = -40t$$

Divide both sides of the equation by − 40.

$$\frac{-320}{-40} = \frac{-40t}{-40}$$
$$8 = t$$
$$t = 8$$

It takes 8 min for the hot air balloon to touch the ground.

This relation can be portrayed graphically by plotting the given points and drawing a line through them. Other points can then be found by interpolation and extrapolation.

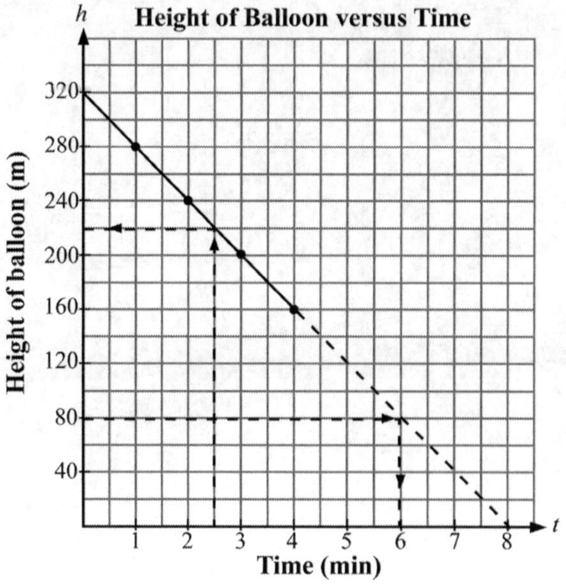

Interpolation and Extrapolation

Interpolation is used to find values within the given data points or line. For example, you can interpolate the height, h, at 2.5 min by locating 2.5 along the x-axis and moving up to the line. Then move directly across to the y-axis and read the resulting value of $h = 220$ m.

Extrapolation is used to find values outside of the given data points or line. To do this, extend the line (as shown by the dotted line on the graph), and read the information as indicated previously. For example, you can extrapolate the time, t, at which the height is 80 m by locating 80 along the y-axis and moving directly across to the line. Then move down to the x-axis and read the resulting value of $t = 6$ min.

Practice Questions

Use the following information to answer the next two questions.

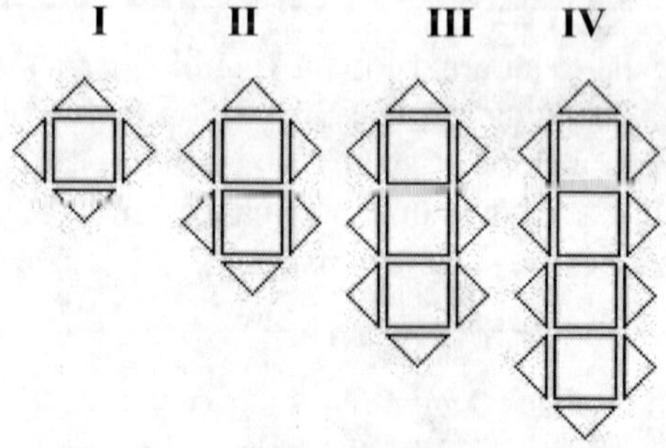

Picture	Number of Squares	Number of Triangles
I	1	4
II	2	6
III		
IV		
V	?	?

47. How many squares and triangles will be in Picture V?

A. 4 squares and 10 triangles

B. 6 squares and 14 triangles

C. 5 squares and 12 triangles

D. 3 squares and 8 triangles

CHALLENGER QUESTION

48. How many triangles will be in a picture with 15 squares?

A. 24

B. 27

C. 30

D. 32

Use the following information to answer the next question.

Tanya has a summer job picking blueberries at a farm. The equation $W = 20 + 2.50n$ represents the relationship between Tanya's daily wage, W, in dollars and the number of baskets of blueberries, n, she picks in a day.

49. In one day, Tanya picks 22 baskets of blueberries. How much does she earn on that day?

A. $42.00

B. $49.50

C. $55.00

D. $75.00

Use the following information to answer the next question.

The cost of buying jerseys for a basketball team is shown in the graph.

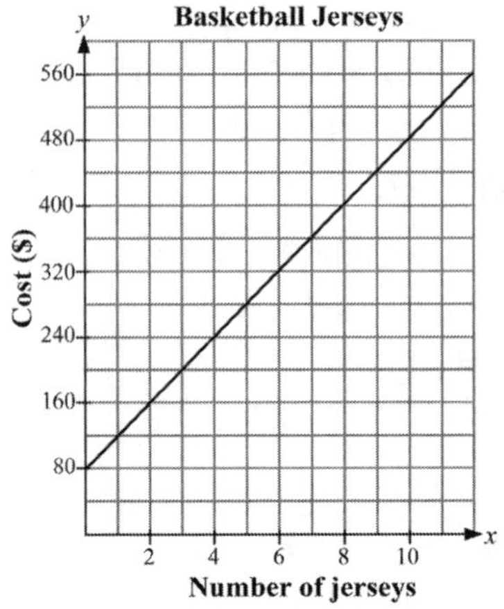

50. What is the cost of buying 11 jerseys?

A. $880

B. $520

C. $440

D. $400

Open Response

Keep Fit

A fitness club charges a one-time membership fee of $200 and a weekly fee of $18.50.

3.

a) Complete the table below.

Number of Weeks at the Fitness Club	Total Cost ($)
2	237
4	
6	
8	
10	

b) Determine the equation that represents the linear relationship between the total cost, C, and the number of weeks, n, that an individual is enrolled at the fitness club. Show your work.

c) How many weeks could Ron be enrolled at the fitness club for a total cost of $607? Justify your answer.

LR4.02 describe a situation that would explain the events illustrated by a given graph of a relationship between two variables

Explaining a Relationship between Two Variables in a Graph

A graph provides a picture of a relationship between two variables. To describe a situation that reflects each part of a graph, you must be aware of the rate of change in each section.

Example

The graph below portrays how a car's volume of fuel in litres varies with the time elapsed in hours during a trip.

How Fuel Consumption Varies with Time

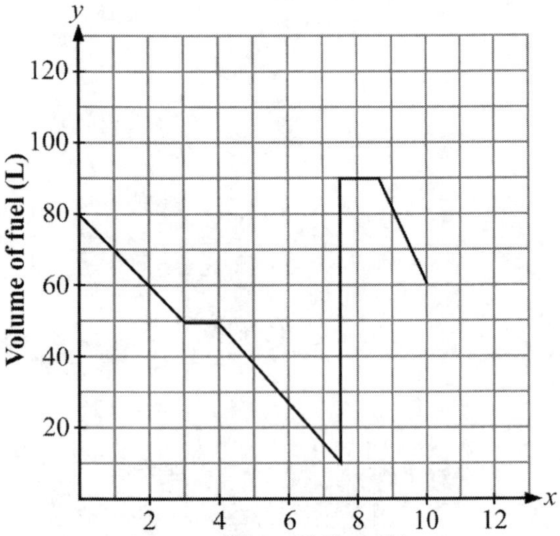

To describe the graph, look at each of these sections:

- **From 0 to 3 hours:** The car went at a constant speed, burning about 10 L for every hour driven. The level of fuel in the tank dropped from 80 to 50 L.
- **Form 3 to 4 hours:** The volume of the fuel stayed fixed at 50 L, which means the car was not moving (the driver took a one-hour break).
- **From 4 to 7.5 hours:** The driver continued travelling at constant speed, burning about 10 L for every hour driven. The level of fuel in the tank dropped from 50 to 10 L.
- **At 7.5 hours:** The fuel level rose suddenly from 10 L to 90 L (the car was filled up with gas).
- **From 7.5 hours to 8.5 hours:** Since the volume of fuel stayed at 90 L, the car stopped again.
- **From 8.5 to 10 hours:** The car continued at a constant speed, burning about 30 L of fuel, and finally stopped at the 10th hour.

Practice Questions

Use the following information to answer the next question.

Each day after work, Steve goes for a walk from his home. The diagram represents Steve's walk on a particular day.

Steve's Walk from Home

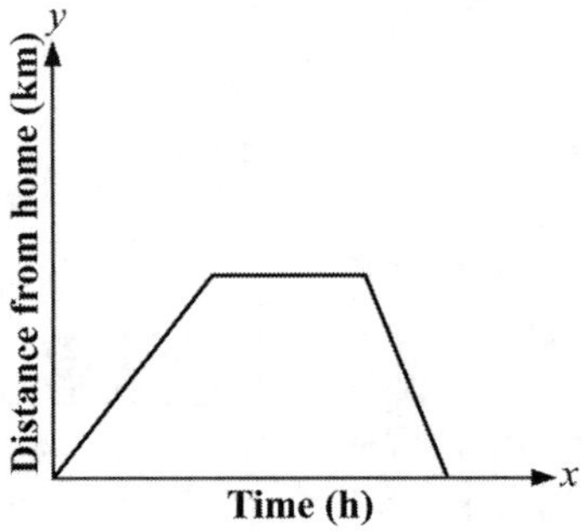

51. Which of the following statements best describes Steve's walk from home on that day?

A. Steve walks at a constant rate, stops for a period of time, and then walks home at a constant rate.

B. Steve walks at an increasing rate, then walks at a constant rate, and finally walks at a decreasing rate until he returns home.

C. Steve walks at a fast constant rate, then walks at a slower rate, turns around, and finally walks back home at a fast constant rate.

D. Steve starts out slowly, increases his speed, walks at a constant rate, and finally decreases his speed until he comes to a stop at home.

52. A cellphone company charges $20 for the first 200 minutes of cellphone usage each month. For each minute over 200 minutes, the charge is $0.50/min. Which of the following graphs illustrates the relationship between the total charges for a month and the number of minutes of cellphone usage?

A.

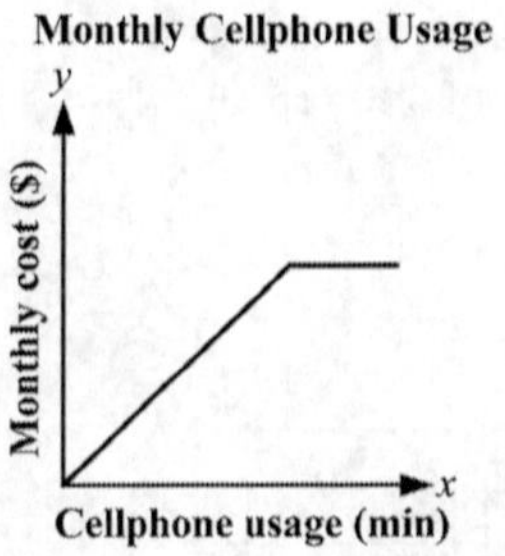

B.

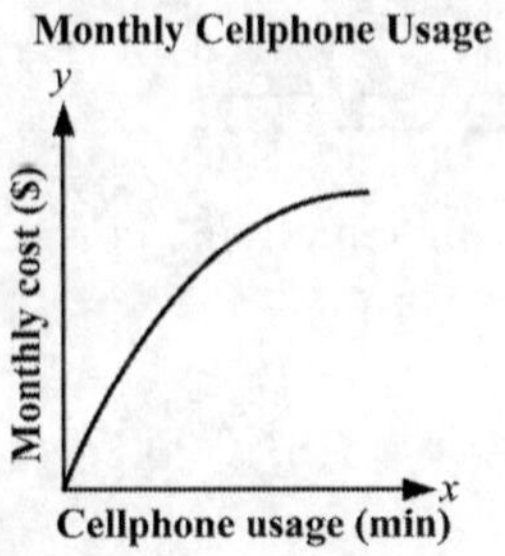

C.

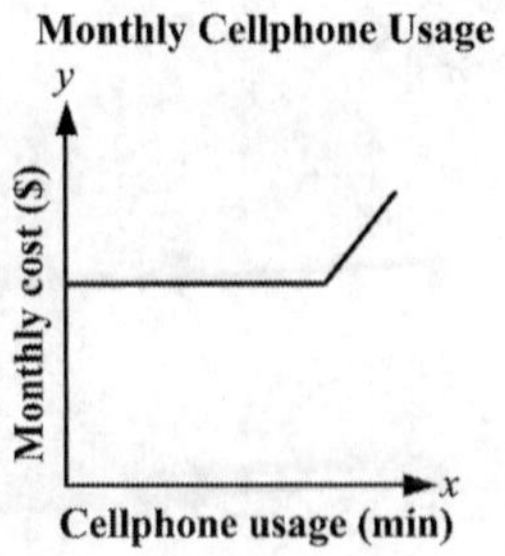

D.

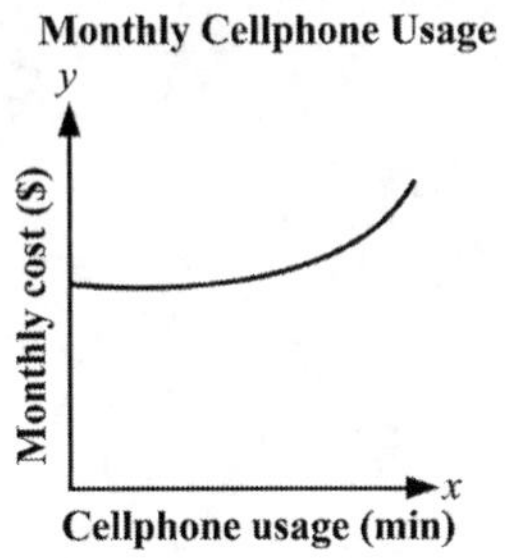

LR4.03 determine other representations of a linear relation arising from a realistic situation, given one representation

Representing a Real-Life Linear Relation

In order to determine other representations of a linear relation arising from a real-life situation, you must be aware of the constant rate of change and use it to confirm the initial value (vertical intercept).

Example

The data below compares the distance, *d*, in kilometres, a person is from a lightning flash to the time, *t*, in seconds, it takes the person to see the lighting and hear the thunder.

t **(s)**	***d*** **(km)**
3	1
6	2
9	3
12	4
15	5

You could represent this linear relation graphically:

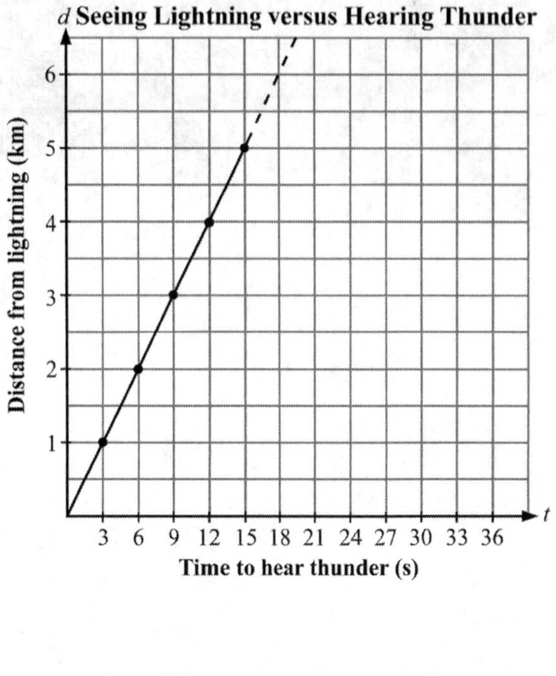

The constant rate of change is $\frac{1}{3}$, since for every 3 s (run), the distance increases 1 km (rise). If you extend the line in a downward direction, it passes through the origin (0, 0). This means the initial value at $t = 0$ s is $d = 0$ km.

This linear relation can also be represented algebraically as $d = \frac{1}{3}t$.

You can verify the algebraic model by substituting a point from the graph into the equation to validate the initial value (b) in the equation $y = mx + b$.

$d = \frac{1}{3}t$	
$3 = \frac{1}{3}(9) + b$	Substitute (9, 3) into the equation.
$3 = \frac{9}{3} + b$	
$3 = 3 + b$	
$3 - 3 = 3 - 3 + b$	Subtract 3 from both sides.
$0 = b$	

Therefore, $d = \frac{1}{3}t$ is the correct algebraic representation.

PRACTICE QUESTIONS

Use the following information to answer the next question.

After a snowstorm, Jesse must shovel the snow from his 80-m driveway. Jesse shovels at a constant rate of 10 m/h. The data in the following table shows the amount of driveway left to shovel, d, in metres in relation to the time spent shovelling, t, in hours.

t	d
2	60
4	40
5	30
7	10

53. Which of the following equations represents the data given in this table?

A. $d = 30t$

B. $d = -10t$

C. $d = 10t + 80$

D. $d = -10t + 80$

Use the following information to answer the next question.

Chandra constructed a partial graph to show the relationship between the time she spent working at a car wash, t, in hours and the money she earned, E, in dollars.

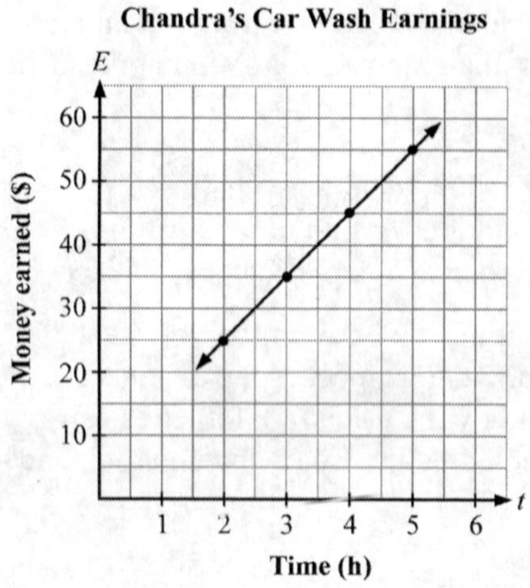

54. The graph of the line shown is defined by the equation

A. $E = 10t$

B. $E = \frac{25}{2}t$

C. $E = 5t + 10$

D. $E = 10t + 5$

LR4.04 solve problems that can be modelled with first-degree equations, and compare the algebraic method to other solution methods

MODELLING PROBLEMS USING FIRST-DEGREE EQUATIONS

Real-life word problems can be solved using linear equations.

Example

The temperature outside at noon was 12°C. During the next hour, the temperature dropped 1.5°C and then continued to drop at this constant rate. At what time would the temperature reach 0°C? What would the temperature be at midnight?

Build the linear equation in the form $y = mx + b$ by finding the initial value b and then the constant rate of change m.

The constant rate of change is $m = -1.5$, since the temperature drops 1.5°C every hour.

The initial value is $b = 15$°C, which occurs at the time of $t = 0$ (or noon).

Therefore, the equation representing this problem is $T = -1.5t + 12$, where T is the outside temperature in degrees Celsius and t is the number of hours after noon.

To find the time at which the temperature reaches 0°C, substitute $T = 0$, and solve for the time t.

$T = -1.5t + 12$	Substitute 0 for T.
$0 = -1.5t + 12$	
$0 - 12 = -1.5t + 12 - 12$	Subtract 12 from both sides of the equation.
$-12 = -1.5t$	
$\frac{-12}{-1.5} = \frac{-1.5t}{-1.5}$	Divide both sides of the equation by −1.5.
$8 = t$	Realign the equation.
$t = 8$	

The value 8 indicates the number of hours after noon that the temperature reached 0°C, so adding 8 to 12 P.M. gives you 8 P.M.

To find the temperature at midnight, substitute 12 for t (since midnight is 12 hours after noon) into the equation, and solve for T:

$$T = -1.5t + 12$$
$$T = -1.5(12) + 12$$
$$T = -18 + 12$$
$$T = -6$$

The temperature outside at midnight is –6°C. This problem could also have been solved by graphing the relation and interpolating values from the graph or creating a table of values and using its pattern to find other values.
These methods were discussed in lesson 4.01.

Practice Questions

CHALLENGER QUESTION

A family of six, two adults and four children drove go-carts at an amusement park.
The following charges were in effect:

Flat charge: \$20 per adult and \$10 per child

Rate charge: \$0.05 per 15 seconds per driver

55. If each member of the family spent 45 min driving go-carts, what was the total cost?

A. \$174

B. \$134

C. \$80

D. \$54

CHALLENGER QUESTION

56. The total cost, C, to print n graduation programs is a linear relation. The fixed cost is \$35, and there is a charge of \$0.10 for every 5 programs. If the total cost was \$48, how many programs were printed?

A. 36

B. 130

C. 480

D. 650

LR4.05 describe the effects on a linear graph and make the corresponding changes to the linear equation when the conditions of the situation they represent are varied

The Effects of Changing Values

When the initial fixed value and the constant rate of change are altered for a given real-life context, the graph and equation are also altered.

Example

A trucking company charges a flat rate of \$80 plus \$1/km to move furniture from the warehouse to a particular residence.

The relationship between the total cost, C, in dollars with respect to the distance, d, travelled by the truck in kilometres can be represented by the following equation and graph:

$$C = 1.00d + 80$$

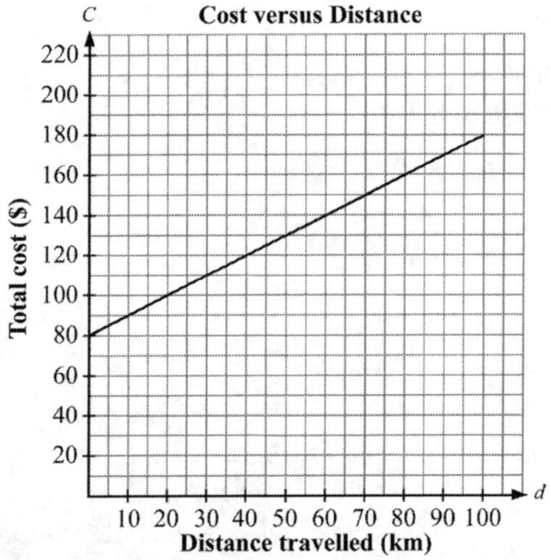

Another trucking company charges a flat rate of \$20 plus \$2/km to move furniture from the warehouse to a particular residence. How will the equation and graph change?

Since the flat rate is less than before, the initial value in the equation is also lower (80 compared to 20), and the graph will show a lower vertical intercept (80 compared to 20).

The rate increases from \$1 per kilometre to \$2 per kilometre. This change will increase the numerical coefficient of the variable d to $2.00d$ ($1.00d$ increases to $2.00d$).

On the graph, the line becomes steeper from left to right, since the constant rate of change $\left(\frac{\text{rise}}{\text{run}}\right)$ has changed from $\frac{1.00}{1}$ to $\frac{2.00}{1}$.

These changes are portrayed in the new equation and graph shown below:

$C = 2.00d + 20$

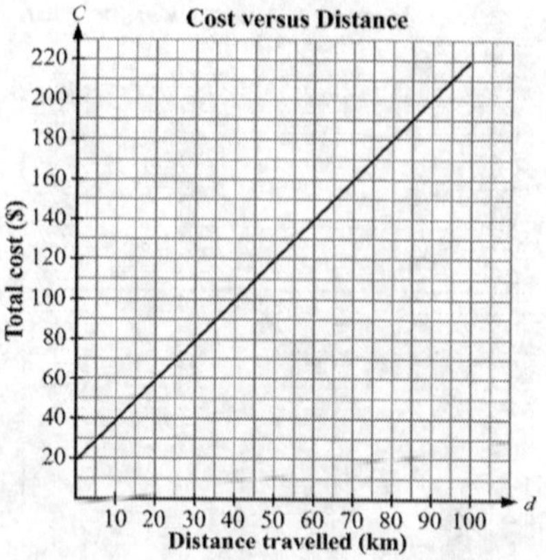

PRACTICE QUESTIONS

Use the following information to answer the next question.

> Two different car repair companies advertise the following charges for car repairs:
> **A^{+} Car Repair:** Service charge of $40 plus $25 per hour
> **AR Car Repair:** Service charge of $80 plus $20 per hour
>
> The graph and the equation representing the total cost, C, in dollars with respect to the time, t, in hours required to fix a car at A^{+} Car Repair are shown.
>
> 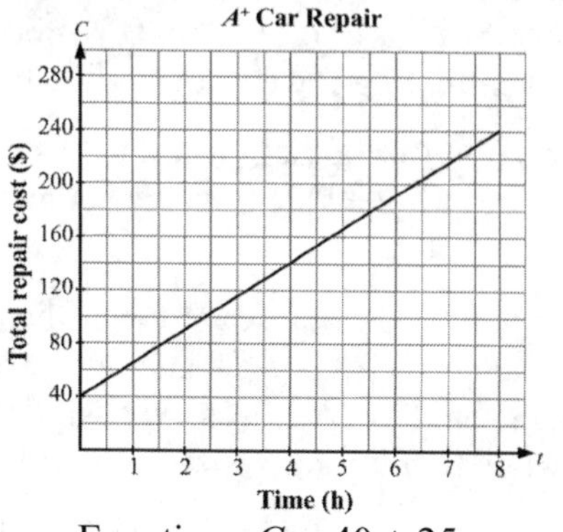
>
>
> Equation: $C = 40 + 25t$

57. Which of the following statements about the cost to fix a car at AR Car Repair is **true**?

A. The total cost is represented by the equation $C = 20 + 8t$, and the corresponding graph shows a line that is steeper from left to right than the graph of the line representing the total cost to fix a car at A+ Car Repair.

B. The total cost is represented by the equation $C = 80 + 20t$, and the corresponding graph shows a line that is steeper from left to right than the graph of the line representing the total cost to fix a car at A^{+} Car Repair.

C. The total cost is represented by the equation $C = 20 + 80t$, and the corresponding graph shows a line that is less steep from left to right than the graph of the line representing the total cost to fix a car at A^{+} Car Repair.

D. The total cost is represented by the equation $C = 80 + 20t$, and the corresponding graph shows a line that is less steep from left to right than the graph of the line representing the total cost to fix a car at A^{+} Car Repair.

Use the following information to answer the next question.

Each of the following four scenarios are modelled by the equation $C = an + b$, where C is the total cost of producing n items.

Scenario 1: The total cost, C, of producing n stuffed toys is \$200 plus an additional \$4 per toy.

Scenario 2: The total cost, C, of producing n rings is \$300 plus an additional \$4 per ring.

Scenario 3: The total cost, C, of producing n baseball caps is \$4 plus an additional \$6 per cap.

Scenario 4: The total cost, C, of producing n cups is \$200 plus an additional \$8 per cup.

58. When modelled by the equation $C = an + b$, which of the scenarios described have the same value of a?

A. Scenarios 1 and 2

B. Scenarios 1 and 3

C. Scenarios 1, 2, and 3

D. Scenarios 1, 2, 3, and 4

LR4.06 determine graphically the point of intersection of two linear relations, and interpret the intersection point in the context of an application

DETERMINING POINTS OF INTERSECTION

Two lines that are not parallel and distinct will eventually intersect at a point. When two lines representing two different conditions for the same real-life context intersect, at the **point of intersection**, the x-variable and the y-variables for *both* lines are equal. Points below or above the points of intersection also provide valuable information regarding the differences in the two conditions of the real-life context.

Example

A video rental company has two monthly plans:
Plan A: A flat fee of \$40/month is charged for unlimited rentals.
Plan B: A fixed fee of \$8 is charged, plus \$4 for every video rented.
You can analyze these two plans by drawing their representative lines.

Video Rental of Plan A versus Plan B

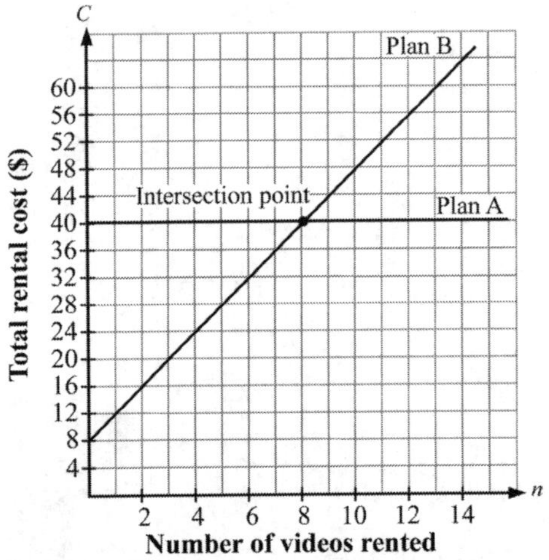

The intersection point of the two lines is (8, 40). This point represents the condition where both plans have the same total cost. When eight videos are rented, the cost is \$40 under Plan A and \$40 under Plan B.

Examine points to the left of the intersection point and determine which plan is better for the customer.

Since the points for Plan B are below the points for Plan A (from $n = 0$ to $n = 8$), it indicates that Plan B is less expensive than Plan A.
For example, at $n = 4$, the total cost is \$24 for Plan B and \$40 for Plan A. Plan B is a better choice when renting fewer than eight videos.

Examine points to the right of the intersection point and determine which plan is better for the customer.

Since the points for Plan A are lower than the points for Plan B (from $n = 8$ and up),
it indicates that Plan A is less expensive than Plan B when renting more than eight videos.

For example, at $n = 12$, the total cost is \$40 under Plan A and \$56 under Plan B.

PRACTICE QUESTIONS

Use the following information to answer the next question.

A ski rental shop has two different monthly plans for renting skis. Plan A charges a flat fee of $30 per month for unlimited rentals. Plan B charges $9 per month plus $3 per ski rental. A snapshot from a graphing calculator showing the lines representing each respective plan and the point of intersection of the two plans is given.

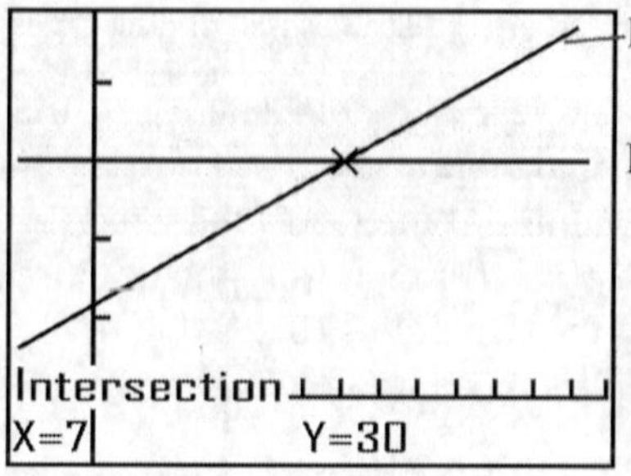

59. Which of the following statements is **true**?

A. Plan B is more cost efficient for monthly ski rentals.

B. Plan A is more cost efficient for monthly ski rentals.

C. Plan B is more cost efficient when renting skis less than seven times a month.

D. Plan B is more cost efficient when renting skis more than seven times a month.

CHALLENGER QUESTION

Breanna and Jacob decided to jog around a track. Jacob left the starting point first, running at a constant speed of 4 m/s. Breanna waited 3 s and then left from the same starting point, running at a constant speed of 5 m/s. The graph portrays their progress around the track.

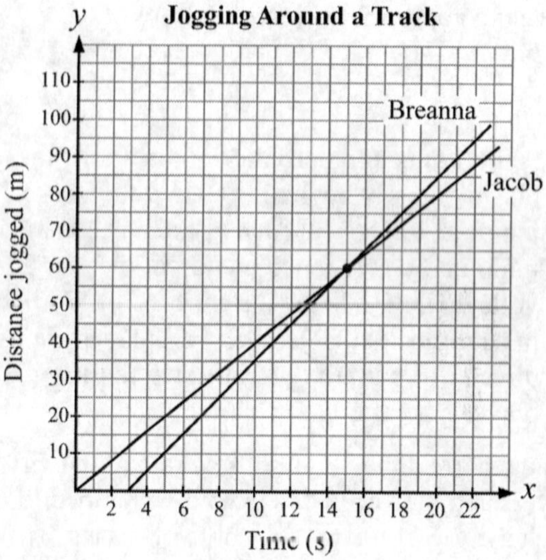

60. The intersection point of the lines that represent the two given linear relations is *i*, and at 10 s, *ii* is ahead by *iii*.
The row that completes this statement is

	i	*ii*	*iii*
A.	(15, 60)	Jacob	5 m
B.	(15, 60)	Breanna	10 m
C.	(60, 15)	Jacob	5 m
D.	(60, 15)	Breanna	10 m

LR4.07 select a topic involving a two-variable relationship, pose a question on the topic, collect data to answer the question, and present its solution using appropriate representations of the data

TWO-VARIABLE RELATIONSHIPS

Real-life problems involving two variable relationships can be solved by collecting data and using appropriate representations of the data.

Example

Alice wants to record the heights (h) of the players on a volleyball team and the vertical jumping heights (v) each of them needs to jump in order to touch the top of the volleyball net. Is the distance, v, in centimetres that a volleyball player jumps directly or partially proportional to the player's height, h, in centimetres?

Alice recorded the height of several volleyball players and the vertical heights they jumped to touch the top of the net in a table of values, as shown.

Vertical jumping height (cm)	**Height of player (cm)**
66	150
60	155
26	185
14	195
31	180
55	160
43	170
37	175
20	190
49	165

The corresponding graph of this data can be portrayed as shown:

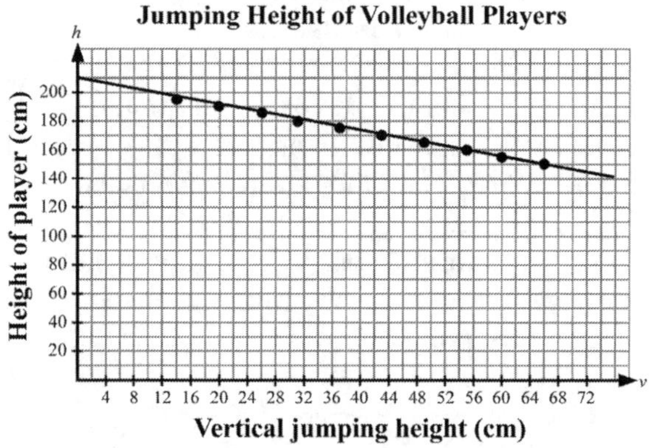

You could also represent this data by writing its representative algebraic equation. Extend the line of best fit until it intersects the y-axis. This point is (0, 210); therefore, the initial value is 210 using the two points (0, 210) and (66, 150). The constant rate of change

$$= \frac{\text{rise}}{\text{run}} = \frac{150-210}{66-0} = \frac{-60}{66} = -0.91$$

The equation representing the linear graph is $h = -0.91v + 210$.

From the equation, you can infer that a 210 cm tall player would not have to jump to touch the top of the net ($h = 210$ when $v = 0$).

When the net is placed higher, the initial value rises, but the rate of change stays the same. Since the line of best fit is a straight line that does not go through the origin, it is a partial variation.

Practice Questions

Use the following information to answer the next question.

Marcel wanted to investigate the relationship between different speeds and times of a bobsled travelling down a particular bobsled run. He stated the following hypothesis:

"There is a linear relationship between the average speed, v, and the time, t, that a bobsled takes to travel down a bobsled run."

Marcel collected the following data using a radar gun and an electronic timer for runs made by various bobsleds.

Time (s)	Speed (m/s)
30	50
40	37
60	25
80	18
100	15
120	13
140	11

To analyze the relationship between average speed and time, Marcel drew the following graph of the given data:

Speed of Bobsled versus Time

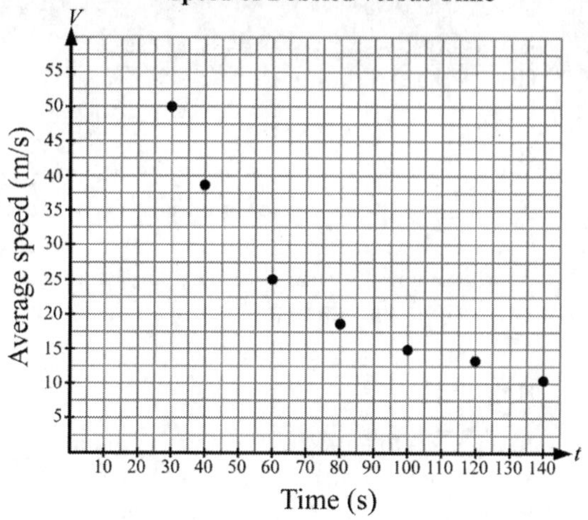

61. Which of the following statements about Marcel's hypothesis is true?

A. Marcel's hypothesis is correct, and $v = 2t - 5$.

B. Marcel's hypothesis is correct, and $v = 5 - 2t$

C. Marcel's hypothesis is incorrect because the points rise and then fall.

D. Marcel's hypothesis is incorrect because the points do not represent a constant rate of change.

ANSWERS AND SOLUTIONS—PRACTICE QUESTIONS

1. B	12. C	OR1. **	35. A	OR2. **	57. D
NR1. 4	13. C	24. D	36. A	47. C	58. A
2. D	14. C	25. A	37. D	48. D	59. C
3. C	15. B	26. C	38. B	49. D	60. A
4. A	16. C	27. C	39. B	50. B	61. D
5. B	17. A	28. B	40. D	OR3. **	
6. B	18. B	29. D	41. C	51. A	
7. D	19. B	30. A	42. D	52. C	
8. D	20. D	31. C	43. A	53. D	
9. A	21. A	32. D	44. A	54. D	
10. A	22. D	33. C	45. A	55. B	
11. C	23. C	34. A	46. B	56. D	

**** SEE SOLUTIONS**

1. B

The lowest outside temperature can be found by locating the point that has the smallest *y*-coordinate. This point is (7, –6), so the lowest outside temperature is –6° (the *y*-coordinate), and the corresponding time of day is 7 a.m. (the *x*-coordinate).

NR1. 4

There are four points with a smaller *y*-coordinate (lower outside temperatures) than the *y*-coordinate of the point one hour earlier. They are:

(7, –6)→2°C lower than at 6 a.m. (6, –4)

(10, 1)→1°C lower than at 9 a.m. (9, 2)

(1, 5)→1°C lower than at 12:00 p.m. (12, 6)

(4, 8)→1°C lower than at 15:00 (3, 9)

2. D

The point (34, 375) has an *x*-coordinate (shaft speed) of 34 and a *y*-coordinate (power) of 375; however, the point (34, 375) actually represents a shaft speed of 34 000 rpm (34 × 1 000) and a power output of 375 000 W (375 × 1 000).

3. C

The *x*-coordinate represents the time of day. For the given point, (2, –6), the time is 2:00 p.m. The *x*-coordinate for the new point is 2:00 p.m. + 2h = 2 + 2 = 4:00 p.m.
The *y*-coordinate represents the outside temperature. For the given point, (2, –6), the outside temperature is –6°C. The *y*-coordinate for the new point is –6°C + rise of 3°C = –6 + 3 = –3°C. The new point is (4, –3).

4. A

By definition, a hypothesis is a best guess about the relationship between two variables.

5. B

A student with very poor attendance will most likely receive a low final mark. This hypothesis is more likely true than any of the other three hypotheses.

6. B

In addition to a plastic cup and ice water, Josette needs a thermometer to measure temperature change and a clock to record the time.

7. D

From the given data, the points that need to be indicated on the scatter plot are (0, 0.5), (4, 2), (8, 4), (12, 6.5), (16, 8.5), (20, 11), (24, 13.5). The scatter plot in alternative **D** correctly shows these points.

8. D

Since a thermal mug is insulated, the temperature of the ice water would rise more slowly compared to ice water in a plastic cup. After 24 min, the temperature of the ice water in the thermal mug would be lower than the ice water in the plastic cup. The temperature of the ice water still rises, but in smaller intervals, as shown in the table in alternative **D**.

9. A

As age increases in list 1, the height of the students increases in list 2. The only exception is the 16-year-old student whose height is 145 cm. When (16, 145) is excluded, the approximate change in height per year is about 8 cm.
163 – 155 = 8 cm,
171 – 163 = 8 cm,
180 – 171 = 9 cm,
187 – 180 = 7 cm,
195 – 187 = 8 cm
As age increases, height increases at a rate of about 8 cm per year.

10. A

Since 145 is the smallest number in L_2, the point (16, 145) most likely represents a 16-year-old student who is shorter than most other students his or her age. There is no information provided about a 12-year-old student, so it is not possible to compare the height of the 13-year-old student.

11. C

The given data shows that the percentage of rural and non-farm-based Canadians increased slightly from 1951 to 1986 (an increase of 4%).

12. C

The amount of daily sunlight on December 21, 2007, is the lowest all year. After December 21, the amount of daily sunlight increases up to the first day of summer on June 21, 2007, after which the amount of daily sunlight decreases again until the first day of winter on December 21, 2008. Therefore, the correct inference is made by Ramsay.

13. C

Carmen's Canoe Company charges a flat fee of \$20 plus \$1.20 for every 30 minutes of use.
After 30 minutes of usage, it costs
\$20 + 1.20 = \$21.20
After 60 minutes of usage, it costs
\$20 + 2(\$1.20) = \$22.40
In other words, the cost rises \$1.20 ÷ 3 = \$0.40 for every 10 minutes of usage.

Thus, L_1 and L_2 should represent the points (0, 20.00), (10, 20.40), (20, 20.80), (30, 21.20), (40, 21.60), (50, 22.00), (60, 22.40).

14. C

The point (0, 52) is located on the *y*-axis; therefore, the number of tickets that Stephan started with was 52.

The next point to the right is (5, 48). This means he had 48 tickets left to sell after 5 minutes. This pattern continues in a linear manner. Stephan started with 52 tickets and sold 4 tickets every 5 minutes.

15. B

As the snail moves, its distance from the sidewalk decreases by a constant rate of 4 cm per minute or –4 cm/min. Every two minutes, the snail's distance from the sidewalk decreases at a constant rate of $\frac{4\times 2}{1\times 2}=\frac{8\text{ cm}}{2\text{ min}}$, or –8 cm/2 min. The table in alternative **B** represents this change in distance over time:

Time (min)	Distance (cm)
0	40
2	40 – 8 = 32
4	32 – 8 = 24
6	24 – 8 = 16
8	16 – 8 = 8

16. C

Since a typist earns \$10 for the first 400 lines, the initial value in the table for 0 extra lines is 10. The typist earns \$0.10 per additional line over 400, which represents a constant rate of change of \$0.10 per additional line.
The constant rate of change for 10 additional lines over 400 is $\$0.10 \times 10 = \$1.00$.
This situation represents a partial variation.
The table that correctly represents the initial value and constant rate of change is as follows:

Number of extra lines	Earnings (\$)
0	10
10	$10 + 1 = 11$
20	$11 + 1 = 12$
30	$12 + 1 = 13$
40	$13 + 1 = 14$

The correct table of values is displayed in alternative **C**.

17. A

The points follow a non-linear rather than a linear pattern; thus, the line on the graph is not a straight line. The data in the given table is best represented by a curve of best fit.
The graph in alternative **A** is the only graph showing a curve of best fit.

18. B

If a line of best fit is drawn such that there is an equal number of points above and below the line, then a point on the line of best fit with a y-coordinate of 200 000 has a corresponding x-coordinate of about 110. Thus, a 110 m^2 house costs about \$200 000 to build.

19. B

For every 10 m^2 of increment increase from the x-coordinate of one point to the next point on the line of best fit, the corresponding y-coordinates increase by slightly more than one scale value. Since each scale value on the y-axis represents an increase of \$50 000, a little more than one scale value represents an increase of about \$60 000. The total cost of a house increases by about \$60 000 for every increase of 10 m^2 in size.

20. D

This is a non-linear relationship, since for every constant increase in the length of each side, l, the value, V, does not increase by a constant amount,
as illustrated below.

$27 - 8 = 19$
$64 - 27 = 37$
$125 - 64 = 61$
$216 - 125 = 91$
$343 - 216 = 127$

21. A

Since gas prices decreased at a constant rate from the spring to the fall, the relationship between gas prices and time of year is linear. The graph portraying this relationship is a line segment that falls from the left to the right, such as the graph illustrated in alternative **A**.

22. D

Look at the first differences of the y-values in the table to see the constant rate of change of the corresponding graph.

n	C
200	—
400	$19 - 20 = -1.0$
600	$17.5 - 19 = -1.5$
800	$15.5 - 17.5 = -2.0$
1 000	$13 - 15.5 = -2.5$
1 200	$10 - 13 = -3.0$

Since the first differences are not constant, this relation is non-linear. Also since the values of the rate of change are negative, the non-linear curve of the graph moves downward from the left to the right of the graph.

23. C

The cost of fencing the field is \$0.25 for every metre of fencing. The constant rate of change is \$0.25/m.For every 25 m of fencing, it costs

$\frac{0.25 \times 25}{1 \times 25} = \$6.25$ per 25 m of fencing.

The initial value is \$0 for 0 m of fencing.
This situation represents a direct variation.
The table of values that correctly represents the initial value and constant rate of change is as shown:

Fencing (m)	Cost ($)
0	0
25	0 + 6.25 = 6.25
50	6.25 + 6.25 = 12.50
75	12.50 + 6.25 = 18.75
100	18.75 + 6.25 = 25.00

The correct table of values is displayed in alternative **C**.

OR 1.

a)

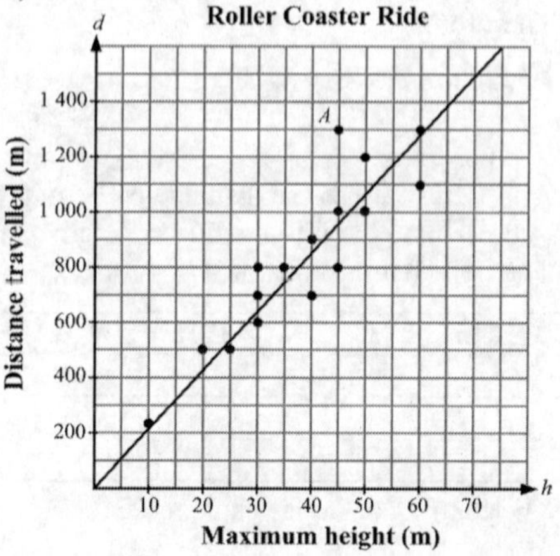

b)

Locate 55 on the *x*-axis, and then move vertically up from 55 until you intersect the line of best fit. Move horizontally from this point of intersection until you intersect the *y*-axis. Your answer is this point of intersection on the *y*-axis. In this case, the answer should be between 1 100 m and 1 200 m.

c)
Answers may vary.
Cheyenne's interpretation is incorrect. Point A represents a high maximum height (45 m); however, the corresponding distance travelled by the roller coaster is 1 300 m, which is a long rather than a short distance.

24. D

For every increase of 1°C, the temperature in Kelvin also increases 1 K. To go from 291.15 K to 304.15 K, there are 13 increases of 1 K (304.15 – 291.15 = 13). Since there is an increase of 13 K, there is also an increase of 13°C. For 304.15 K, the new temperature in Celsius is 18 + 13 = 31°C.

25. A

From point $A(-2, -6)$ to point $D(2,0)$, the run is $2-(-2)=4$ units horizontally to the right, and the rise is $0-(-6)=6$ units vertically upward.

Therefore, the rate of change $=\frac{\text{rise}}{\text{run}}=\frac{6}{4}=\frac{3}{2}$.

From point D to C, the run is $6-2=4$ units horizontally to the right, and the rise is $6-0=6$ units vertically upward. Therefore, the rate of change $=\frac{\text{rise}}{\text{run}}=\frac{6}{4}=\frac{3}{2}$. The rate of change of the given line is $\frac{3}{2}$.

26. C

The run of the line shown in the graph in alternative **C** is 4 units horizontally to the right ($0-4=-4$ units). The rise is 12 units vertically downward ($12-0=12$ units). The rate of change $=\frac{\text{rise}}{\text{run}}=-\frac{12}{4}=-3$. **Note:** the rates of change are $3, -\frac{1}{3}$, and $\frac{2}{3}$, respectively, for the lines shown in the graphs in alternatives **A, B,** and **D**.

27. C

The constant rate of change on a graph is $\frac{\text{rise}}{\text{run}}$, where the rise indicates the change of *y*-coordinates and the run indicates the change of *x*-coordinates. From point $P(3, -2)$ to $Q(5, -8)$,
$\frac{\text{rise}}{\text{run}}=\frac{-2\xrightarrow{-6}-8}{3\xrightarrow{+2}5}=\frac{-6}{2}=-3$. The constant rate of change between points $P(3, -2)$ and $Q(5, -8)$ on a linear graph is $\frac{\text{rise}}{\text{run}}=\frac{-6}{2}=-3$.

28. B

To find the constant rate of change, take any two points on the given line, say (1, 2 250) and (2, 4 500).

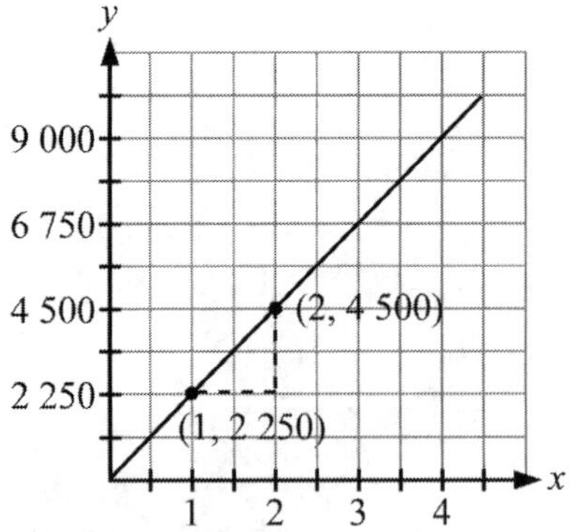

Constant rate of change

$$= \frac{\text{rise}}{\text{run}} = \frac{\text{vertical change}}{\text{horizontal change}}$$

$$= \frac{4\,500 - 2\,250}{2 - 1} = \frac{2\,250}{1} = 2\,250$$

The constant rate of change of the line is 2 250.

29. D

In order for table 1 to represent a linear relation, the value of n must be halfway between –3 and –13. The number –8 is halfway between –3 and –13; thus, $n = -8$. The first differences are then found by subtracting consecutive y-values as follows:

$$-8 - (-3) = -8 + 3 = -5$$
$$-13 - (-8) = -13 + 8 = -5$$

(In table 2, $n = 3$, and the first differences are all 4.)

Therefore, $n = -8$, and the first differences are all –5 in table 1.

30. A

The rate of change of the height of the snow bank with respect to time is –2 cm/h. This means that for a run of 1 unit horizontally to the right, there is a fall of 2 units vertically down (–2). The graph in alternative **A** shows that if you move 1 unit right (1 hour), the height drops by 2 units (–2 cm); therefore,

$$\frac{\text{rise}}{\text{run}} = -2.$$

31. C

This scenario represents a partial variation, since the taxi is rented on the basis of a fixed charge and an additional constant rate per kilometre driven. The constant rate of change charged by the taxi driver is found as follows:

$$\text{Constant rate of change} = \frac{\text{rise}}{\text{run}}.$$

The rise is the change in charge:
\$33 – \$23 = \$10.
The run is the change in distance:
15 – 10 = 5
Therefore,

$$\text{Constant rate of change} = \frac{10}{5} \text{ or}$$

\$10 per 5 km.
Apply this rate so the distance is 0 km in order to determine the initial value or fixed charge. The table below illustrates this process.

Charge (\$)	**Distance (km)**
23	10
23 – 10 = 13	10 – 5 = 5
13 – 10 = 3	5 – 0 = 5

The flat fee, or initial value, is \$3.

32. D

Two times the initial distance is $2(120) = 240$ m. Substitute this value for d, and solve for t in the given equation.

$$d = 5t + 120$$
$$240 = 5t + 120$$

Subtract 120 from both sides.

$$240 - 120 = 5t + 120 - 120$$
$$120 = 5t$$

$$\frac{120}{5} = \frac{5t}{5}$$

$$24 = t$$

It will take Aidan 24 s to be at a position that is two times the initial distance from his house.

33. **C**

$V = 4t$ (equation I) is a direct variation, as the initial value is 0. $V = 30 - 2t$ (equation II) portrays a partial variation, where 30 is the initial value and –2 represent the constant rate of change. $V = 6t + 13$ (equation III) portrays a partial variation, where 13 is the initial value and 6 represents the constant rate of change. $V = 14t - 3t$ (equation IV) can be simplified to $V = 11t$. This is a direct variation, as the initial value is 0. Equations II and III represent partial variations between the velocity of the particle and the time.

34. **A**

The graph of a direct variation must be a straight line passing through (0, 0).
The graph given in alternative **A** starts at (0, 0) and has a constant rate of change (a straight line is formed); therefore, the graph in alternative **A** shows a direct variation between the cost of renting a car and the distance travelled.

35. **A**

The initial value for a partial variation cannot be zero; however, a partial variation must have a constant rate of change. Instructor I has an initial value of \$45 and a constant rate of change of \$12 per class. This represents a partial variation between the total cost of instruction and the number of classes taken. Only the fees of Instructor I result in a partial variation.

36. **A**

The given graph shows that the initial value is 10; thus, at a time of 0 hours, Meg's workplace is 10 km from her house.

37. **D**

The initial value is \$35, and the constant rate of change is 39¢ per letter, which can be represented by $0.39n$. The cost of placing an advertisement in the paper can be expressed as $C = 35 + 0.39n$.

38. **B**

The rate of change is 2, since it is the numerical coefficient of n in the equation $C = 20 + 2n$. This means that for every 1 unit increase in n, C will increase by 2 units. When $n = 1$, $C = 20 + 2 = 22$. Similarly, when $n = 2$, $C = 20 + 2 + 2 = 24$, when $n = 3$, $C = 20 + 2 + 2 + 2 = 26$, when $n = 4$, $C = 20 + 2 + 2 + 2 + 2 = 28$. These values are represented in the table in alternative **B**.

39. **B**

From the graph, observe that for every 100 km to the right in the x-direction (run), there is a drop of 10 L in the y-direction (rise).
Therefore, the rate of change is

$$\frac{\text{rise}}{\text{run}} = \frac{-10}{100} = -\frac{1}{10}.$$

The initial value is 60 (when $d = 0$, $F = 60$).
The equation that defines the line segment is

$$F = 60 - \frac{1}{10}d.$$

40. **D**

The initial value in the table is 75 (75 eggs are laid when there are 0 new hens). The constant rate of change is 7 ($82 - 75 = 7$, $89 - 82 = 7$, $96 - 89 = 7$, and $103 - 96 = 7$), which is indicated by the pattern of increase in the total number of eggs laid for every new hen purchased. Therefore, the equation representing the total number of eggs laid in one week with respect to the number of new hens purchased is $E = 75 + 7H$.

41. **C**

The fixed cost of \$700 represents an initial value of 700. The two values \$0.50 and \$3.50 represent the constant rate of change for every yearbook printed. The constant rate of change is \$4.00. (\$0.50 + \$3.50). Therefore, the equation representing the total cost, C, and the number of yearbooks purchased is $C = 700 + 4.00n$.

42. D

The initial value is 12. If Dirk has 12 incorrect answers, he will score 0 points. For every increase of 4 units horizontally to the right, there is a corresponding decrease of 2 units vertically downward, which can be represented by –2. Thus, the constant rate of change $= \frac{\text{rise}}{\text{run}} = \frac{-2}{4} = -0.5$.

The equation of the line of best fit illustrating the relationship between the number of incorrect answers, A, and the number of points scored, P, is
$A = 12 - 0.5P$.

43. A

The initial value is 60, since 60 L is the amount of fuel Geoff has in his tank at the start of his trip. The rate of change is negative, since the fuel decreases.
The constant rate of change is –5 L per 50 km, which is $\frac{-5\text{ L}}{50\text{ km}}$ or –0.10 L/km.

The equation that could be used to determine the number of kilometres Geoff could drive on 60 L of fuel is $F = 60 - 0.1d$.
The graph that enables Geoff to determine the value of d when $F = 0$ has an initial value of 60 (the F-intercept) and portrays a negative rate of change of –5 L/50 km. A line that has a negative rate of change falls from left to right. The graph and equation in alternative **A** satisfy these requirements.

44. A

Examine the table of values to see the following pattern:

0 to 1 hours	–8°C to –2°C is an increase of 6°C, Since (–2) – (–8) = (–2) + 8 = 6.
1 to 2 hours	–2°C to 4°C is an increase of 6°C, Since (4) – (–2) = 4 + 2 = 6.
2 to 3 hours	4°C to 10°C is an increase of 6°C, Since (10) – (4) = 6.
3 to 4 hours	10°C to 16°C is an increase of 6°C, Since (16) – (10) = 6.

Therefore, the constant rate of change in the table of values is 6, which means that the temperature rose at a rate of 6°C per hour.

45. A

The initial value is 17, which represents the fixed cost of \$17 for the t-shirt and the logo (\$15 + \$2). The constant rate of change, 0.25, represents the cost of \$0.25 for each letter placed on the back of the t-shirt.

46. B

In the equation $C = 20 + 13n$, the value 20 is the initial value, or fixed rate, while the numerical coefficient 13 is the constant rate of change.
Therefore, the scenario of boarding a dog at a fixed fee of \$20 and at a constant rate of change of \$13 per day represents the equation $C = 20 + 13n$.

OR 2.

a)
Jasmine's fixed daily rate of pay can be determined by examining the given graph and observing which ordered pair is located on the vertical axis.

The ordered pair (0, 24) portrays Jasmine's daily wage (\$24) when 0 crates are packed. Jasmine's fixed daily rate of pay is \$24.

b)
Let's choose the points (6, 72) and (12, 120). The constant rate of change is given by $\frac{\text{rise}}{\text{run}}$. For these ordered pairs, the rise is 48 (120 – 72), and the run is 6 (12 – 6).
The constant rate of change is 8 (48 ÷ 6), which represents \$8 per crate.

c)
The fixed daily rate of pay is \$24, and the constant rate of change is \$8 per crate. If n represents the number of crates packed, then the equation that describes the relationship between Jasmine's daily wage, W, and the number of crates she packs is $W = 24 + 8n$.

47. C

Observe the following:

Picture I:1 square and 4 triangles
Picture II:2 squares and 6 triangles
Picture III:3 squares and 8 triangles
Picture IV:4 squares and 10 triangles
Picture V:5 squares and 12 triangles

Therefore, in Picture V, there will be 5 squares and 12 triangles.

48. D

Begin by looking for a pattern.
Notice that in each case, the number of triangles, y, can be found by multiplying the number of squares, x, by 2 and then adding 2 to this product. In terms of an equation, write $y = 2x + 2$.
To determine the number of triangles in a picture with 15 squares, substitute 15 for x in the equation $y = 2x + 2$ and solve for y as follows:

$y = 2x + 2$
$y = 2(15) + 2$
$= 30 + 2$
$y = 32$

There will be 32 triangles in a picture with 15 squares.

49. D

Since n represents the number of baskets of blueberries picked, substitute 22 for n in the equation $W = 20 + 2.50n$, and solve for W as follows:

$W = 20 + 2.50n$
$W = 20 + 2.50(22)$
$W = 20 + 55$
$W = 75$

If Tanya picked 22 baskets of blueberries in one day, her wage would be \$75.

50. B

Locate 11 on the x-axis and then move vertically upward until you intersect the line. From this point of intersection, move horizontally across to the y-axis. The resulting value is 520. The cost of buying 11 jerseys is \$520.

OR 3.

a)
The completed table is shown below:

Number of Weeks at the Fitness Club	Total Cost ($)
2	237
4	274
6	311
8	348
10	385

b)
The fixed amount is \$200 (the initial membership fee) and the constant rate of change is \$18.50 per week.

The equation that represents the linear relationship between the total cost, C, and the number of weeks, n, that an individual is enrolled at the fitness club is $C = 200 + 18.50n$.

c)
It is given that the total cost, C, is \$607. Solve for the number of weeks, n, by making use of the equation $C = 200 + 18.50n$ as follows:

$C = 200 + 18.50n$
Substitute 607 for W.
$607 = 200 + 18.50n$
$607 - 200 = 200 - 200 + 18.50n$
$407 = 18.50n$
$\frac{407}{18.50} = \frac{18.50}{18.50}n$
$22 = n$

Ron could be enrolled at the fitness club for 22 weeks for a total cost of \$607.

51. A

Steve walks at a constant rate away from his home, stops (his distance from home does not change) and then returns home (his distance from home is decreasing) at a constant rate.

52. C

The charge for the first 200 minutes of cell phone usage is \$20. This can be illustrated by a horizontal line (the rate does not change for the first 200 minutes). After 200 minutes, the constant of increase is \$0.50 per minute. This portion of the graph should be a straight line rising to the right. The graph that best illustrates the total monthly charge in relation to the number of minutes of cell phone usage is shown in alternative **C**.

53. D

Since the driveway is 80 m long, the initial value is 80 (at time $t = 0$ hours, the amount of driveway to shovel is 80 m). The constant rate of change is given as –10 m/h (after every hour, there are 10 fewer metres of driveway to shovel). The equation that represents the data given in the table is as follows:

$$d = 80 - 10t$$
$$= -10t + 80$$

An alternate solution is shown below.

Choose any two ordered pairs represented by the data in the given table; for example, (2, 60) and (7, 10). From these two points, the run is 5 (7 – 2), and the rise is –50 (10 – 60).
The constant rate of change

$$= \frac{\text{rise}}{\text{run}} = \frac{-50}{5} = -10 \text{ m/h}.$$

Now, build an equation to determine the initial value, V. That equation is $d = V - 10t$ (the coefficient of t is –10 since the constant rate of change is –10 m/h).
Choose another ordered pair from the table, perhaps (5, 30), and solve for V as follows:

$d = V - 10t$
Substitute 5 for t and 30 for d.
$30 = V - 10(5)$
$30 = V - 50$
$80 = V$

The required equation is $d = -10t + 80$.

54. D

Begin by choosing any two points on the given line; for example, (2, 25) and (3, 35). From these two points, the run is 1 (3 – 2), and the rise is 10 (35 – 25). The constant rate of change $= \frac{\text{rise}}{\text{run}} = \frac{10}{1} = \$10/\text{h}$.
Now, build an equation to determine the initial value, V. That equation is $E = V + 10t$ (the coefficient of t is 10 because the constant rate of change is \$10/h.) Choose another point on the line, perhaps (5, 55), and solve for V as follows:

$E = V + 10t$
Substitute 5 for t and 55 for E.
$55 = V + 10(5)$
$55 = V + 50$
$5 = V$
$V = 5$

The equation of the line shown is $E = 10t + 5$.

55. B

The total flat charge for the family is $2 \times \$20 + 4 \times \$10 = \$80$. The rate of change per person to drive a go-cart is

$$\frac{\$0.05}{15 \text{ s}} = \frac{x}{60 \text{ s}}$$
$$x = \frac{0.05 \times 60}{15}$$
$$x = \$0.20/\text{min}$$

Therefore, the rate charge per person to drive a go-cart for 45 min is $\$0.20 \times 45 = \$9$. The total rate charge for a family of six to drive go-carts is $\$9 \times 6 = \$54$. Thus, the total cost for the family to drive go-carts for 45 min is $\$80 + \$54 = \$134$.

56. D

The initial value is the fixed cost of \$35. The constant rate of change is \$0.10 per 5 programs

$$= \frac{\$0.10}{5} = \$0.02 \text{ per program}$$

The linear equation representing the total cost of printing the graduation programs with an initial value of 35 and a constant rate of change of 0.02 is $C = 0.02n + 35$.
Solve for n when $C = 48$ as follows:

$C = 0.02n + 35$
Substitute 48 for C.
$48 = 0.02n + 35$

Subtract 35 from both sides.

$48 - 35 = 0.02n + 35 - 35$
$13 = 0.02n$
$\frac{13}{0.02} = \frac{0.02n}{0.02}$
$650 = n$

Thus, 650 programs can be printed for a total cost of \$48.

57. D

The initial value of a repair at AR Car Repair is 80, which represents the service charge of \$80. The constant rate of change for AR Car Repair is 20, which represents the charge of \$20 per hour. The equation representing the total cost to fix a car at AR Car Repair is $C = 80 + 20t$. The graph of the line defined by the equation $C = 80 + 20t$ is flatter than the line defined by the equation $C = 40 + 25t$ (the total cost to fix a car at A^+ Car Repair) because the rate of change is lower for AR Car Repair than it is for A^+ Car Repair (\$20 per hour is less than \$25 per hour).

58. **A**

The value of the constant rate of change ($4) in scenarios 1 and 2 is the same. Since a represents the numerical value of the constant rate of change, alternative **A** is correct.

59. **C**

The intersection point of the two plans is located at (7, 30). Notice that the *y*-coordinates of the points on the line representing Plan B are lower than the corresponding *y*-coordinates on the line representing Plan A when *x* is between 0 and 7. Plan B is more cost efficient if skis are rented fewer than seven times per month.

60. **A**

The two lines intersect at the point (15, 60). Remember to write the *x* coordinate first in an ordered pair. At the 10-second mark, Jacob has jogged 40 m and Breanna has jogged 35 m. At 10 s, Jacob is 5 m(40 – 35) ahead of Breanna.

61. **D**

The relationship between average speed and time is not linear because the given points do not form a line (there is not a constant rate of change). Marcel's hypothesis is incorrect because the points do not represent a constant rate of change.

UNIT TEST—LINEAR RELATIONS

Use the following information to answer the next question

Based on measurements from field specimens, a palaeontologist derived a linear relationship between the Maiasaura dinosaur's average length and height throughout its lifespan, as shown on the graph.

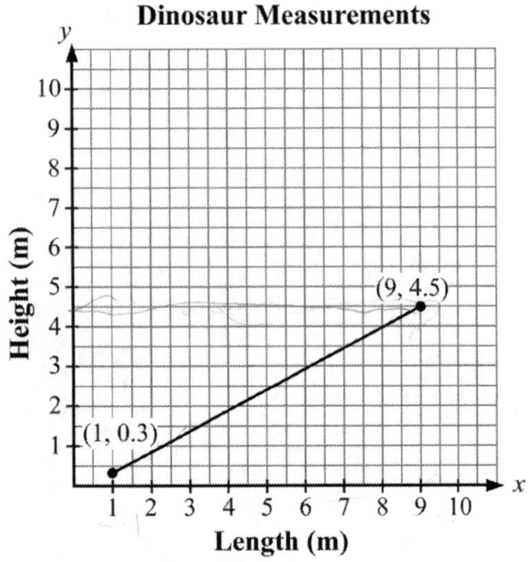

1. The point (9, 4.5) on the graph illustrates that the dinosaur's
   - **A.** height was two times its length
   - **B.** length was two times its height
   - **C.** length was 4.5 times more than its height
   - **D.** height was 4.5 times more than its length

Use the following information to answer the next question.

To analyze the relationship between wind speed and the wind-chill equivalent temperature at a fixed air temperature of –10°C, a forecaster analyzed the scatter plot shown.

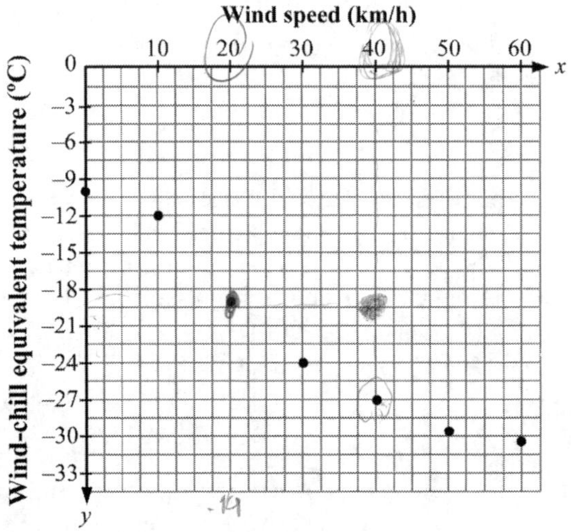

2. The point (20, –19) represents a wind speed of 20 km/h creating a wind-chill temperature of –19°C. When the wind speed is 40 km/h, how much lower is the wind-chill temperature compared to the wind-chill temperature at 20 km/h?
   - **A.** 8°C
   - **B.** 10°C
   - **C.** 12°C
   - **D.** 27°C

3. Which of the following statements is a poor hypothesis about the age and height of children under 12 years of age?
   A. As children get older, their heights increase.
   B. Children who increase in height also increase in age.
   C. For every year that a child gets older, the child's height increases by a large amount.
   D. For every year that a child gets older, the child's height increases by a small amount.

Use the following information to answer the next question.

An experiment was conducted to determine the height to which a particular ball rebounds when it is dropped from various heights. The data collected during the experiment is shown in the following chart:

Height of Dropped Ball (cm)	Rebound Height (cm)
100	25
200	55
300	80
400	110
500	125
600	150
700	180
800	210
900	220
1 000	255

4. Which of the following scatter plots correctly illustrates the data provided in the chart?
   A.

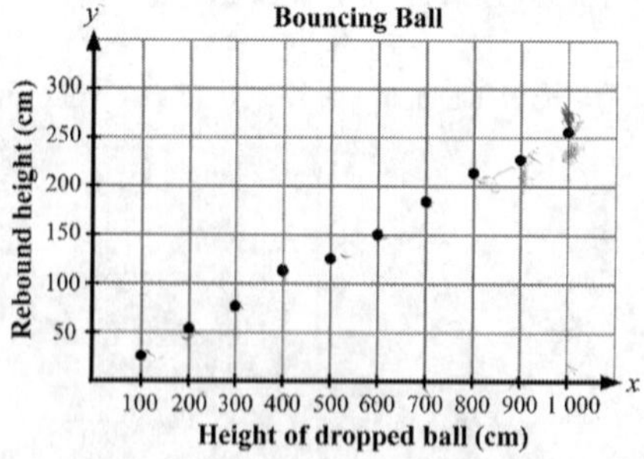

   B.

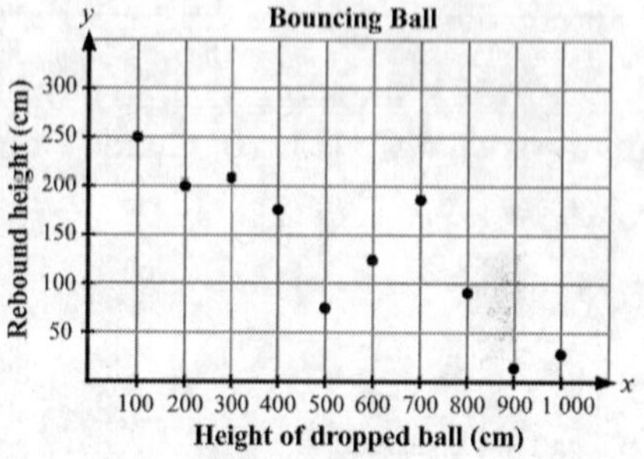

   C.

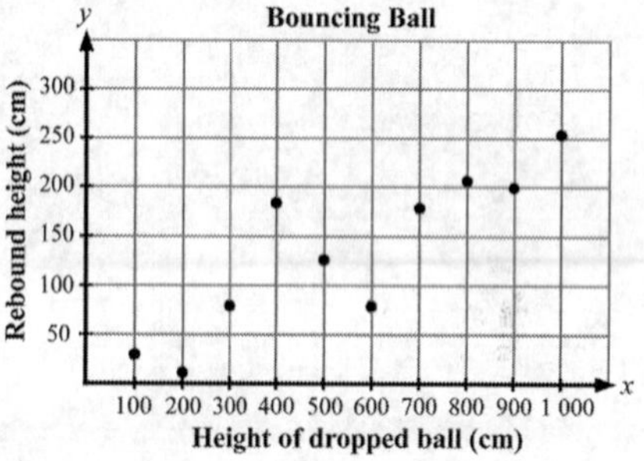

   D.

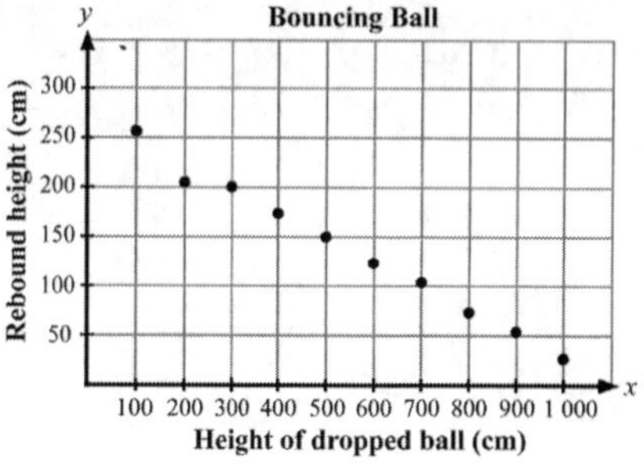

Use the following information to answer the next question

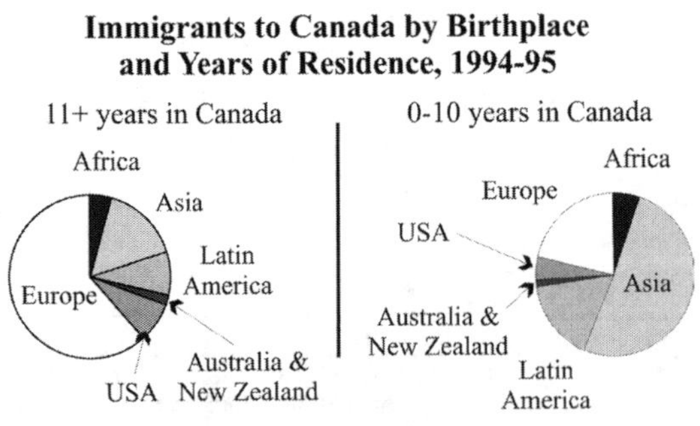

5. Prior to 1985, the largest number of immigrants to Canada originated from

A. Asia

B. Europe

C. the USA

D. Latin America

CHALLENGER QUESTION

The graph shows the final marks of students attending a particular class.

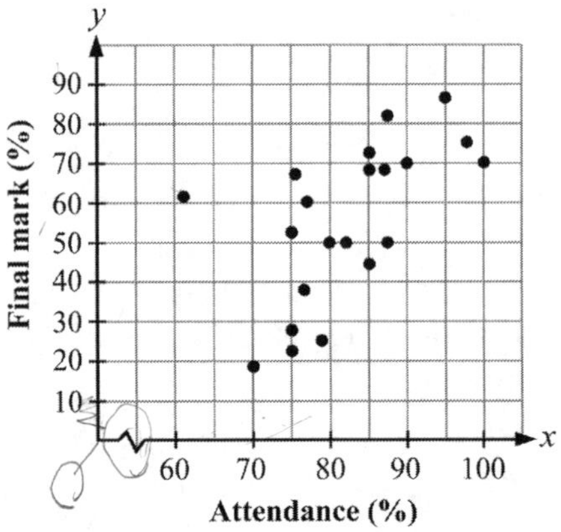

6. Which of the following statements **best** describes the correlation between the percentage of total days attending class and a student's final mark?

A. There is a reasonable correlation between the percentage of total days attended and students' final marks.

B. There is no correlation between the percentage of total days attended and students' final marks.

C. All students have the same final marks when they have the same percentage of total days attended.

D. All students attain better final marks when they have a better percentage of total days attended.

following information to answer the next question.

The graph below portrays the relationship between the practice time and golf scores of a particular golfer.

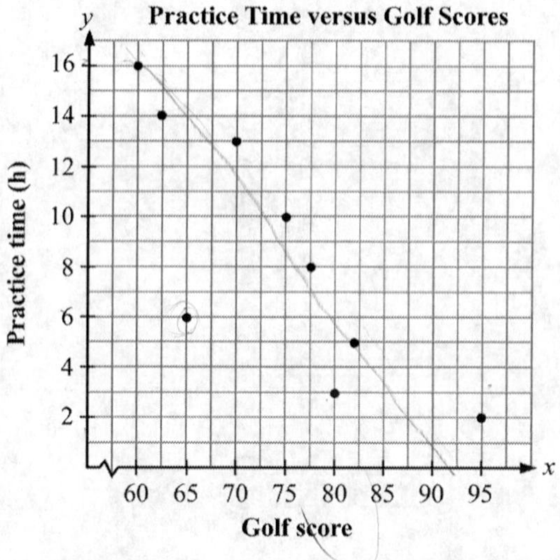

As the amount of practice time increases, the golf scores *i*. However, *ii* points do not follow this trend of the relationship.

7. The row that correctly completes these statements is

	i	*ii*
A.	increase	three
B.	increase	two
C.	decrease	three
D.	decrease	two

Use the following information to answer the next question.

A catering company charges $220 for setup plus $18 per plate to cater a wedding.
A partial table showing the number of guests attending and the total cost of catering is shown.

Number of guests attending	Total cost ($)
0	220
20	
40	940
60	
80	
100	*M*
120	*N*

8. What is the total cost for the entries labelled *M* and *N*?

A. M = $1 800
N = $2 240

B. M = $1 800
N = $2 820

C. M = $2 020
N = $2 380

D. M = $2 020
N = $2 840

Use the following information to answer the next question.

Bob is a weightlifter. When he starts his conditioning program, he can lift 180 pounds. For every two days of conditioning, the weight he can lift increases by 10 pounds. A partial table of the weight he lifts in pounds with respect to the conditioning time is shown.

Conditioning time (days)	**Weight lifted (pounds)**
0	180
2	190
4	200
6	210
8	220
10	230
12	240

9. Which of the following scatter plots portrays the relationship between weight lifted and conditioning time for Bob?

A.

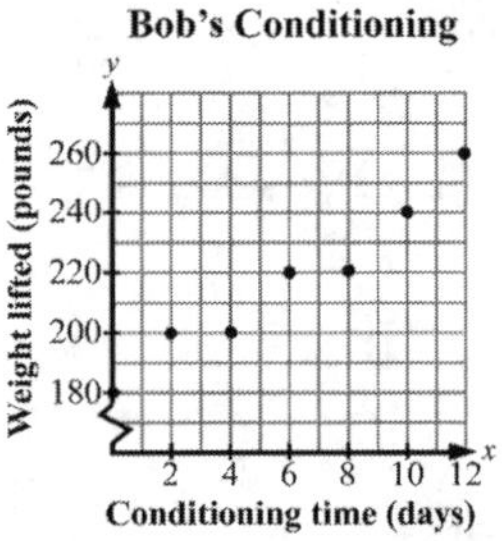

B.

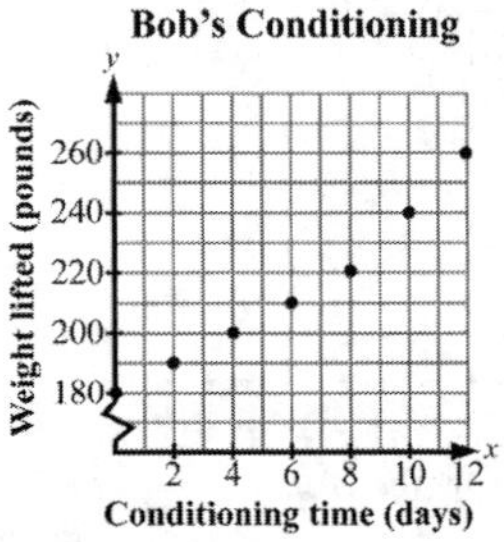

C.

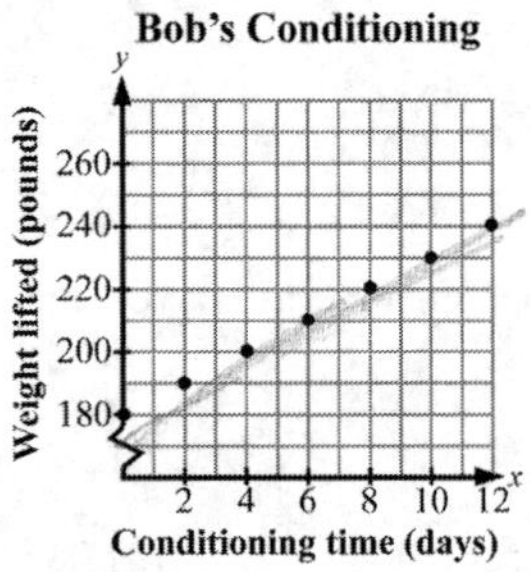

D.

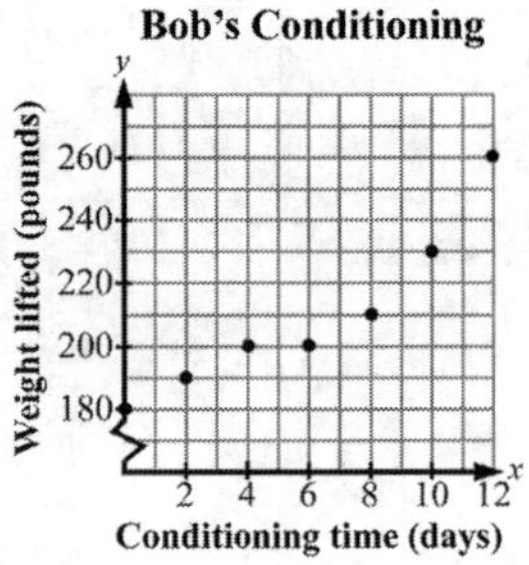

Use the following information to answer the next two questions.

A pulp and paper company operates a tree nursery to provide seedlings for reforestation. To analyze the relationship between the heights and root diameters of tree seedlings, a biologist completed the scatter plot shown, including a line of best fit.

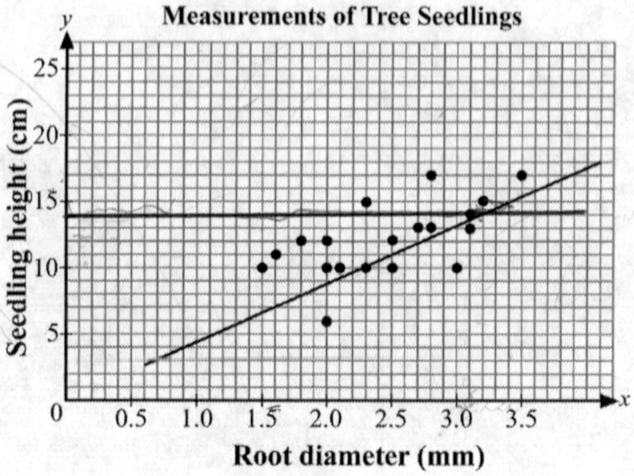

10. According to the line of best fit, what is the predicted root diameter for a seedling with a height of 14 cm?

A. 2.6 mm

B. 2.7 mm

C. 3.2 mm

D. 3.3 mm

11. According to the line of best fit, for every 1.0 mm increase in root diameter, a seedling's height increases by approximately

A. 5.5 cm

B. 4.5 cm

C. 2.1 cm

D. 1.0 cm

Use the following information to answer the next question.

Each of the following tables expresses speed as a function of time.

Table A		Table B	
Time (s)	Speed (m/s)	Time (s)	Speed (m/s)
0	2	0	20
1	4	1	32
2	8	2	38
3	16	3	50
4	32	4	56

Table C		**Table D**	
Time (s)	Speed (m/s)	Time (s)	Speed (m/s)
0	35	0	28
1	32	1	23
2	28	2	18
3	20	3	13
4	8	4	8

12. Which table has data that represents a linear function?

A. Table A

B. Table B

C. Table C

D. Table D

13. As the price of oil steadily increases, the Alberta government receives corresponding increases in oil royalties. Which of the following graphs illustrates this relationship?

A.

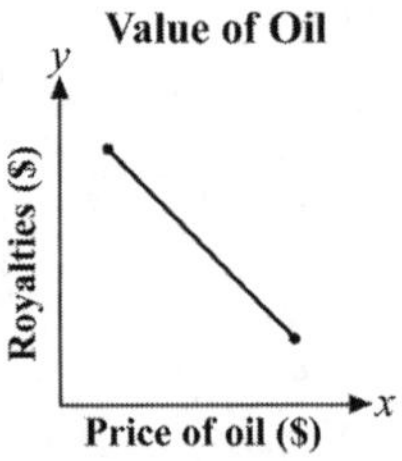

B.

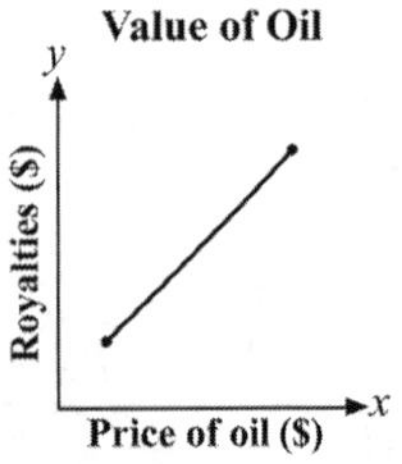

C.

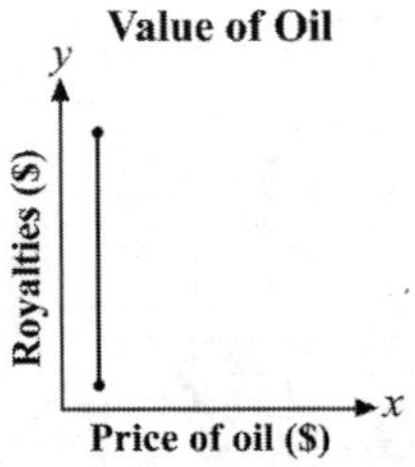

D.

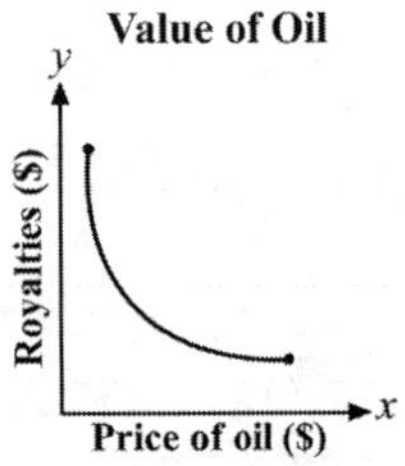

14. The graph of a linear relation has a constant rate of change of $-\frac{1}{2}$. Which of the following statements about the graph of this linear relation is **true**?

A. The run is 2 units to the right, and the rise is 1 unit upward.

B. The run is 1 unit to the right, and the rise is 2 units upward.

C. The run is 1 unit to the right, and the rise is 2 units downward.

D. The run is 2 units to the right, and the rise is 1 unit downward.

15. Which of the following graphs illustrates a linear relation with a constant rate of change of 5?

A.

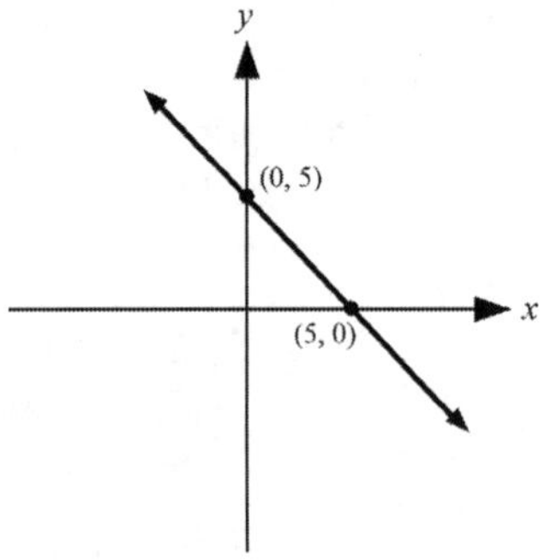

B.

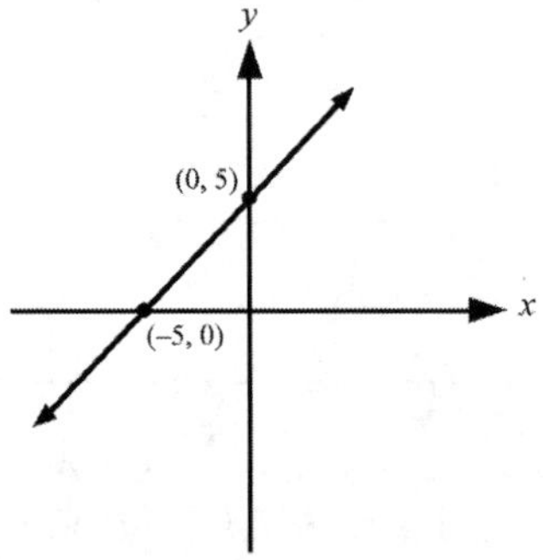

C.

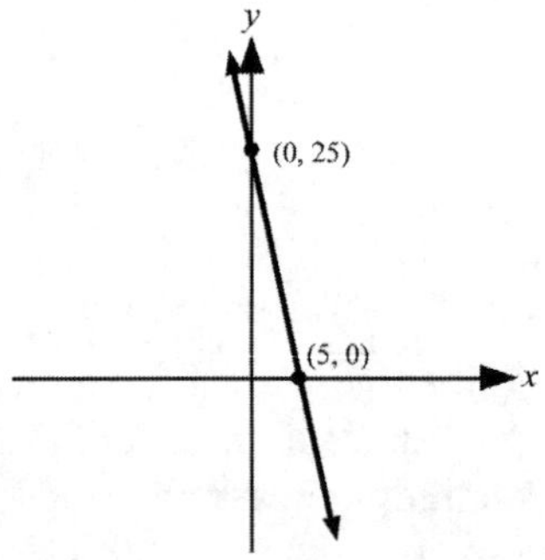

D.

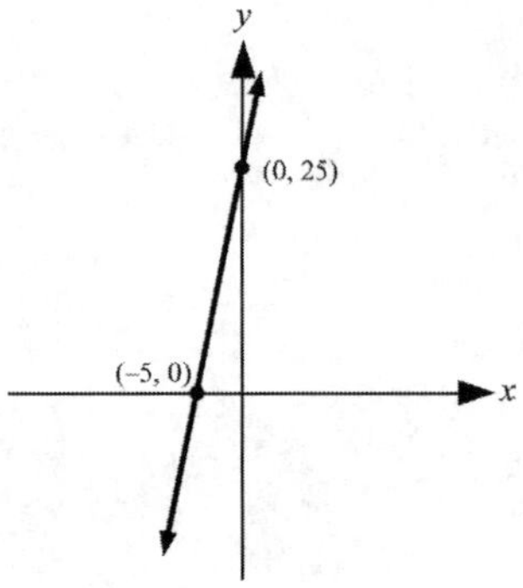

16. As a tool salesman, Jacy earns $66 per day plus $6.50 for every set of tools, n, he sells. Which of the following statements about Jacy's daily salary, S, is **true**?

A. $S = 66 + 6.50n$, and the constant rate of change is 66.

B. $S = 6.50 + 66n$, and the constant rate of change is 66.

C. $S = 6.50 + 66n$, and the constant rate of change is 50.

D. $S = 66 + 6.50n$, and the constant rate of change is 6.50.

17. The odometer reading in Mia's car at the start of a particular drive through the city is 10 101 km. If Mia travels at a constant speed of 80 km/h, which of the following tables of values correctly represents Mia's odometer reading for the given intervals of time?

A.

Time (min)	Odometer (km)
0	10 101
30	10 181
60	10 261
90	10 341
120	10 421
150	10 501

B.

Time (min)	Odometer (km)
0	10 101
30	10 141
60	10 181
90	10 221
120	10 261
150	10 301

A.

Time (min)	Odometer (km)
0	10 101
30	10 261
60	10 421
90	10 581
120	10 741
150	10 901

B.

Time (min)	Odometer (km)
0	10 101
30	10 201
60	10 301
90	10 401
120	10 501
150	10 601

18. Which of the following graphs represents a direct variation?

A.

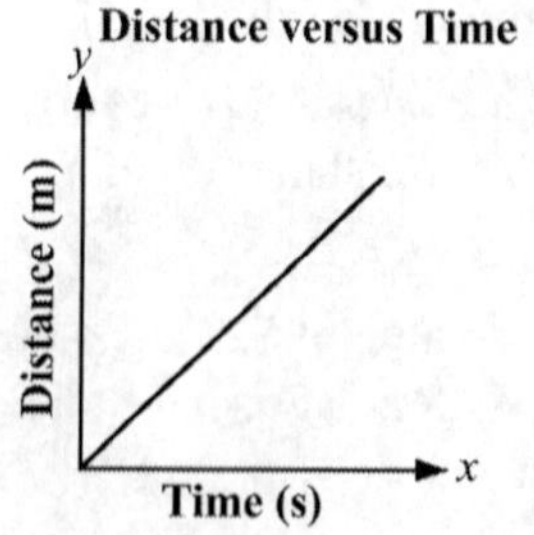

B.

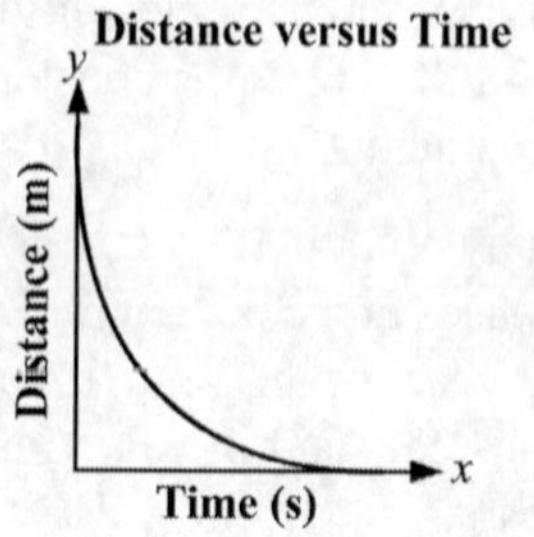

C.

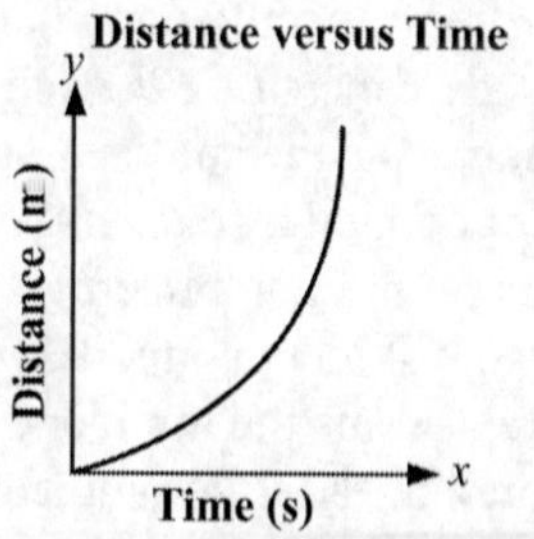

D.

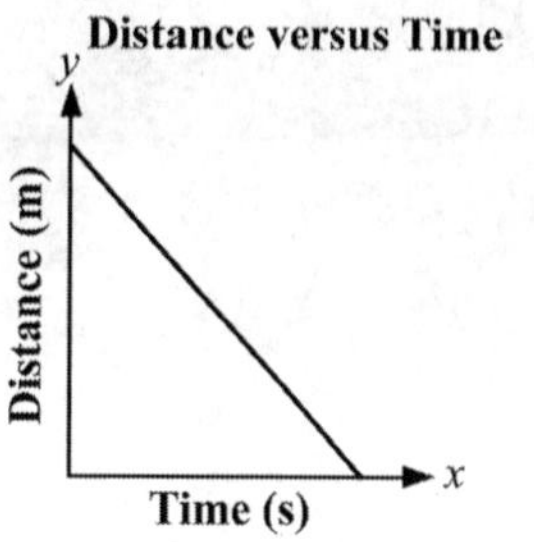

19. Given that there is a partial variation between the numbers of years a collector has a rare coin and its value, which of the following statements is **true**?

A. Starting at a value of \$0, a coin's value increases at a constant rate of \$2 000 per year.

B. Starting at a value of \$2 000, a coin's value increases at a constant rate of \$2 000 per year.

C. Starting at a value of \$0, a coin's value increases at \$2 000 per year for the first 10 years and then remains constant in value for the next 10 years.

D. Starting at a value of \$2 000, a coin's value increases at a constant rate of \$2 000 per year for the first 10 years and then remains constant in value for the next 10 years.

20. As a fundraiser, the student council at a school sells candy canes for 20¢ each. Each candy cane costs the student council 5¢. The student council also spends \$20 on posters advertising the fundraiser. If P represents the student council's profit in dollars and n represents the number of candy canes sold, which of the following equations is **true**?

A. $P = 20 + 0.05n$

B. $P = 20 + 0.15n$

C. $P = 0.15n - 20$

D. $P = 0.20n - 20$

Use the following information to answer the next question.

An otter dives into a river. The position, d, in centimetres of the top of the otter's head with respect to the surface of the river at time, t, in seconds is illustrated in the diagram shown.

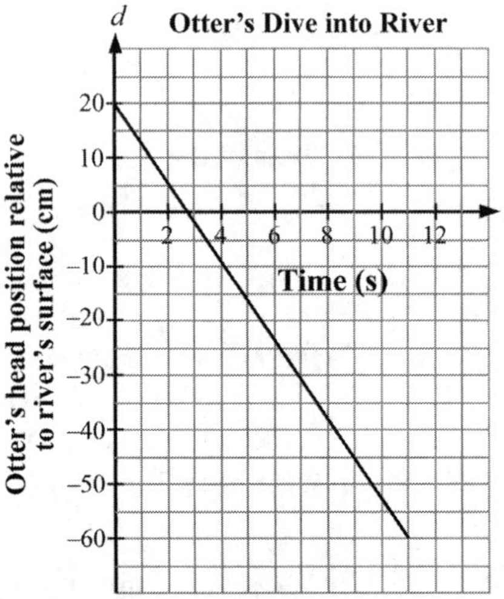

21. The equation of the graph that represents the relationship between the position of the otter's head and the time is

A. $d = 20 - 3t$

B. $d = 20 - \frac{20}{3}t$

C. $d = 20 + \frac{20}{3}t$

D. $d = 20t - \frac{20}{3}$

22. Which of the following scenarios could be modelled by the equation $C = 6n + 20$, where C represents the total cost?

A. The total cost of making 20 toys at a rate of \$6 per hour, where n is the number of hours worked

B. The total cost of making 6 toys at a rate of \$20 per hour, where n is the number of hours worked

C. The total cost of making toys where the rate of cost is \$20 per toy with a fixed start-up cost of \$6, and where n is the number of toys made

D. The total cost of making toys where the rate of cost is \$6 per toy with a fixed start-up cost of \$20, and where n is the number of toys made

Use the following information to answer the next question.

Shawn investigated the stretch distance of a spring when different masses were attached to it. The spring stretched a distance of 12 cm when no mass was attached. When a mass of 100 g was attached to the end of the spring, the stretch distance was 16 cm. When a mass of 200 g was attached, the stretch distance was 20 cm. When a mass of 300 g was attached, the stretch distance was 24 cm. This pattern continued when Shawn attached masses of 400 g, 500 g, 600 g, and up to 1 000 g.

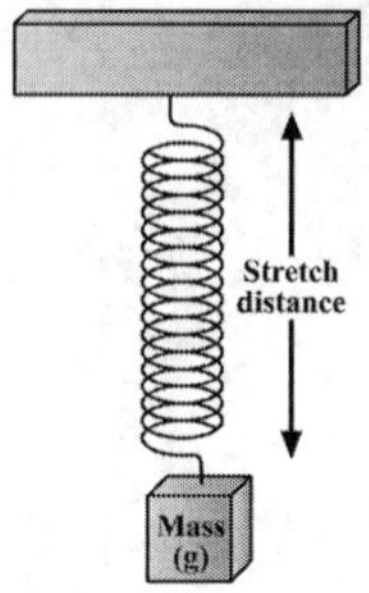

Shawn plotted his data as points on a graph. The mass, m, in grams, represented the x-values, and the stretch distances of the spring, d, in centimetres represented the y-values of his points. The graph of points formed a linear pattern.

23. Which of the following statements correctly describes the graph of this linear relation?

A. The initial value is 12 cm, and the constant rate of change is 4 cm per 100 g.

B. The initial value is 16 cm, and the constant rate of change is 4 cm per 100 g.

C. The initial value is 12 cm, and the constant rate of change is $\frac{1}{4}$ cm per 100 g.

D. The initial value is 16 cm, and the constant rate of change is $\frac{1}{4}$ cm per 100 g.

Use the following information to answer the next question.

Emmanuel works for a computer company called CompuWare. The table shows his annual salary for the last four years.

Year	Annual Salary (\$)
1	38 000
2	39 800
3	41 600
4	43 400

24. If this linear trend continues, then Emmanuel's annual salary in year 9 will be

A. \$45 200

B. \$49 200

C. \$50 600

D. \$52 400

Use the following information to answer the next question.

At Hidden Valley Golf Course, Stacey pays an annual membership fee of $800 plus $23 for each round of golf that she plays.

25. The equation $C = 23n + 800$ represents the relationship between Stacey's total annual cost, C, to play golf at Hidden Valley Golf Course with respect to the number of rounds of golf, n, that she plays in a year. How many rounds of golf did Stacey play at Hidden Valley in a given year if her total annual cost was $1 352?

A. 24 **B.** 35

C. 59 **D.** 94

Use the following information to answer the next question.

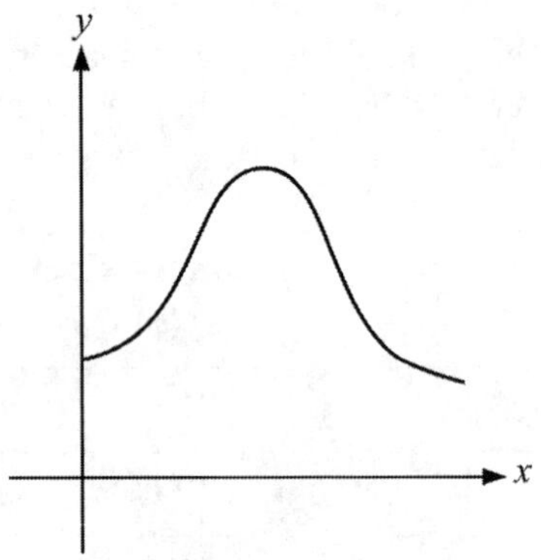

26. Which of the following situations is modelled by the graph shown?

A. The relationship between the day of the month and the amount of precipitation that falls each day in a town situated in a desert

B. The relationship between the number of hours of daylight in a day and the time of year in the city of Ottawa

C. The relationship between the cost of renting a car and the number of kilometres that it is driven

D. The relationship between the volume of a sphere and the radius of the sphere

27. Samantha works at a hardware store. She earns $10/h for her first 15 hours of work in a week. For each additional hour she works, she earns $15/h. Which of the following graphs shows the relationship between Samantha's earnings and the number of hours that she works in a week?

A.

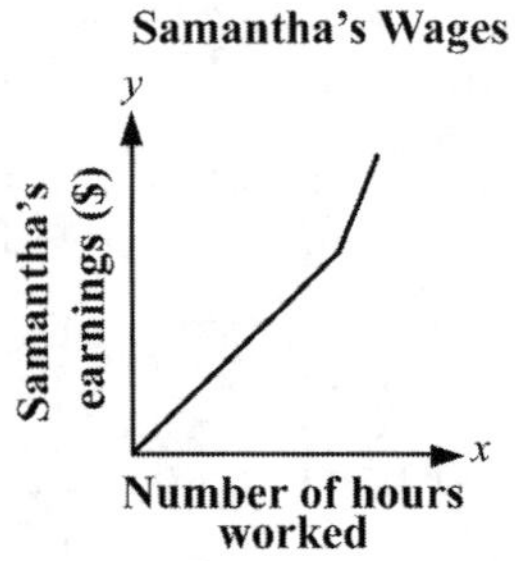

B.

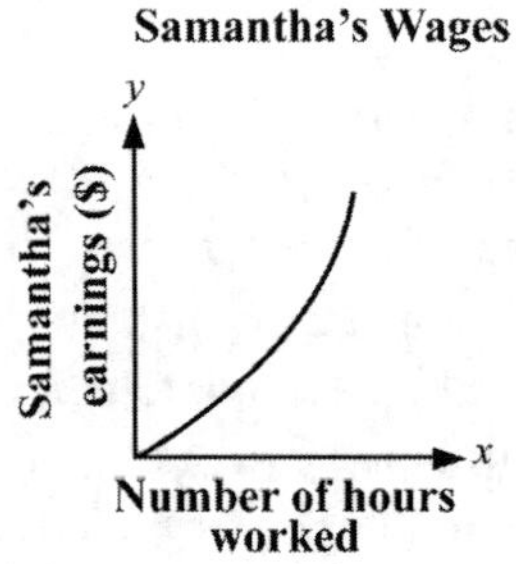

C.

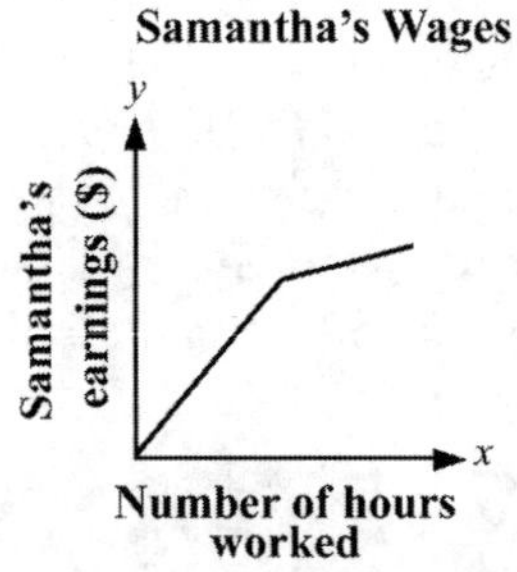

D.

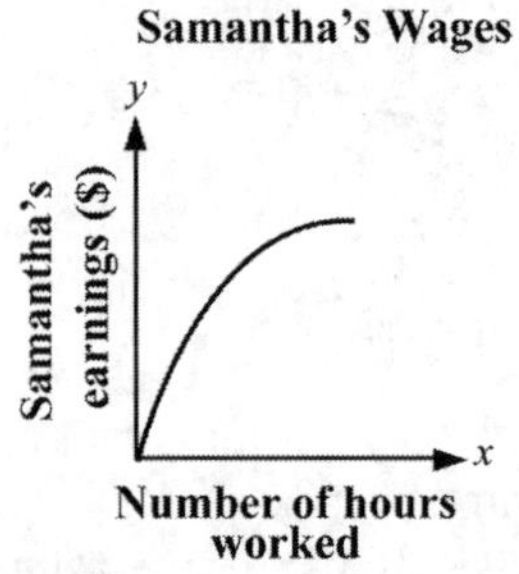

Use the following information to answer the next question.

A fitness centre pays a fixed annual amount for operating costs. Each member of the fitness centre is charged an annual membership fee. The relationship between the annual profit, *P*,
in dollars made by the fitness centre and the number of members, *n*, is linear. The table shown presents some data collected by the fitness centre.

Number of members	Profit ($)
100	5 000
120	10 000
140	15 000
160	20 000

28. The equation that correctly represents the relationship between annual profit and number of members at the fitness centre is

A. $P = 50n$

B. $P = 250n$

C. $P = 250n + 5\,000$

D. $P = 250n - 20\,000$

Use the following information to answer the next question.

A contractor has building materials delivered from a lumberyard to various construction sites. The delivery cost, *C*, is based on a fixed amount plus a per-kilometre cost. The delivery cost and the distance, *d*, of the construction sites from the lumberyard is illustrated in the diagram shown.

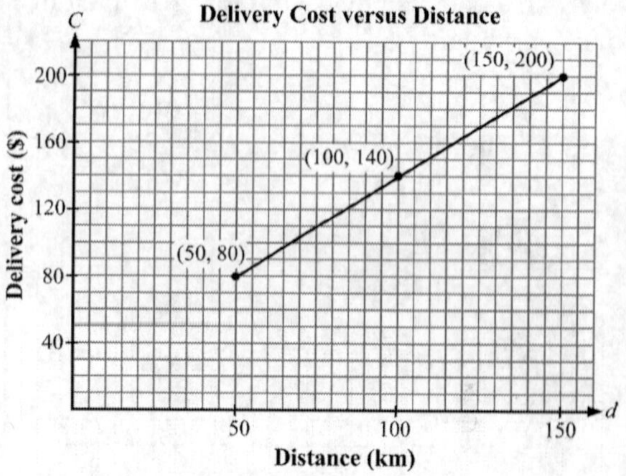

29. The graph of the given line is defined by the equation

A. $C = \frac{6}{5}d + 80$

B. $C = \frac{6}{5}d + 20$

C. $C = \frac{8}{5}d$

D. $C = 12d$

30. Bianca's parents give her $108 a month to spend on lunch at school. Her average cost for each lunch is $6. How many days in a given month can Bianca have lunch at school if she wants to have $72 in lunch money left over at the end of the month?

A. 30

B. 12

C. 10

D. 6

Use the following information to answer the next question.

Yolanda begins working at a farm at a starting wage of \$15/h. Every two months, Yolanda's hourly wage will increase by \$0.80/h. Yolanda asks four friends to help her calculate the number of months, n, it will take before she earns \$21.40/h. The equations and answers generated by each friend are given in the chart below:

Friend	**Equation**	**Number of Months**
Jill	$W = 0.80n + 15$	8
Sasha	$W = 0.40n + 15$	16
Jasmine	$W = 15.8n$	5
Rachel	$W = 15.4n$	6

31. Which of Yolanda's friends came up with the correct equation and the correct answer?

A. Jill

B. Sasha

C. Jasmine

D. Rachel

Use the following information to answer the next two questions.

The total cost of printing summer catalogues for a particular department store is based on fixed setup costs plus a cost per book.

Line A represents the total cost of printing the catalogues last year. Line B represents the total cost of printing the catalogues this year.

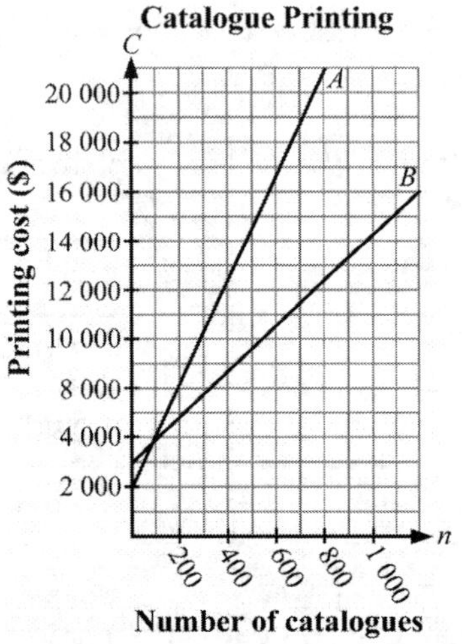

32. Which of the following statements is **true**?

A. The fixed setup costs for printing catalogues last year and this year are the same.

B. The cost per catalogue for printing last year was more than the cost per catalogue for printing this year when more than 100 catalogues are printed.

C. The cost per catalogue for printing this year is more than the cost per catalogue for printing last year.

D. The fixed setup cost for printing catalogues this year is lower than the fixed setup cost for printing catalogues last year.

33. If the equation for line A is written as $C = an + b$ and the equation for line B is written as $C = cn + d$, which of the following statements about the relationship of values a to c and b to d is true?

A. a is greater than c, and b is greater than d.

B. a is greater than c, and b is less than d.

C. a is less than c, and b is greater than d.

D. a is less than c, and b is less than d.

Use the following information to answer the next question.

Natasha wants to sign up for Internet service. She analyzes the monthly plans offered by two different Internet companies: Surfcom and Netsurf. In the given graph, each line illustrates the relationship between the cost, C, in dollars and the number of minutes, t, of Internet usage with each company.

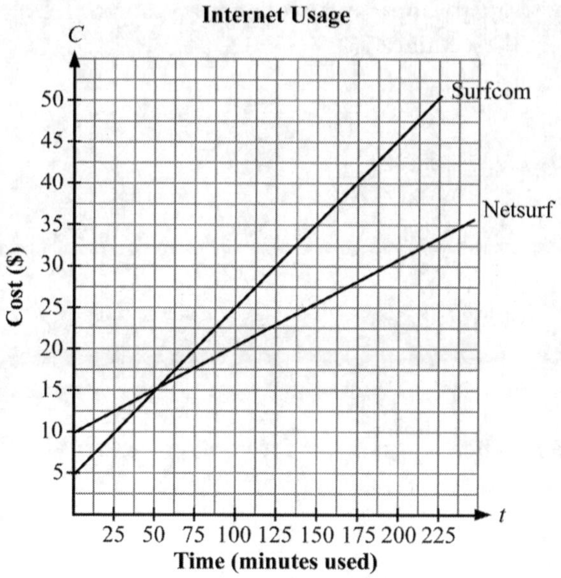

34. Which of the following statements is **true**?

A. Netsurf is cheaper when more than 50 minutes are used.

B. Surfcom is cheaper when more than 50 minutes are used.

C. Netsurf is cheaper regardless of the number of minutes used.

D. Surfcom is cheaper regardless of the number of minutes used.

Use the following information to answer the next question.

Four different plans for renting a particular car are shown in the given graph. Each line illustrates a relationship between total cost and distance travelled.

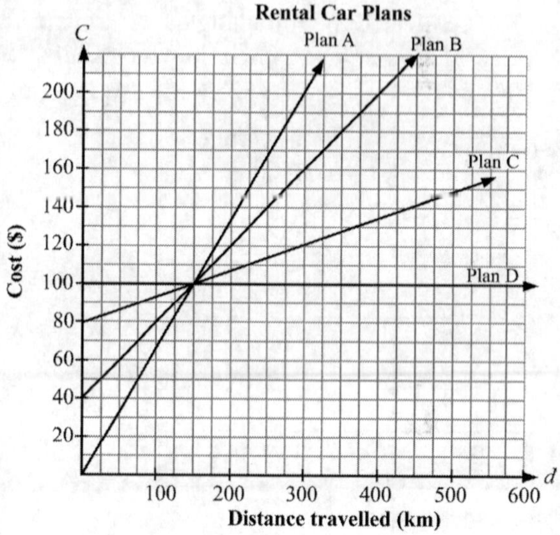

35. Which of the following statements is **true**?

A. Plan D is the least expensive regardless of the number of kilometres driven.

B. Plan A is the most expensive when the car is driven more than 150 km and the least expensive when the car is driven less than 150 km.

C. The four plans cost the same when the car is driven exactly 150 km, but Plan C is the least expensive when the car is driven more than 150 km.

D. Plan A is the least expensive when the car is driven exactly 150 km, and Plan B is the most expensive when the car is driven exactly 300 km.

Open Response

Kara collected the following data in science class during an experiment in which she heated a liquid.

Time (s)	Temperature (°C)
0	12
60	17
120	22
180	27
240	32
300	37
360	42

1. Determine whether the relationship between temperature and time is linear or non-linear. Justify your answer.

2. Two lawnmower repair shops charge different rates for repairs. At both shops, the total cost, *C*, is related to the time, *t*, in hours needed to make the repair. The following two tables of values show this relationship for both shops:

Mower Incorporated		**Green's Mower Service**	
Time (h)	**Cost ($)**	**Time (h)**	**Cost ($)**
0	28	0	0
1	46	1	22
2	64	2	44
3	82	3	66
4	100	4	88

a) Determine the hourly rates of repair for both repair shops, and explain how you arrived at these values.

b) When will the cost for both repair shops be the same?

c) Which repair shop has a fixed cost? Justify your answer.

A volleyball player's movements during the events of one play are represented in the following graph. The graph shows the relationship between the distance, d, in metres of the player from the net and the time, t, in seconds during the play.

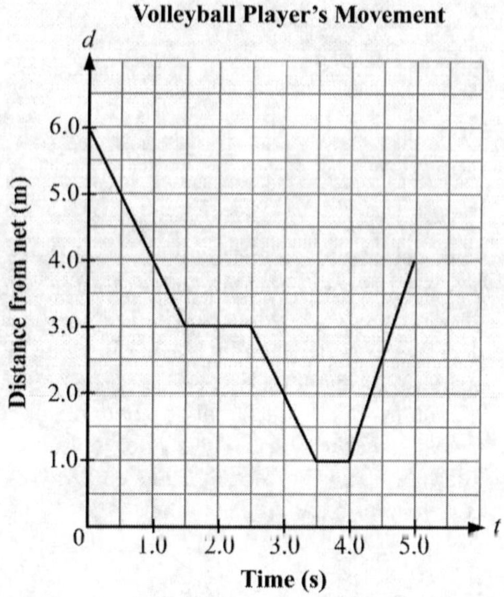

3. Describe the volleyball player's movement over the duration of the five-second play, mentioning speed, direction, and distance from the net.

ANSWERS AND SOLUTIONS—UNIT TEST

1. B	**8. C**	**15. D**	**22. D**	**29. B**	**OR1. ****
2. A	**9. C**	**16. D**	**23. A**	**30. D**	**OR2. ****
3. C	**10. C**	**17. B**	**24. D**	**31. B**	**OR3. ****
4. A	**11. B**	**18. A**	**25. A**	**32. B**	
5. B	**12. D**	**19. B**	**26. B**	**33. B**	
6. A	**13. B**	**20. C**	**27. A**	**34. A**	
7. D	**14. D**	**21. B**	**28. D**	**35. B**	

**** SEE SOLUTIONS**

1. B

The x-coordinate of the point (9, 4.5) is 9, which represents the length of the dinosaur. The y-coordinate of the point (9, 4.5) is 4.5, which represents the height of the dinosaur. Since $9 = 4.5 \times 2$, the length of the dinosaur was two times its height.

2. A

The point (20, –19) represents a wind speed of 20 km/h (the x-coordinate) and a wind-chill temperature of –19°C (the y-coordinate). The wind-chill temperature at 40 km/h was –27°C. $(-19) - (-27) = (-19) + (+27) = 8°C$ The wind-chill temperature with a 40 km/h wind is 8°C lower than the wind-chill temperature with a 20 km/h wind.

3. C

Children who get older get taller; however, it is very unlikely that their heights increase by a large amount from one year to the next. If this were the case, children would become impossibly tall.The hypothesis in alternative **C** is a poor hypothesis.

4. A

The scatter plots in alternatives **B** and **D** are incorrect because the data values for the various heights to which the ball rebounds are decreasing rather than increasing in value. The scatter plot in alternative C is incorrect because it contains data values that do not correspond to values in the chart. The scatter plot in alternative **A** is correct, since its data values correspond to the values in the chart.

5. B

The two pie charts present information about the origins of immigrants to Canada as of 1994 to 1995. The pie chart on the left gives information about people who immigrated to Canada prior to 1985, since these immigrants have lived in Canada for at least 11 years. The pie chart shows that before 1985, the majority of immigrants (about 60%) came from Europe.

6. A

In general, as the percentage of total days attended increases, students' final marks also increase. This is not always the case, however. For example, the student who attended 62% of the total classes got a final mark of 62%, whereas the student who attended 70% of the total classes got a much lower final mark of 19%. The statement that best describes the relationship between the percentage of total days attended and a student's final mark is that there is a reasonable correlation between the percentage of total days attended and the final marks.

7. **D**

Ordered pair (70, 13) shows an increased score as practice time increases from 6 to 13 hours. Ordered pair (82, 5) shows an increased score as practice time increases from 3 to 5 hours. These are the only two times that the golf scores increase as the practice time increases; therefore, as the amount of practice time increases, the golf scores decrease, but there are two points that do not follow this trend of the relationship.

8. **C**

It costs \$18 per plate, so to solve for *M*, multiply \$18 by 100, then add the fixed charge of \$220.
$\$18 \times 100 + \$220 = \$2\,020$
To solve for *N*, multiply \$18 by 120 and add \$220.
$\$18 \times 120 + \$220 = \$2\,380$
The value of *M* is \$2 020, and the value of *N* is \$2 380.

9. **C**

Since the weight Bob can lift increases by 10 pounds every two days, the complete table of values is as shown:

Conditioning time (days)	Weight lifted (pounds)
0	180
2	190
4	200
6	210
8	220
10	230
12	240

The scatter plot that corresponds to the data given in the table is shown in alternative **C**.

10. **C**

First locate 14 cm on the *y*-axis. Next, move horizontally to the right from 14 cm until you intersect the line of best fit. Finally, move vertically down from the point of intersection until you intersect the *x*-axis. The resulting *x*-value is 3.2 mm. Therefore, a seedling with a height of 14 cm has a predicted root diameter of 3.2 mm.

11. **B**

Read to the right along the *x*-axis to the value of 1.0 mm, and then move vertically up to intersect the line of best fit. You will find a corresponding *y*-value of about 4.5 cm. Therefore, for every 1.0 mm in root diameter, a seedling's height increases by approximately 4.5 cm. **Note:** You could locate any point (x_1, y_1) on the line of best fit and a second point (x_2, y_2) on the line of best fit such that $x_2 - x_1 = 1$ mm. The value $y_2 - y_1$ also gives the correct answer.

12. **D**

For a linear function, the value of the first differences must be constant. In the table in alternative **D**, *y* decreases by a constant value of 5 for every increase of 1 in the *x*-value.

$28 - 23 = 5$
$23 - 18 = 5$
$18 - 13 = 5$
$13 - 8 = 5$

Since the first differences are the same, the data in the table in alternative **D** represents a linear function.

13. **B**

The graph that shows a constant increase of the value of *x* (royalties) and a constant increase of the value of *y* (price of oil) is the graph given in alternative **B**.
Note: The graph of a linear function will always be a straight line.

14. **D**

A rate of change of $-\frac{1}{2}$ can be written as $\frac{-1}{2}$.
Since the rate of change is defined as rise divided by run, the rise is –1, and the run is 2
The run is 2 units to the right, and the rise is 1 unit downward.

15. D

Since the rate of change has a positive value (5), the corresponding graph must rise from the left to the right. Only the graphs in alternatives B and D rise from the left to the right.
In alternative D, the rise is 25 (25 – 0), and the run is 5(0 –(–5)) The rate of change is defined as rise divided by run. The rate of change for the graph in alternative **D** is 25 ÷ 5 = 5.

16. D

Jacy's daily salary is given by the equation $S = 66 + 6.50n$. The number 6.50 represents the constant rate of change (for every increase of 1 for n, the value of S increases by 6.50). The correct numerical coefficient of n is 6.50. Jacy's daily salary is given by the equation $S = 66 + 6.50n$, and the constant rate of change is 6.50.

17. B

The constant rate of change, or the speed of 80 km/h, indicates that the odometer reading increases by 80 km for every hour travelled. This could also be represented by a 40 km increase in the odometer reading for every increase of half an hour (or 30 minutes). Therefore, the correct table of values should portray a constant rate of increase of 40 km for every increase of 30 minutes

$$10\,101 \xrightarrow{+40} 10\,141 \xrightarrow{+40} 10\,181 \xrightarrow{+40} 10\,221 \xrightarrow{+40} 10\,261 \xrightarrow{+40} 10\,301$$

18. A

The graph of a direct variation is a straight line passing through the origin (0, 0). The correct graph is shown in alternative **A**.

19. B

A partial variation is a linear relation with a constant rate of change and an initial value that is not zero. A coin with an initial value of \$2 000 that increases at a constant rate of change of \$2 000 per year represents a partial variation.

20. C

For the fundraiser, the constant rate of change of the profit is 15¢ (20¢ – 5¢) per candy cane sold. Since the profit is expressed in dollars, the numerical coefficient of n (the number of candy canes sold) is 0.15. The fixed cost for advertising is \$20. The correct equation for the profit is $P = 0.15n - 20$.

21. B

Initially, the top of the otter's head is 20 cm above the surface of the river (when $t = 0$ seconds, the value of d is 20 cm). The constant rate of change $= \frac{\text{rise}}{\text{run}} = -\frac{20}{3}$, since for every increase of 3 s (run) to the right in the t-direction, there is a decrease of 20 cm (rise) in the d-direction.
Therefore, the resulting equation is $d = 20 - \frac{20}{3}t$.

22. D

The constant rate of change in the given equation is 6 (the coefficient of n). The fixed quantity in the given equation is 20. The constant rate of change is \$6, the cost per toy, and the fixed start-up cost is \$20. The equation $C = 6n + 20$ could model the total cost of making toys where the rate of cost is \$6 per toy with a fixed start-up cost of \$20, and where n is the number of toys made.

23. A

The initial value of the graph represents the spring's initial stretch distance of 20 cm when no mass is attached ($m = 0$ g). The constant rate of change of the graph represents the change in stretch distance for every change of 100 g. When the mass added goes from 0 to 100 g, the stretch distance change is 16 – 12 = 4 cm. When the mass added goes from 100 g to 200 g, the stretch distance change is $20 - 16 = 4$ cm. The stretch distance change of 4 cm for every increase of 100 g occurs as 300 g, 400 g, and up to 1 000 g are added, which means that the constant rate of change for the linear relation is 4 cm per 100 g. The initial value is 12 cm, and the constant rate of change is 4 cm per 100 g.

24. D

Using the given table of values, determine Emmanuel's annual rate of salary increase.
\$39 800 – \$38 000 = \$1 800
\$41 600 – \$39 800 = \$1 800
\$43 400 – \$41 600 = \$1 800
To determine Emmanuel's annual salary in year 9, add five times \$1 800 to Emmanuel's annual salary in year 4.

$$\$43\ 400 + \$1\ 800 + \$1\ 800 + \$1\ 800 + \$1\ 800 + \$1\ 800 = \$52\ 400.$$

Emmanuel's annual salary in year 9 will be \$52 400.

25. A

In order to determine the number of rounds of golf, *n*, that Stacey played at Hidden Valley in the given year, substitute \$1 352, the total annual cost, for *C*, and then solve for *n* as follows:

$$C = 23n + 800$$
$$1\ 352 = 23n + 800$$

Subtract 800 from both sides of the equation.

$$1\ 352 - 800 = 23n + 800 - 800$$
$$552 = 23n$$

Divide both sides of the equation by 23.

$$\frac{552}{23} = \frac{23n}{23}$$
$$24 = n$$
$$n = 24$$

Stacey played 24 rounds of golf at Hidden Valley Golf Course in the given year.

26. B

The graph portrays the relationship between the number of hours of daylight in a day and the time of year in Ottawa. In January (left side of the graph), there are fewer hours of daylight per day, as illustrated by the *y*-intercept. The number of hours of daylight per day increases from January until the end of June (top of curve). From the end of June until the latter part of December, the number of hours of daylight per day decreases (right side of graph).

27. A

Samantha's rate of pay over the first 15 hours of work rises at a constant rate of \$10/h, as represented by the first rising line segment. From 15 hours on, her rate increases to \$15/h, which is represented by the steeper (second) line segment. This is shown in graph **A.**

28. D

The constant rate of change can be determined from any two successive values in the table. For example, for every 20 members (120 – 100) the rate of profit is \$5 000 (\$10 000 – \$5 000).
This rate of change can be expressed as \$5 000 ÷ 20 = \$250 per member; therefore, the annual membership fee is \$250 per member.
Build an equation to solve for the fixed annual operating costs, *V*. This equation is $P = 250n + V$
To solve for *V*, substitute any pair of corresponding data values into the derived equation, perhaps $n = 140$ and $P = 15\ 000$.

$$P = 250n + V$$
$$15\ 000 = 250(140) + V$$
$$15\ 000 = 35\ 000 + V$$

Subtract 35 000 from both sides

$$15\ 000 - 35\ 000 = 35\ 000 - 35\ 000 + V$$
$$-20\ 000 = V$$
$$V = -20\ 000$$

The equation $P = 250n - 20\ 000$ represents the given relationship.

29. B

Begin by choosing any two points on the graph in order to determine the constant rate of change. For example, *P*(50, 80) and *Q*(100, 140). From these two points, the rise is 60 (140 – 80 = 60), and the run is 50 (100 – 50 = 50). The constant rate of change can now be found as follows:

The constant rate of change $= \frac{\text{rise}}{\text{run}} = \frac{60}{50} = \frac{6}{5}$.

Build an equation to solve for the unknown initial value, *V*.

This equation is $C = \frac{6}{5}d + V$.

To solve for V, choose one point on the graph, perhaps (150, 200), and substitute the appropriate values into the derived equation.

$$C = \frac{6}{5}d + V$$
$$200 = \frac{6}{5}(150) + V$$
$$200 = \frac{900}{5} + V$$
$$200 = 180 + V$$

Subtract 180 from both sides.

$$200 - 180 = 180 - 180 + V$$
$$20 = 0 + V$$
$$20 = V$$
$$V = 20$$

The equation $C = \frac{6}{5}d + 20$ represents the graph of the given line segment.

30. D

Bianca receives $108 a month for school lunches. She spends her money at the rate of $6 per lunch. Since Bianca wants to have $72 left over at the end of the month, use the equation

$108 - 6t = 72$, where t is the number of days Bianca has lunch at school.
Solve for t as follows:

$$72 = 108 - 6t$$

Subtract 108 from both sides.

$$72 - 108 = 108 - 108 - 6t$$
$$-36 = -6t$$

Divide both sides by -6.

$$\frac{-36}{-6} = \frac{-6t}{-6}$$
$$6 = t$$

Bianca can have six lunches at school and still have $72 of her lunch money remaining at the end of the month.

31. B

Yolanda's starting wage is $15/h, and the constant rate of change of her hourly wage is $0.40 per month ($0.80 ÷ 2 months).
If W represents Yolanda's hourly wage, then build an equation in order to solve for the number of months, n.
This equation is $W = 0.40n + 15$.
Solve for n by substituting 21.40 for W as shown.

$$21.40 = 0.40n + 15$$

Subtract 15 from both sides.

$$21.40 - 15 = 0.40n + 15 - 15$$
$$6.40 = 0.40n$$

Divide both sides by 0.40.

$$\frac{6.40}{0.40} = \frac{0.40n}{0.40}$$
$$16 = n$$

Sasha came up with the correct equation and the correct answer.

32. B

The fixed setup cost portrayed by each graph is given by the initial value, or vertical intercept, C, of each respective line. The fixed setup cost portrayed by line B (this year's catalogues) is **greater** than the fixed setup cost portrayed by line A (last year's catalogues). Next, examine the positioning of each line. The steeper the line, the more each catalogue costs. Since line A is steeper than line B, it means that the cost per catalogue for printing last year was more than the cost per catalogue for printing this year.

33. B

The constant rate of change $\left(\frac{\text{rise}}{\text{run}}\right)$ of line A is greater than the constant rate of change of line B since line A is steeper than line B. The numerical coefficient a in the equation representing line A is greater than the numerical coefficient c in the equation representing line B. The initial value (vertical intercept) of line A is less than the initial value (vertical intercept) of line B. Value b in the equation representing line A is less than value d in the equation representing line B. a is greater than c, and b is less than d.

34. A

The intersection point for the two lines is (50, 15). This means that at 50 minutes of Internet usage, each plan will cost $15. To the right of the intersection point, the points on the line representing Netsurf are lower than the points on the line representing Surfcom. Since the points are lower, it means that a customer pays less per minute of Internet usage with Netsurf than with Surfcom. Netsurf is cheaper when using the Internet for more than 50 minutes.

35. B

The intersection point for all four lines is located at (150, 100). This means that when the car is driven exactly 150 km, the cost under all four plans is $100. Observe that from 0 km to 150 km, the cost of renting a car is least expensive under Plan A. For any *x*-coordinate before 150, the *y*-coordinate for any point on the line representing Plan A is smaller than the *y*-coordinate for any point on the line representing any of the other three plans. Similarly, for any distance greater than 150 km, the cost of renting a car is most expensive under Plan A. For any *x*-coordinate greater than 150, the *y*-coordinate for any point on the line representing Plan A is greater than the *y*-coordinate for any point on the line representing any of the other three plans. Plan A is the most expensive when the car is driven for more than 150 km and the least expensive when the car is driven less than 150 km.

OR 1.

To determine whether the data is linear or non-linear, determine whether or not there is a constant rate of change. The rate of change is given by the ratio $\frac{\text{rise}}{\text{run}}$.

This rate of change must be constant (the same) for any two rows in the table. For example, in row 2, the time is 60 s, and the temperature is 17°C.

In row 5, the time is 240 s, and the temperature is 32°C. For the ordered pairs (60, 17) and (240, 32), the rise is 15 (32 – 17), and the run is 180 (240 – 60); thus, the rate of change is 0.083 (15 ÷ 180). Regardless of the two ordered pairs chosen, the rate of change equals 0.083. Since there is a constant rate of change, the relationship between time and temperature is linear.

OR 2.

a)
The rate charged by Mower Incorporated is $18 per hour.

$46 – $28 = $18
$82 – $64 = $18
$100 – $82 = $18

The rate charged by Green's Mower Service is $22 per hour.

$22 – $0 = $22
$44 – $22 = $22
$66 – $44 = $22
$88 – $66 = $22

b)
One possible solution is to extend the table representing time and cost for each repair shop until the values for time and cost match as follows:

Mower Incorporated	
Time (h)	**Cost ($)**
0	28
1	46
2	64
3	82
4	100
5	118
6	136
7	154

Green's Mower Service	
Time (h)	**Cost ($)**
0	0
1	22
2	44
3	66
4	88
5	110
6	132
7	154

At the 7th hour, the cost of repairs at each shop will be the same ($154).

Alternate solution:
The initial charge for Mower Incorporated is \$28, and the hourly charge is \$18 per hour; therefore, the equation representing the cost, C, for n hours of repair is $C = 28 + 18n$.
The initial charge for Green's Mower Service is \$0, and the hourly charge is \$22 per hour; therefore, the equation representing the cost, C, for n hours of repair is $C = 0 + 22n$ or $C = 22n$.
Since the cost is the same at both repair shops (at this point in time), it follows that $28 + 18n = 22n$. Now, solve for n as shown:

$$28 + 18n = 22n$$
$$28 + 18n - 18n = 22n - 18n$$
$$28 = 4n$$

$$\frac{28}{4} = \frac{4}{4}n$$

$$7 = n \text{ or}$$
$$n = 7$$

At the 7th hour, the cost of repairs will be the same at each shop.

c)
Mower Incorporated has a fixed charge of \$28 that the customer pays in addition to the hourly rate regardless of how long the repair takes. Green's Mower Service does not have a fixed charge.

OR 3.

First, consider the interval from 0 s to 1.5 s. For this interval, the rise is 3 – 6 = –3 and the run is 1.5 – 0 = 1.5. In other words, for the first 1.5 s, the volleyball player's distance from the net decreases at a constant rate of –3 ÷ 1.5 = –2, which represents a constant rate of change of –2 m/s. The volleyball player moves from 6 m to 3 m from the net at a constant rate of 2 m/s from 0 to 1.5 s. Next, from 1.5 s to 2.5 s, the volleyball player's distance from the net does not change.
The player stays at a distance of 3 m from the net. From 2.5 s to 3.5 s, the rise is 1 – 3 = –2, and the run is 1 (3.5 – 2.5); thus, from 2.5 s to 3.5 s, the rate of change is –2 (–2 ÷ 1), which represents a constant rate of change of –2 m/s. The volleyball player moves from 3 m to 1 m from the net at a constant rate of 2 m/s from 2.5 s to 3.5 s.

From 3.5 s to 4.0 s, the volleyball player's distance from the net does not change.
The player stays at a distance of 1.0 m from the net. Finally, from 4.0 s to 5.0 s, the rise is

3 (4.0 – 1.0 = 3), and the run is 1 (5.0 – 4.0 = 1). In other words, from 4.0 s to 5.0 s, the rate of change is 3 (3 ÷ 1 = 3), which represents a constant rate of change of 3 m/s. The volleyball player moves from 1 m to 4 m from the net at a constant rate of 3 m/s from 4 s to 5 s.

Measurement and Geometry

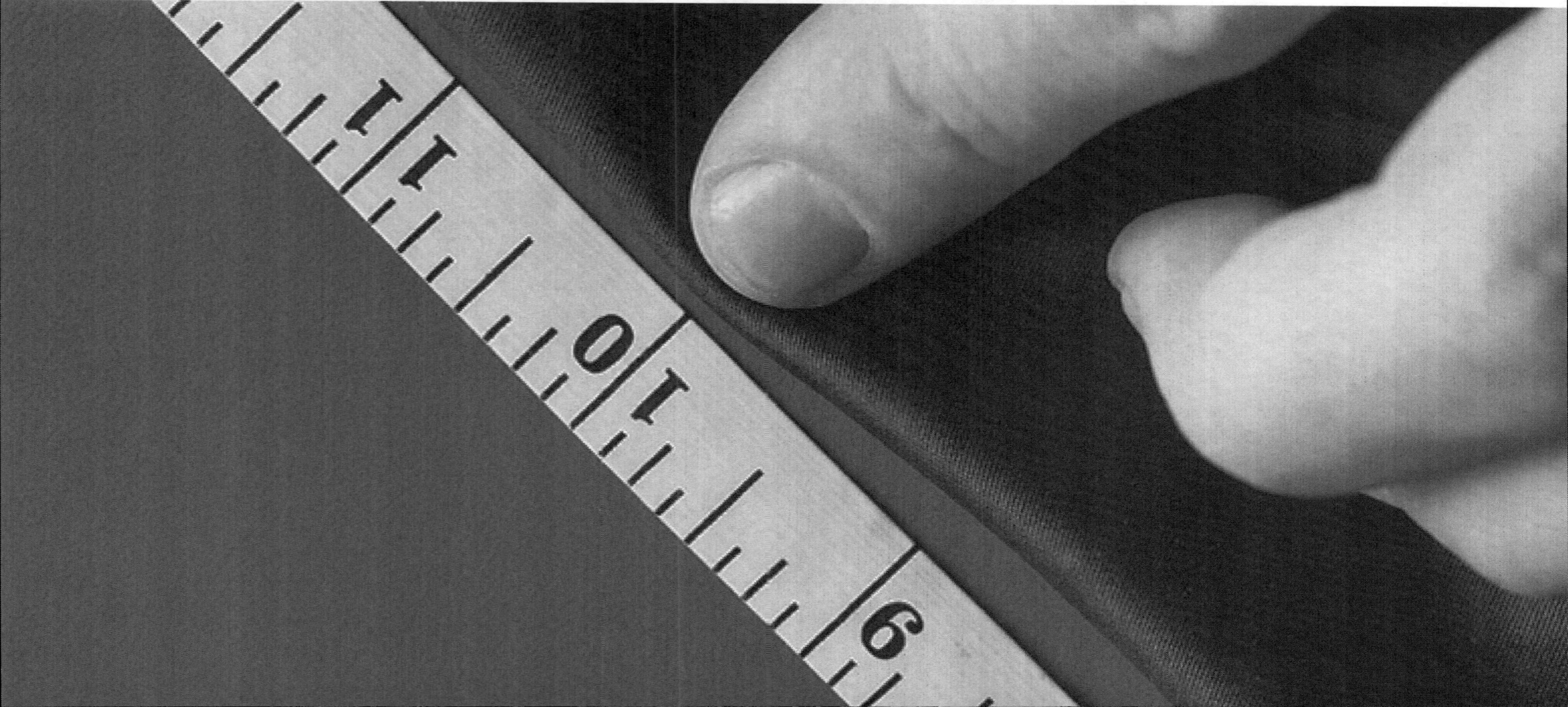

MEASUREMENT AND GEOMETRY

Table of Correlations			
	Specific Expectation	**Practice Questions**	**Unit Test Questions**
MG1.01	*determine the maximum area of a rectangle with a given perimeter by constructing a variety of rectangles, using a variety of tools, and by examining various values of the area as the side lengths change and the perimeter remains constant*	1, 2, 3, 4	1, 2
MG1.02	*determine the minimum perimeter of a rectangle with a given area by constructing a variety of rectangles, using a variety of tools, and by examining various values of the side lengths and the perimeter as the area stays constant*	5, 6, 7	3
MG1.03	*solve problems that require maximizing the area of a rectangle for a fixed perimeter or minimizing the perimeter of a rectangle for a fixed area*	8, 9, 10, 11	4, 5, 6
MG2.01	*relate the geometric representation of the Pythagorean theorem to the algebraic representation* $a^2 + b^2 = c^2$	12, 13, 14	7, 8, 9
MG2.02	*solve problems using the Pythagorean theorem, as required in applications*	15, 16, 17, 18, 19, 20	10
MG2.03	*solve problems involving the areas and perimeters of composite two-dimensional shapes (i.e., combinations of rectangles, triangles, parallelograms, trapezoids, and circles)*	21, 22, 23, 24, OR1	11, 12
MG2.04	*develop, through investigation, the formulas for the volume of a pyramid, a cone, and a sphere*	25, 26	14
MG2.05	*solve problems involving the volumes of prisms, pyramids, cylinders, cones, and spheres*	27, 28, 29, 30	13, 15, 16
MG3.01	*determine, through investigation using a variety of tools, and describe the properties and relationships of the interior and exterior angles of triangles, quadrilaterals, and other polygons, and apply the results to problems involving the angles of polygons*	31, 32, 33, NR1	17, 18
MG3.02	*determine, through investigation using a variety of tools, and describe the properties and relationships of the angles formed by parallel lines cut by a transversal, and apply the results to problems involving parallel lines*	34, 35, 36, 37, OR2	19, 20, OR2
MG3.03	*create an original dynamic sketch, paper-folding design, or other illustration that incorporates some of the geometric properties from this section, or find and report on some real-life application(s) of the geometric properties*	38, 39	

MEASUREMENT AND GEOMETRY

MG1.01 determine the maximum area of a rectangle with a given perimeter by constructing a variety of rectangles, using a variety of tools, and by examining various values of the area as the side lengths change and the perimeter remains constant

FINDING MAXIMUM AREA GIVEN THE PERIMETER

Different rectangles with equal perimeters can enclose different areas. By constructing a variety of rectangles with the same perimeter, you can identify the shape with the maximum possible area.

Example

Examine various rectangles with fixed perimeters of 320 m, and determine their respective areas.

Rectangle 1

$w = 40$ m

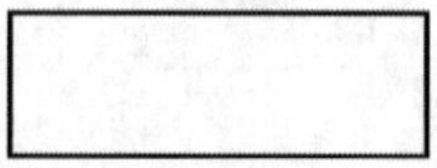

$l = 120$ m

$A_1 = 40 \times 120$

$A_1 = 4\ 800\ \text{m}^2$

Rectangle 2

$w = 60$ m

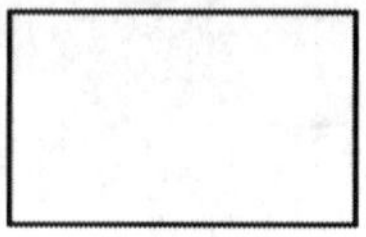

$l = 100$ m

$A_2 = 60 \times 100$

$A_2 = 6\ 000\ \text{m}^2$

Rectangle 3

$w = 80$ m

$l = 80$ m

$A_3 = 80 \times 80$

$A_3 = 6\ 400\ \text{m}^2$

Observe that Rectangle 3 has the maximum possible area. Notice that the maximum possible area of 6 400 m^2 occurs when the width and length of the rectangle are equal. When the rectangle is a square, the maximum area is formed.

In general:

The maximum area of a rectangle with a fixed perimeter, *P*, occurs when

$$w = l = \frac{\text{perimeter}}{4} = \frac{P}{4}$$

The value of this maximum area, *A*, is

$A = (l)(w)$

You can use these formulas to verify the observations made in the above example. The maximum area of the rectangle occurs when the width, *w*, equals the length, *l*.

Therefore, since $w = l = \dfrac{320\ \text{m}}{4} = 80\ \text{m}$,

the dimensions of the rectangle with a maximum area are 80 m by 80 m. Likewise, the maximum area, *A*, of the rectangle with a fixed perimeter, $P = 320$ m, occurs when

$A = (l)(w) = (80)(80) = 6\ 400\ \text{m}^2$.

PRACTICE QUESTIONS

1. Which of the following dimensions will give the maximum area of a rectangle with a perimeter of 100 cm?

   A. 10 cm× 5 cm

   B. 25 cm × 25 cm

   C. 25 cm × 2 cm

   D. 25 cm × 4 cm

2. If the perimeter of a sandbox is 20 m then what is the maximum area the sandbox could have?

A. 20 m^2 **B.** 25 m^2

C. 100 m^2 **D.** 400 m^2

Use the following information to answer the next question.

James drew the rectangle shown.

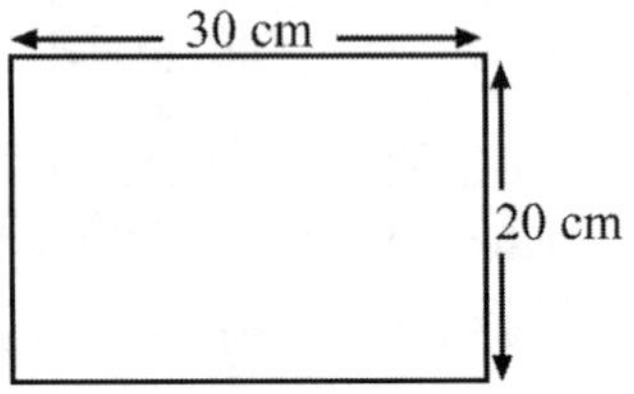

3. Which of the following expressions describes the maximum area of a different rectangle with the same perimeter as the rectangle shown?

A. $\left(\dfrac{50 \text{ m}}{4}\right)\left(\dfrac{50 \text{ m}}{4}\right)$

B. $\left(\dfrac{60 \text{ m}}{4}\right)\left(\dfrac{60 \text{ m}}{4}\right)$

C. $\left(\dfrac{100 \text{ m}}{4}\right)\left(\dfrac{100 \text{ m}}{4}\right)$

D. $\left(\dfrac{100 \text{ m}}{16}\right)\left(\dfrac{100 \text{ m}}{16}\right)$

4. A rectangle has a length, *l*, of 20 m and a width, *w*, of 10 m. If the perimeter remains fixed, which of the following expressions involving the original dimensions creates a rectangle with a maximum area?

A. $l-5$ and $w+5$

B. $l+5$ and $w-5$

C. $\dfrac{l}{2}$ and 2w

D. $\dfrac{l}{2}$ and $\dfrac{w}{2}$

MG1.02 determine the minimum perimeter of a rectangle with a given area by constructing a variety of rectangles, using a variety of tools, and by examining various values of the side lengths and the perimeter as the area stays constant

FINDING MINIMUM PERIMETER GIVEN THE AREA

Rectangle 1

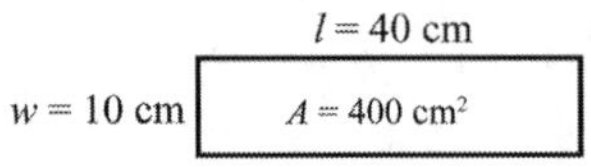

$$\begin{aligned} P_1 &= 2(l+w) \\ &= 2(40+10) \\ &= 2(50) \\ &= 100 \text{ cm} \end{aligned}$$

Rectangle 2

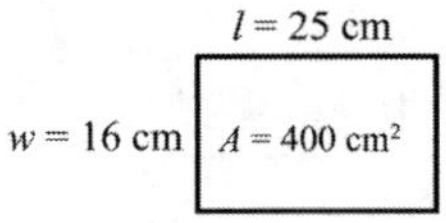

$$\begin{aligned} P_2 &= 2(l+w) \\ &= 2(25+16) \\ &= 2(41) \\ &= 82 \text{ cm} \end{aligned}$$

Rectangle 3

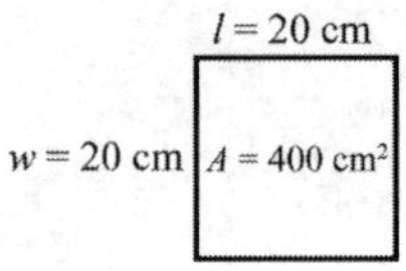

$$\begin{aligned} P_3 &= 2(l+w) \\ &= 2(20+20) \\ &= 2(40) \\ &= 80 \text{ cm} \end{aligned}$$

Different rectangles with the same area will have different values for their respective perimeters. By constructing a variety of rectangles with the same area, you can identify the shape with the minimum perimeter.

Example

Examine rectangles with a fixed area of $400\ \text{cm}^2$, and determine their respective perimeters.

Observe that Rectangle 3 has the minimum possible perimeter. Notice that the minimum possible perimeter of 80 cm occurs when the width and length of the rectangle are equal. When the rectangle is a square, the minimum perimeter is formed.

In general:

The minimum perimeter of a rectangle with a fixed area, A, occurs when $w = l = \sqrt{\text{area}} = \sqrt{A}$

The value of this minimum perimeter, P, is $P = 2(l + w)$.

You can use the formulas to verify the observations made in the above example.
For the fixed area $A = 400\ \text{cm}^2$, the minimum perimeter of the rectangle occurs when the width, w, and the length, l, are equal; therefore, since $w = l = \sqrt{400\ \text{cm}^2} = 20\ \text{cm}$, the dimensions of the rectangle with a minimum perimeter are 20 cm by 20 cm. Likewise, the value of the minimum perimeter, P, of the rectangle with an area $A = 400\ \text{cm}^2$ occurs when $P = 2(l + w) = 2(20 + 20) = 2(40) = 80\ \text{cm}$.

Practice Questions

CHALLENGER QUESTION

Two rectangles have the same area of $144\ \text{cm}^2$ as shown below. The measure of one side is given for each rectangle. The rectangles are not drawn to scale.

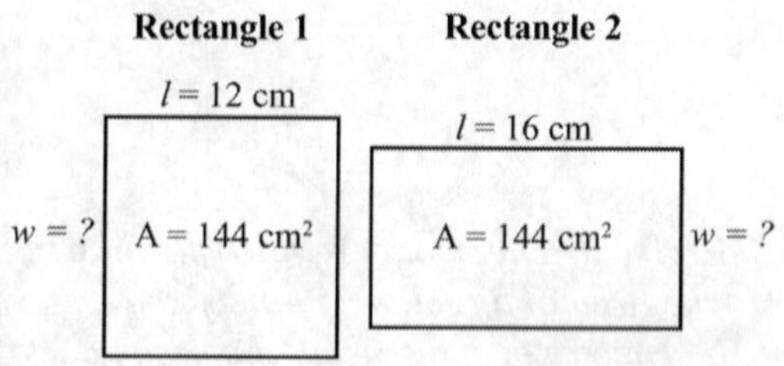

5. Which of the following statements regarding the perimeter and area of the rectangles is correct?

A. Rectangle 1 has a greater perimeter than Rectangle 2.

B. Rectangle 1 and Rectangle 2 have the same perimeter.

C. After calculating w, Rectangle 1 has the minimum perimeter for a rectangle with an area of $144\ \text{cm}^2$.

D. After calculating w, Rectangle 2 has the minimum perimeter for a rectangle with an area of $144\ \text{cm}^2$.

6. A rectangle has an area of $200\ \text{cm}^2$. To the nearest tenth, the minimum perimeter of the rectangle is

A. 14.1 cm

B. 28.2 cm

C. 56.6 cm

D. 100.0 cm

7. The perimeter of a rectangle is P. If P remains fixed, then which of the following formulas produces the correct length, l, to form a rectangle with a maximum area?

A. $l = P^2$

B. $l = \sqrt{P}$

C. $l = \frac{P}{2}$

D. $l = \frac{P}{4}$

MG1.03 solve problems that require maximizing the area of a rectangle for a fixed perimeter or minimizing the perimeter of a rectangle for a fixed area

MAXIMIZING AREA AND MINIMIZING PERIMETER

You can use the formulas discussed in the previous two lessons to determine the maximum area or minimum perimeter of a rectangular region divided into one or more sections having one length and multiple width designations. To clarify the meaning of the perimeter of the rectangular region, P, since it excludes one length, the perimeter refers to the amount of fencing needed.

MAXIMIZING AREA FOR A GIVEN AMOUNT OF FENCING

The maximum enclosed area, A, of a rectangular region divided into one or more sections, given a fixed amount of fencing, occurs when the length is equal to the number of sections multiplied by the width.

This process could be applied to rectangular regions with identical areas placed side by side against a fixed length.

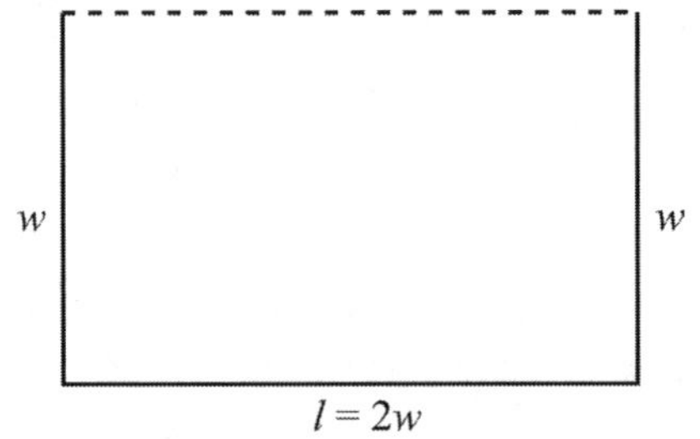

For a rectangular region, given a fixed amount of fencing for one length, l, and two widths, w, $l = 2w$.

Let P = the fencing for the one length and the two widths.

$P = 2(w) + l$, and since $l = 2w$,

$P = 2w + 2w$
$P = 4w$

Therefore, $w = \frac{P}{4}$

The maximum area, A, is $A = (l)(w)$, and since $l = 2w$, $A = (2w)(w)$.

Example

Mrs. Davies has purchased 40 m of fencing. She wants to use the fencing to enclose a rectangular garden. One side of the garden, which is bordered by her house, requires no fencing. She also wants to divide the rectangular garden into three sections, as illustrated in the diagram below.

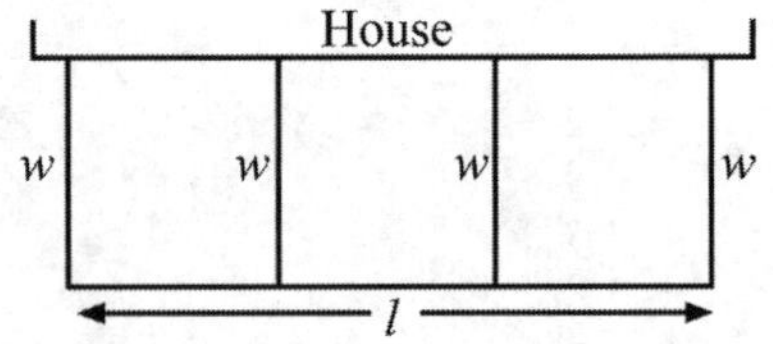

If the fencing required for the garden is 40 m what are the dimensions of the garden producing the maximum possible area? What is the maximum possible area of Mrs. Davies' garden?

Solution

The maximum area of a rectangular region with three sections requiring fencing for one length and four sections of equal width occurs when $l = 4w$.

The dimensions needed to maximize the area of the rectangular region divided into three sections are 20 m by 5 m. The maximum area is $A = (l)(w) = (20)(5) = 100\text{ m}^2$.

Minimizing the Amount of Fencing for Given Areas

The minimum amount of fencing, *P*, required for a fixed area, *A*, of a rectangular region divided into one or more sections occurs when the length is equal to the number of sections multiplied by the width.

For a rectangular region given a fixed area requiring fencing for one length and three sections of equal width, $l = 3w$

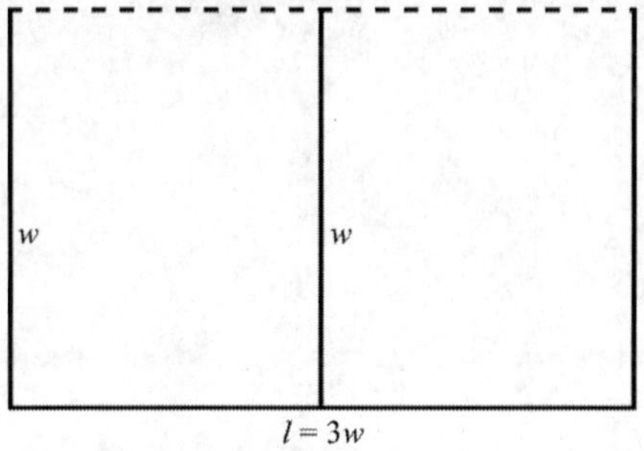

Let A = the fixed area

$A = (l)(w)$, and since $l = 3w$

$A = (3w)(w)$

$A = 3w^2$

Therefore, $w^2 = \frac{A}{3}$ **or** $w = \sqrt{\frac{A}{3}}$

The minimum amount of fencing, *P*, required for one length, *l*, and three sections of width, *w*, is $P = 3w + l$, and since $l = 3w$,

$P = 3w + 3w = 6w.$

Example

A rectangular playground next to a school is to be fenced. Fencing is required for one length and two widths. No fencing is required along the side of the school, as illustrated below.

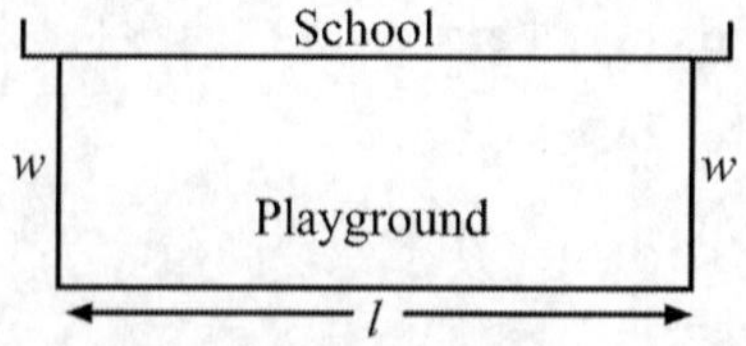

If the area of the playground is 200 m², then what are the dimensions of the playground requiring the minimum amount of fencing? What is the minimum amount of fencing?

For the rectangular region, the minimum amount of fencing, *P*, required for one length, *l*, and two widths, *w*, occurs when $l = 2w$.

Let A = the fixed area

$A = (l)(w)$, and since $l = 2w$

$A = (2w)(w)$

$A = 2w^2$

Therefore, $w^2 = \frac{A}{2}$ $\quad w = \sqrt{\frac{A}{2}}$

Substitute 200 for *A*.

$w = \sqrt{\frac{200}{2}}$

$w = \sqrt{100}$

$w = 10\text{ m}$

Substitute 10 for *w*

$l = 2w$

$l = 2(10)$

$l = 20\text{ m}$

The dimensions of the rectangular playground creating the minimum amount of fencing are

20 m by 10 m.

The minimum amount of fencing required for one length and two widths of the playground is $P = 2w + l = 2(10) + 20 = 40\text{ m}$.

Practice Questions

8. A picture frame has an area of 100 cm^2 with a minimum perimeter. What are the dimensions of the frame?

A. 10 cm × 10 cm

B. 25 cm × 4 cm

C. 20 cm × 5 cm

D. 50 cm × 2 cm

Use the following information to answer the next question.

The promoters of a rock concert want to fence off a rectangular area directly in front of the stage for a VIP section. They plan on using 16 m of fencing, including the gate.
The fencing is to be used for all sides of the VIP area except for the side bordering the stage.

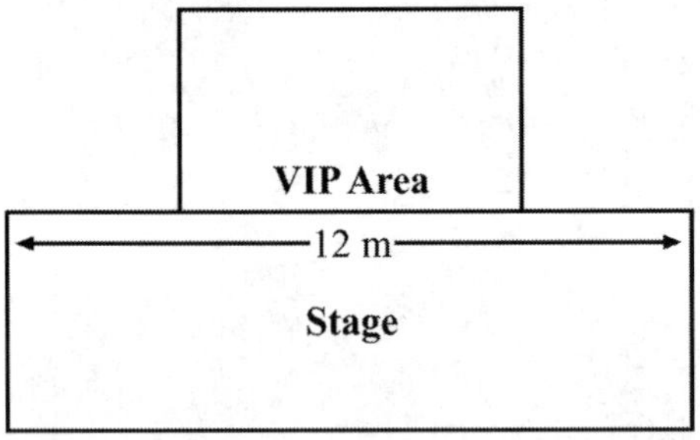

9. If the length of the stage is 12 m, what is the maximum area that can be fenced off using 16 m of fencing?

A. 16 m^2

B. 32 m^2

C. 48 m^2

D. 60 m^2

Use the following information to answer the next question

A rectangular field is to be fenced off against one side of a school as illustrated

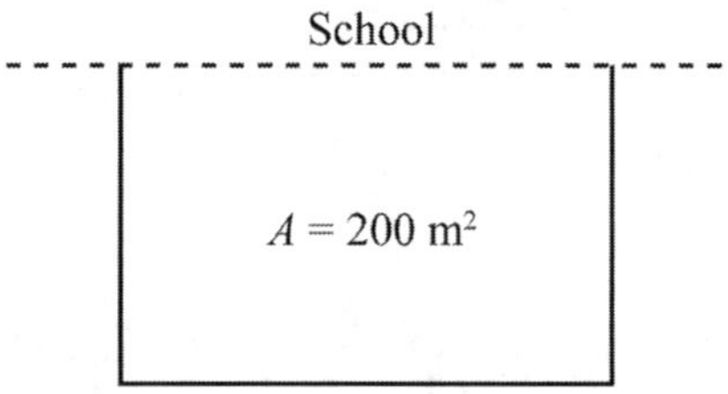

10. The cost of labour and materials to construct the three sides of the fence is \$30/m. If the area of the rectangular field must be 200 m^2, then the minimum cost of building the fence is

A. \$900

B. \$1 200

C. \$3 000

D. \$6 000

CHALLENGER QUESTION

In an art museum, Roxanne and Damian are asked to build a rectangular barrier dividing the museum into several sections around three famous artifacts. The barrier material will only be used for the length of the barrier and the widths of the sections of the barrier. The wall of the art museum is to be used as one side of the barrier, and the area of the rectangular enclosure must be 900 m^2. Their planned rectangular barriers with the divided sections are shown below.

Roxanne

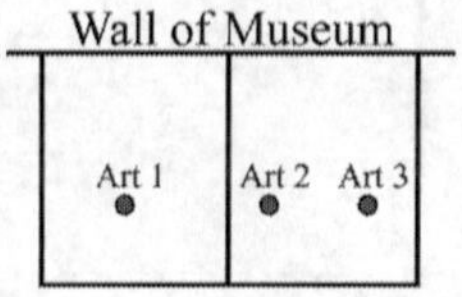

Damian

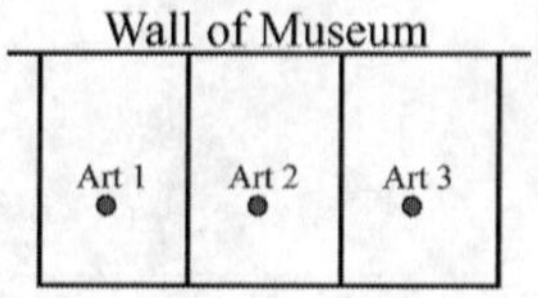

11. If both Roxanne and Damian use the minimum amount of barrier material for their 900 m^2 enclosure, which of the following statements is true?

A. Roxanne uses 5.7 m more barrier material than Damian.

B. Damian uses 5.7 m more barrier material than Roxanne.

C. Roxanne uses 16.1 m more barrier material than Damian.

D. Damian uses 16.1 m more barrier material than Roxanne.

MG2.01 relate the geometric representation of the Pythagorean theorem to the algebraic representation $a^2 + b^2 = c^2$

UNDERSTANDING THE PYTHAGOREAN THEOREM

The Pythagorean theorem states that for any right triangle, the area of the square formed on the longest side is equal to the sum of the areas of the squares formed on the other two sides. The following diagram shows the geometric representation of the Pythagorean theorem.

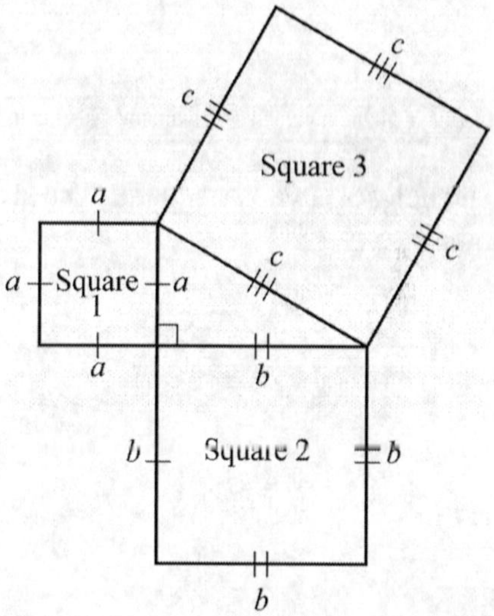

The area of a square is given by the formula $A = s^2$, where s is the length of a side of the square. In the above diagram, the area of Square 1 is a^2, the area of Square 2 is b^2, and the area of Square 3 is c^2. According to the Pythagorean theorem, the area of Square 3 is equal to the sum of the areas of squares 1 and 2.

$$a^2 + b^2 = c^2 \quad \text{or} \quad c^2 = a^2 + b^2$$

In the above diagram, side c is called the **hypotenuse** of the right triangle, since it is the longest side of the triangle and is opposite to the right angle. The square of the length of the hypotenuse (c) equals the sum of the squares of the lengths of the other two sides (a and b).

Example

Show that Area 1 + Area 2 = Area 3 when $a = 3$, $b = 4$, and $c = 5$.

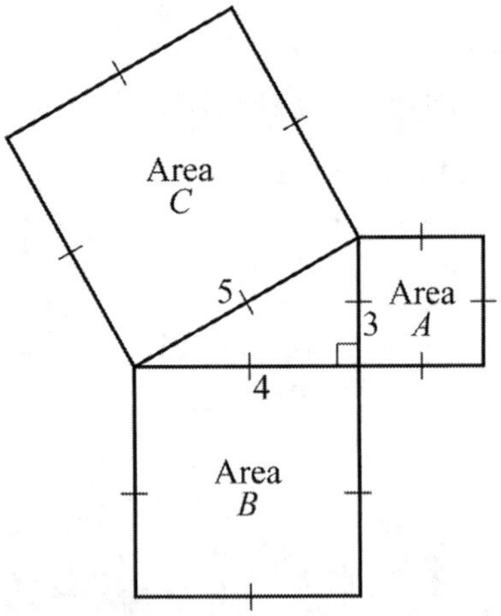

Each enclosed area is a square. The area of a square is $A = s^2$.

$$\begin{aligned}\text{Area } A &= s^2\\ &= 3^2\\ &= 9\end{aligned}$$

$$\begin{aligned}\text{Area } B &= s^2\\ &= 4^2\\ &= 16\end{aligned}$$

$$\begin{aligned}\text{Area } C &= s^2\\ &= 5^2\\ &= 25\end{aligned}$$

Thus, $a^2 + b^2 = c^2$

$$\begin{aligned}9 + 16 &= 25\\ 25 &= 25\end{aligned}$$

This equality shows that:
Area *A* + Area *B* = Area *C*.

PRACTICE QUESTIONS

Use the following information to answer the next question.

Rico draws a right triangle and then draws a square on each of its sides, as shown.

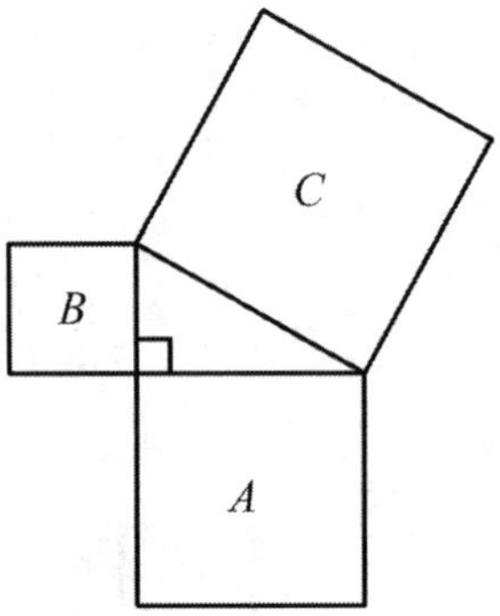

12. If square *B* has an area of 9 cm^2 and square *A* has an area of 16 cm^2, what is the area of square *C*?

A. 9 cm^2

B. 16 cm^2

C. 25 cm^2

D. 32 cm^2

CHALLENGER QUESTION

The area of square *A* is 36 cm^2, and the area of square *B* is 64 cm^2. What is the length of side *c* in square *C*?

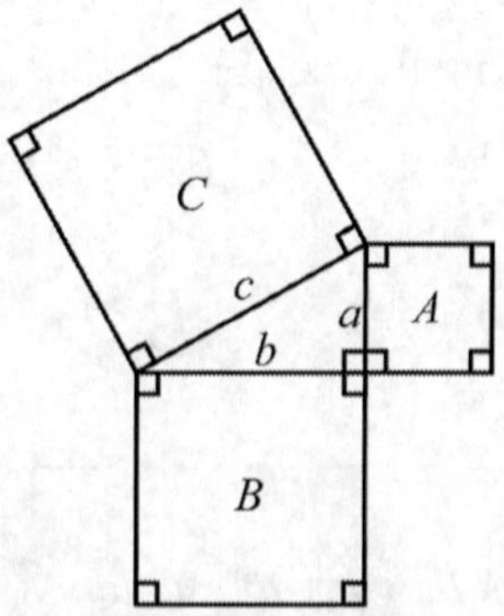

13. What is the length of side *c* in square *C*?

A. 100 cm

B. 28 cm

C. 14 cm

D. 10 cm

Use the following information to answer the next question.

This isosceles right triangle has two equal sides, both labelled *x*, and a hypotenuse of 20 cm.

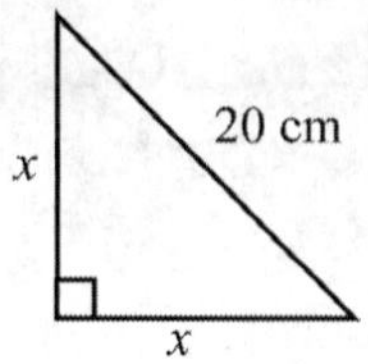

14. The value of *x* is determined by which of the following expressions?

A. $\sqrt{400}$

B. $\sqrt{20}$

C. $\sqrt{\frac{400}{2}}$

D. $\sqrt{\frac{20}{2}}$

MG2.02 solve problems using the Pythagorean theorem, as required in applications

Applying the Pythagorean Theorem to Solve Problems

The Pythagorean theorem, $a^2 + b^2 = c^2$ or $c^2 = a^2 + b^2$, can be used to solve for a missing side length of a right triangle when the measures of the other two sides are known. Remember that *c* is the length of the hypotenuse, and *a* and *b* are the lengths of the other two sides.

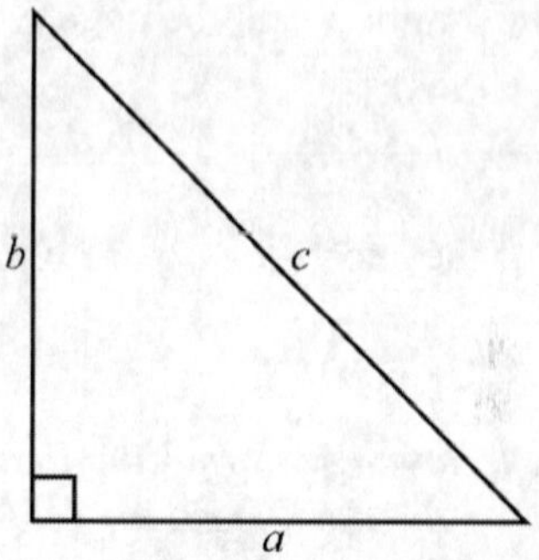

Example

If the length of the two shorter sides of a right triangle are $a = 5$ cm and $b = 5$ cm what is the length of the hypotenuse, *c*, to the nearest hundredth of a centimetre?

Solution

$c^2 = a^2 + b^2$
$c^2 = 5^2 + 5^2$
$c^2 = 25 + 25$
$c^2 = 50$
$c = \pm\sqrt{50}$,

but since the length cannot be negative, $-\sqrt{50}$ is discarded;
Therefore, $c = +\sqrt{50}$ or $\sqrt{50} \approx 7.07$

The length of the hypotenuse is 7.07 cm

Example

If the length of one of the shorter sides is $a = 6$ cm and the length of the hypotenuse is $c = 9$ cm, what is the length of the other short side, b, to the nearest hundredth centimetre?

$$a^2 + b^2 = c^2$$
$$6^2 + b^2 = 9^2$$
$$36 + b^2 = 81$$
$$36 - 36 + b^2 = 81 - 36$$
$$b^2 = 45$$
$$b = \pm\sqrt{45}$$

But since the length cannot be negative, $-\sqrt{45}$ is discarded;

Therefore, $b = \sqrt{45} \approx 6.71$.

The length of the short side is 6.71 cm

PRACTICE QUESTIONS

Use the following information to answer the next question.

A ladder is 4.70 m long and reaches a height of 4.40 m on a wall as illustrated.

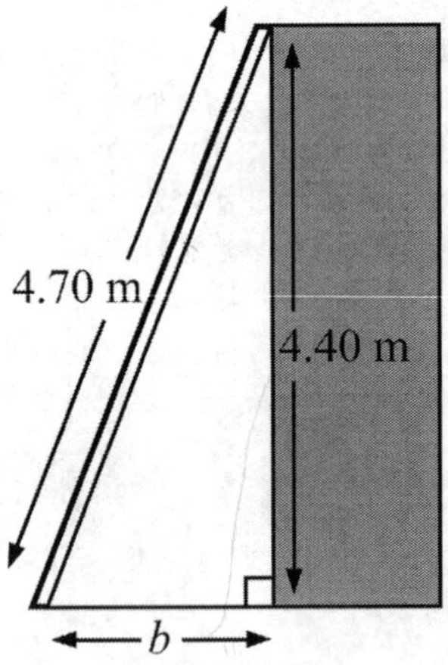

15. To the nearest hundredth, how far is the foot of the ladder from the base of the wall?

A. 0.30 m

B. 1.65 m

C. 2.73 m

D. 6.44 m

CHALLENGER QUESTION

16. Jean, Fritz, and Colin are playing catch. Fritz is standing 20 m directly in front of Jean, and Colin is standing 15 m directly to Jean's right. To the nearest tenth, how far is Fritz from Colin?

A. 5.0 m

B. 13.2 m

C. 25.0 m

D. 35.0 m

Use the following information to answer the next question.

A right circular cone with a base diameter of 20 cm and a slant length of 24 cm is shown.

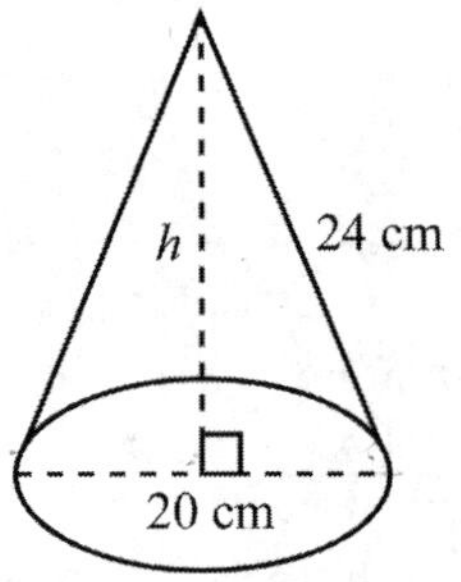

17. To the nearest tenth, what is the height, h, of the cone?

A. 13.2 cm

B. 14.0 cm

C. 21.8 cm

D. 31.2 cm

Use the following information to answer the next question.

Jill is flying a kite. She is holding the end of the kite string 1 m above the ground, and she has let out 126 m of string. Becky is standing directly below the kite, 54 m away from Jill, as shown in the diagram.

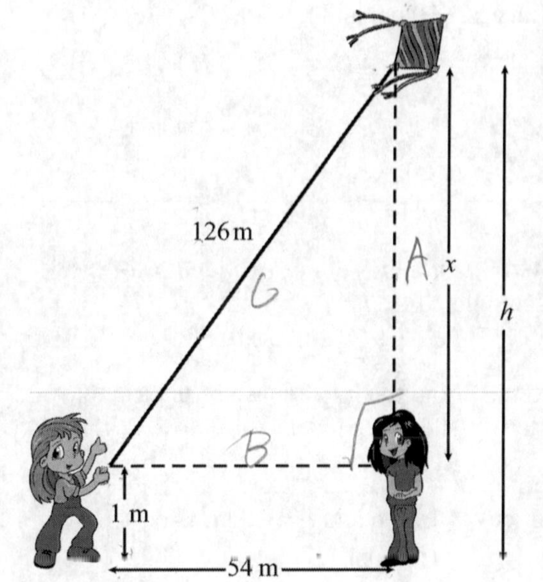

18. To the nearest tenth, the height, h, of the kite above the ground is

A. 113.8 m

B. 114.8 m

C. 137.1 m

D. 138.1 m

Use the following information to answer the next question.

A trapezoid with the following dimensions is given.

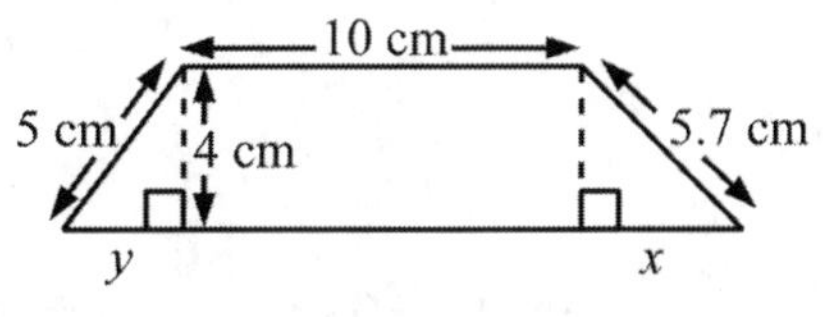

l is the base of the trapezoid.

19. What is the length, l, to the nearest hundredth?

A. 13.36 cm

B. 16.00 cm

C. 17.06 cm

D. 23.36 cm

20. A shorter side of a right triangle has a length of 4 cm. If the hypotenuse is two times the length of this shorter side, which of the following equations solves for the length of the other missing side, x?

A. $x = \sqrt{8 - 4}$

B. $x = \sqrt{16 - 4}$

C. $x = \sqrt{32 - 16}$

D. $x = \sqrt{64 - 16}$

MG2.03 solve problems involving the areas and perimeters of composite two-dimensional shapes (i.e., combinations of rectangles, triangles, parallelograms, trapezoids, and circles)

CALCULATING AREA AND PERIMETER OF A COMPOSITE 2-D SHAPE

A **composite two-dimensional** shape consists of any number of two-dimensional shapes connected with each other in some way.

CALCULATING THE PERIMETER OF A COMPOSITE 2-D SHAPE

The perimeter of a 2-D shape is the distance around it. The perimeter, P, of any polygon can be expressed in terms of the sum of all its sides, s:

$$P = s_1 + s_2 + s_3 + s_4 + s_5 + s_6$$

For circles, the perimeter is referred to as the **circumference** (C). The circumference of a circle can be calculated using the diameter (d) or the radius (r).

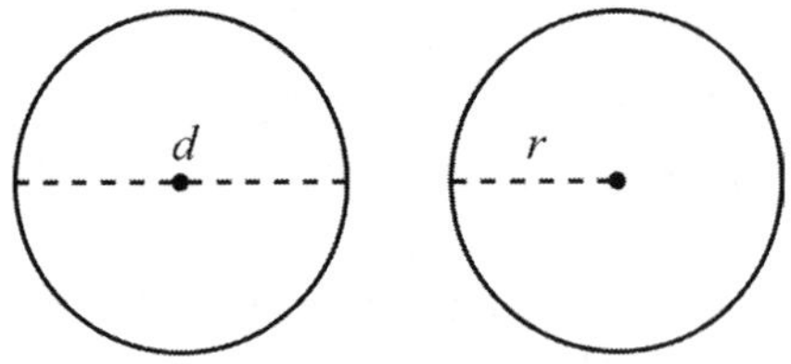

$C = \pi d$ $\quad$ $C = 2\pi r$

Note: The **diameter**, d, is equal to two times the length of the radius, r; thus, $d = 2r$.
The constant π is an irrational number with an approximate value of 3.141592654.

When calculating the perimeter of a composite 2-D shape, divide the shape into its smaller pieces, and then determine the perimeter of the smaller pieces, using the appropriate formulas. Ignore the lengths of the adjoining sides. Finally, add these values together to get the perimeter of the complete 2-D composite shape.

CALCULATING THE AREA OF A COMPOSITE 2-D SHAPE

The area of a 2-D shape is the number of square units contained in the shape. When calculating the area of a composite 2-D shape, divide the shape into its smaller pieces, and then determine the area of the smaller pieces using the appropriate formulas. Finally, add these values together to get the area of the composite 2-D shape.

Example

To the nearest hundredth of a centimetre, what is the perimeter of the 2-D shape below? What is the area to the nearest hundredth of a square centimetre?

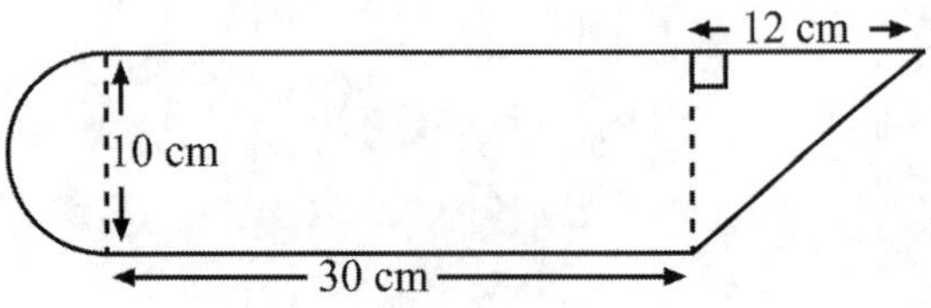

Perimeter

Step 1: Find the perimeter of semicircle.

The perimeter of the semicircle is one-half the circumference of a circle.

$$P_{\text{semicircle}} = \frac{C_{\text{circle}}}{2} = \frac{2\pi r}{2} = \pi r$$

Since $d = 10$ cm and $d = 2r$,

$$r = \frac{10}{2} = 5 \text{ cm.}$$

$$\begin{aligned} P_{\text{semicircle}} &= \pi r \\ &= \pi(5) \\ &\approx 15.71 \text{ cm} \end{aligned}$$

Step 2: Find the sum of two lengths of the rectangle. Since $l = 30$ cm, then

$$l + l = 2l = 3(30) = 60 \text{ cm}$$

Step 3: Find the hypotenuse of the triangle and add it to the given side.

$$c^2 = a^2 + b^2$$

Since $a = 10$ cm and $b = 12$ cm, then

$$\begin{aligned} c^2 &= 10^2 + 12^2 \\ c^2 &= 100 + 144 \\ c^2 &= 244 \\ c &= \sqrt{244} \\ &\approx 15.62 \end{aligned}$$

The sum of the sides: $15.62 + 12 = 27.62$ cm.

Step 4: Find the perimeter of the composite shape by adding sides together.

$$\begin{aligned} P_{\text{total}} &= 15.71 + 60 + 27.62 \\ &= 103.33 \text{ cm} \end{aligned}$$

The perimeter of the composite shape is 103.33 cm.

Area

Step 1: Find the area of the semicircle.

The area of the semicircle is one-half the area of a circle.

$$A_{\text{semicircle}} = \frac{A_{\text{circle}}}{2} = \frac{\pi r^2}{2} \text{ or } \frac{1}{2}\pi r^2$$

Since $d = 10$ cm and $d = 2r$, $r = \frac{10}{2} = 5$ cm.

$$\begin{aligned} A_{\text{semicircle}} &= \frac{1}{2}\pi r^2 \\ &= \frac{1}{2}\pi(5)^2 \\ &= \frac{1}{2}\pi(5)(5) \\ &\approx 39.27 \text{ cm}^2 \end{aligned}$$

Step 2
Find the area of the rectangle.

$A_{\text{rectangle}} = (l)(w)$

Since $l = 30$ cm and $w = 10$ cm, then

$A_{\text{rectangle}} = (30)(10) = 300 \text{ cm}^2$

Step 3
Find the area of the triangle.

$A_{\text{triangle}} = \frac{1}{2}bh$

Since the base $b = 12$ cm
and the height $h = 10$ cm, then

$A_{\text{triangle}} = \frac{1}{2}(12)(10) = 60 \text{ cm}^2$

Step 4
Find the area of the composite shape by adding all the areas together.

$$\begin{aligned} A_{\text{total}} &= 39.27 + 300 + 60 \\ &= 399.27 \text{ cm}^2 \end{aligned}$$

The area of the composite shape is 399.27 cm^{20}.

PRACTICE QUESTIONS

Use the following information to answer the next two questions.

The original shape of a park is that of an isosceles trapezoid. The park is to be altered by attaching a square section to its shortest side, as shown below.

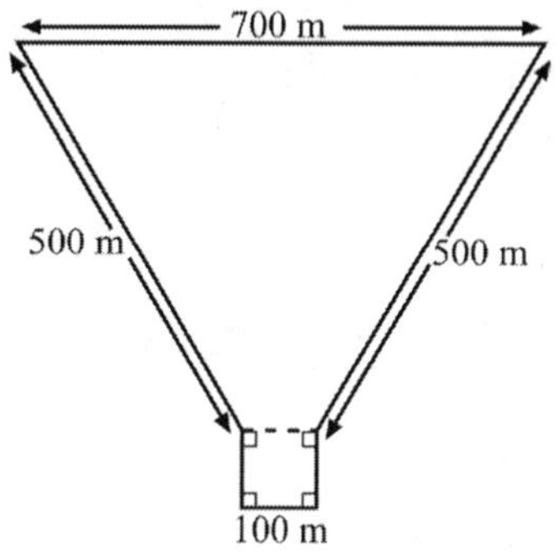

21. If a fence is to be placed all along the outside of the altered park, how much fencing is required?

A. 1 800 m
B. 1 900 m
C. 2 000 m
D. 2 100 m

22. If the altered park is to be fully sodded with grass, how much sod will be required?

A. 130 000 m^2
B. 160 000 m^2
C. 170 000 m^2
D. 210 000 m^2

CHALLENGER QUESTION

The front of a t-shirt with particular dimensions is shown. The neck of the shirt is a semicircle with a diameter of 20 cm.

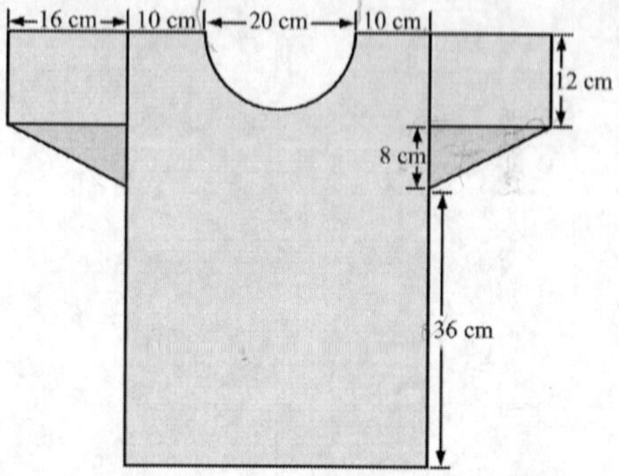

23. To the nearest whole number, what is the total surface area of the front of the t-shirt?

A. 2 083 cm^2
B. 2 339 cm^2
C. 2 438 cm^2
D. 2 595 cm^2

Use the following information to answer the next question.

A composite shape is made up of a square and a semicircle, as shown.

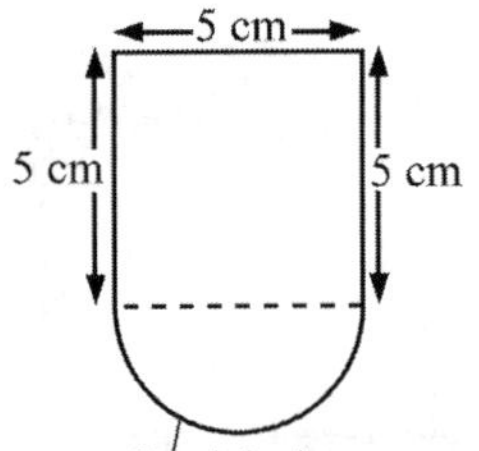

24. Which of the following expressions describes the perimeter of this shape?

A. $3(5)+\pi(5)$

B. $3(5)+\dfrac{\pi(2.5)^2}{2}$

C. $3(5)+\dfrac{\pi(2.5)}{2}$

D. $3(5)+\pi(2.5)$

Open Response

1. Mr. and Mrs. Glover want to build a deck against their house having a maximum area that will require a railing of 12 m to go around its two widths and one length. They also want to have a flower bed area against a different side of their house with the particular dimensions as shown in the below.

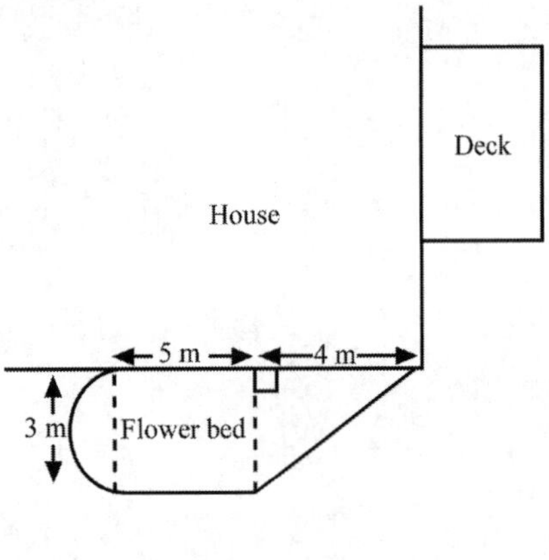

a) Determine the maximum area for the deck requiring 12 m of railing.

b) If the flower bed is made up of three shapes, a semicircle, a rectangle, and a triangle, then find its total area.

c) Find the length of edging needed to form a border around the outside edge of the flower bed. Record your answer to the nearest tenth.

MG2.04 develop, through investigation, the formulas for the volume of a pyramid, a cone, and a sphere

DETERMINING THE VOLUME OF A PYRAMID, CONE, AND SPHERE

You can investigate the relationship between a cylinder and a cone, a prism and a cylinder, and a cylinder and a sphere by carrying out three simple activities.

RELATING THE VOLUME OF A CYLINDER TO THE VOLUME OF A CONE

To show the relationship between a cylinder and a cone, make a conical paper cup with a height of h (e.g., 10 cm) and a radius of r (e.g., 3 cm) and a cylindrical paper cup with the same height of h and radius of r, as shown below.

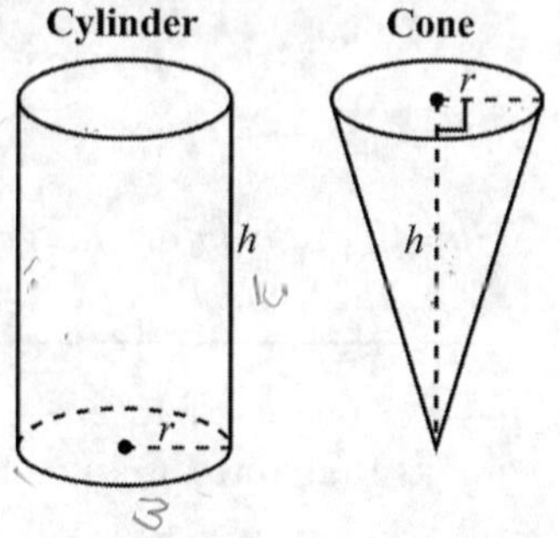

If you were to fill the cone to the top with sand or water and then pour it into the cylinder, you would find that the cylinder would be one-third full. In other words, it would take three cones of sand or water to fill the cylinder. The volume of a cylinder is three times the volume of a cone.

$$3 \times V_{\text{cone}} = V_{\text{cylinder}}$$
$$3 \times V_{\text{cone}} = (\text{area of base})(\text{height})$$
$$3 \times V_{\text{cone}} = (\pi r^2)(h)$$
$$V_{\text{cone}} = \frac{(\pi r^2)(h)}{3}$$
$$V_{\text{cone}} = \frac{1}{3}\pi r^2 h$$

Note: The formulas given above and the other formulas used in this section can be found at the back of your book on the formula sheet.

RELATING THE VOLUME OF A PRISM TO THE VOLUME OF A PYRAMID

A similar relation exists between a prism and a pyramid with the same base areas and heights.

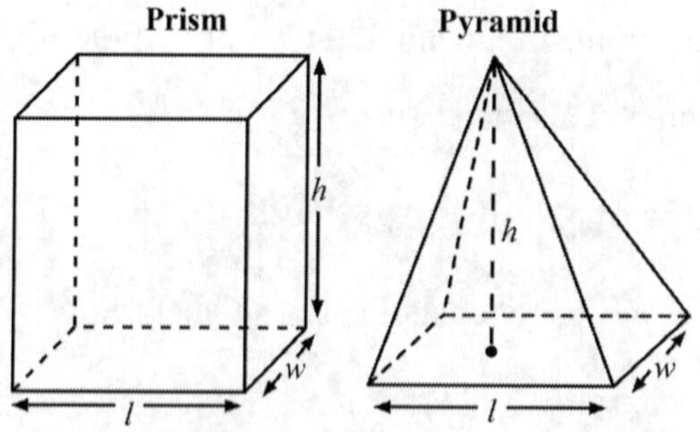

The volume of a prism is three times the volume of a pyramid.

$$3 \times V_{\text{pyramid}} = V_{\text{prism}}$$
$$3 \times V_{\text{pyramid}} = (\text{area of base})(\text{height})$$
$$3 \times V_{\text{pyramid}} = lwh$$
$$V_{\text{pyramid}} = \frac{lwh}{3}$$
$$V_{\text{pyramid}} = \frac{1}{3}(lwh)$$

RELATING THE VOLUME OF A CYLINDER TO THE VOLUME OF A SPHERE

A similar relation also exists between a cylinder with radius r and height $2r$ and a sphere with the same radius. You could put the sphere inside the cylinder, fill the cylinder with water, then remove the sphere and examine the amount of water remaining.

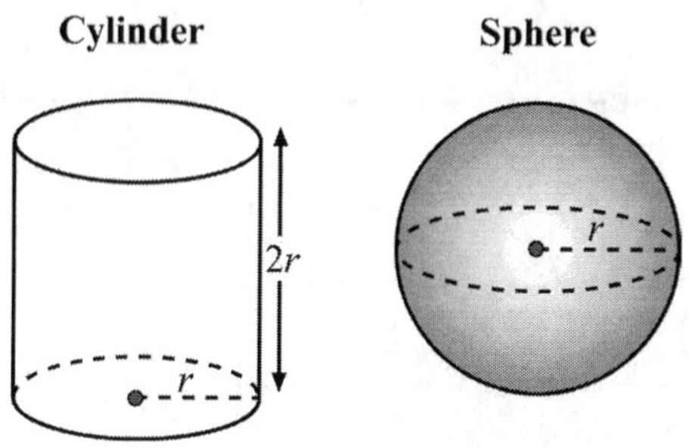

You would find that there would be two-thirds of the cylinder of water left. This indicates that it takes $1\frac{1}{2}$ or $\frac{3}{2}$ spheres to fill the cylinder.

The volume of a cylinder is $1\frac{1}{2}$ or $\frac{3}{2}$ times the volume of a sphere.

$$\frac{3}{2}\times V_{\text{sphere}} = V_{\text{cylinder}}$$
$$\frac{3}{2}\times V_{\text{sphere}} = (\text{area of base})(\text{height})$$
$$\frac{3}{2}\times V_{\text{sphere}} = (\pi r^2)\times 2r$$
$$\frac{3}{2}\times V_{\text{sphere}} = 2\pi r^3$$
$$\frac{2}{3}\times\frac{3}{2}\times V_{\text{sphere}} = \frac{2}{3}\times 2\pi r^3$$
$$V_{\text{sphere}} = \frac{4}{3}\pi r^3$$

PRACTICE QUESTIONS

Use the following information to answer the next question.

Trevor described three shapes that had equal dimensions:

Cylinder: The volume of the cylinder is 400 cm^3

Sphere: The sphere has the same radius, *r*, as the cylinder, and a diameter, *d*, equal to the height, *h*, of the cylinder.

Cone: The cone has the same radius, *r*, as the cylinder, and the same height, *h*, as the cylinder.

25. In relation to the cylinder's volume, the volume of the sphere and the cone is

A. $V_{\text{sphere}} = \frac{400\text{ cm}^3}{3}$, $V_{\text{cone}} = \frac{400\text{ cm}^3}{3}$

B. $V_{\text{sphere}} = \frac{800\text{ cm}^3}{3}$, $V_{\text{cone}} = \frac{400\text{ cm}^3}{3}$

C. $V_{\text{sphere}} = \frac{400\text{ cm}^3}{3}$, $V_{\text{cone}} = \frac{800\text{ cm}^3}{3}$

D. $V_{\text{sphere}} = \frac{800\text{ cm}^3}{3}$, $V_{\text{cone}} = \frac{800\text{ cm}^3}{3}$

Use the following information to answer the next question.

A cylinder has a diameter of 12 cm and a height of *h* cm, as illustrated in the diagram.

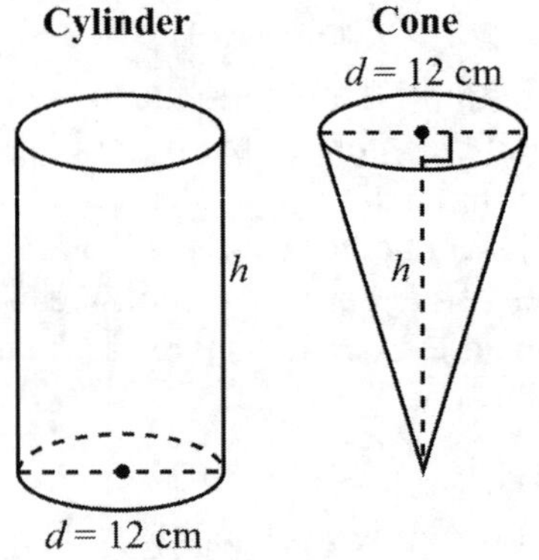

The cone has the same base diameter and height as the given cylinder.

26. Which of the following equations can be used to determine the volume of the cone?

A. $V = 12\pi h$ **B.** $V = 36\pi h$

C. $V = 48\pi h$ **D.** $V = 144\pi h$

MG2.05 solve problems involving the volumes of prisms, pyramids, cylinders, cones, and spheres

Volume of Prisms, Pyramids, Cylinders, Cones, and Spheres

Problems involving the volume of prisms, pyramids, cylinders, cones, and spheres can be solved by applying the formulas from lesson 2.04. These can be found on the formula sheet at the back of your book.

Problem

If a sugar cube measures 12 mm by 12 mm by 12 mm, how many sugar cubes will fit in a box that has dimensions of 120 mm by 120 mm by 120 mm?

The volume of the sugar cube is the same as the volume of a prism, where all three sides are equal.

$$\begin{aligned}V_{\text{cube}} &= (l)(w)(h)\\ &= (12)(12)(12)\\ &= 1\ 728\text{ mm}^3\end{aligned}$$

The volume of the box is also the volume of a prism, where all three sides are equal.

$$\begin{aligned}V_{\text{box}} &= (l)(w)(h)\\ &= (120)(120)(120)\\ &= 1\ 728\ 000\text{ mm}^3\end{aligned}$$

The number of sugar cubes that will fit inside the box can be found as follows:

$$\begin{aligned}\text{Number of sugar cubes} &= \frac{\text{volume of box}}{\text{volume of sugar cube}}\\ &= \frac{1\ 728\ 000\text{ mm}^3}{1\ 728\text{ mm}^3}\\ &= 1\ 000\end{aligned}$$

Therefore, 1 000 sugar cubes will fit inside the box.

Problems involving composite volumes (more than one shape) can also be solved.

Problem

If three tennis balls fit exactly into a cylindrical container with a height of 21 cm, what is the volume of the container **not** occupied by the three tennis balls, to the nearest tenth of a cubic centimetre?

Solution

Since a tennis ball is spherical and three tennis balls fit into the container, the sum of the diameters, *d*, of the three tennis balls equals the height of the container.

$$\begin{aligned}\text{Thus, } d+d+d &= 21\text{cm}\\ 3d &= 21\text{ cm}\\ d &= \frac{21\text{ cm}}{3}\\ d &= 7\text{ cm}\end{aligned}$$

The radius, *r*, of each tennis ball is $7\text{ cm} \div 2 = 3.5\text{ cm}$.

The volume of each ball, *V*, is calculated as follows:

$$V = \frac{4}{3}\pi r^3$$

$$V = \frac{4}{3}\pi(3.5)^3 \qquad \text{Substitute 3.5 for } r.$$

$$V = \frac{4}{3}\pi(3.5)(3.5)(3.5)$$

$$V = \frac{4}{3}\pi(42.875)$$

$$V \approx 179.59438$$

$$V \approx 179.6\text{ cm}^3$$

Since there are three tennis balls, the total volume of the three balls is about $3 \times 179.6\text{ cm}^3 = 538.8\text{ cm}^3$.

The volume of the cylindrical container is calculated as follows:

$V = \pi r^2 h$
$V = \pi(3.5)^2(21)$
$V = \pi(3.5)(3.5)(21)$
$V \approx 808.1747101$
$V \approx 808.2 \text{ cm}^3$

When you subtract the volume of the container from the volume occupied by the three tennis balls, you get a remaining volume of
$808.2 \text{ cm}^3 - 538.8 \text{ cm}^3 = 269.4 \text{ cm}^3$.

The volume of the container not occupied by the three tennis balls is approximately 269.4 cm^3.

PRACTICE QUESTIONS

CHALLENGER QUESTION

The dimensions of a 350-g cereal box are shown in the following illustration:

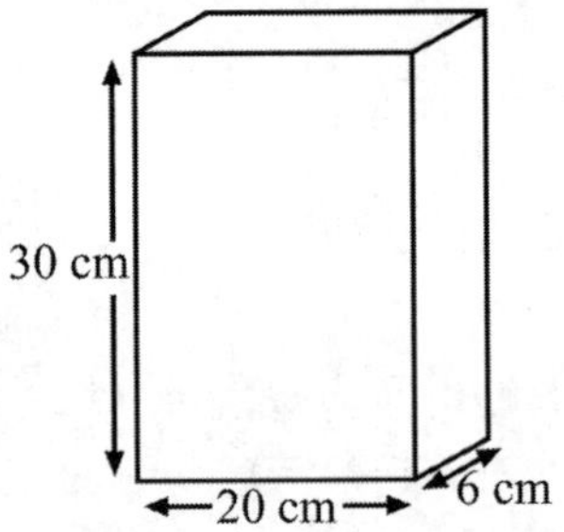

27. This brand of cereal is also available in a larger box with dimensions of 40 cm × 24 cm × 18 cm. What is the maximum amount of cereal that could be contained in the larger box?

A. 1 728 g

B. 1 680 g

C. 1 200 g

D. 480 g

Use the following information to answer the next question.

A particular toy figure is made so that it has a cylindrical bottom and a conical top as shown.

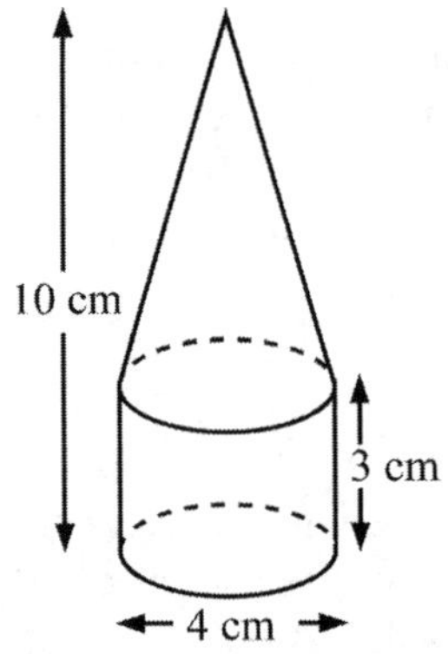

28. To the nearest tenth of a cubic centimetre, what is the volume of the toy figure?

A. 67.0 cm^3

B. 79.6 cm^3

C. 268.1 cm^3

D. 318.3 cm^3

Use the following information to answer the next question.

The garbage bin shown is built with a cylindrical bottom and a hemispherical top.

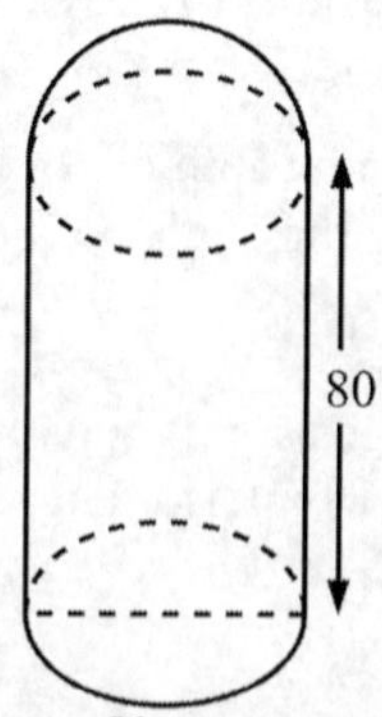

29. To the nearest whole cubic centimetre, what is the volume of garbage that the garbage bin can hold if it is completely filled?

A. 189 805 cm^3

B. 236 529 cm^3

C. 418 879 cm^3

D. 668 043 cm^3

30. A cat box has a volume defined by V_C. If the size of a dog box is such that each dimension is two times as long as each dimension of the cat box, what is the volume of the dog box defined by V_D?

A. $V_D = 2V_C$

B. $V_D = 4V_C$

C. $V_D = 8V_C$

D. $V_D = 16V_C$

MG3.01 determine, through investigation using a variety of tools, and describe the properties and relationships of the interior and exterior angles of triangles, quadrilaterals, and other polygons, and apply the results to problems involving the angles of polygons

PROPERTIES AND RELATIONSHIPS OF THE INTERIOR AND EXTERIOR ANGLES OF POLYGONS

INTERIOR AND EXTERIOR ANGLES OF TRIANGLES

You can draw a triangle and determine the measure of each of its **interior angles** using a protractor. For example, the triangle shown below has interior angles of 30°, 60°, and 90°. The sum of these angles is $30° + 60° + 90° = 180°$.

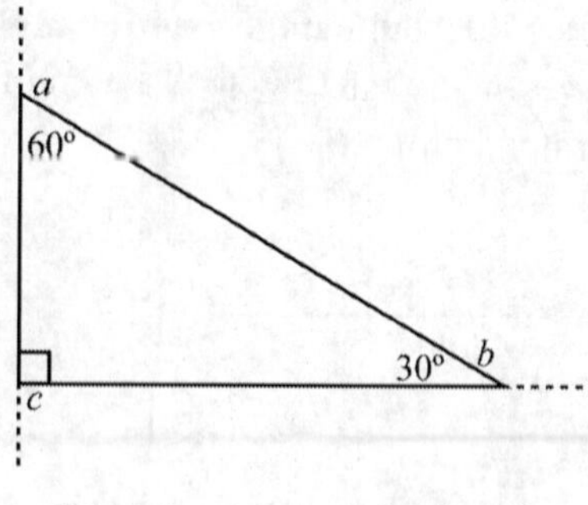

The sum of the measures of the interior angles of any triangle will always equal 180°.

You can also determine the measure of each **exterior angle** $(\angle a, \angle b, \text{and } \angle c)$ of a triangle by recalling that the measure of a straight line is 180°.

$$\angle a = 180° - 60° = 120°$$
$$\angle b = 180° - 30° = 150°$$
$$\angle c = 180° - 90° = 90°$$

The sum of the measures of the exterior angles of this triangle is 120° + 150° + 90° = 360°

For any triangle, the sum of the measures of the exterior angles is always 360°.

Interior and Exterior Angles of Quadrilaterals

Next, you could investigate the measures of the angles of a four-sided quadrilateral. Divide the quadrilateral into two triangles, as shown below.

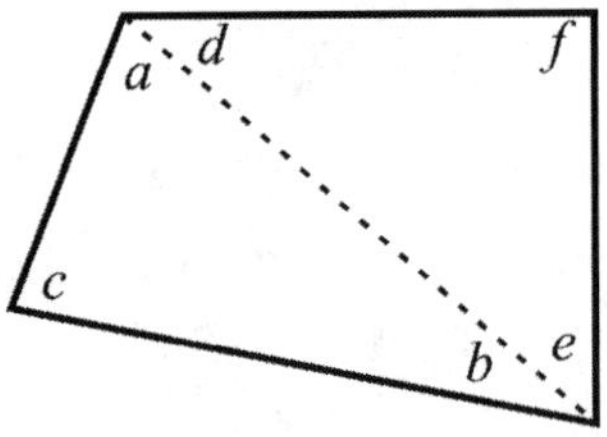

Since you already know that the sum of the measures of the interior angles of any triangle is 180°, $\angle a+\angle b+\angle c=180°$ and $\angle d+\angle e+\angle f=180°$.

The sum of the measures of the interior angles of any quadrilateral must be $180°+180°=360°$.

Next, you could examine the exterior angles ($\angle a, \angle b, \angle c$, and $\angle d$) of a quadrilateral like the one illustrated below.

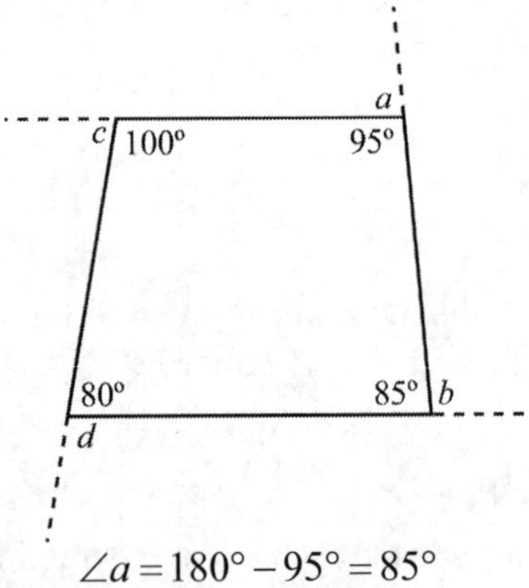

$$\angle a=180°-95°=85°$$
$$\angle c=180°-100°=80°$$
$$\angle b=180°-85°=95°$$
$$\angle d=180°-80°=100°$$

The sum of the measures of the exterior angles of the above quadrilateral is equal to $85°+95°+80°+100°=360°$.

For any quadrilateral, the sum of the measures of the exterior angles is 360°.

Interior and Exterior Angles of a Polygon

For any polygon with n sides, the sum, S, of the measures of its interior angles is $S = 180°(n-2)$. The sum of the measures of the exterior angles of any polygon is 360°

These two rules can be applied to solve various problems involving the angles of polygons.

Example

How many sides does a polygon have if the sum of the measures of its interior angles is 1 620?

$$S=180°(n-2)$$
$$1\,620°=180°(n-2)$$
$$\frac{1\,620°}{180°}=\frac{180°}{180°}(n-2)$$
$$9=n-2$$
$$9+2=n-2+2$$
$$11=n$$

The polygon has 11 sides.

Practice Questions

Use the following information to answer the next question.

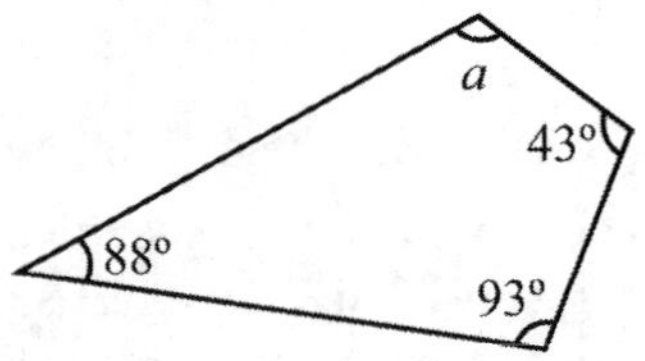

31. What is the measure of angle a in the quadrilateral?

A. 107° **B.** 117°

C. 136° **D.** 150°

32. The sum of the interior angles of a particular polygon is 3 240°. How many sides does the polygon have?

A. 18 **B.** 19

C. 20 **D.** 21

CHALLENGER QUESTION

A pentagon with labeled interior angles is shown.

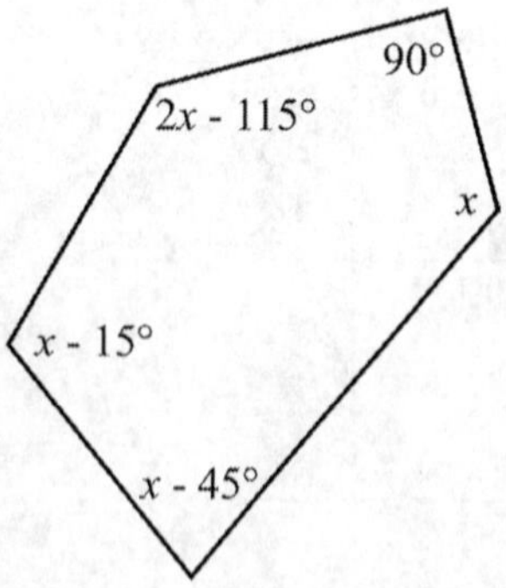

33. What is the measure of angle x?

A. 108°

B. 125°

C. 135°

D. 156°

NUMERICAL RESPONSE

3. What is the difference between the measure of each exterior angle and the measure of each interior angle of a regular five-sided polygon? ________

MG3.02determine, through investigation using a variety of tools, and describe the properties and relationships of the angles formed by parallel lines cut by a transversal, and apply the results to problems involving parallel lines

PROPERTIES AND RELATIONSHIPS OF ANGLES FORMED BY PARALLEL LINES CUT BY A TRANSVERSAL

A line that intersects two or more parallel lines is called a **transversal**. Eight angles are formed when a transversal intersects two parallel lines, as shown below.

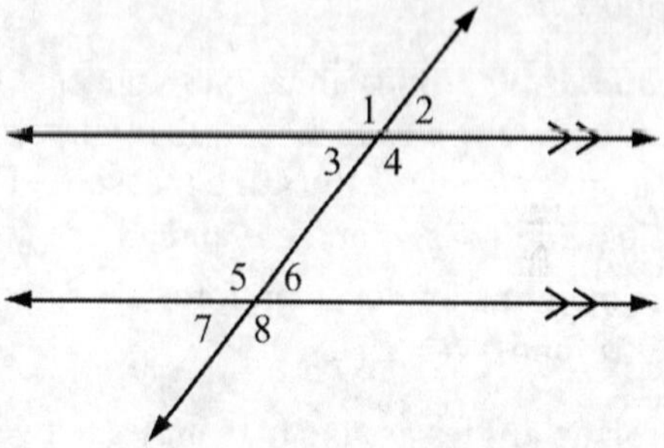

You can investigate the relationship of these eight angles using a protractor.

Example

Given the angle of 60° in the following diagram, find the measures of the other seven angles.

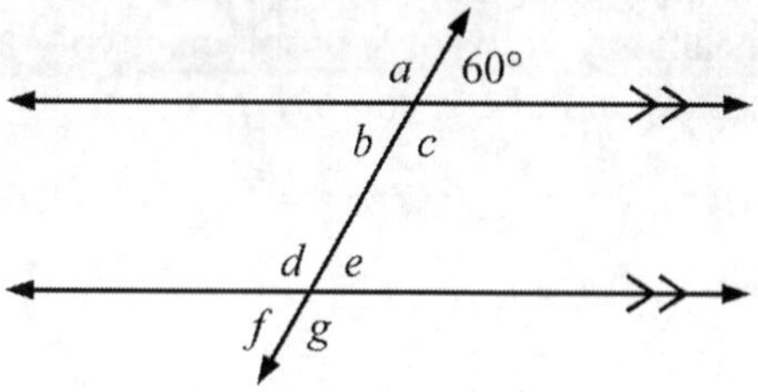

Since a straight line has a measure of 180° you should come up with the following values: $\angle a = 120°$, $\angle b = 60°$, $\angle c = 120°$, $\angle d = 120°$, $\angle e = 60°$, $\angle f = 60°$, $\angle g = 120°$

The following relationships are identified from this investigation:

Vertically opposite angles are angles across two intersecting lines. These angles have the same measure. For example, $\angle a$ and $\angle c$ are vertically-opposite angles; therefore, $\angle a = \angle c$. Other pairs of vertically opposite angles that are equal are $\angle b = 60°$, $\angle d = \angle g$ and $\angle e = \angle f$

Alternate interior angles are diagonal to one another about the transversal. These angles have the same measure. For example, $\angle b$ and $\angle e$ are alternate interior angles; therefore, $\angle b = \angle e$. Another pair of alternate interior angles is $\angle c$ and $\angle d$.

Corresponding angles are angles connected to the parallel lines on each side of the transversal. These angles also have the same measure. For example, $\angle a$ and $\angle d$ and $\angle b$ and $\angle f$ are pairs of corresponding angles; therefore, $\angle a = \angle d$ and $\angle b = \angle f$.

Co-interior angles are the two angles between the parallel lines on each side of the transversal. The measures of these angles are supplementary, which means that the sum of their measures is equal to 180°
For example, $\angle b$ and $\angle d$ are co-interior angles; therefore, $\angle b + \angle d = 180°$

Understanding these relationships between angles enables you to solve problems involving parallel lines and one or more transversals.

Example

To find the measures of $\angle a$, $\angle b$, $\angle c$, $\angle d$, $\angle e$, and $\angle f$ in the diagram shown below, use the properties and relationships of angles formed by parallel lines cut by a transversal.

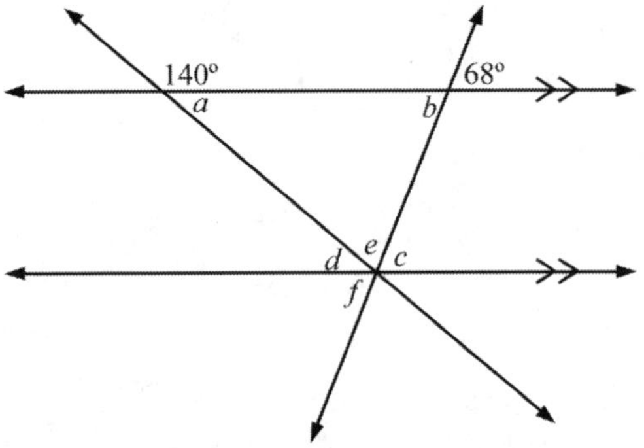

$\angle a$ and 140° share the same line, so they are supplementary angles.

$\angle a + 140° = 180°$, and it follows that $\angle a = 40°$.

$\angle b$ and 68° are vertically-opposite angles.

$\angle b = 68°$.

$\angle b$ and $\angle c$ are alternate interior angles. Since $\angle b = 68°$, it follows that $\angle c = 68°$.

$\angle a$ and $\angle d$ are alternate interior angles. Since $\angle a = 40°$, it follows that $\angle d = 40°$.

Observe that $\angle d + \angle e + \angle c$ form a straight line.

$$\begin{aligned} \angle d + \angle e + \angle c &= 180° \\ 40° + \angle e + 68° &= 180° \\ 108° + \angle e &= 180° \\ 108° - 108° + \angle e &= 180° - 108° \\ \angle e &= 72° \end{aligned}$$

or

The sum of the measures of the interior angles of a triangle is equal to 180°; therefore,

$$\begin{aligned} \angle a + \angle b + \angle e &= 180° \\ 40° + 68° + \angle e &= 180° \\ 108° + \angle e &= 180° \\ 108° - 108° + \angle e &= 180° - 108° \\ \angle e &= 72° \end{aligned}$$

Practice Questions

Use the following information to answer the next question.

A diagram of two parallel lines and two transversals is shown.

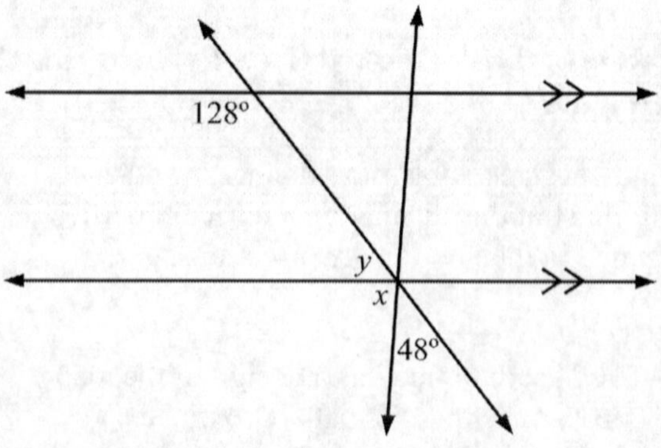

34. What is the sum of the measures of $\angle x$ and $\angle y$?

A. 128°

B. 132°

C. 152°

D. 176°

Use the following information to answer the next question.

A transversal passes through two parallel lines *AB* and *CD*

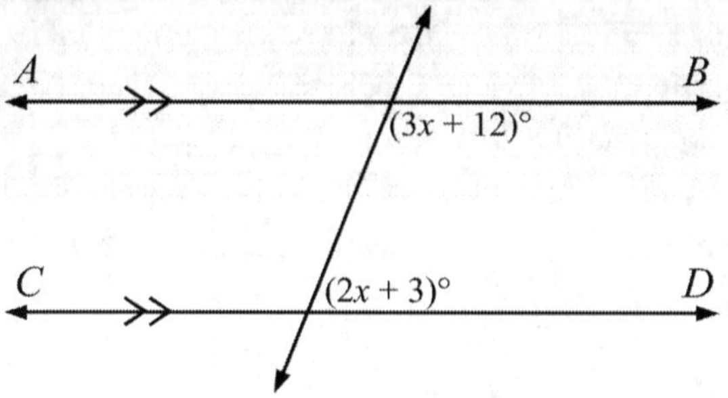

35. The value of *x* is

A. 15

B. 29

C. 33

D. 39

CHALLENGER QUESTION

On a construction site, a carpenter put braces between three vertical and parallel studs and between two horizontal top and bottom plates, as shown.

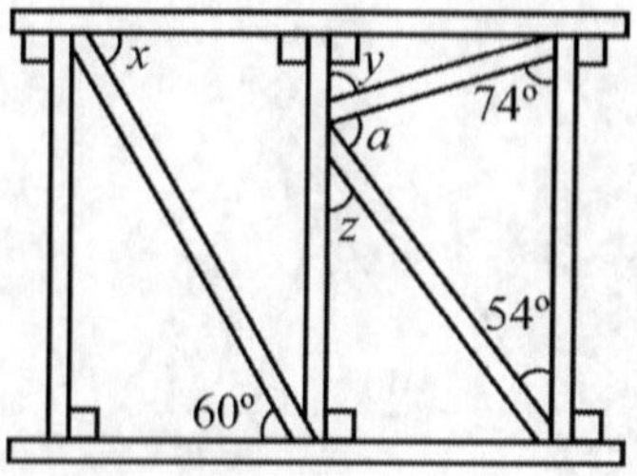

36. The sum of the measures of angles $\angle a$, $\angle x$, $\angle y$, and $\angle z$ is

A. 222°

B. 240°

C. 242°

D. 260°

Use the following information to answer the next question.

A transversal intersects two parallel lines such that $\angle a$ and $\angle b$ are co-interior angles, $\angle a$ and $\angle c$ are corresponding angles, and $\angle c$ and $\angle d$ are vertically opposite angles

A student makes the following four statements:

Statement I: $\angle a = \angle b$

Statement II: $\angle a = \angle c$

Statement III: $\angle d = \angle a$

Statement IV: $\angle d = \angle b$

37. If $\angle a \neq 90°$, then which of the student's statements are true?

A. Statements II and III

B. Statements III and IV

C. Statements I, II, and III

D. Statements II, III, and IV

Open Response

2. A student designed a new logo for his outdoor hiking club.

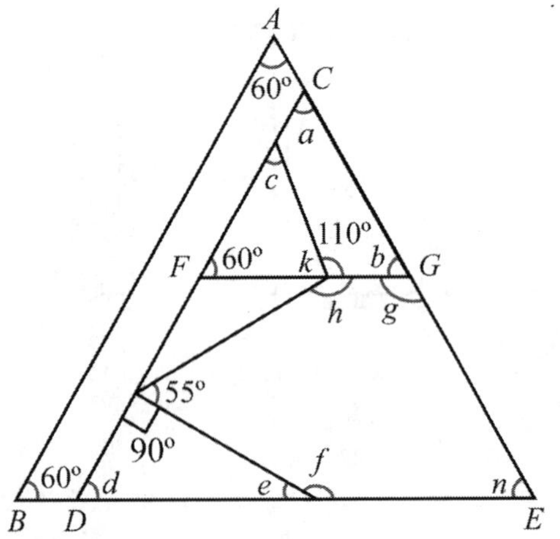

Side AB is parallel to line segment CD, and the line segments FG and BE are also parallel.

a) Find the measures of $\angle a, \angle b, \angle d$ and $\angle g$

b) Find the measures of $\angle c, \angle e, \angle f$ and $\angle h$

MG3.03create an original dynamic sketch, paper-folding design, or other illustration that incorporates some of the geometric properties from this section, or find and report on some real-life application(s) of the geometric properties

PROPERTIES OF ANGLES IN UNIQUE SHAPES

Many designs, dynamic sketches, or other real-life illustrations display geometric properties studied in the previous two sections.

Example

A Canadian flag has a design of the maple leaf in the middle that approximates a polygon with many sides. How many sides does the maple leaf have, and what is the sum of its interior angles?

The maple leaf design approximates a 25-sided polygon. If you counted each side of the three leaf segments and the bottom stem, you would see that the maple leaf has 25 sides.

Recall that the sum, S, of the measures of the interior angles of an n-sided polygon is equal to $S = 180°(n - 2)$. Since the maple leaf has 25 sides $(n = 25)$,

$$\begin{aligned} S &= 180°(25 - 2) \\ &= 180°(23) \\ &= 4\ 140° \end{aligned}$$

The approximate sum of the measures of the interior angles of the Canadian maple leaf is 4 140°.

PRACTICE QUESTIONS

Use the following information to answer the next two questions.

The Canadian loonie is an 11-sided regular polygon, called a hendecagon. Two Canadian loonies are shown with sides touching.

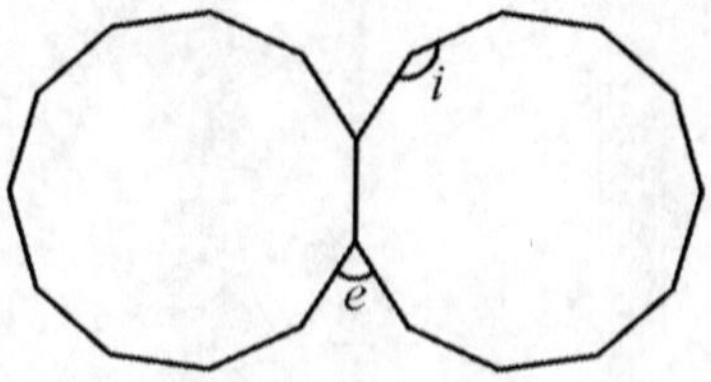

38. To the nearest tenth of a degree, what is the measure of the interior $\angle i$?

A. 135.0°

B. 147.3°

C. 162.0°

D. 163.6°

39. To the nearest tenth of a degree, what is the measure of the exterior $\angle e$ between the two sides where the loonies touch?

A. 32.7°

B. 45.0°

C. 58.2°

D. 65.4°

ANSWERS AND SOLUTIONS—PRACTICE QUESTIONS

1. B	12. C	23. D	33. B
2. B	13. D	24. D	NR1. 36°
3. C	14. C	OR1. **	34. B
4. A	15. B	25. B	35. C
5. C	16. C	26. A	36. B
6. C	17. C	27. B	37. A
7. D	18. B	28. A	OR2. **
8. A	19. C	29. A	38. B
9. B	20. D	30. C	39. D
10. B	21. C	31. C	
11. D	22. C	32. C	

****SEE SOLUTIONS**

1. B

The maximum area of a rectangle occurs when $w = l = \frac{P}{4}$.

Since $P = 100$ cm, $w = l = \frac{100}{4} = 25$ cm

The maximum area occurs when the width and length are each 25 cm.
The rectangle has dimensions of 25 cm × 25 cm.

2. B

The maximum area, A, of a rectangle occurs when $A = \frac{P}{4}$.

Since $P = 20$ m,

$A = \frac{20}{4} = 5$ cm

$A = (l)(w)$
$= (5 \text{ cm})(5 \text{ cm})$
$= 25 \text{ cm}^2$

The maximum area of a rectangular sandbox with a perimeter of 20 m is 25 m^2.

3. C

First, find the perimeter of the given rectangle.
$P = 2l + 2w$
Substitute 30 cm for l and 20 cm for w.
$= 2(30) + 2(20)$
$= 60 + 40$
$= 100$ cm

The maximum area, A, of the new rectangle is given by $A = \frac{P^2}{16}$.

Since $P = 100$ cm, $A = \frac{(100 \text{ m})^2}{16}$.

The expression describing the maximum area of a rectangle with a perimeter of 100 m is $\frac{(100 \text{ m})^2}{16}$,

or

$\left(\frac{100 \text{ m}}{4}\right)\left(\frac{100 \text{ m}}{4}\right)$.

4. **A**

The perimeter of the rectangle is
$P = 2l + 2w$
Substitute 20 for l and 10 for w.
$P = 2 \times 20 + 2 \times 10$
$P = 40 + 20$
$P = 60$ m
The dimensions of a rectangle of maximum area can be found by $S = \frac{P}{4}$, as it is a square.
$S = \frac{P}{4}$
Substitute 60 for P.
$S = \frac{60}{4}$
$S = 15$ m
The sides of the square are 15 m. Subtract 5 from the original length ($20 - 5 = 15$), and add 5 to the original width ($10 + 5 = 15$).
The correct expression is $l - 5$ and $w + 5$.

5. **C**

The rectangle with the smallest perimeter has dimensions of $w = l = \sqrt{A}$.
Since each of the given rectangles has an area of 144 cm^2, $w = l = \sqrt{144 \text{ cm}^2} = 12$ cm.
Therefore, the rectangle with the smallest perimeter must have dimensions of 12 cm by 12 cm.
Rectangle 1 has dimensions of 12 cm by 12 cm.
Therefore, Rectangle 1 has the smallest possible perimeter for a rectangle of area 144 cm^2.

6. **C**

The minimum perimeter, P, of a rectangle of area, A, is given by $P = 4\sqrt{A}$.
$P = 4\sqrt{A}$
Substitute 200 for A.
$= 4\sqrt{200}$
$\approx 4(14.14213562)$
≈ 56.6 cm
The minimum perimeter is 56.6 cm.

7. **D**

A rectangle that produces the maximum area is a square. The perimeter of a square is $P = 4s$.
Substitute l for s.
$P = 4l$
Divide by 4.
$\frac{P}{4} = l$
$l = \frac{P}{4}$
The formula that produces the correct length, l, to form a rectangle with a maximum area is $l = \frac{P}{4}$.

8. **A**

The dimensions of a rectangle with a minimum perimeter for an area, A, occurs when $w = l = \sqrt{A}$.
Since $A = 100$ cm^2, $w = l = \sqrt{100} = 10$ cm.
The dimensions of the picture frame are 10 cm × 10 cm.

9. **B**

When a fixed amount of fencing is used for one length and two sides of a rectangular area, the maximum area occurs when the length is two times the width ($l = 2w$)
The required amount of fencing material is given by $P = 2w + l$.

$P = 2w + l$
Substitute $2w$ for l.
$P = 2w + 2w$

$P = 4w$
$w = \frac{P}{4}$

Substitute 16 for P.
$w = \frac{16}{4}$
$w = 4$ m
Since $l = 2w$, $l = 2(4) = 8$ m.

The maximum area that can be fenced off can be determined as follows:
$A = (l)(w)$
$= (8)(4)$
$= 32$ m^2
The maximum area that can be fenced off is 32 m^2.

10. B

When the sum of the length of three sides of a rectangle is fixed, the minimum perimeter occurs when the length is two times the width ($l = 2w$). The perimeter of the required fencing material is given by $P = 2w + l$.
First, determine the value of w and l:

$A = (l)(w)$

Substitute $2w$ for l.

$A = (2w)(w)$
$A = 2w^2$
$w^2 = \frac{A}{2}$
$w = \sqrt{\frac{A}{2}}$

Substitute 200 m^2 for A.

$w = \sqrt{\frac{200\text{ m}^2}{2}}$
$w = \sqrt{100\text{ m}^2}$
$w = 10$ m

Since $l = 2w$, $l = 2(10\text{ m}) = 20$ m

$P = 2w + l$
$P = 2(10) + 20$
$P = 20 + 20$
$P = 40$ m

The minimum cost, C, to build this fence is $C = \$30/\text{m} \times 40\text{ m} = \$1\ 200$.

11. D

The minimum area for Roxanne's enclosure occurs when the length is three times the width ($l = 3w$). The perimeter of Roxanne's enclosure is given by $P = 3w + l$. Solve for w and l as follows:

$A = (l)(w)$

Substitute $3w$ for l.

$A = (3w)(w)$
$A = 3w^2$
$w^2 = \frac{A}{3}$
$w = \sqrt{\frac{A}{3}}$

Substitute 900 for A.

$w = \sqrt{\frac{900}{3}}$
$w \approx 17.32$ m

Since $l = 3w$, $l \approx 3(17.32\text{ m}) \approx 51.96$ m
Recall $P = 3w + l$
Substitute 17.32 for w and 51.96 for l.

$\approx 3(17.32) + 51.96$
≈ 103.9 m

The minimum area for Damian's enclosure occurs when the length is four times the width ($l = 4w$).
The perimeter of Damian's enclosure is given by $P = 4w + l$.
Solve for w and l as follows:

$A = (l)(w)$

Substitute $4w$ for l.

$A = (4w)(w)$
$A = 4w^2$
$w^2 = \frac{A}{4}$
$w = \sqrt{\frac{A}{4}}$

Substitute 900 for A.

$w = \sqrt{\frac{900}{4}} = \sqrt{225}$
$w = 15$ m

Since $l = 4w$, $l = 4(15\text{ m}) = 60$ m

Recall $P = 4w + l$
Substitute 15 for w and 60 for l.

$P = 4(15) + 60$
$P = 60 + 60$
$P = 120$ m

Damian uses 120 m – 103.9 m = 16.1 m more barrier material than Roxanne.

12. C

The area of the squares on two sides of the right-angle triangle is given. The Pythagorean theorem can be applied to find the area of the square on the third side.In the problem $a^2 + b^2 = c^2$, where a^2 is the area of square A, b^2 is the area of square B, and c^2 is the area of square C:

$a^2 + b^2 = c^2$

Substitute 16 for a^2 and 9 for b^2.

$16 + 9 = c^2$
$25 = c^2$

The area of square C is 25 cm^2.

13. D

The Pythagorean theorem states that Area C = Area A + Area B; therefore, substitute 36 for Area A and 64 for Area B.
Area $C = 36 + 64$
Area $C = 100\text{ cm}^2$
The area of square C is given by
$A = (c)(c) = c^2$.
Thus,
$100 = c^2$
$c = \sqrt{100}$
$c = 10\text{ cm}$
The length of side c in square C is 10 cm.

14. C

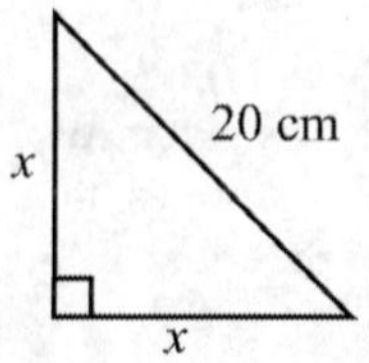

$a^2 + b^2 = c^2$	Pythagorean theorem
$x^2 + x^2 = 20^2$	Substitute x for a and b and 20 for c.
$2x^2 = 20^2$	
$x^2 = \frac{20^2}{2}$	Divide by 2.
$x = \sqrt{\frac{400}{2}}$	Take the square root.

The value of x is determined by the expression
$x = \sqrt{\frac{400}{2}}$.

15. B

Placing the ladder against the wall creates a right-angle triangle. The lengths of two sides are given. Use the Pythagorean theorem to determine the distance of the base of the ladder from the wall. Consider the diagram shown in the question, and let $a = 4.40$ m and $c = 4.70$ m. Using the Pythagorean theorem, it follows that
$a^2 + b^2 = c^2$
$(4.40)^2 + b^2 = (4.70)^2$
Now, solve this equation to find the value of b:
$19.36 + b^2 = 22.09$
$b^2 = 22.09 - 19.36$
$b^2 = 2.73$

$b = \sqrt{2.73}$
$b = 1.65\text{ m}$
To the nearest hundredth metre, the foot of the ladder is 1.65 m from the base of the wall.

16. C

Illustrate the problem graphically to make it easier to solve. Fritz (F) is standing 20 m directly in front of Jean (J), and Colin (C) is 15 m to the right of Jean.

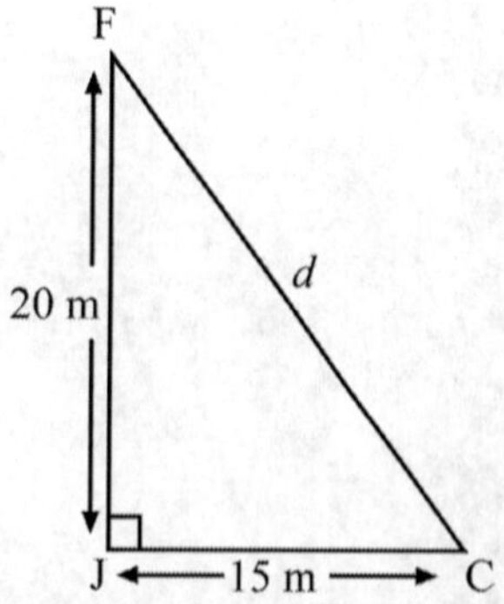

Solve for distance d from Fritz to Colin using the Pythagorean theorem.
$(20)^2 + (15)^2 = d^2$
$400 + 225 = d^2$
$625 = d^2$

$d = \sqrt{625} = 25\text{ m}$
The distance between Fritz and Colin is 25.0 m.

17. C

The radius is equal to half of the diameter; therefore, the radius is 10 cm (20 cm ÷ 2). Use the Pythagorean theorem to find the missing height, h.
$a^2 + b^2 = c^2$
$10^2 + h^2 = 24^2$
$100 + h^2 = 576$
$h^2 = 576 - 100$
$h^2 = 476$

$h = \sqrt{476}$

$h \approx 21.817$ cm
To the nearest tenth of a centimetre,
the height of the right circular cone is 21.8 cm.

18. B

Find the length of x using the Pythagorean theorem:

$a^2 + b^2 = c^2$

$54^2 + x^2 = 126^2$

$2\,916 + x^2 = 15\,876$

$x^2 = 15\,876 - 2\,916$

$x^2 = 12\,960$

$x = \sqrt{12\,960}$

$x \approx 113.8$ m

The height is 1 m more than x; therefore, $h = 1$ m + 113.8 m = 114.8 m

19. C

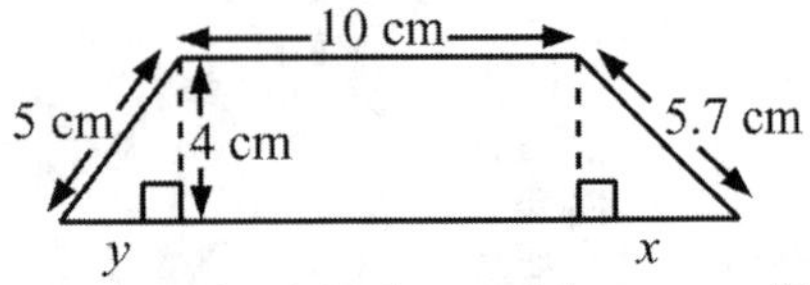

The length of the base of the trapezoid is $y + 10 + x$.

Find the length of y using the Pythagorean theorem, as shown:

$a^2 + b^2 = c^2$

Substitute y for a, 4 for b, and 5 for c.

$y^2 + 4^2 = 5^2$

$y^2 + 16 = 25$

Subtract 16 from both sides.

$y^2 + 16 - 16 = 25 - 16$

$y^2 = 9$

$y = 3$

Find the length of x using the Pythagorean theorem, as shown:

$a^2 + b^2 = c^2$

Substitute 4 for a, x for b, and 5.7 for c.

$4^2 + x^2 = 5.7^2$

$16 + x^2 = 32.49$

Subtract 16 from both sides.

$x^2 + 16 - 16 = 32.49 - 16$

$x^2 = 16.49$

$x = 4.06$

The length of the base of the trapezoid is $3 + 10 + 4.06 = 17.06$

20. D

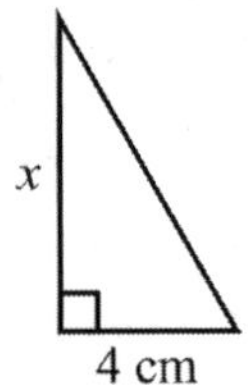

$a^2 + b^2 = c^2$

Substitute 4 for a, x for b, and 8 for c.

$4^2 + x^2 = 8^2$

$16 + x^2 = 64$

Subtract 16 from both sides.

$x^2 + 16 - 16 = 64 - 16$

$x = \sqrt{64 - 16}$

The equation that solves for the missing side, x, is $x = \sqrt{64 - 16}$

21. C

The amount of fencing required is equal to the perimeter, P, of the figure. The distance around the three sides of the isosceles trapezoid and the three equal sides of the square is as follows:

$P = 700 + 2(500) + 3(100)$

$= 700 + 1\,000 + 300$

$= 2\,000$ m

The amount of fencing required is 2 000 m.

22. C

The amount of the sod required is equal to the area of the park. The area of the park is formed by two geometric figures: an isosceles trapezoid and a square.

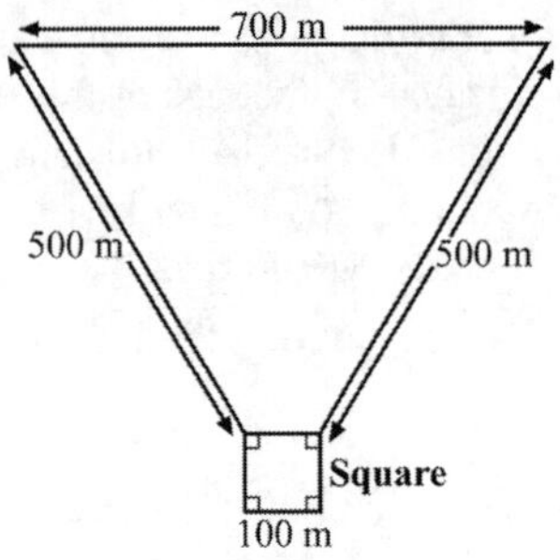

$A_{\text{square}} = s^2$

$= (100)^2$

$= 10\,000 \text{ m}^2$

$$A_{\text{trapezoid}} = \frac{1}{2}h(b_1 + b_2)$$

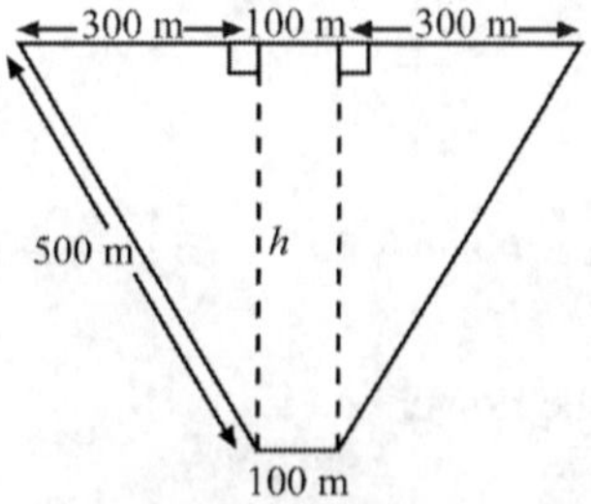

Begin by solving for h. Apply the Pythagorean theorem as follows:

$$500^2 = 300^2 + h^2$$
$$250\,000 = 90\,000 + h^2$$
$$250\,000 - 90\,000 = h^2$$
$$160\,000 = h^2$$

$$h = \sqrt{160\,000}$$

$$h = 400 \text{ m}$$

Now, substitute the values for h, b^1, and b^2 into the area formula for a trapezoid.

$$\begin{aligned} A_{\text{trapezoid}} &= \frac{1}{2}h(b_1 + b_2) \\ &= \frac{1}{2}(400)(700 + 100) \\ &= (200)(800) \\ &= 160\,000 \text{ m}^2 \end{aligned}$$

The total area that will be sodded is $160\,000 \text{ m}^2 + 10\,000 \text{ m}^2 = 170\,000 \text{ m}^2$.

23. D

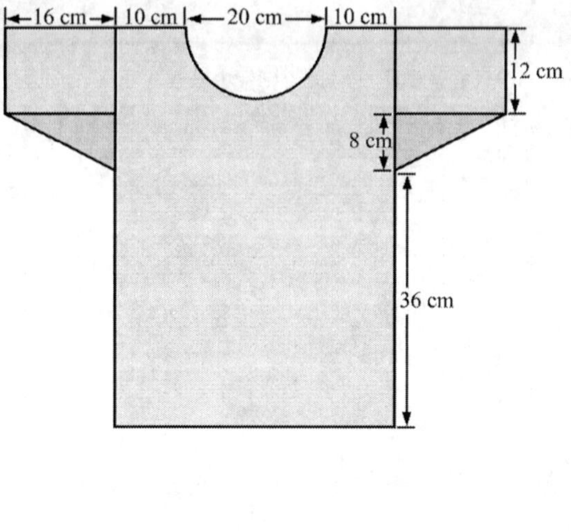

In order to calculate the total surface area of the front of the t-shirt, consider the defined geometric shapes from which it is constructed. The front middle part of the t-shirt is a rectangle minus a semicircle. The rectangle is 40 cm (10 cm + 20 cm + 10 cm) in width and 56 cm (36 cm + 8 cm + 12 cm) in length. The semicircle is 10 cm (20 cm ÷ 2) in radius. The surface area, A, of the front middle part of the t-shirt can be determined as follows:

Body of shirt:

$$A_1 = A_{\text{rectangle}} - A_{\text{semicircle}}$$
$$A_1 = lw - \frac{\pi r^2}{2}$$
$$A_1 = (56)(40) - \frac{\pi(10)^2}{2}$$
$$A_1 \approx 2\,240 - 157.08$$
$$A_1 \approx 2\,082.92 \text{ cm}^2$$

Each sleeve is made up of a rectangle and a triangle. The rectangle is 12 cm in width and 16 cm in length. The triangle is 8 cm in height and has a base of 16 cm.

The surface area, A_2, of the two sleeves can be determined as follows:

Sleeves:

$$A_2 = 2 \times A_{\text{rectangle}} + 2 \times A_{\text{triangle}}$$
$$A_2 = 2(lw) + 2\left(\frac{1}{2}bh\right)$$
$$A_2 = 2(16 \times 12) + 2\left(\frac{1}{2} \times 16 \times 8\right)$$
$$A_2 = 2(192) + 2(64)$$
$$A_2 = 384 + 128$$
$$A_2 = 512 \text{ cm}^2$$

The total surface area of the t-shirt is $A_1 + A_2 \approx 2\,082.92 \text{ cm}^2 + 512 \text{ cm}^2 \approx 2\,594.92 \text{ cm}^2$

To the nearest whole number, the total surface area of the t-shirt is 2 595 cm^2.

24. D

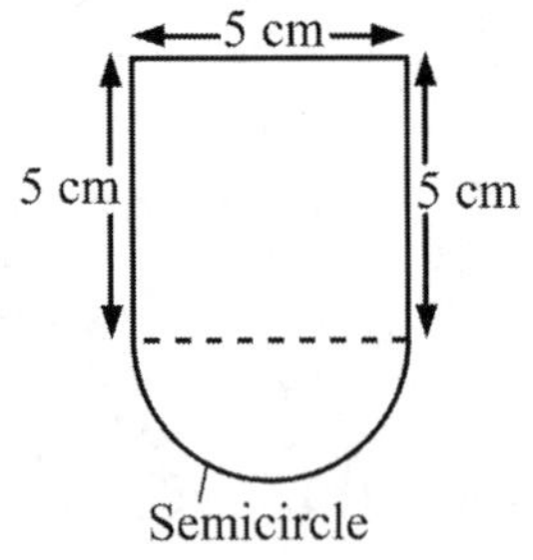

The perimeter is the sum of three sides of the square plus the circumference of the semicircle.

$C_{\text{semicircle}} = \pi r$
$C_{\text{semicircle}} = \pi(2.5)$
Perimeter $= 3(5) + \pi(2.5)$
The perimeter of this shape is described by the expression $3(5) + \pi(2.5)$.

OR 1.

a)
The maximum area of a rectangle is fixed when the length is two times the width ($l = 2w$); thus, $P = 2w + l$.
You can solve for l and w as follows:
$P = 2w + l$
Substitute $2w$ for l.
$P = 2w + 2w$
$P = 4w$
$w = \dfrac{P}{4}$ Substitute 12 m for P.
$w = \dfrac{12 \text{ m}}{4} = 3 \text{ m}$
Since $l = 2w$, the length is 6 m (2 × 3 m).
The maximum area of the deck can be found as follows:
$A = (l)(w)$
$A = (6 \text{ m})(3 \text{ m})$
$A = 18 \text{ m}^2$

b)
To find the total area of the flower bed, find the sum of the areas of the semicircle, rectangle, and triangle.

$A_{\text{semicircle}} = \dfrac{\pi r^2}{2}$

Substitute $1.5, (3 \div 2)$, for r $= \dfrac{\pi(1.5)^2}{2}$

$\approx \dfrac{7.0686}{2}$

$\approx 3.5 \text{ m}^2$

$A_{\text{rectangle}} = (l)(w)$
Substitute 5 for l and 3 for w.
$= (5)(3)$
$= 15 \text{ m}^2$

$A_{\text{triangle}} = \dfrac{(b)(h)}{2}$

Substitute 4 for b and 3 for h. $= \dfrac{(4)(3)}{2}$ The

$= 6 \text{ m}^2$

total area of the flower bed is
$6 \text{ m}^2 + 15 \text{ m}^2 + 3.5 \text{ m}^2 = 24.5 \text{ m}^2$

c)
To find the length of the edging, find the perimeter of the flower bed (not including the house).
To find the perimeter of the right triangular section, use the Pythagorean Theorem $c^2 = a^2 + b^2$ to solve for c, where c is the longest side.

Substitute 3 for a and 4 for b.
$c^2 = 3^2 + 4^2$
$c^2 = 9 + 16$
$c^2 = 25$
$c = \sqrt{25}$
$c = 5 \text{ m}$
Find the circumference (perimeter) of the semicircle as follows:
$P = \dfrac{2\pi r}{2}$
$= \pi r$
Substitute 1.5 for r.
$= \pi(1.5)$
$= 4.7 \text{ m}$
The outside length of the rectangle is 5 m.
$5 \text{ m} + 4.7 \text{ m} + 5 \text{ m} = 14.7 \text{ m}$
The total amount of edging required is 14.7 m.

25. **B**

The volume of the sphere is $\frac{2}{3}$ the volume of the cylinder.

$$V_{\text{sphere}} = \frac{2}{3}V_{\text{cylinder}}$$
$$= \frac{2}{3}(400)$$
$$= \frac{800\text{ cm}^3}{3}$$

The volume of the cone is $\frac{1}{3}$ the volume of the cylinder.

$$V_{\text{cone}} = \frac{1}{3}V_{\text{cylinder}}$$
$$= \frac{1}{3}(400)$$
$$= \frac{400\text{ cm}^3}{3}$$

In relation to the cylinder's volume, the volume of the sphere and the cone is

$V_{\text{sphere}} = \frac{800\text{ cm}^3}{3}$, $V_{\text{cone}} = \frac{400\text{ cm}^3}{3}$.

26. **A**

The formula for the volume of a cylinder is $V = \pi r^2 h$. The formula for the volume of a cone with the same base diameter and height is $V = \frac{\pi r^2 h}{3}$.

$$V_{\text{cylinder}} = \pi r^2 h$$

Substitute 6 for r.

$$V_{\text{cylinder}} = \pi\left(6^2\right)h$$
$$V_{\text{cylinder}} = 36\pi h$$

$$V_{\text{cone}} = \frac{\pi r^2 h}{3}$$
$$V_{\text{cone}} = \frac{36\pi h}{3}$$
$$V_{\text{cone}} = 12\pi h$$

The equation that can be used to determine the volume of the cone is $V_{\text{cone}} = 12\pi h$.

27. **B**

The volume of the 350 g cereal box is

$V = (l)(w)(h)$
$V = 20 \times 6 \times 30$
$V = 3\ 600\text{ cm}^3$

The volume of the larger cereal box is

$V = (l)(w)(h)$
$V = 18 \times 24 \times 40$
$V = 17\ 280\text{ cm}^3$

Now, find how many times greater the volume of the larger cereal box is compared to the volume of the smaller cereal box.

$$\text{Number of times greater} = \frac{V_{\text{larger box}}}{V_{\text{smaller box}}}$$
$$= \frac{17\ 280\text{ cm}^3}{3\ 600\text{ cm}^3}$$
$$= 4.8$$

Since the larger cereal box is 4.8 times greater in volume than the smaller box, it holds 4.8 times the amount of cereal in the smaller box.

$4.8 \times 350\text{ g} = 1\ 680\text{ g}$

The larger cereal box could hold a maximum of 1 680 g of cereal.

28. **A**

The cone and cylinder both have radii measuring 2 cm (4 cm ÷ 2).

The height of the cone is
10 cm – 3 cm = 7 cm

The volume of the cone can be found as follows:

$$V_{\text{cone}} = \frac{1}{3}\pi r^2 h$$
$$= \frac{1}{3}\pi(2)^2(7)$$
$$\approx 29.3\text{ cm}^3$$

The volume of the cylinder can be found as follows:

$$V_{\text{cylinder}} = \pi r^2 h$$
$$= \pi(2)^2(3)$$
$$\approx 37.7\text{ cm}^3$$

Add the volumes together.

$29.3\text{ cm}^3 + 37.7\text{ cm}^3 = 67.0\text{ cm}^3$

The total volume of the figure is 67.0 cm^3.

29. A

The cylinder and hemisphere both have radii measuring 25 cm (50 cm ÷ 2). The volume of the cylinder can be found as follows:

$$V_{\text{cylinder}} = \pi r^2 h$$
$$= \pi(25)^2(80)$$
$$\approx 157\,079.6 \text{ cm}^3$$

The volume of a hemisphere is one-half the volume of a sphere. The volume of the hemisphere can be found as follows:

$$V_{\text{hemisphere}} = \frac{V_{\text{sphere}}}{2}$$
$$= \frac{4}{3}\pi r^3 \div 2$$
$$= \left(\frac{4}{3}\pi(25)^3\right) \div 2$$
$$\approx 32\ 724.9 \text{ cm}^3$$

157 079.6 cm^3 + 32 724.9 cm^3
= 189 804.5 cm^3
To the nearest whole number, the volume the bin can hold if it is completely full is 189 805 cm^3.

30. C

Solve the problem by example.

Cat's Bed	**Dog's Bed**
$V_c = lwh$	$V_d = lwh$
$V_c = 1 \times 2 \times 3$	$V_d = 2 \times 4 \times 6$
$V_c = 6 \text{ unit}^3$	$V_d = 48 \text{ unit}^3$

The volume of the dog's bed is $\frac{48}{6} = 8$ times the volume of the cat's bed. The volume of the dog's bed compared to the volume of the cat's bed is $V_d = 8V_c$.

31. C

The sum of the interior angles of a quadrilateral is 360°.

$$\angle a + 43° + 93° + 88° = 360°$$
$$\angle a + 224° = 360°$$

Subtract 224° from both sides.

$$\angle a = 360° - 224°$$
$$\angle a = 136°$$

Angle *a* measures 136°.

32. C

The sum of the interior angles of an *n*-sided polygon is given by the formula $S = 180°(n - 2)$.

Substitute 3 240° for the sum.

$$3\ 240° = 180°(n-2)$$

Divide both sides by 180°.

$$\frac{3\ 240°}{180°} = \frac{180°(n-2)}{180°}$$
$$18 = n - 2$$
$$20 = n$$

A polygon with interior angles that add up to 3 240° has 20 sides.

33. B

The sum of the interior angles of a pentagon can be found using $S = 180°(n - 2)$, where *n* is the number of sides.

$S = 180°(n - 2)$
Substitute 5 for *n*.
$S = 180°(5 - 2)$
$S = 180° \times 3$
$S = 540°$

The sum of the interior angles of a pentagon is 540°.
Add the interior angles.
$2x - 115 + x - 15 + x - 45 + x + 90 = 540$
Collect like terms.
$5x - 85 = 540$
Add 85 to both sides.
$5x - 85 + 85 = 540 + 85$
$5x = 625$
Divide by 5.
$\frac{5x}{5} = \frac{625}{5}$
$x = 125$
The value of *x* is 125°.

NR 1 36°

The sum of the interior angles of a regular polygon can be found using the formula $S_{5\text{-sidedpolygon}} = 180°(n - 2)$, where *n* is the number of sides.

$S_{5\text{-sidedpolygon}} = 180°(n - 2)$
$= 180°(5 - 2)$
$= 180° \times 3$
$= 540°$

The size of each interior angle is

$540 \div 5 = 108°$
The size of each exterior angle can be found by dividing 360 by the number of sides, or
$360 \div 5 = 72°$
The difference between the size of an interior angle and an exterior angle is $108° - 72° = 36°$

34. B

$\angle y$ and 128° are co-interior angles. Since co-interior angles are supplementary,
$\angle y + 128° = 180°$
Subtract 128° from both sides.
$\angle y = 180° - 128°$
$\angle y = 52°$
$\angle x$, $\angle y$, and 48° are angles on a straight line.
The sum of the measures of angles on a straight line is 180°; therefore,
$\angle x + \angle y + 48° = 180°$
$\angle x + 52° + 48° = 180°$
$\angle x + 100° = 180°$
Subtract 100° from both sides. The sum of
$\angle x = 180° - 100°$
$\angle x = 80°$
$\angle x$ and $\angle y$ is
$80° + 52° = 132°$

35. C

The two angles illustrated in the diagram are co-interior angles. Since co-interior angles are supplementary, $(3x + 12) + (2x + 3) = 180°$.
Now, solve for x as follows:
$$(3x+12)+(2x+3)=180$$
$$3x+12+2x+3=180$$
Collect like terms.
$$5x+15=180$$
Subtract 15 from both sides.
$$5x+15-15=180-15$$
$$5x=165$$
Divide both sides by 5.
$$\frac{5x}{5}=\frac{165}{5}$$
$$x=33$$
The value of x is 33.

36. B

$\angle x$ is an alternate interior angle to 60°. Since alternate interior angles are equal, $\angle x = 60°$.
$\angle y$ is an alternate interior angle to 74°. Since alternate interior angles are equal, $\angle y = 74°$.
$\angle z$ is an alternate interior angle to 54°; therefore, $\angle z = 54°$.
A straight line has a measure of 180°; therefore, $\angle y + \angle a + \angle z = 180°$.
You can solve for $\angle a$ as follows:
Substitute 74° for $\angle y$
and 54° for $\angle z$.
$74° + \angle a + 54° = 180°$ **or**
$\angle a + 128° = 180°$
$\angle a = 52°$
$\angle a + 74° + 54° = 180°$, since the sum of the interior angles of a triangle is 180°.
$\angle a + 128° = 180°$
$\angle a = 52°$
The sum of the measures of
$\angle a$, $\angle x$, $\angle y$, and $\angle z$ is 240°
(52° + 60° + 74° + 54°).

37. A

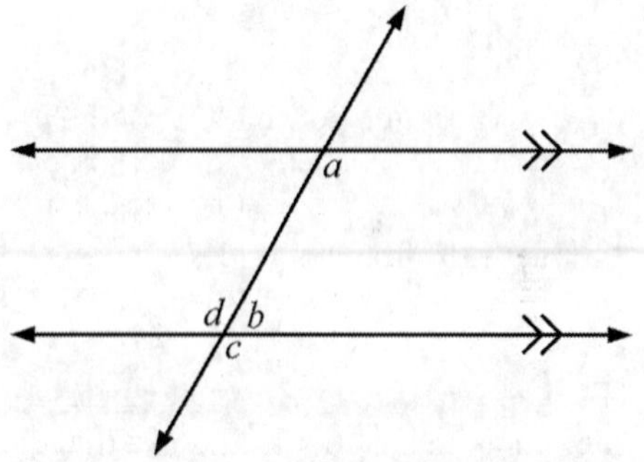

$\angle a = \angle c$	Corresponding angles
$\angle c = \angle d$	Vertically opposite angles
$\angle a = \angle d$	Alternate angles

Statements II and III are true.

OR 2.

a)

$\angle a$ is a corresponding angle to $\angle BAE$, $\angle b$ is a corresponding angle to $\angle AEB$, and $\angle d$ is a corresponding angle to $\angle ABE$. Since corresponding angles are equal, and $\angle BAE = \angle AEB = \angle ABE = 60°$,

$\angle a = \angle b = \angle d = 60°$.

$\angle g$ is a co-interior angle with $\angle AEB$. Since co-interior angles are supplementary,

$$\angle g + \angle AEB = 180°$$
$$\angle g + 60° = 180°$$

Subtract 60° from both sides.

$$\angle g + 60° = 180° - 60°$$
$$\angle g = 120°$$

$\angle a$, $\angle b$, and $\angle d$ equal 60°, and $\angle g$ equals 120°.

b)

The shape containing angle c is a triangle. Since the sum of the angles of a triangle is 180°, $\angle k + 110°$ forms a straight line.

$$\angle k + 110° = 180°$$

Subtract 110° from both sides.

$$\angle k + 110° - 110° = 180° - 110°$$
$$\angle k = 70°$$

$$\angle c + 60° + \angle k = 180°$$

Substitute 70° for $\angle k$.

$$\angle c + 60° + 70° = 180°$$
$$\angle c + 130° = 180°$$

Subtract 130° from both sides.

$$\angle c + 130° - 130° = 180° - 130°$$
$$\angle c = 50°$$

The shape containing $\angle e$ is a triangle. The sum of the interior angles in a triangle is 180°; therefore,

$$\angle e + \angle d + 90° = 180°$$
$$\angle e + 60° + 90° = 180°$$
$$\angle e + 150° = 180°$$

Subtract 150° from both sides.

$$\angle e + 150° - 150° = 180° - 150°$$
$$\angle e = 30°$$

$\angle e$ and $\angle f$ form a straight line, so

$$\angle f + \angle e = 180°$$
$$\angle f + 30° = 180°$$

Subtract 30° from both sides.

$$\angle f + 30° - 30° = 180° - 30°$$
$$\angle f = 150°$$

The shape containing $\angle h$ is a pentagon (five-sided polygon). It has a sum of interior angles of 180° (5 – 2) = 180°(3) = 540°. The sum of the angles of a triangle is 180°. The angles of the large triangle are 60°, 60°, and n°; therefore, $\angle n = 60°$

$$\angle h + \angle g + \angle n + \angle f + 55° = 540°$$
$$\angle h + 120° + 60° + 150° + 55° = 540°$$
$$\angle h + 385° = 540°$$

Subtract 385° from both sides.

$$\angle h + 385° - 385° = 540° - 385°$$
$$\angle h = 155°$$

$\angle c$ measures 50°, $\angle e$ measures 30°, $\angle f$ measures 150°, and $\angle h$ measures 155°.

38. B

The sum, S, of the interior angles of an n-sided polygon is given by the formula $S = 180°(n - 2)$.

The sum of the interior angles of a Canadian loonie can be determined as follows:

$S = 180°(n - 2)$

Substitute 11 for n.

$= 180(11 - 2)$

$= 180(9)$

$= 1\ 620°$

Since there are 11 interior equal angles in a Canadian loonie, 1 620 ÷ 11, $i = 147.3°$.

39. D

The sum of the two interior angles between the two sides that form $\angle e$, and $\angle e$ is equal to 360°. The measure of $\angle e$ can be determined as follows:

$$\angle e + 147.3° + 147.3° = 360°$$
$$\angle e + 294.6° = 360°$$
$$\angle e = 65.4°$$

UNIT TEST—MEASUREMENT AND GEOMETRY

Use the following information to answer the next question.

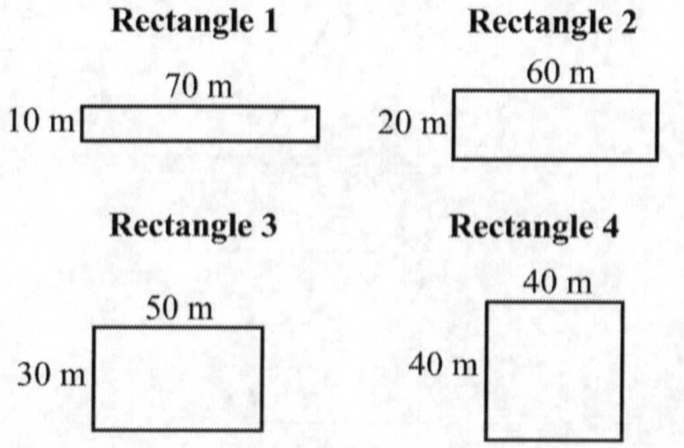

1. Which rectangle illustrates the rectangle with the maximum area?

A. Rectangle 1 **B.** Rectangle 2

C. Rectangle 3 **D.** Rectangle 4

Use the following information to answer the next question.

Wesley wishes to construct a rectangular enclosure from two identical boards, each with a length of 20 feet as shown. To make this enclosure, he plans to cut each board once, producing a total of four pieces.

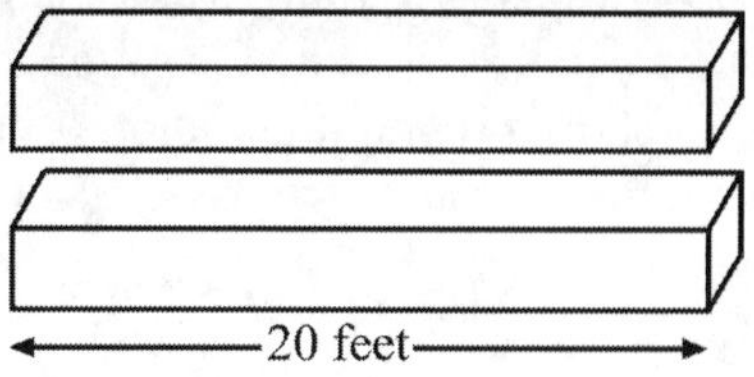

2. In order to construct the rectangular enclosure with the maximum possible area, Wesley should cut each board at

A. 10 feet **B.** 8 feet

C. 6 feet **D.** 4 feet

3. Ana is a lifeguard at a swimming pool. She needs to rope off a 60 m^2 rectangular area of the pool for swimming lessons. To the nearest tenth of a metre, what is the minimum length of rope needed to enclose this area?

A. 15.5 m

B. 16.0 m

C. 31.0 m

D. 32.0 m

4. A rectangular picture frame has a total area of 400 cm^2. If the cost for the frame is \$2.00/cm, then which of the following expressions describes the minimum cost, C, of the required framing material?

A. $C = \$2.00\,/\,\text{cm} \times 100\ \text{cm}$

B. $C = \$2.00\,/\,\text{cm} \times 80\ \text{cm}$

C. $C = \$2.00\,/\,\text{cm} \times 40\ \text{cm}$

D. $C = \$2.00\,/\,\text{cm} \times 20\ \text{cm}$

Use the following information to answer the next question.

Sam and Jill each have 200 m of fencing material to use to enclose rectangular gardens at their homes. Sam uses all of his material to build a four-sided rectangle around his garden. Jill uses all of her material to build a three-sided rectangle around her garden. She does not fence along the side of the garden bordering her house

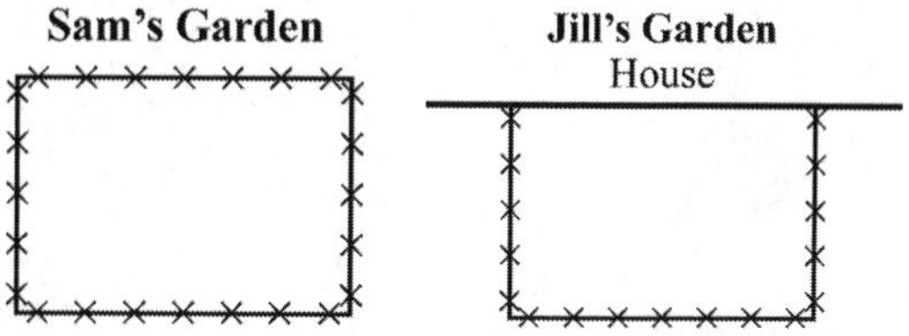

5. If Sam and Jill each chose dimensions that maximized the respective areas of their gardens, how much more area has Jill enclosed with her fence compared to Sam?

A. 2 500 m^2

B. 4 000 m^2

C. 5 000 m^2

D. 7500 m^2

Use the following information to answer the next question.

A rectangular enclosure is to be fenced off on three sides, with the other side bordered by the wall of a building. The enclosure is then to be divided into four smaller rectangular sections by erecting three fences perpendicular to the building, as shown.

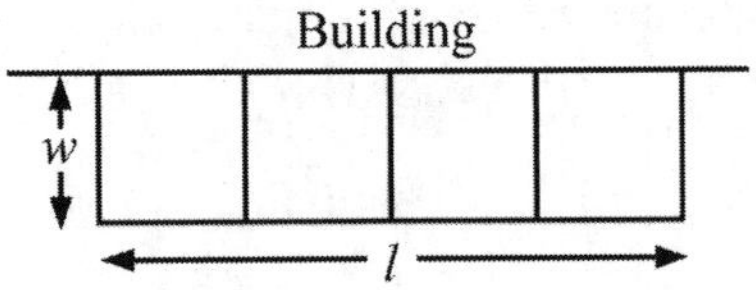

6. If no fencing is needed on the side of the enclosure that is next to the building, and 1 000 m of fencing is available for the entire project, then what are the values of the width, w, and the length, l, such that the entire rectangular enclosure has a maximum area?

A. $w = 200$ m, l=800 m

B. $w = 167$ m, $l = 167$ m

C. $w = 100$ m, $l = 500$ m

D. $w = 80$ m, l=600 m

Use the following information to answer the next question.

In the diagram shown, the areas of squares A, B, and C are 36 cm^2, 64 cm^2, and 100 cm^2, respectively.

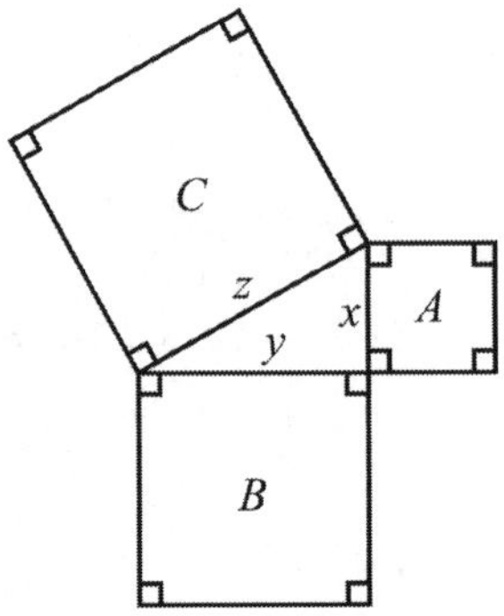

7. Which of the following equations describing the relationships between the sides or areas of the squares is **incorrect**?

A. $36 = 100 - 64$

B. $6^2 + 8^2 = 10^2$

C. $x^2 + y^2 = z^2$

D. $x + y = z$

Use the following information to answer the next question.

Monique draws a right triangle and then constructs a square on each side of the triangle, as shown in the illustration. The sides of the squares are given as x, y, and z.

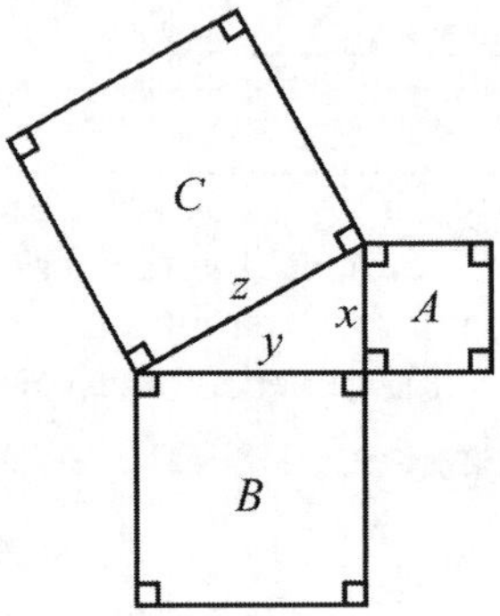

8. If square C has an area of 169 cm^2 and square A has an area of 144 cm^2, what is the sum of the lengths of sides x and y?

A. 1 cm **B.** 17 cm

C. 18 cm **D.** 25 cm

Use the following diagram to answer the next question.

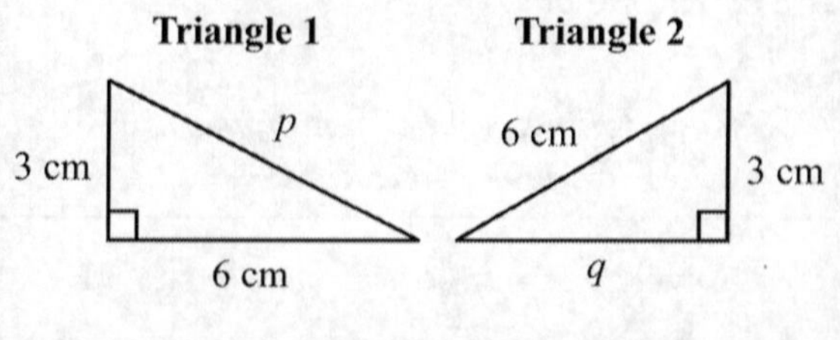

9. The value of the expression $p+q$ is

A. $\sqrt{3^2+6^2}+\sqrt{6^2+3^2}$

B. $\sqrt{3^2+6^2}+\sqrt{6^2-3^2}$

C. $\sqrt{3^2+6^2+6^2-3^2}$

D. $\sqrt{3^2+6^2+6^2+3^2}$

Use the following information to answer the next question.

Mark, a mountain climber, stands at the top of a cliff. From the edge of the cliff, he can see his base camp in the valley below. Mark calculates that the distance from the edge of the cliff to the edge of his base camp is 900 m and that he is 61 m higher than the level of his base camp, as shown.

10. Mark climbs straight down from the cliff. What is the distance, x, to the nearest tenth of a metre that he must now travel to get to the base camp?

A. 839.0 m **B.** 897.9 m

C. 902.1 m **D.** 961.0 m

Use the following information to answer the next question.

The garden plot shown is a composite shape consisting of a semicircle, triangle, and parallelogram.

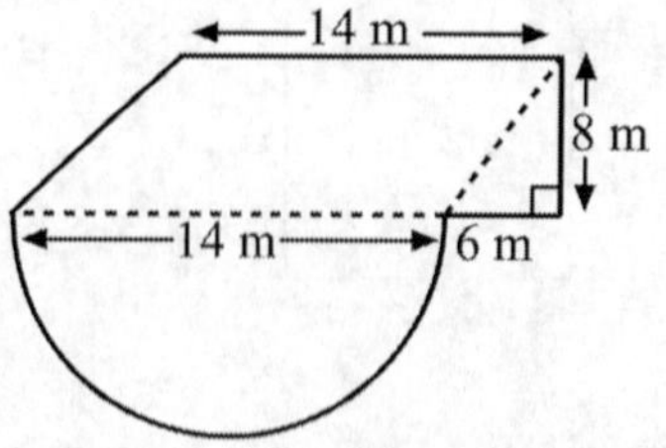

11. Plastic edging is set up around the outside of the garden plot. To the nearest metre, what is the length of the plastic edging?

A. 58 m **B.** 60 m

C. 82 m **D.** 90 m

Use the following information to answer the next question.

The floor plan of a hotel lobby is shown below:

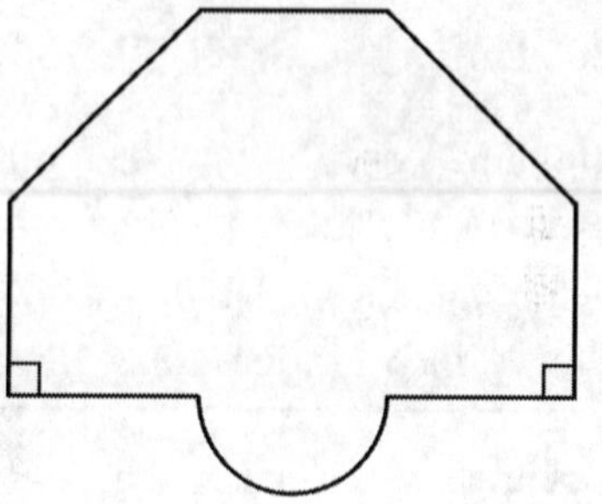

12. Which of the following formulas would **not** be useful in determining the area of the hotel lobby?

A. $A=\frac{1}{2}(a+b)h$

B. $A=\frac{\pi r^2}{2}$

C. $A=lw$

D. $A=\pi r$

Use the following information to answer the next question.

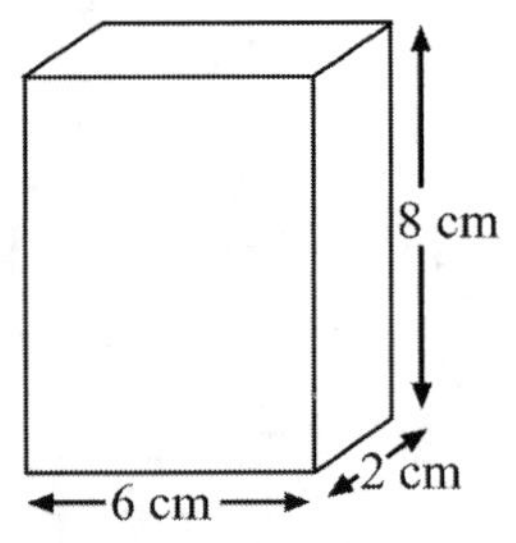

13. The maximum volume of the pyramid that would fit snugly inside the illustrated prism is

A. 96 cm^3 **B.** 48 cm^3

C. 32 cm^3 **D.** 16 cm^3

14. A cone has the same radius and height as a cylinder. A sphere has the same radius as a cylinder and a diameter equal to the height of the cylinder. If the volume of the cone is 200 cm^3 what is the volume of the sphere?

A. 200 cm^3 **B.** 300 cm^3

C. 400 cm^3 **D.** 600 cm^3

Use the following information to answer the next question.

A prism-shaped water tank and a pyramid-shaped water tank with particular dimensions are shown.

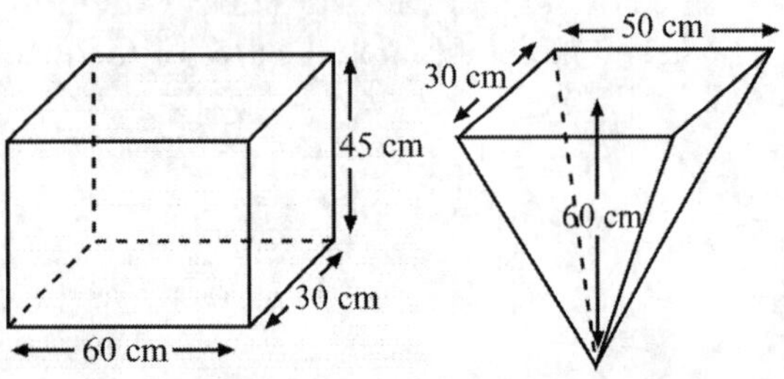

15. How much more water can the prism-shaped water tank hold compared to the pyramid-shaped water tank?

A. $9\ 000\text{ cm}^3$

B. $30\ 000\text{ cm}^3$

C. $51\ 000\text{ cm}^3$

D. $81\ 000\text{ cm}^3$

Use the following information to answer the next question.

A package of three golf balls is shown.

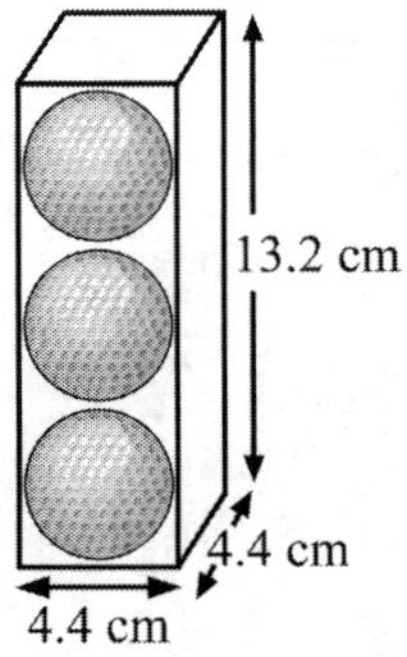

16. If the radius of each golf ball is 2.2 cm, how much extra space, correct to the nearest tenth, is there in a package of three golf balls $(\pi = 3.14)$?

A. 121.8 cm^3

B. 133.8 cm^3

C. 145.9 cm^3

D. 211.0 cm^3

17. A regular polygon has 24 sides. What is the measure of each interior angle?

A. 155°

B. 165°

C. 170°

D. 180°

Use the following information to answer the next question.

Pentagon *ABCDE* is shown, with each labelled interior angle

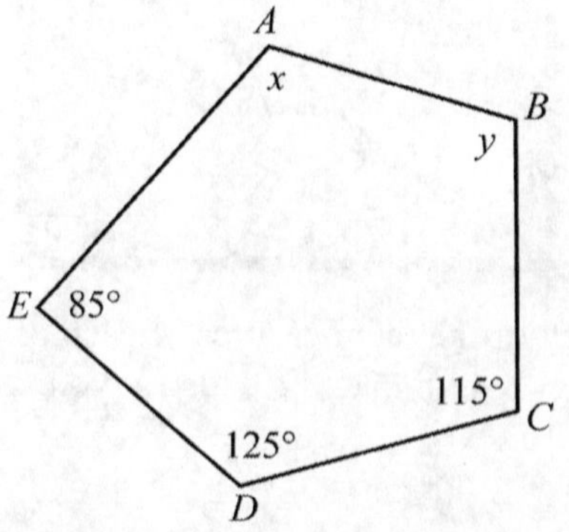

18. The sum of the measures of angles x and y is

A. 180°

B. 200°

C. 215°

D. 325°

Use the following information to answer the next question.

A diagram of two parallel lines and two transversals is shown.

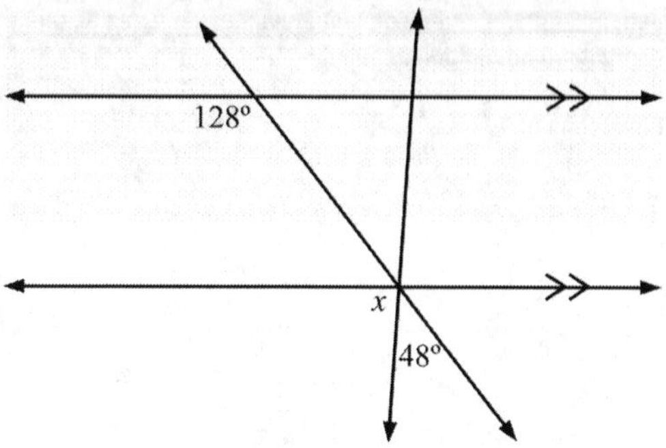

19. The measure of angle x is

A. 42°

B. 73°

C. 80°

D. 86°

Use the following information to answer the next question.

A special ramp was built in the shape of the trapezoid *ABCD*, where sides *BC* and *AD* are parallel.

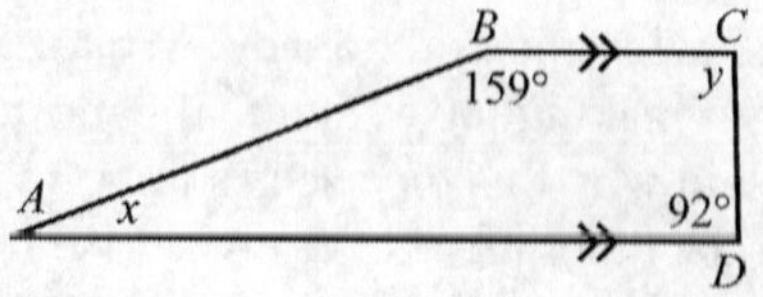

20. What are the measures of angles x and y?

A. $\angle x = 19°$, $\angle y = 90°$

B. $\angle x = 17°$, $\angle y = 88°$

C. $\angle x = 17°$, $\angle y = 92°$

D. $\angle x = 21°$, $\angle y = 88°$

Open Response

1 A company designing a new game needs to make three different solid game pieces: a cylindrical, conical, and spherical piece, with the dimensions shown.

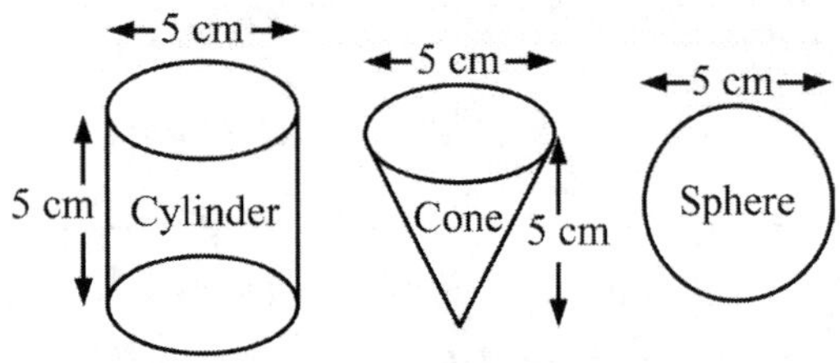

a) The aluminum used to make each of these game pieces costs 0.5¢/ cm^3 What is the cost of making the cylindrical game piece? Explain why this piece costs more to make than the other pieces.

b) Describe the relationship between the cost of a conical game piece compared to the cost of a cylindrical game piece.

c) Describe the relationship between the cost of a spherical game piece compared to the cost of a cylindrical game piece.

2 Farmer Dell built a gate with two cross brackets. The gate with the cross brackets and some angle measurements are shown.

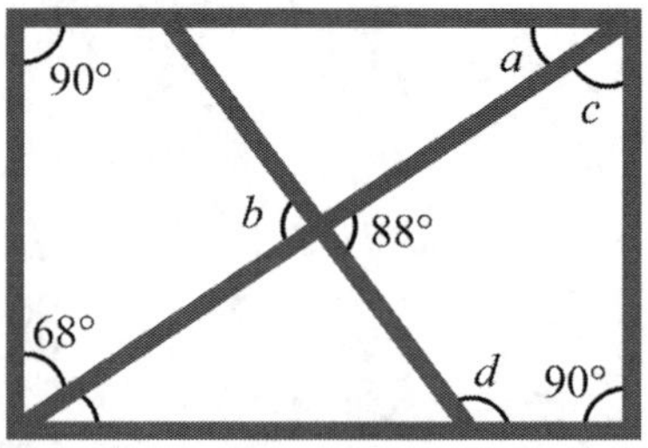

Determine the measures of each of the angles *a*, *b*, *c*, and *d*. Justify your answers.

ANSWERS AND SOLUTIONS—UNIT TEST

1. D	**7. D**	**13. C**	**19. C**
2. A	**8. B**	**14. C**	**20. D**
3. C	**9. B**	**15. C**	**OR 1. ****
4. B	**10. B**	**16. A**	**OR 2. ****
5. A	**11. B**	**17. B**	
6. C	**12. D**	**18. C**	

****SEE SOLUTIONS**

1. **D**

The rectangle with the maximum area occurs when $w = l = \frac{P}{4}$.

Since the perimeter, P, is 160 m,

$w = l = \frac{160}{4} = 40 \text{ m.}$

Rectangle 4, with a width of 40 m and a length of 40 m, has the maximum area for a rectangle with a perimeter of 160 m.

2. **A**

The total perimeter, P, of the two boards that will be used to make the rectangular enclosure is $20 \text{ feet} + 20 \text{ feet} = 40 \text{ feet}$.

The rectangle with the maximum area occurs when $w = l = \frac{P}{4}$.

Since P equals 40 feet, $w = l = \frac{40}{4} = 10 \text{ feet}$.

Each board must be cut at 10 feet to produce four cut pieces of equal length. The rectangular enclosure will be 10 feet by 10 feet.

3. **C**

The perimeter is represented by the rope needed to enclose the rectangular swimming area. The minimum length of rope required to enclose the given area occurs when $P = 4\sqrt{A}$.

Since $A = 60 \text{ m}^2$,

$$\begin{aligned} P &= 4\sqrt{60} \\ &\approx 4(7.746) \\ &\approx 31.0 \text{ m} \end{aligned}$$

The shortest rope required to enclose the given swimming area is 31.0 m.

4. **B**

To find the expression for the minimum cost, find the minimum perimeter to frame the area of the picture.

The minimum perimeter occurs when $P = 4\sqrt{A}$.

Since $A = 400 \text{ cm}^2$,

$$\begin{aligned} P &= 4\sqrt{400} \\ &= 4(20) \\ &= 80 \text{ cm} \end{aligned}$$

Since the framing material costs $2.00/cm and the perimeter of the picture is 80 cm, the correct expression for the minimum cost to frame the picture is $C = \$2.00/\text{cm} \times 80 \text{ cm}$.

5. **A**

Sam uses his fencing material, P, to enclose two lengths and two widths of his rectangular garden. The maximum area, A, of his garden occurs when $w = l = \frac{P}{4}$.

Since $P = 200 \text{ m}$,

$w = l = \frac{200}{4} = 50 \text{ m}$.

The maximum area, A, of Sam's rectangular garden can be determined as follows:

$$\begin{aligned} A &= (l)(w) \\ &= (50)(50) \\ &= 2\,500 \text{ m}^2 \end{aligned}$$

Jill uses her fencing material, P, to enclose only one length and two widths of her rectangular garden, since her house borders the other side.

The maximum area, A, of her garden occurs when the length is two times the width: $l = 2w$.

$P = l + 2w$

$P = 2w + 2w$ Substitute $2w$ for l.

$P = 4w$

$w = \frac{P}{4}$

$w = \frac{200}{4}$ Substitute 200 for P.

$w = 50$ m

Since $l = 2w$, the value of $l = 2 \times 50 = 100$ m.

The maximum area, A, of Jill's rectangular enclosure can be determined as follows:

$$A = (l)(w) = (100)(50) = 5\ 000 \text{ m}^2$$

Jill has enclosed $5\ 000 \text{ m}^2 - 2\ 500 \text{ m}^2 = 2\ 500 \text{ m}^2$ more area with her fence than Sam.

6. **C**

The rectangular enclosure is divided into four rectangular sections of equal area, and there is 1 000 m of fencing, P, available. The maximum area, A, of the rectangular enclosure occurs when the length is five times the width $(l = 5w)$.

$P = l + 5w$

$P = 5w + 5w$ Substitute $5w$ for l.

$P = 10w$

$w = \frac{P}{10}$

$w = \frac{1\ 000}{10}$ Substitute 1 000 m for P.

$w = 100$ m

Since $l = 5w$, the value of $l = 5 \times 100 = 500$ m.

The maximum area of the rectangular enclosure occurs when $w = 100$ m and $l = 500$ m.

7. **D**

The area of a square can be found by applying the formula $A = s^2$.

Using this formula enables you to find the lengths of the sides of the three squares.

Square A: Area = 36 cm^2

$$A = x^2$$
$$36 = x^2$$
$$\sqrt{36} = \sqrt{x^2}$$
$$6 = x$$

Square B: Area = 64 cm^2

$$A = y^2$$
$$64 = y^2$$
$$\sqrt{64} = \sqrt{y^2}$$
$$8 = y$$

Square C: Area = 100 cm^2

$$A = z^2$$
$$100 = z^2$$
$$\sqrt{100} = \sqrt{z^2}$$
$$10 = z$$

According to the formula, Area C = Area A + Area B. The correct equations describing the relationships between the sides or areas of the squares are the following:

$$x^2 + y^2 = z^2$$
$$36 + 64 = 100 \text{ or } 36 = 100 - 64$$
$$6^2 + 8^2 = 10^2$$

The equation $x + y = z$ is an incorrect description of the relationship between the sides of the squares $(6 + 8 \neq 10)$.

8. **B**

According to the Pythagorean theorem, Area C = Area A + Area B

or

$$\text{Area } B = \text{Area } C - \text{Area } A = 169 - 144 = 25$$

The area of a square can be found by applying the formula $A = s^2$. Recall that $x^2 + y^2 = z^2$. Using this formula enables you to find the length of the sides of the three squares.

Square A: Area = 144 cm^2

$$A = x^2$$
$$144 = x^2$$
$$\sqrt{144} = \sqrt{x^2}$$
$$12 \text{ cm} = x$$

Square B: Area = 25 cm^2

$$A = y^2$$
$$25 = y^2$$
$$\sqrt{25} = \sqrt{y^2}$$
$$5 \text{ cm} = y$$

Square C Area = 169 cm^2

$$A = z^2$$
$$169 = z^2$$
$$\sqrt{169} = \sqrt{z^2}$$
$$13 \text{ cm} = z$$

The sum of the sides is
$x + y = 12 \text{ cm} + 5 \text{ cm} = 17 \text{ cm}$.

9. B

Using the Pythagorean theorem $c^2 = a^2 + b^2$, find the missing length of each triangle.

Triangle 1: $c^2 = a^2 + b^2$

$$p^2 = (3)^2 + (6)^2$$
$$p = \sqrt{3^2 + 6^2}$$

Triangle 2: $c^2 = a^2 + b^2$

$$(6)^2 = (3)^2 + (q)^2$$
$$6^2 - 3^2 = q^2$$
$$q^2 = 6^2 - 3^2$$
$$q = \sqrt{6^2 - 3^2}$$

The value of the expression $p + q$ is
$\sqrt{3^2 + 6^2} + \sqrt{6^2 - 3^2}$.

10. B

Using the Pythagorean theorem $c^2 = a^2 + b^2$, find the missing distance, x, that Mark must travel to reach the base camp.

$c^2 = a^2 + b^2$

Substitute 900 m for c and 61 m for a

$900^2 = 61^2 + x^2$

$810\ 000 = 3\ 721 + x^2$

Subtract 3 721 from both sides

$810\ 000 - 3\ 721 = 3\ 721 - 3\ 721 + x^2$

$810\ 000 - 3\ 721 = x^2$

$806\ 279 = x^2$

$\sqrt{806\ 279} = x$

$x = \sqrt{806\ 279}$

$x \approx 897.9$

The distance, x, that Mark must travel to reach the base camp is 897.9 m.

11. B

In order to determine the length of the plastic edging, find the perimeter of each section of the composite shape.

The perimeter (circumference) of a semicircle is half the circumference of a circle.

$$C_{\text{semicircle}} = \frac{C_{\text{circle}}}{2} = \frac{\pi d}{2}$$

Since $d = 14$ m,

$$C_{\text{semicircle}} = \frac{\pi(14)}{2} \approx 22 \text{ m}$$

The missing side of the parallelogram can be found using the Pythagorean theorem $c^2 = a^2 + b^2$:

$c^2 = (8)^2 + (6)^2$

$c^2 = 8^2 + 6^2$

$c^2 = 64 + 36$

$c^2 = 100$

$c = \sqrt{100}$

$c = 10$ m

To find the total distance, P, around the whole garden plot, add all the sides of the shape together:

$$P = 14 + 8 + 6 + 22 + 10 = 60 \text{ m}$$

The total length of the plastic edging is 60 m.

12. D.

The following three formulas are useful in determining the area of the hotel lobby:

$A = \frac{1}{2}(a + b)h$, since it is the formula used to find the area of a trapezoid.

$A = \frac{\pi r^2}{2}$, since it is the formula used to find the area of a semicircle.

$A = lw$, since it is the formula used to find the area of a rectangle.The formula $A = \pi r$ is not useful, since it does not describe the area of the semicircle. To be useful, r must be a two-dimensional variable (r^2) reflecting the area of a circle.

13. C

The volume of a pyramid is $\frac{1}{3}$ the volume of a prism with the same length, width, and height. Determine the maximum volume of the pyramid as follows:

$$V_{\text{pyramid}} = \frac{1}{3}V_{\text{prism}}$$
$$= \frac{1}{3}(lwh)$$

Substitute 6 cm for *l*, 2 cm for *w*, and 8 cm for *h*.

$$= \frac{1}{3}(6 \times 2 \times 8)$$
$$= \frac{1}{3}(96)$$
$$= 32 \text{ cm}^3$$

The maximum volume of the pyramid that would fit snugly inside the prism is 32 cm^3.

14. C

The volume of a cone that has the same radius and height as a cylinder is $\frac{1}{3}$ the volume of a cylinder. Determine the volume of the cylinder as follows:

$$V_{\text{cone}} = \frac{1}{3}V_{\text{cylinder}}$$
$$3V_{\text{cone}} = V_{\text{cylinder}}$$
$$3(200) = V_{\text{cylinder}}$$
$$V_{\text{cylinder}} = 600 \text{ cm}^3$$

It is given that the volume of a sphere with the same radius as a cylinder and a diameter equal to the height of a cylinder is $\frac{2}{3}$ the cylinder's volume.
Determine the volume of the sphere as follows:

$$V_{\text{sphere}} = \frac{2}{3}V_{\text{cylinder}}$$
$$= \frac{2}{3}(600)$$
$$= \frac{1\ 200}{3}$$
$$= 400 \text{ cm}^3$$

The volume of the sphere is 400 cm^3.

15. C

The volume of the prism-shaped water tank with the dimensions $l = 60$ cm, $w = 30$ cm, and $h = 45$ cm can be determined as follows:

$$V_{\text{prism}} = (l)(w)(h)$$
$$= (60)(30)(45)$$
$$= 81\ 000 \text{ cm}^3$$

The volume of the pyramid-shaped water tank with the dimensions $l = 50$ cm, $w = 30$ cm, and $h = 60$ cm can be determined as follows:

$$V_{\text{pyramid}} = \frac{(l)(w)(h)}{3}$$
$$= \frac{(50)(30)(60)}{3}$$
$$= 30\ 000 \text{ cm}^3$$

The difference between these two volumes is $81\ 000 \text{ cm}^3 - 30\ 000 \text{ cm}^3 = 51\ 000 \text{ cm}^3$.
The prism-shaped water tank can hold $51\ 000 \text{ cm}^3$ more water than the pyramid-shaped water tank.

16. A

The package is in the shape of a prism.
Its volume can be determined as follows:

$$V_{\text{prism}} = (l)(w)(h)$$
$$= (4.4)(4.4)(13.2)$$

Substitute 4.4 cm for *l*, 4.4 cm for *w*, and 13.2 cm for *h*.

$$\approx 255.6 \text{ cm}^3$$

Each ball is spherical. The diameter,*d*, of each ball is 4.4 cm. The radius can be determined as follows:

$$r = \frac{d}{2} = \frac{4.4 \text{ cm}}{2} = 2.2 \text{ cm}$$

The volume occupied by each ball can be determined as follows:

$$V_{\text{sphere}} = \frac{4}{3}\pi r^3$$

Substitute 2.2 cm for *r*.

$$= \frac{4\pi(2.2)^3}{3}$$
$$\approx 44.6 \text{ cm}^3$$

The volume occupied by all three balls is $V_{\text{golfballs}} = 44.6 \times 3 = 133.8 \text{ cm}^3$.

The volume of the extra space is the difference between the volume of the package and the volume of the three golf balls.

$$\begin{aligned} V_{\text{space}} &= V_{\text{prism}} - V_{\text{golf balls}} \\ &= 255.6\ \text{cm}^3 - 133.8\ \text{cm}^3 \\ &= 121.8\ \text{cm}^3 \end{aligned}$$

17. B

The sum, *S*, of the measures of the interior angles of a 24-sided polygon can be found using the formula $S = 180°(n-2)$, where $n = 24$.

$$\begin{aligned} S &= 180°(n-2) \\ &= 180°(24-2) \\ &= 180°(22) \\ &= 3\ 960° \end{aligned}$$

Since it is a regular polygon, the measure of each interior angle, *a*, is the same.

$$a = \left(\frac{3\ 960}{24}\right) = 165°$$

For a 24-sided regular polygon, the measure of each interior angle is 165°.

18. C

The sum, *S*, of the measures of the interior angles of a pentagon can be found using the formula $S = 180°(n-2)$, where $n = 5$.

$$\begin{aligned} S &= 180°(n-2) \\ &= 180°(5-2) \\ &= 180°(3) \\ &= 540° \end{aligned}$$

Since the sum of the angles is 540°, you can find the values of angles *x* and *y* as follows:

$$\begin{aligned} 85° + 125° + 115° + x + y &= 540° \\ 325° + x + y &= 540° \end{aligned}$$

Subtract 325° from both sides.

$$\begin{aligned} 325° - 325° + x + y &= 540° - 325° \\ x + y &= 215° \end{aligned}$$

The sum of the measures of *x* and *y* is 215°.

19. C

The angle 128º and the angle on the other side of the bottom parallel line next to angle $\angle x$ are co-interior angles. Since co-interior angles are supplementary, the measure of that angle is 180º – 128º = 52º.

The sum of the measures of angles $\angle x$, 48º, and 52º is 180º, since the measure of a straight line is 180º. Determine the measure of $\angle x$ as follows:

$$\begin{aligned} \angle x + 48° + 52° &= 180° \\ \angle x + 100° &= 180° \end{aligned}$$

Subtract 100° from both sides

$$\begin{aligned} \angle x + 100° - 100° &= 180° - 100° \\ \angle x &= 80° \end{aligned}$$

The measure of angle *x* is 80°.

20. D

The angle measuring 92º and $\angle y$ are co-interior angles. Since co-interior angles are supplementary,

$$\angle y + 92° = 180°$$

Subtract 92° from both sides.

$$\begin{aligned} \angle y + 92° - 92° &= 180° - 92° \\ \angle y &= 88° \end{aligned}$$

The sum of the measures of the interior angles of a quadrilateral is 360º; therefore,

$$\angle x + 159° + \angle y + 92° = 360°$$

Substitute 88° for $\angle y$.

$$\begin{aligned} \angle x + 159° + 88° + 92° &= 360° \\ \angle x + 339° &= 360° \end{aligned}$$

Subtract 339° from both sides.

$$\begin{aligned} \angle x + 339° - 339° &= 360 - 339° \\ \angle x &= 21° \end{aligned}$$

$\angle x = 21°$ and $\angle y = 88°$.

OR 1 A

$$V_{\text{cylinder}} = \pi r^2 h\ ,$$

where $r = \frac{d}{2} = \frac{5}{2} = 2.5$ cm

Substitute 2.5 cm for *r* and 5 cm for *h*.

$$\begin{aligned} &= \pi(2.5)^2(5) \\ &\approx 98.175\ \text{cm}^3 \end{aligned}$$

$$V_{\text{cone}} = \frac{1}{3}\left(\pi r^2 h\right)$$

Substitute 2.5 cm for *r* and 5 cm for *h*.

$$\begin{aligned} &= \frac{1}{3}\pi(2.5)^2(5) \\ &\approx 32.725\ \text{cm}^3 \end{aligned}$$

$$V_{\text{sphere}} = \frac{4}{3}\pi r^3$$

Substitute 2.5 for *r*

$$\begin{aligned} &= \frac{4}{3}\pi(2.5)^3 \\ &\approx 65.45\ \text{cm}^3 \end{aligned}$$

The cost of the cylindrical game piece is as follows:

$$\begin{aligned} C &= 98.175\ \text{cm}^3 \times 0.5¢/\text{cm}^3 \\ &= 98.175\ \text{cm}^3 \times \$0.005/\text{cm}^3 \\ &= \$0.49 \end{aligned}$$

Since the game pieces are solid and the volume of the cylinder is more than the volume of the cone and the volume of the sphere, the cylinder requires more material to construct.

b)

The formula for the volume of a cone $\left(V = \frac{1}{3}\pi r^2 h\right)$ and the formula for the volume of a cylinder $\left(V = \pi r^2 h\right)$

show that the volume of the cone is $\frac{1}{3}$ the volume of the cylinder.

This can be verified as follows:

$$\frac{1}{3}\left(V_{\text{cylinder}}\right) = V_{\text{cone}}$$

$$\frac{1}{3}\left(98.175\ \text{cm}^3\right) = 32.725\ \text{cm}^3$$

$$32.725\ \text{cm}^3 = 32.725\ \text{cm}^3$$

It costs $\frac{1}{3}$ the price of a cylindrical game piece to make a conical game piece, or

$\frac{1}{3} \times \$0.49 = \$0.16$.

c)

Observe that the volume of the sphere is two times the volume of the cone. This can be verified as follows:

$$2\left(V_{\text{cone}}\right) = V_{\text{sphere}}$$

$$2\left(32.725\ \text{cm}^3\right) = 65.45\ \text{cm}^3$$

$$65.45\ \text{cm}^3 = 65.45\ \text{cm}^3$$

Furthermore, since

$V_{\text{cone}} = \frac{1}{3}V_{\text{cylinder}}$ and $V_{\text{cone}} = \frac{1}{2}V_{\text{sphere}}$, then

$$\frac{1}{2}V_{\text{sphere}} = \frac{1}{3}V_{\text{cylinder}}$$

Multiply both side by 2

$$2 \times \frac{1}{2}V_{\text{sphere}} = 2 \times \frac{1}{3}V_{\text{cylinder}}$$

$$V_{\text{sphere}} = \frac{2}{3}V_{\text{cylinder}}$$

It costs $\frac{2}{3}$ the price of a cylindrical game piece to make a spherical game piece, or

$\frac{2}{3} \times \$0.49 = \$0.32$.

OR 2

$\angle c$ and 68° are alternate interior angles, since the two sides of the gate are parallel. Alternate interior angles are equal; thus, $\angle c = 68°$.

$\angle b$ and 88° are vertically-opposite angles. Since vertically-opposite angles have equal measures, $\angle b = 88°$.

$\angle a$, 68°, and 90° are the interior angles of the right triangle in the upper-left half of the gate.

Subtract 158° from both sides

$$\angle a + 158° - 158° = 180° - 158°$$

$$\angle a = 22°$$

Finally, $\angle d$, $\angle c$, 88°, and 90° are the interior angles of the quadrilateral in the bottom-right side of the gate. The sum of the measures of the interior angles of a quadrilateral is 360°; therefore,

$$\angle d + \angle c + 88° + 90° = 360°$$

$$\angle d + 68° + 88° + 90° = 360°$$

$$\angle d + 246° = 360°$$

Subtract 246° from both sides

$$\angle d + 246° - 246° = 360° - 246°$$

$$\angle d = 114°$$

Thus,

$\angle a = 22°$, $\angle b = 88°$, $\angle c = 68°$, and $\angle d = 114°$.

Key Strategies for Success on Tests

KEY STRATEGIES FOR SUCCESS ON TESTS

THINGS TO CONSIDER WHEN TAKING A TEST

It is normal to feel anxious before you write a test. You can manage this anxiety by using the following strategies:

- Think positive thoughts. Imagine yourself doing well on the test.
- Make a conscious effort to relax by taking several slow, deep, controlled breaths. Concentrate on the air going in and out of your body.
- Before you begin the test, ask questions if you are unsure of anything.
- Jot down key words or phrases from any instructions your teacher gives you.
- Look over the entire test to find out the number and kinds of questions on the test.
- Read each question closely, and reread if necessary.
- Pay close attention to key vocabulary words. Sometimes, these words are **bolded** or *italicized*, and they are usually important words in the question.
- If you are putting your answers on an answer sheet, mark your answers carefully. Always print clearly. If you wish to change an answer, erase the mark completely, and ensure that your final answer is darker than the one you have erased.
- Use highlighting to note directions, key words, and vocabulary that you find confusing or that are important to answering the question.
- Double-check to make sure you have answered everything before handing in your test.
- When taking tests, students often overlook the easy words. Failure to pay close attention to these words can result in an incorrect answer. One way to avoid this is to be aware of these words and to underline, circle, or highlight them while you are taking the test.
- Even though some words are easy to understand, they can change the meaning of the entire question, so it is important that you pay attention to them. Here are some examples.

all	always	most likely	probably	best	not
difference	usually	except	most	unlikely	likely

Example

1. Which of the following expressions is **incorrect**?

A. $3 + 2 \geq 5$

B. $4 - 3 < 2$

C. $5 \times 4 < 15$

D. $6 \times 3 \geq 18$

Test Preparation and Test-Taking Skills

Helpful Strategies for Answering Multiple-Choice Questions

A multiple-choice question gives you some information and then asks you to select an answer from four choices. Each question has one correct answer. The other choices are distractors, which are incorrect.

The following strategies can help you when answering multiple-choice questions:

- Quickly skim through the entire test. Find out how many questions there are, and plan your time accordingly.
- Read and reread questions carefully. Underline key words, and try to think of an answer before looking at the choices.
- If there is a graphic, look at the graphic, read the question, and go back to the graphic. Then, you may want to underline the important information from the question.
- Carefully read the choices. Read the question first and then each choice that goes with it.
- When choosing an answer, try to eliminate those choices that are clearly wrong or do not make sense.
- Some questions may ask you to select the best answer. These questions will always include words like *best*, *most appropriate*, or *most likely*. All of the choices will be correct to some degree, but one of the choices will be better than the others in some way. Carefully read all four choices before choosing the answer you think is the best.
- If you do not know the answer, or if the question does not make sense to you, it is better to guess than to leave it blank.
- Do not spend too much time on any one question. Make a mark (*) beside a difficult question, and come back to it later. If you are leaving a question to come back to later, make sure you also leave the space on the answer sheet, if you are using one.

- Remember to go back to the difficult questions at the end of the test; sometimes, clues are given throughout the test that will provide you with answers.
- Note any negative words like *no* or *not*, and be sure your answer fits the question.
- Before changing an answer, be sure you have a very good reason to do so.
- Do not look for patterns on your answer sheet, if you are using one.

Helpful Strategies for Answering Written-Response Questions

A written response requires you to respond to a question or directive indicated by words such as explain, predict, list, describe, show your work, solve, or calculate. The following strategies can help you when answering written-response questions:

- Read and reread the question carefully.
- Recognize and pay close attention to directing words such as *explain*, *show your work*, and *describe*.
- Underline key words and phrases that indicate what is required in your answer, such as *explain*, *estimate*, *answer*, *calculate*, or *show your work*.
- Write down rough, point-form notes regarding the information you want to include in your answer.
- Think about what you want to say, and organize information and ideas in a coherent and concise manner within the time limit you have for the question.
- Be sure to answer every part of the question that is asked.
- Include as much information as you can when you are asked to explain your thinking.
- Include a picture or diagram if it will help to explain your thinking.
- Try to put your final answer to a problem in a complete sentence to be sure it is reasonable.
- Reread your response to ensure you have answered the question.
- Ask yourself if your answer makes sense.
- Ask yourself if your answer sounds right.
- Use appropriate subject vocabulary and terms in your response.

About Mathematics Tests

What You Need to Know about Mathematics Tests

To do well on a mathematics test, you need to understand and apply your knowledge of mathematical concepts. Reading skills can also make a difference in how well you perform. Reading skills can help you follow instructions and find key words, as well as read graphs, diagrams, and tables. They can also help you solve mathematics problems.

Mathematics tests usually have two types of questions: questions that ask for understanding of mathematics ideas and questions that test how well you can solve mathematics problems.

How You Can Prepare for Mathematics Tests

The following strategies are particular to preparing for and writing mathematics tests:

- Know how to use your calculator, and, if it is allowed, use your own for the test.
- Note taking is a good way to review and study important information from your class notes and textbook.
- Sketch a picture of the problem, procedure, or term. Drawing is helpful for learning and remembering concepts.
- Check your answer to practice questions by working backward to the beginning. You can find the beginning by going step by step in reverse order.
- Use the following steps when answering questions with graphics (pictures, diagrams, tables, or graphs):
  1. Read the title of the graphic and any key words.
  2. Read the test question carefully to figure out what information you need to find in the graphic.
  3. Go back to the graphic to find the information you need.
  4. Decide which operation is needed.
- Always pay close attention when pressing the keys on your calculator. Repeat the procedure a second time to be sure you pressed the correct keys.

TEST PREPARATION COUNTDOWN

If you develop a plan for studying and test preparation, you will perform well on tests.

Here is a general plan to follow seven days before you write a test.

COUNTDOWN: 7 DAYS BEFORE THE TEST

1. Use "Finding Out about the Test" to help you make your own personal test preparation plan.
2. Review the following information:
   - Areas to be included on the test
   - Types of test items
   - General and specific test tips
3. Start preparing for the test at least seven days before the test. Develop your test preparation plan, and set time aside to prepare and study.

COUNTDOWN: 6, 5, 4, 3, 2 DAYS BEFORE THE TEST

1. Review old homework assignments, quizzes, and tests.
2. Rework problems on quizzes and tests to make sure you still know how to solve them.
3. Correct any errors made on quizzes and tests.
4. Review key concepts, processes, formulas, and vocabulary.
5. Create practice test questions for yourself, and answer them. Work out many sample problems.

COUNTDOWN: THE NIGHT BEFORE THE TEST

1. Use the night before the test for final preparation, which includes reviewing and gathering materials needed for the test before going to bed.
2. Most importantly, get a good night's rest, and know you have done everything possible to do well on the test.

TEST DAY

1. Eat a healthy and nutritious breakfast.
2. Ensure you have all the necessary materials.
3. Think positive thoughts, such as "I can do this," "I am ready," and "I know I can do well."
4. Arrive at your school early, so you are not rushing, which can cause you anxiety and stress.

SUMMARY OF HOW TO BE SUCCESSFUL DURING A TEST

You may find some of the following strategies useful for writing a test:

- Take two or three deep breaths to help you relax.
- Read the directions carefully, and underline, circle, or highlight any important words.
- Look over the entire test to understand what you will need to do.
- Budget your time.
- Begin with an easy question or a question you know you can answer correctly rather than follow the numerical question order of the test.
- If you cannot remember how to answer a question, try repeating the deep breathing and physical relaxation activities. Then, move on to visualization and positive self-talk to get yourself going.
- When answering questions with graphics (pictures, diagrams, tables, or graphs), look at the question carefully, and use the following steps:
    1. Read the title of the graphic and any key words.
    2. Read the test question carefully to figure out what information you need to find in the graphic.
    3. Go back to the graphic to find the information you need.
- Write down anything you remember about the subject on the reverse side of your test paper. This activity sometimes helps to remind you that you do know something and are capable of writing the test.
- Look over your test when you have finished, and double-check your answers to be sure you did not forget anything.

NOTES

Practice Tests

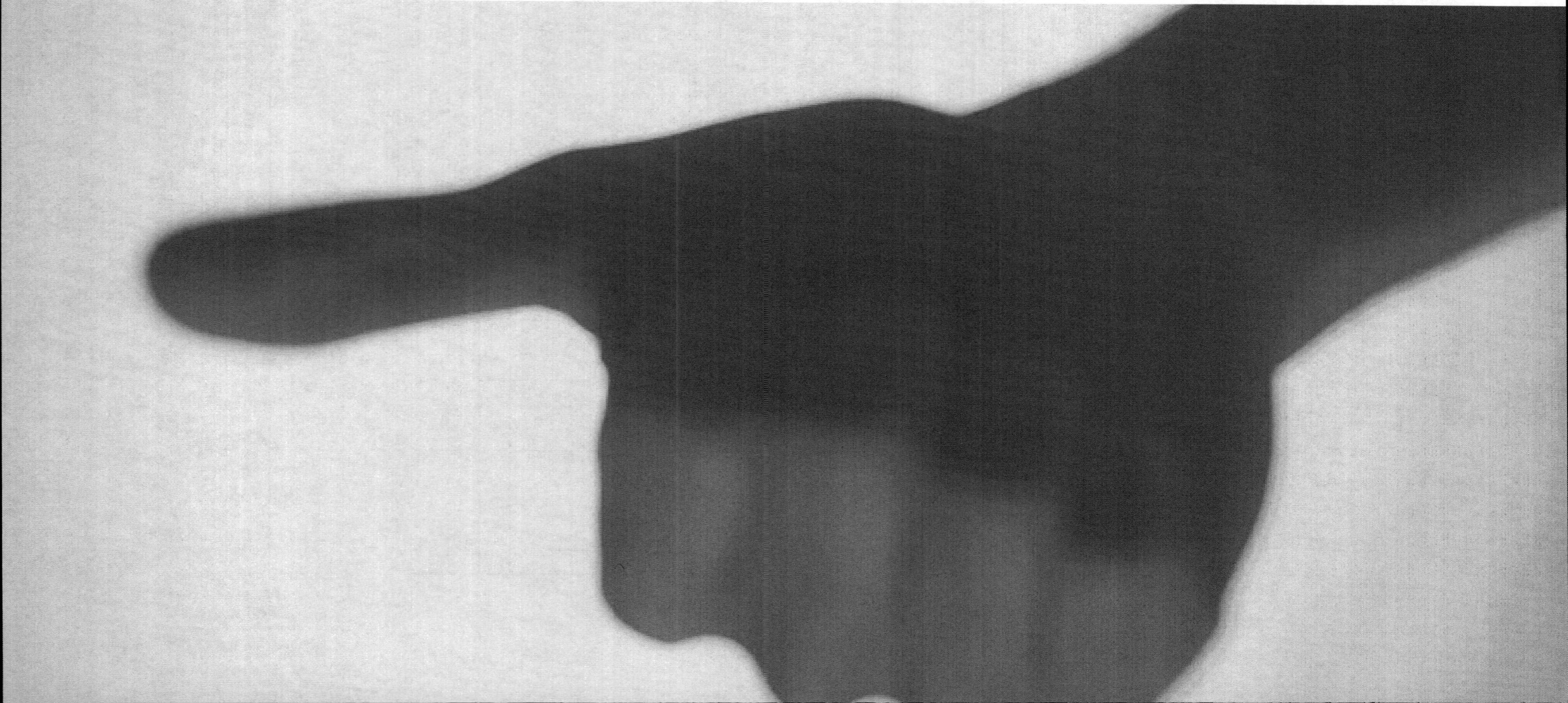

PRACTICE TESTS

Table of Correlations		
Specific Expectation	**Practice Test 1**	**Practice Test 2**
Solving Problems Involving Proportional Reasoning		
NA1.01 *illustrate equivalent ratios, using a variety of tools*	1	
NA1.02 *represent, using equivalent ratios and proportions, directly proportional relationships arising from realistic situations*		1
NA1.03 *solve for the unknown value in a proportion, using a variety of methods*	2	2
NA1.04 *make comparisons using unit rates*	3	
NA1.05 *solve problems involving ratios, rates, and directly proportional relationships in various contexts*	4, 5	3
NA1.06 *solve problems requiring the expression of percents, fractions, and decimals in their equivalent forms*		4, 5
Simplifying Expressions and Solving Equations		
NA2.02 *relate their understanding of inverse operations to squaring and taking the square root, and apply inverse operations to simplify expressions and solve equations*	9	
NA2.03 *describe the relationship between the algebraic and geometric representations of a single-variable term up to degree three [i.e., length, which is one dimensional, can be represented by x; area, which is two dimensional, can be represented by (x)(x) or x^2; volume, which is three dimensional, can be represented by (x)(x)(x), $(x^2)(x)$, or x^3]*	6	
NA2.04 *substitute into and evaluate algebraic expressions involving exponents (i.e., evaluate expressions involving natural-number exponents with rational-number bases)*		6
NA2.05 *add and subtract polynomials involving the same variable up to degree three, using a variety of tools*	7	9
NA2.06 *multiply a polynomial by a monomial involving the same variable to give results up to degree three, using a variety of tools*		7
NA2.07 *solve first-degree equations with non-fractional coefficients, using a variety of tools and strategies*	8	
NA2.08 *substitute into algebraic equations and solve for one variable in the first degree*		8
Using Data Management to Investigate Relationships		
LR1.01 *interpret the meanings of points on scatter plots or graphs that represent linear relations, including scatter plots or graphs in more than one quadrant*	10	10
LR 1.04 *describe trends and relationships observed in data, make inferences from data, compare the inferences with hypotheses about the data, and explain any differences between the inferences and the hypotheses*	14	11
Determining Characteristics of Linear Relations		
LR 2.01 *construct tables of values and graphs, using a variety of tools, to represent linear relations derived from descriptions of realistic situations*	11	12

LR 2.02 *construct tables of values, scatter plots, and lines or curves of best fit as appropriate, using a variety of tools, for linearly related and non-linearly related data collected from a variety of sources*	12	
LR 2.03 *identify, through investigation, some properties of linear relations (i.e., numerically, the first difference is a constant, which represents a constant rate of change; graphically, a straight line represents the relation), and apply these properties to determine whether a relation is linear or non-linear*	13	13, 14
Investigating Constant Rate of Change		
LR3.01 *determine, through investigation, that the rate of change of a linear relation can be found by choosing any two points on the line that represents the relation, finding the vertical change between the points (i.e., the rise) and the horizontal change between the points (i.e., the run), and writing the ratio* $\frac{\text{rise}}{\text{run}}$ *(i.e., rate of change* $= \frac{\text{rise}}{\text{run}}$*)*	15	
LR3.02 *determine, through investigation, connections among the representations of a constant rate of change of a linear relation*	18	15
LR3.03 *compare the properties of direct variation and partial variation in applications, and identify the initial value*	16	18
LR3.04 *express a linear relation as an equation in two variables, using the rate of change and the initial value*		16
LR3.05 *describe the meaning of the rate of change and the initial value for a linear relation arising from a realistic situation, and describe a situation that could be modelled by a given linear equation*	17	17
Connecting Various Representations of Linear Relations and Solving Problems Using the Representations		
LR4.01 *determine values of a linear relation by using a table of values, by using the equation of the relation, and by interpolating or extrapolating from the graph of the relation*	19	19
LR4.02 *describe a situation that would explain the events illustrated by a given graph of a relationship between two variables*	20	
LR4.03 *determine other representations of a linear relation arising from a realistic situation, given one representation*		20, 23
LR4.04 *solve problems that can be modelled with first-degree equations, and compare the algebraic method to other solution methods*	21	
LR4.05 *describe the effects on a linear graph and make the corresponding changes to the linear equation when the conditions of the situation they represent are varied*		21
LR4.06 *determine graphically the point of intersection of two linear relations, and interpret the intersection point in the context of an application*	22, 23	22
Investigating the Optimal Values of Measurements of Rectangles		
MG1.01 *determine the maximum area of a rectangle with a given perimeter by constructing a variety of rectangles, using a variety of tools, and by examining various values of the area as the side lengths change and the perimeter remains constant*	24	
MG1.02 *determine the minimum perimeter of a rectangle with a given area by constructing a variety of rectangles, using a variety of tools, and by examining various values of the side lengths and the perimeter as the area stays constant*		24
MG1.03 *solve problems that require maximizing the area of a rectangle for a fixed perimeter or minimizing the perimeter of a rectangle for a fixed area*	25	

Solving Problems Involving Perimeter, Area, and Volume		
MG2.01 *relate the geometric representation of the Pythagorean theorem to the algebraic representation* $a^2 + b^2 = c^2$		25
MG2.02 *solve problems using the Pythagorean theorem, as required in applications*	26	
MG2.03 *solve problems involving the areas and perimeters of composite two-dimensional shapes (i.e., combinations of rectangles, triangles, parallelograms, trapezoids, and circles)*	28	26
MG2.04 *develop, through investigation, the formulas for the volume of a pyramid, a cone, and a sphere*	27	
MG2.05 *solve problems involving the volumes of prisms, pyramids, cylinders, cones, and spheres*		27, 28
Investigating and Applying Geometric Relationships		
MG3.01 *determine, through investigation using a variety of tools, and describe the properties and relationships of the interior and exterior angles of triangles, quadrilaterals, and other polygons, and apply the results to problems involving the angles of polygons*	29, 31	29
MG3.02 *determine, through investigation using a variety of tools, and describe the properties and relationships of the angles formed by parallel lines cut by a transversal, and apply the results to problems involving parallel lines*	30	30, 31
MG3.03 *create an original dynamic sketch, paper-folding design, or other illustration that incorporates some of the geometric properties from this section, or find and report on some real-life application(s) of the geometric properties*		

PRACTICE TEST 1

1. Matteo draws a rectangle with a width-to-area ratio of 4:20. Which of the following rectangles has an equivalent width-to-area ratio to Matteo's rectangle?

A

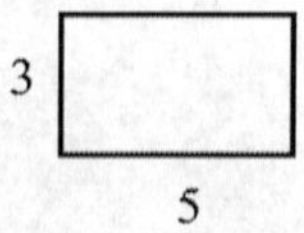

B

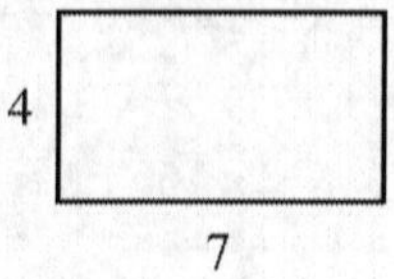

C

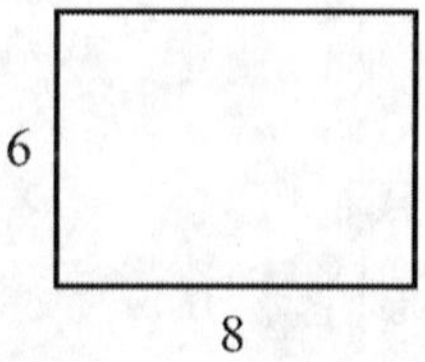

D

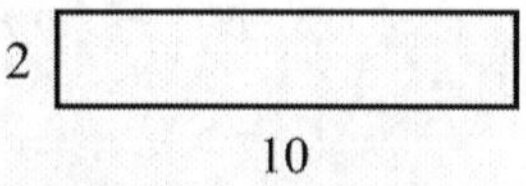

2. Gumball machine 1 contains 20 red, 14 green, and 16 white gumballs. Gumball machine 2 contains a different number of gumballs in the same ratio of red to green to white. If gumball machine 2 contains a total of 300 gumballs, how many green gumballs does it contain?

F. 84

G. 120

H. 140

J. 210

3. A photograph of a child is shown.

The scale factor of the picture height to the actual height is 20.4 cm : 1.80 m.
If the child's height in the picture is 16 cm, then what is the child's actual height?

A. 44.2 cm

B. 81.6 cm

C. 141.2 cm

D. 160.0 cm

4. A customer at a local grocery store is trying to decide from the following choices of boxes of tea which is the best buy.

Box 1: 24 tea bags for $1.98
Box 2: 36 tea bags for $2.70
Box 3: 60 tea bags for $3.60
Box 4: 144 tea bags for $9.36

Which box of tea is the best buy?

F. Box 1

G. Box 2

H. Box 3

J. Box 4

Open Response

5 Cross-country Running

Dammond is preparing for a cross-country race. He goes for a jog and runs at a constant rate. It takes him 55 s to cover a distance of 308 m. If he continues at the same rate, how far will he travel in 2 minutes? Show your work.

6. A geometric shape is shown below with algebraic expressions representing the length of each side.

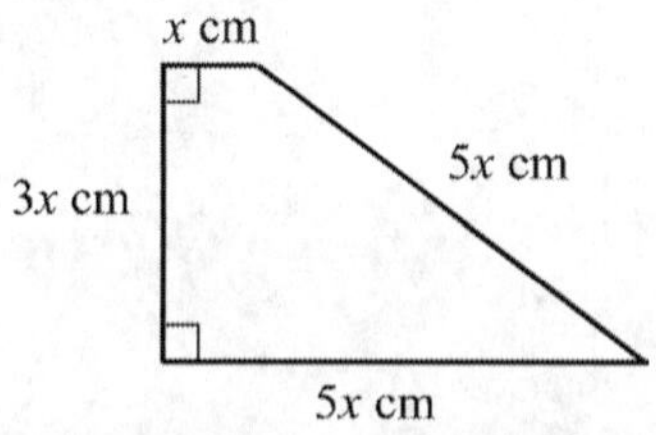

What is the correct algebraic expression representing the perimeter of this shape?

A. $6x$ cm

B. $14x$ cm

C. $15x$ cm

D. $75x$ cm

7. The algebra tiles below represent an algebraic term or numerical value

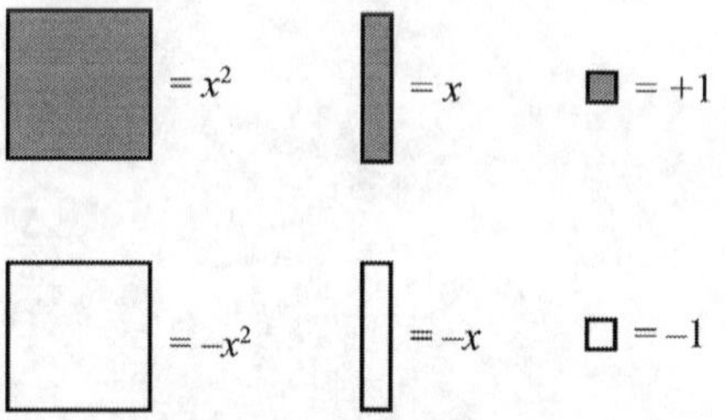

Which of the following algebra tile models represents the simplified form of the subtraction of the two polynomials $(2x^2 + x + 1) - (3x^2 + x - 4)$?

F

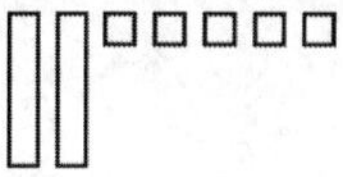

G

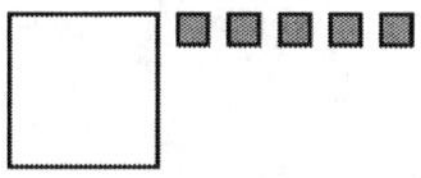

H

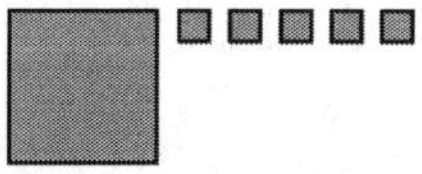

J

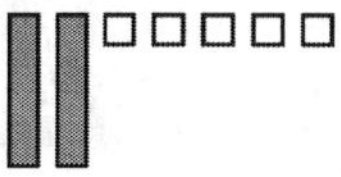

8. The following scale is balanced.

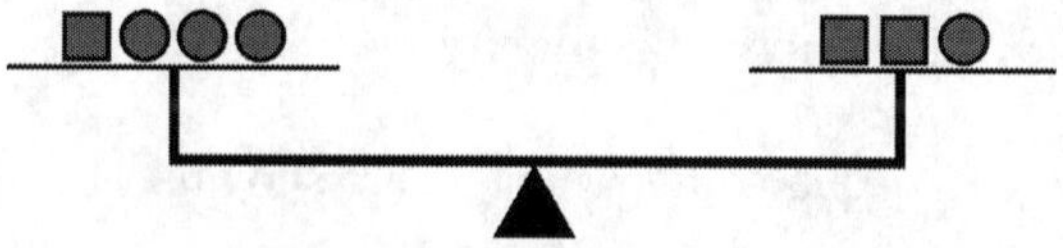

All figures with the same shape have the same mass, and ■ represents the variable x and ● represents *1*.

Which of the following scales is balanced?

A

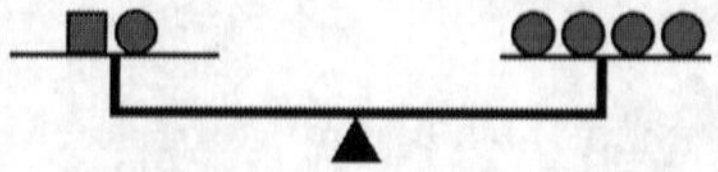

B

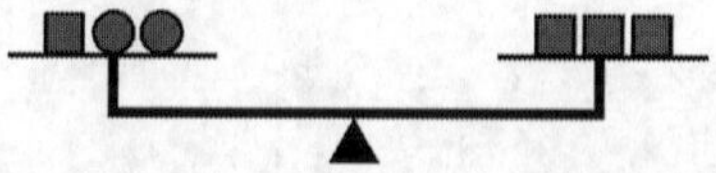

C

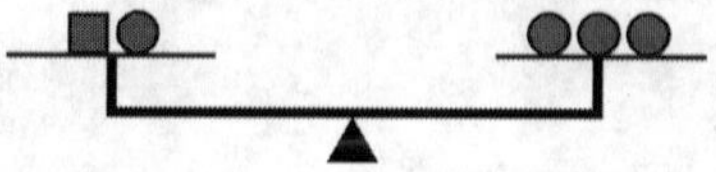

D

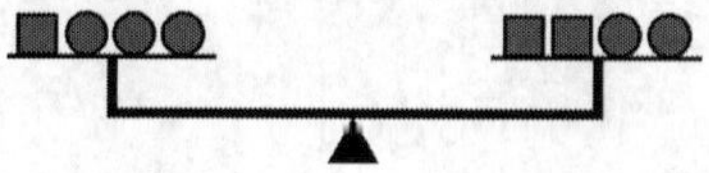

Open Response

9. Perimeter Perplexity

A square and rectangle are shown.

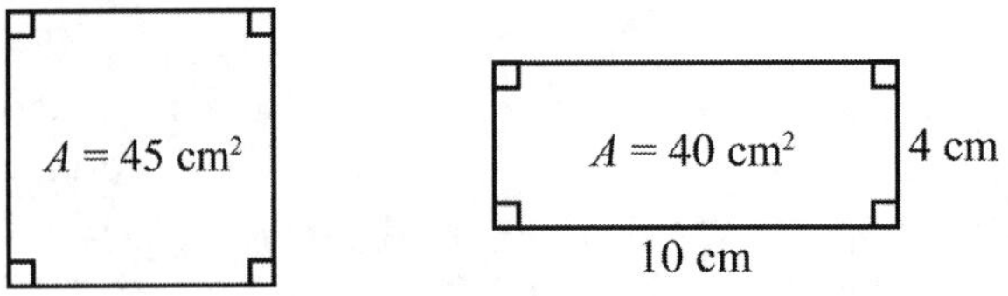

Which shape has the largest perimeter? Justify your answer

10. The scatter plot below shows the number of hours of practice time versus golf scores by a particular golfer.

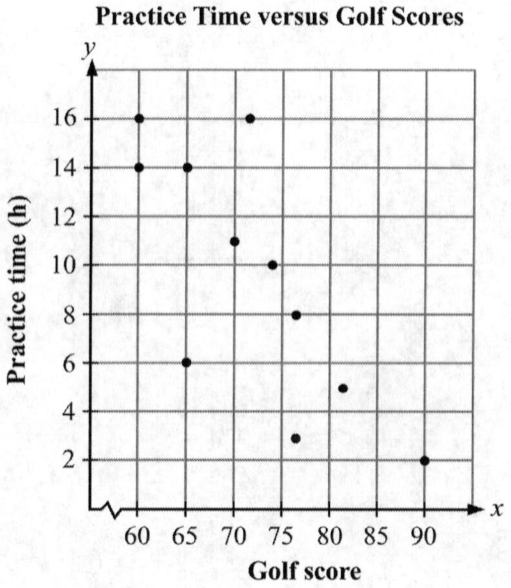

Which point on the scatter plot shows the most practice time with the lowest golf score?

F. (60, 16)

G. (73, 16)

H. (77, 3)

J. (90, 2)

11. On March 1, 48 cm of snow fell. Each day thereafter, Tammy measures the height of the snow in her backyard and records that the height decreases by 2.5 cm each day.

If x represents the number of days after March 1 and y represents the height of the snow for that day, then which of the following tables of values correctly represents this relationship?

A.

x	y
2	45.5
4	43.0
6	40.5
8	38.0
10	35.5
12	33.0

B.

x	y
2	43.0
4	38.0
6	33.0
8	28.0
10	23.0
12	18.0

C.

x	y
2	50.5
4	53.0
6	55.5
8	35.0
10	60.5
12	63.0

D.

x	y
2	53.0
4	58.0
6	63.0
8	68.0
10	73.0
12	78.0

12. Adele wanted to study the relationship between the volume of a square-based prism, V, and the side length, l, for a fixed height of 2 cm.

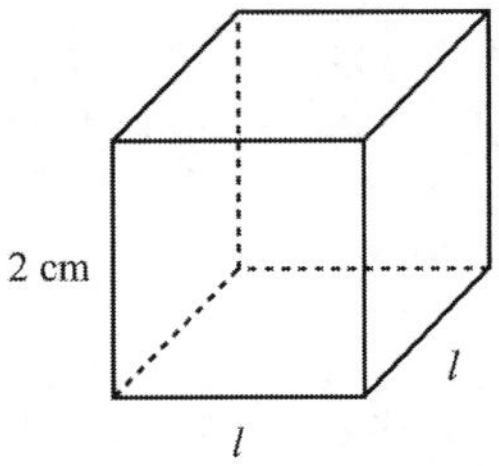

The formula for the volume, V, of a square-based prism is $V = (l)(l)(h)$. Thus, the volume of Adele's prism is $V = 2(l)(l) = 2l^2$. Adele created the following table of values for several side length measurements.

Side length	Volume (cm^3)
0	0
1	2
2	8
3	18
4	32
5	50
6	72

Which of the following graphs represents the relationship between the side length and the volume of the prism?

F

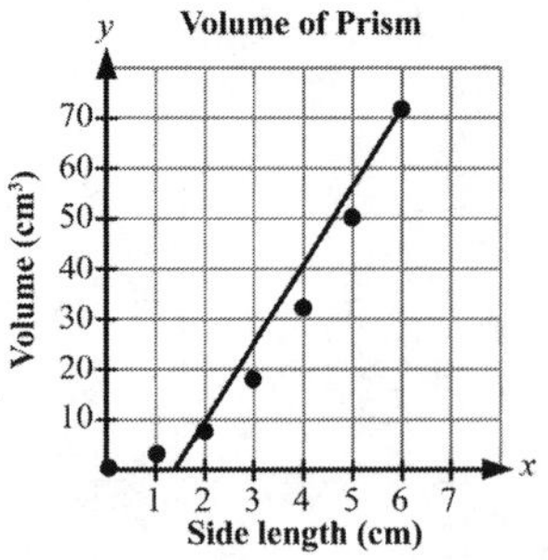

G

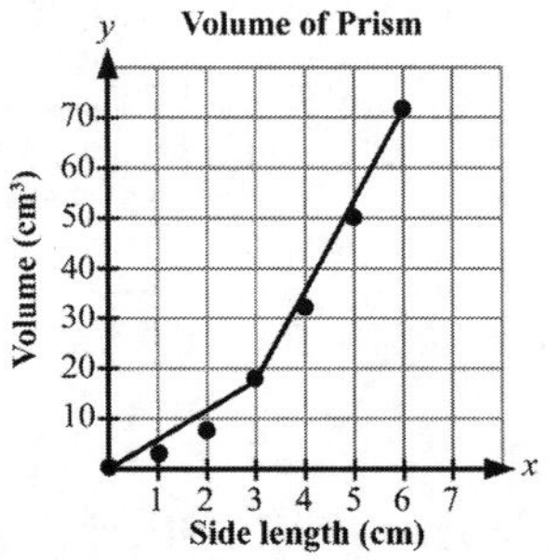

H

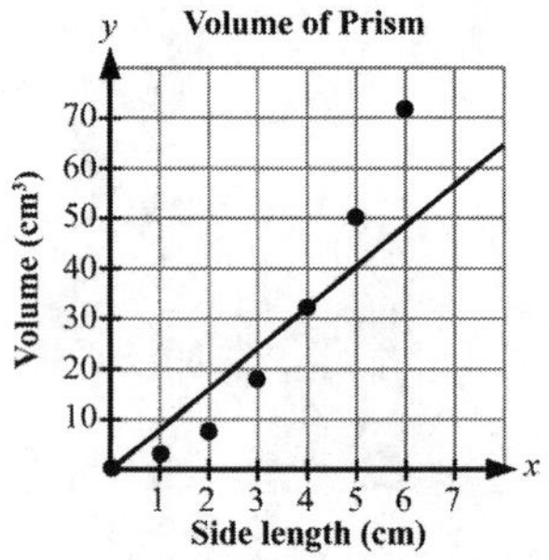

J

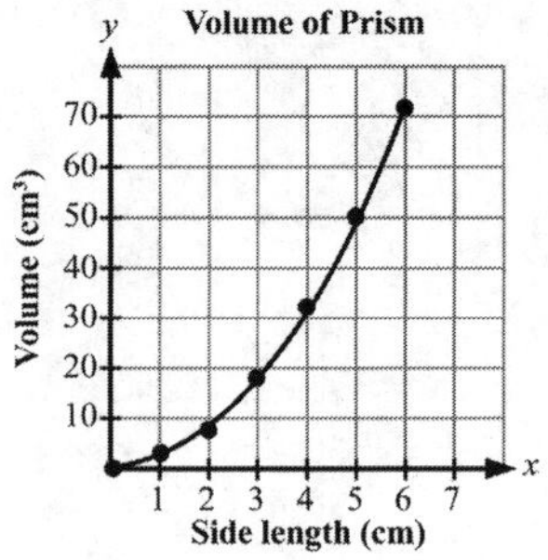

13. The area, A, of a square is related to the length of its side, s.

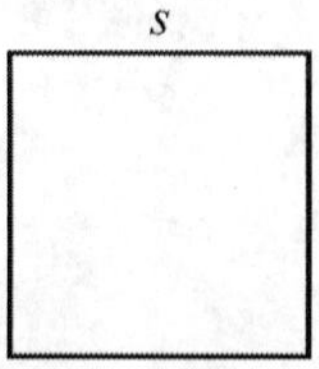

Adele created the following table of values for several side length measurements.

Side length (cm)	Area (cm^2)
0	0
1	1
2	4
3	9
4	16
5	25
6	36

According to the pattern of data in the table, which of the following statements correctly describes the relationship between the area of a square and its side length?

A. The area, A, increases linearly as l increases, since the first differences are constant.

B. The area, A, increases linearly as l increases, since the first differences are not constant.

C. The area, A, increases non-linearly as l increases, since the first differences are constant.

D. The area, A, increases non-linearly as l increases, since the first differences are not constant.

OPEN RESPONSE

14. Hit and Miss

A basketball player's percentages of successful shots from different distances from the hoop are shown in the scatter plot.

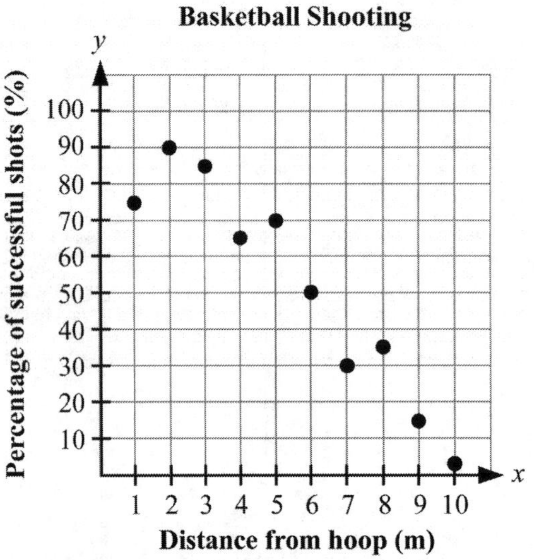

Describe the relationship between the percentages of successful shots and the player's distance from the hoop.

If the basketball player is shooting from more than 4 m away from the hoop, identify the coordinates of the point where he is most successful. Explain a possible reason that the basketball player is more successful at this point.

15. The linear graph shown passes through points *A*, *B*, and *C*.

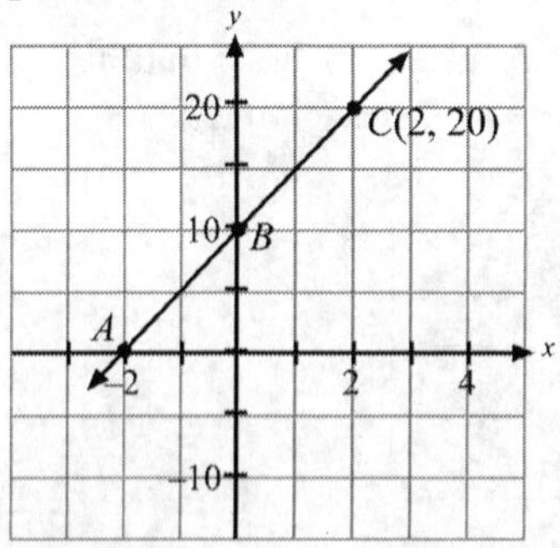

Which of the following equations expresses the constant rate of change of the linear graph?

F. $\frac{20}{2}=10$

G. $\frac{20}{-2}=-10$

H. $\frac{10}{2}=5$

J. $\frac{10}{-2}=-5$

16. A student was walking to school at a constant rate. The data relating his time of walking, *t*, in minutes to the distance from the school, *d*, in metres represents a partial variation. Which of the following tables represents this partial variation?

A.

Time (min)	Distance (m)
0	0
2	400
4	800
6	1 200
8	1 600
10	2 000

B.

Time (min)	Distance (m)
0	0
2	0
4	400
6	800
8	1 200
10	1 600

C.

Time (min)	Distance (m)
0	100
2	500
4	900
6	1 300
8	1 700
10	2 100

D.

Time (min)	Distance (m)
0	100
2	100
4	500
6	500
8	1 000
10	1 500

17. In a robotics lab, students analyzed the relationship between the horizontal position, *x*, and the vertical position, *y*, in centimetres of a robot's movement. The linear graph portraying the robot's movement is shown.

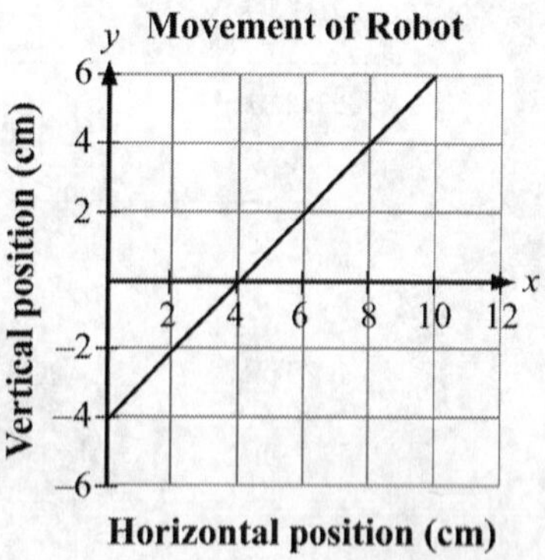

What is the equation representing the graph of this linear relation?

F. $y=-4x$

G. $y=4x-4$

H. $y=1x-4$

J. $y=-1x+4$

OPEN RESPONSE

18. Lawnmower Labour

Samson is paid a flat fee of $10 for mowing his neighbour's lawn and $5 for every hour that he works. The table of values portrays the relationship between Samson's earnings, *E*, in dollars with respect to the time, *t*, in hours that he mowed the lawn.

Time (h)	0	1	2	3	4
Earnings ($)	10	15	20	25	30

Samson decided that the equation describing this relationship was $E = 5t + 10$.

Explain why his equation correctly represents the context of this problem.

19. Recently, an airplane called the Enviroplane established a world record for altitude for a solar-powered aircraft. Temperatures at higher altitudes tend to be lower since there is about a 1°F decrease in temperature for every 1 000 m increase in altitude.
A table of values showing various altitudes and temperatures is shown.

Altitude (m)	Temperature (°F)
0	32
2 000	30
4 000	28
6 000	26
8 000	24

If this pattern continued, what would the temperature be at 51 000 m?

A. –51°F

B. –19°F

C. 19°F

D. 27°F

20. Daniel works full-time at a clothing store. The graph shows the relationship between Daniel's earnings for a week and the number of hours worked.

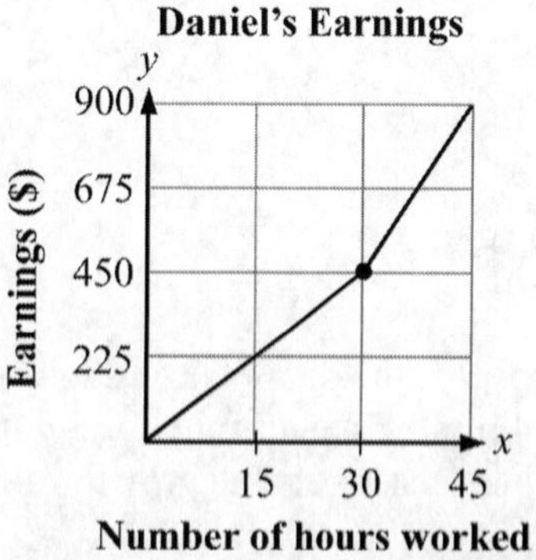

Which statement best describes how Daniel's work conditions change when he works more than 30 hours in a week?

F. He is paid a one-time bonus.

G. He works at an increased rate.

H. He is paid an increased rate of pay.

J. He gets a promotion in the company.

21. The diameter of a seedling tree is 12 mm.

Every six months, the diameter of the tree increases 0.4 mm. Which of the following tables of values describes this growth rate?

A

Time (months)	0	1	2	3	4
Diameter (mm)	12	12.1	12.2	12.3	12.4

B

Time (months)	0	6	12	24	48
Diameter (mm)	12	12.4	12.8	13.2	13.6

C

Time (years)	0	1	2	3	4
Diameter (mm)	12	12.4	12.8	13.2	13.6

D

Time (years)	0	1	2	3	4
Diameter (mm)	12	12.8	13.6	14.4	15.2

22. Two car models with differing starting values depreciate at the rates shown by the two lines.

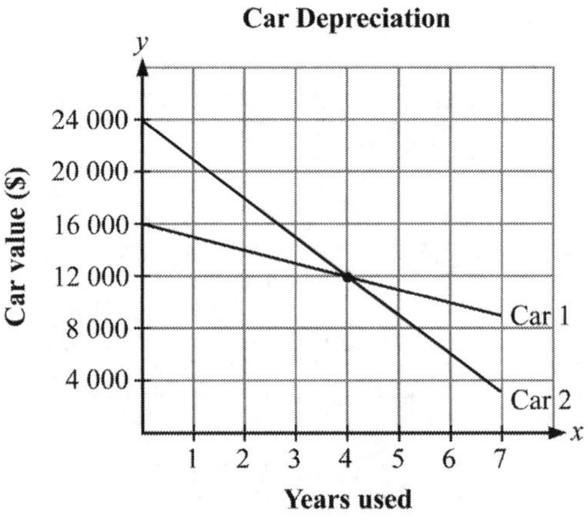

Which of the following statements correctly describes the depreciating values of the two cars over time?

F. Car 1 depreciates at a lesser rate than Car 2.

G. Car 1 depreciates at a greater rate than Car 2.

H. Car 2 has consistently less value than Car 1 throughout the first six years.

J. Car 2 has consistently more value than Car 1 throughout the first six years.

OPEN RESPONSE

23. Pedal Power

Jackie's house is 600 m from the hardware store, and David's house is 500 m from the hardware store as illustrated.

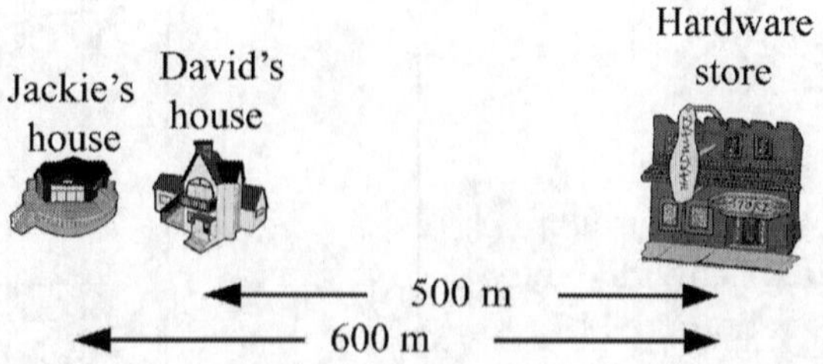

Jackie and David leave their houses at the same time to bike to the hardware store. David bikes at a speed of 4 m/s. The line showing David's distance, *d*, in metres from the store over time, *t*, in seconds is shown in the graph below.

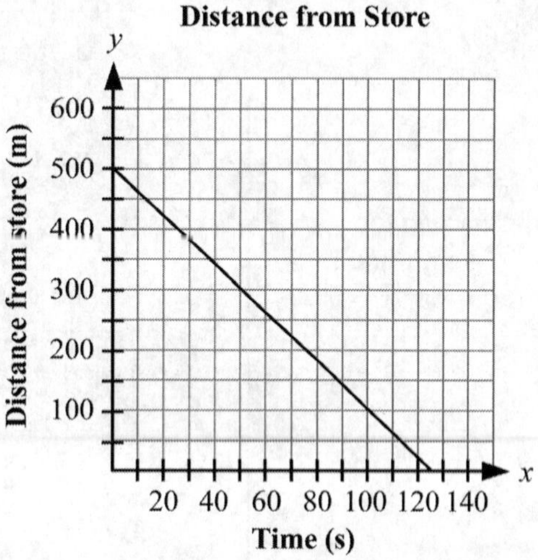

Jackie bikes at a speed of 5 m/s.

Plot points at 10 second intervals indicating Jackie's distance, *d*, in metres from the store, over time, *t*, in seconds, and then draw a line through these points.

Find the point of intersection of the two lines, and explain its meaning in this context.

24. What are the dimensions of a rectangle that would produce the largest possible area for a perimeter of 84 cm?

A. 80 cm × 4 cm

B. 30 cm × 12 cm

C. 24 cm × 18 cm

D. 21 cm × 21 cm

25. Akhil wants to put fencing material around his rectangular garden, which is divided into three sections. The garden is bordered by one side of his house, as portrayed below. He wants to fence the length of the whole garden and the four widths of its three sections.

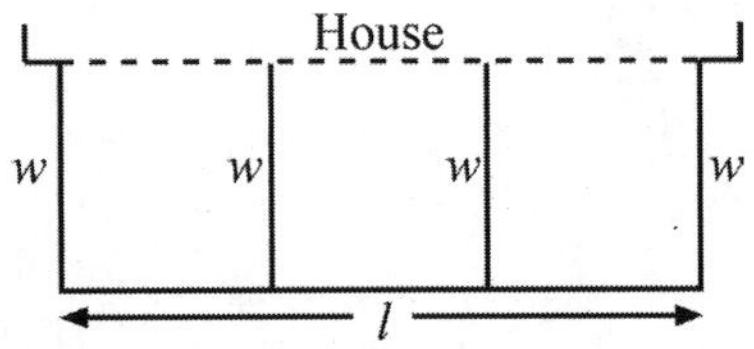

If Akhil wants his rectangular garden to have an area of 36 m^2, what is the minimum amount of fencing material required to enclose it?

F. 24 m

G. 30 m

H. 36 m

J. 48 m

26. In baseball, the distance from home plate to first base is 27.43 m. The distance from first base to second base is also 27.43 m. The first base line is perpendicular to the second base line, as illustrated.

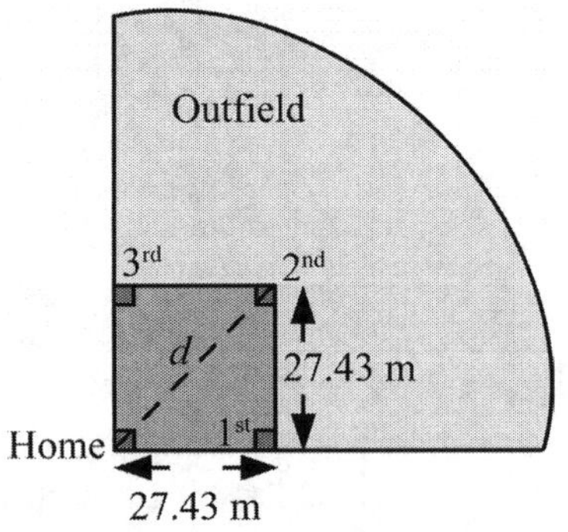

What is the diagonal distance, *d*, from home plate to second base to the nearest hundredth of a metre?

A. 54.86 m

B. 38.79 m

C. 27.43 m

D. 7.41 m

27 A sphere fits snugly into a cylinder. What is the relationship of the volume of the cylinder to the volume of the sphere?

F. $V_{\text{cylinder}} = 3V_{\text{sphere}}$

G. $V_{\text{cylinder}} = 2V_{\text{sphere}}$

H. $2V_{\text{cylinder}} = 3V_{\text{sphere}}$

J. $3V_{\text{cylinder}} = 2V_{\text{sphere}}$

Open Response

28. Fancy Flowerbed

Two composite shapes are proposed to represent a flowerbed in a park.

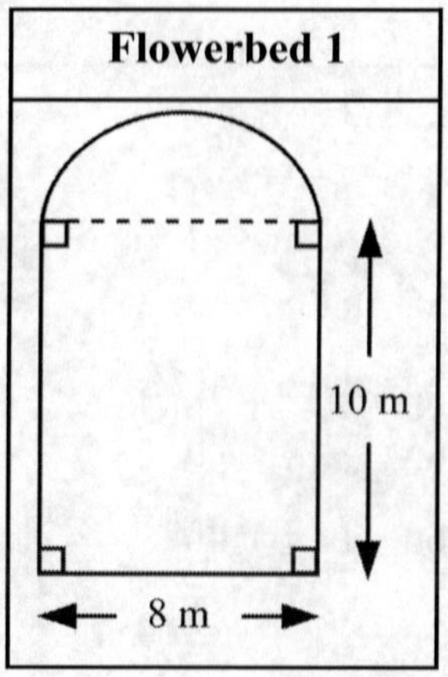

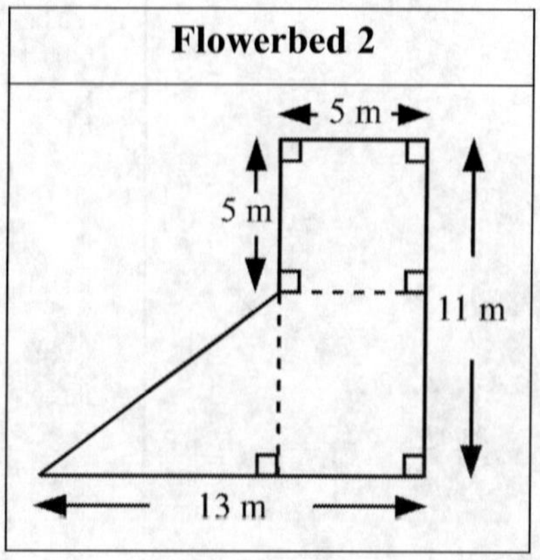

Which proposed flowerbed has the greatest perimeter? Justify your answer.

29. What is the sum of the measures of the exterior angles of a five-sided polygon?

A. 360°

B. 450°

C. 540°

D. 900°

30. A section of a bridge girder is shown below, where line AB is parallel to line CE.

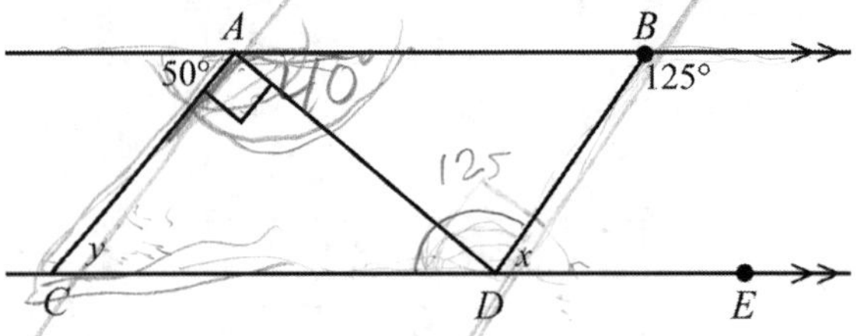

What are the values of x and y?

F. $x = 55°$ and $y = 50°$

G. $x = 55°$ and $y = 40°$

H. $x = 60°$ and $y = 50°$

J. $x = 60°$ and $y = 40°$

OPEN RESPONSE

31. Missing Measures

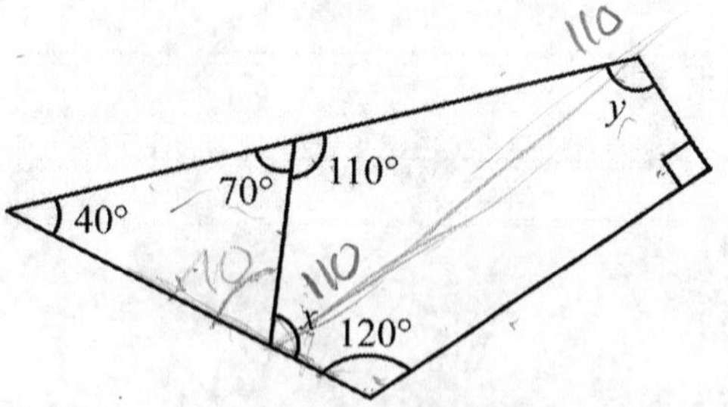

Determine the measures of $\angle x$ and $\angle y$ in the diagram. Show your work.

ANSWERS AND SOLUTIONS—PRACTICE TEST 1

1. A	**9. OR**	**17. H**	**25. F**
2. F	**10. F**	**18. OR**	**26. B**
3. C	**11. B**	**19. B**	**27. H**
4. H	**12. J**	**20. H**	**28. OR**
5. OR	**13. D**	**21. D**	**29. A**
6. B	**14. OR**	**22. F**	**30. F**
7. G	**15. H**	**23. OR**	**31. OR**
8. C	**16. C**	**24. D**	

1. **A**

The width-to-area ratio of Matteo's rectangle is $\frac{4}{20}$. In lowest terms,

this ratio is $\frac{4 \div 4}{20 \div 4} = \frac{1}{5}$.

The area of the 3-by-5 rectangle illustrated in alternative **A** is

$$\begin{aligned} A &= (l)(w) \\ &= (5)(3) \\ &= 15 \end{aligned}$$

The width-to-area ratio of this rectangle is $\frac{3}{15}$.

In lowest terms, this ratio is $\frac{3 \div 3}{15 \div 3} = \frac{1}{5}$.

When stated in lowest terms, the ratios of both these rectangles are the same: $\frac{1}{5} = \frac{1}{5}$

The rectangle illustrated in alternative **A** has an equivalent width-to-area ratio to Matteo's rectangle.

2. **F**

The total number of gumballs in gumball machine 1 is 20 + 14 + 16 = 50; therefore, the ratio of green gumballs to total gumballs in this machine is 14:50. If the number of green gumballs in gumball machine 2 is x, then the ratio of green gumballs to total gumballs in machine 2 is x:300. The correct proportion representing this relationship is $\frac{14}{50} = \frac{x}{300}$.

Use the method of equivalent ratios to solve this question.

$$\frac{14}{50} = \frac{x}{300}$$

Multiply each term in the left ratio by 6.

$$\frac{14 \times 6}{50 \times 6} = \frac{x}{300}$$

$$\frac{84}{300} = \frac{x}{300}$$

$$x = 84.$$

There are 84 green gumballs in gumball machine 2.

3. **C**

Convert 1.80 m to centimetres.
Recall that 1 m = 100 cm; therefore,
$1.80 \times 100 = 180$ cm.
Set up the proportion between the picture height and the actual height, where the child's actual height is represented by x.

$$\frac{20.4 \text{ cm}}{180 \text{ cm}} = \frac{16 \text{ cm}}{x}$$

Use the cross-product rule.
$(20.4)(x) = (16)(180)$
Divide both sides by 20.4.

$$\frac{(20.4)(x)}{20.4} = \frac{(16)(180)}{20.4}$$
$$x = 141.2$$

The child's actual height is 141.2 cm.

4. **H**

Find the unit price per tea bag:

Box 1: $\frac{\$1.98}{24} = \$0.0825/\text{bag}$

Box 2: $\frac{\$2.70}{36} = \$0.075/\text{bag}$

Box 3: $\frac{\$3.60}{60} = \$0.060/\text{bag}$

Box 4: $\frac{\$9.36}{144} = \$0.065/\text{bag}$

The best buy is Box 3, since it has the lowest unit price.

OR5.

To find out how far Dammond ran in two minutes, you must first convert the time into seconds: 2 min × 60 = 120 s.
To find the distance covered, d, in 120 s, you could set up a proportion as follows:

$$\frac{d}{120} = \frac{308}{55}$$

Use the cross-product rule.
$(55)(d) = (120)(308)$
Divide both sides by 55.

$$\frac{(55)(d)}{55} = \frac{(120)(308)}{55}$$
$$d = 672$$

Dammond covered 672 m in two minutes.

6. **B**

The perimeter, P, of this shape can be represented by the expression
$P = s_1 + s_2 + s_3 + s_4$.
$P = x + 3x + 5x + 5x$
$P = (1 + 3 + 5 + 5)x$
$P = 14x$ cm
The algebraic expression that correctly represents the perimeter of this shape is $14x$ cm.

7. **G**

Change all the signs in the second polynomial to switch the expression from a subtraction question to an addition question.
$(2x^2 + x + 1) - (3x^2 + x - 4)$
$= (2x^2 + x + 1) + (-3x^2 - x + 4)$
Simplify by collecting like terms.
$= (2x^2 - 3x^2) + (x - x) + (1 + 4)$
$= -x^2 + 0x + 5$
$= -x^2 + 5$
Since unshaded algebra tiles represent negative terms and shaded algebra tiles represent positive terms, the expression is represented by 1 unshaded square ($-x^2$) and 5 shaded unit squares (5).
The algebra tile model shown in alternative **G** correctly models this solution.

8. **C**

The original scale models one square (x) and three circles (3) on the left side being equal to two squares ($2x$) and one circle (1) on the right side. The equation represented is $x + 3 = 2x + 1$.
Subtract 1 from both sides.

$$x + 3 - 1 = 2x + 1 - 1$$
$$x + 2 = 2x$$

Subtract x from both sides.

$$x - x + 2 = 2x - x$$
$$2 = x$$
$$x = 2$$

The scale modelled in alternative **C** shows one square (x) and one circle (1) on the left side being equal to three circles (3) on the right side.
The equation represented is $x + 1 = 3$.
Subtract 1 from both sides.

$$x + 1 - 1 = 3 - 1$$
$$x = 2$$

The solutions to both equations are the same, so the scale portrayed in alternative **C** is balanced.

OR 9.

The perimeter, P, of the rectangle with a length of 10 cm and a width of 4 cm is as shown:
$P = l + l + w + w$
$P = 10 + 10 + 4 + 4$
$P = 28$ cm
In order to find the perimeter, P, of the square, you must first find the length of the side, s.
The area is given as 45 cm^2.

$$A_{\text{square}} = s^2$$

Substitute 45 for A.

$$45 = s^2$$
$$\pm\sqrt{45} = \sqrt{s^2}$$
$$\pm\sqrt{45} = s$$

The side cannot be negative so discard $-\sqrt{45}$.
$s = \sqrt{45} \approx 6.71$ cm
The perimeter of the square is as shown:
$P = 4s$
$P = 4(6.71)$
$P = 26.84$ cm
The rectangle has a perimeter that is $28 - 26.84 = 1.16$ cm larger than that of the square.

10. F

The longest practice time is represented by the highest y-coordinate, 16. The corresponding lowest x-coordinate representing the lowest golf score is 60. The point that represents this is (60, 16).

11. B

On March 1, 2007, the height of the snow was 48 cm. Since the snow decreases by 2.5 cm per day, the pile decreases 2×2.5 cm $= 5$ cm in two days. The height of the remaining snow two days after March 1 is
48 cm – 5 cm = 43 cm.
Similarly, four days after March 1, the height of the snow has decreased by
4×2.5 cm $= 10$ cm, which means that the height of the snow is 48 cm – 10 cm = 38 cm.
If this pattern continues, there will be 33 cm of snow remaining after 6 days, 28 cm remaining after 8 days, 23 cm remaining after 10 days, and 18 cm remaining after 12 days. The table that illustrates this pattern correctly is the table in alternative **B**.

12. J

The points do not follow a linear pattern. This is evident from the first differences, which are not constant
($2 - 0 = 2$, $8 - 2 = 6$, $18 - 8 = 10$, and so on)
The pattern is non-linear, which is best represented by a curve of best fit, as illustrated in the graph shown in alternative **J**.

13. D

The data points do not follow a constant rate of change, as is shown by the first differences of the area values:

$$0 \xrightarrow{+1} 1 \xrightarrow{+3} 4 \xrightarrow{+5} 9 \xrightarrow{+7} 16 \xrightarrow{+9} 25 \xrightarrow{+11} 36$$

The area, A, increases non-linearly as l increases, since the first differences are not constant.

OR 14.

The relationship between the percentages of successful shots and the player's distance from the hoop is linear. As the distance increases, the percentage of successful shots decreases.
The point where the player is farther away and more successful than at 4 m is (5, 70).
A possible reason that the player might be more successful here is that he is more comfortable shooting here (e.g., shooting from the foul line) than at 4 m. He also may have been concentrating more when shooting from 5 m than when he was shooting from 4 m.

15. H

From points A to C or points B to C, the rate of change = 5.
Points A to C:
Run = 4 units right (-2 to $2 = 4$)
Rise = 20 units up (0 to $20 = 20$)

$$\text{Rate of change} = \frac{\text{rise}}{\text{run}} = \frac{20}{4} = \frac{10}{2} = 5$$

Points B to C:
Run = 2 units right (0 to $2 = 2$)
Rise = 10 units up (10 to $20 = 10$)

$$\text{Rate of change} = \frac{\text{rise}}{\text{run}} = \frac{10}{2} = 5$$

The correct expression for the constant rate of change is $\frac{10}{2} = 5$.

16. C

A partial variation is a relationship between two variables, where the initial value is not 0 and the rate of change is constant. The tables in alternatives C and D both portray initial values that are 100 (not 0) when $t = 0$; however, the first differences in the table in alternative D are not constant ($100 - 100 = 0$, $500 - 100 = 400$, $500 - 100 = 400$, $500 - 500 = 0$, and so on), whereas in the table in alternative **C**, they are constant: ($500 - 100 = 400$, $900 - 500 = 400$, $1\ 300 - 900 = 400$, etc). The table in alternative **C** represents a partial variation between the distance, d, and the time, t.

17. H

From the graph, the initial value or vertical intercept when $x = 0$ is $y = -4$. The constant rate of change $= \frac{\text{rise}}{\text{run}} = \frac{4}{4} = 1$, since for every 4 units to the right in the x-direction (run), there is an increase of 4 in the y-direction (rise). In the equation of the form $y = mx + b$, m represents the constant rate of change of 4, and b represents the initial value of -4. The equation representing this graph is $y = 1x - 4$.

OR 18.

The equation representing this relationship is $E = 5t + 10$ because in the form $y = mx + b$ for a linear equation, m represents the constant rate of change, and b represents the initial value. The constant rate of change in this problem is \$5/h, since for every 1 h increase in work, Samson's earnings increase by \$5. The initial value is the flat fee of \$10, which he receives up front when time $t = 0$ h.

19. B

The table shows a decline of 2°F for every increase in altitude of 2 000 m, or 1°F for every increase in 1 000 m. If this pattern continues, at 51 000 m, the temperature will have dropped $51 \times 1°\text{F} = 51°\text{F}$. Since the original temperature is 32°F at an altitude of 0 m, the temperature at 51 000 m would be $32°\text{F} - 51°\text{F} = -19°\text{F}$.

20. H

Daniel's rate of pay is constant up to 30 hours a week at \$225 for every 15 hours worked. After 30 hours, it increases to a higher rate for every 15 hours worked. This indicates that Daniel is paid an increased rate of pay after 30 hours worked.

21. D

The initial value is 12 mm. The rate of change is 0.40 mm every six months. Since time, t, is in years, this rate must be written in years. One year = 12 months, so the rate of change per year is

$$\frac{0.40\text{ mm}}{6\text{ months}} \times \frac{2}{2} = \frac{0.80\text{ mm}}{12\text{ months}} = \frac{0.80\text{ mm}}{1\text{ year}}$$

or 0.80 mm.
The correct table of values shows an increase of 0.80 mm for every increase in years. This table is shown in alternative **D**.

Time (years)	**Diameter (mm)**
0	12
1	12 + 0.8 = 12.8
2	12.8 + 0.8 = 13.6
3	12.8 + 0.8 = 14.4
4	12.8 + 0.8 = 15.2

22. F

Since the line representing Car 1 drops less than the line representing Car 2, it portrays a rate of change that is smaller than the rate of change of Car 2. Therefore, Car 1 depreciates less quickly than Car 2.

OR 23.

The line showing Jackie's distance, d, in metres from the hardware store with respect to her riding time, t, in seconds is a line starting with an initial value of 600 m and a constant rate of -5 m/s or $\frac{-5 \times 10\text{m}}{1 \times 10\text{s}} = 50$ m per 10 s.

The line below labelled Jackie has an initial value of 600.

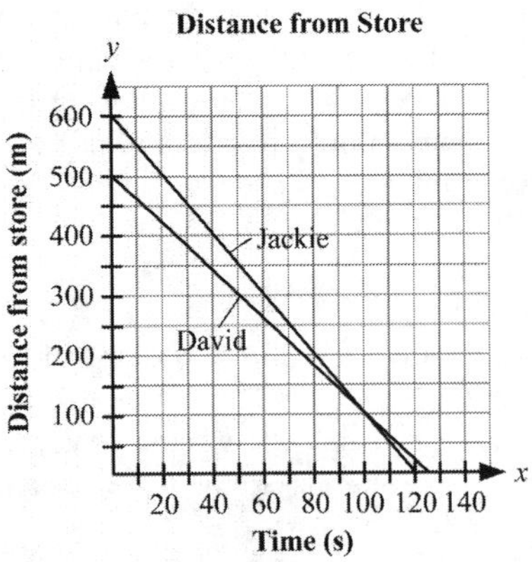

The point of intersection is at about (100, 100). The x-coordinate represents the time pedalled by both Jackie and David (t = 100 s). The y-coordinate represents the distance from the store (d = 100 m). This point (100 m) represents the distance from the store at which Jackie catches up to David.

24. D

The maximum area of a rectangle with a fixed perimeter, P, occurs when the width, w, equals the length, l, and $w = l = \frac{P}{4}$.

Since $P = 84$ cm, $w = l = \frac{84}{4}$

$= 21$ cm

The dimensions of a rectangle that would produce the largest possible area for a perimeter of 84 cm are 21 cm by 21 cm.

25. F

For a rectangular region of fixed area requiring fencing material for one length and four widths of its three sections, $l = 4w$. Thus, since $A = (l)(w)$, and since $l = 4w$.

$A = (4w)(w)$

$A = 4w^2$

$w^2 = \frac{A}{4}$

$w = \sqrt{\frac{A}{4}}$

Substitute 36 for A.

$w = \sqrt{\frac{36}{4}}$

$w = \sqrt{9} = 3$ m

$l = 4w$

$= 4(3)$

$= 12$ m

|The minimum perimeter, P, for one length, l, and four widths, w, is

$P = l + 4w$

$P = 12 + 4(3)$

$P = 12 + 12$

$P = 24$ m

The minimum amount of fencing material required to enclose Akhil's rectangular garden is 24 m.

26. B

The lengths of two sides of a right triangle are given. Use the Pythagorean theorem to find the length of the third side.

$a^2 + b^2 = c^2$, where a is the length of side a, b is the length of side b, and c is the length of the hypotenuse, or side c.

In this case, a is the distance from home plate to first base, and b is the distance from first base to second base.

The distance from home plate to second base, d, is the length of the hypotenuse.

$$a^2 + b^2 = c^2$$
$$27.43^2 + 27.43^2 = d^2$$
$$1\,504.8098 = d^2$$
$$\sqrt{1\,504.8098} = d$$
$$38.79 = d$$

The distance from home plate to second base is 38.79 m.

27. H

The volume of a snugly fitting sphere in a cylinder is $\frac{2}{3}$ the volume of the cylinder.

$$V_{\text{sphere}} = \frac{2}{3}V_{\text{cylinder}}$$

Multiply both sides by 3.

$$3V_{\text{sphere}} = 3\left(\frac{2}{3}V_{\text{cylinder}}\right)$$
$$3V_{\text{sphere}} = \frac{6}{3}V_{\text{cylinder}}$$
$$3V_{\text{sphere}} = 2V_{\text{cylinder}}$$
$$2V_{\text{cylinder}} = 3V_{\text{sphere}}$$

The relationship between the volume of the cylinder and the volume of the sphere is $2V_{\text{cylinder}} = 3V_{\text{sphere}}$.

OR 28.

To find the perimeter, *P*, of Flowerbed 2, find the hypotenuse, *h*, of the triangular section. The height of the triangle is 11 – 5 = 6 m, and the base is 13 – 5 = 8 cm. According to the Pythagorean theorem, $c^2 = a^2 + b^2$, where $a = 6$ m and $b = 8$ m.

The hypotenuse, *h*, (*c*) is found as follows:

$$c^2 = a^2 + b^2$$
$$h^2 = 6^2 + 8^2$$
$$h^2 = 36 + 64$$
$$h^2 = 100$$
$$\sqrt{h^2} = \pm\sqrt{100}$$

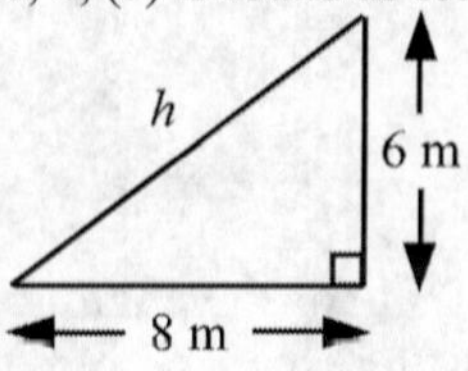

Since a negative value is unrealistic, $-\sqrt{100}$ does not apply.

$$h = +\sqrt{100}$$
$$h = 10\,\text{m}$$

The perimeter, *P*, of Flowerbed 2 is the sum of all sides of the composite shape:

P = 10 + 5 + 5 + 11 + 13 = 44 m.

To find the perimeter, *P*, of Flowerbed 1, find the circumference, *C*, of the semicircular section, where $r = \frac{d}{2} = \frac{8\text{m}}{2} = 4\,\text{m}$.

$$C_{\text{semicircle}} = \frac{C_{\text{circle}}}{2} = \frac{2\pi r}{2} = \pi r = \pi(4) \approx 12.566\,\text{m}$$

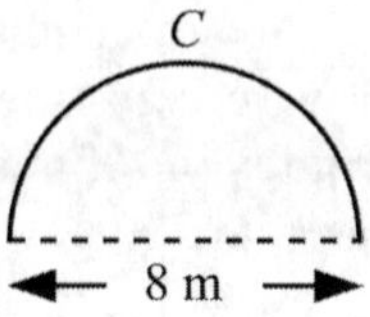

The perimeter, *P*, of Flowerbed 1 is the sum of all sides of the rectangle and the circumference of the semicircle:

$P = 12.566 + 10 + 8 + 10$

$P = 40.566$ m

The perimeter of Flowerbed 2 is 44 – 40.566 = 3.434 m greater than the perimeter of Flowerbed 1.

29. A

The sum of the exterior angles of any polygon is 360°.

30. F

Angle *x* and 125° are co-interior angles. Since co-interior angles are supplementary,

$$\angle x + 125° = 180°$$
$$\angle x + 125° - 125° = 180° - 125°$$
$$\angle x = 55°$$

Angle *y* and 50° are alternate interior angles. Since alternate interior angles are equal, $\angle y = 50°$.

$x = 55°$ and $y = 50°$.

OR 31.

Since the angles of a triangle always add up to 180°, find the other angle, *b*, in the triangle.

$$\angle b + 70° + 40° = 180°$$
$$\angle b + 110° = 180°$$
$$\angle b + 110° - 110° = 180 - 110°$$
$$\angle b = 70°$$

Since $\angle b$ and $\angle x$ form a straight line, they are supplementary.

$$\angle b + \angle x = 180°$$
$$70° + \angle x = 180°$$
$$70° - 70° + \angle x = 180° - 70°$$
$$\angle x = 110°$$

To find $\angle y$, use the formula $S = 180(n-2)$ to find the total sum, *S*, of the angles in a pentagon, where the number of sides is $n = 5$.

$$S = 180°(n-2) = 180°(5-2) = 540°$$

To find $\angle y$, add all the angles in the pentagon, and equate to the sum of 540°.

$$\angle x + 110° + \angle y + 90° + 120° = 540°$$
$$110° + 110° + \angle y + 90° + 120° = 540°$$
$$\angle y + 430° = 540°$$
$$\angle y + 430° - 430° = 540° - 430°$$
$$\angle y = 110°$$

The values of $\angle x$ and $\angle y$ are both equal to 110°.

PRACTICE TEST 2

1. To make 16 cupcakes, Rachel needs 132 g of sugar and 3 cups of flour. Tina wants to make 24 cupcakes with the same proportions of ingredients that Rachel used to make her 16 cupcakes. Which of the following proportions would enable Tina to correctly determine the amount of sugar, n, that she needs for her 24 cupcakes?

A. $\frac{16}{24}=\frac{3}{n}$

B. $\frac{16}{132}=\frac{24}{n}$

C. $\frac{16}{3}=\frac{24}{n}$

D. $\frac{16}{24}=\frac{n}{132}$

2. The ratio of pages in a cookbook to pages in a math textbook is 2:15. If there are 420 pages in the math textbook, how many pages are in the cookbook?

A. 14

B. 28

C. 56

D. 210

3. The CN Tower in Toronto is the tallest freestanding tower in the Americas. The height of the CN Tower in the photograph is 2.77 cm.

If the scale of the photograph is 1:20 000, what is the actual height of the CN Tower?

A. 55.4 m

B. 554 m

C. 5 540 m

D. 55 400 m

4. In 2006, 50% of a sample of 1 000 people in Sudbury agreed that the Federal Government should do more about global warming. In 2008, 56% of another sample of 1 000 people in Sudbury agreed that the Federal Government should do more about global warming. How many **more** people voted in favour of this issue in 2008 compared to 2006?

A. 6

B. 50

C. 60

D. 106

Open-Response

5. Sales Salary

Chantelle works at a furniture store. She earns $15/h and also receives a commission of 4% on her total sales. Determine what Chantelle earns for a 35-hour work week if her total sales are $12 500. Show your work.

6. Tristan was going to solve the expression $-3x^3 - 2x^2$ given the value $x = \frac{3}{4}$.

His solution process is shown in the following steps:

Step 1: $-3\left(\frac{3}{4}\right)^3 - 2\left(\frac{3}{4}\right)^2$

Step 2: $-3\left(\frac{3}{4}\right)\left(\frac{3}{4}\right)\left(\frac{3}{4}\right) - 2\left(\frac{3}{4}\right)\left(\frac{3}{4}\right)$

Step 3: $-5\left(\frac{3}{4}\right)\left(\frac{3}{4}\right)\left(\frac{3}{4}\right)\left(\frac{3}{4}\right)\left(\frac{3}{4}\right)$

Step 4: $-5\left(\frac{3}{4}\right)^3\left(\frac{3}{4}\right)^2$

In which step did Tristan first make an **error**?

A. Step 1

B. Step 2

C. Step 3

D. Step 4

7. The algebra tiles below represent an algebraic term or numerical value.

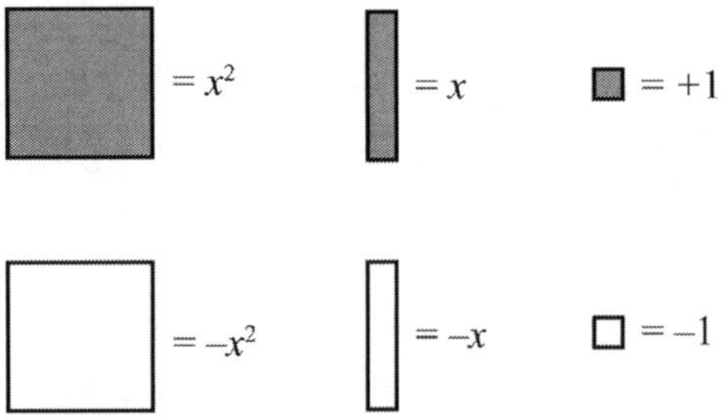

The multiplication of a monomial and polynomial is portrayed by the algebra-tile model shown below.

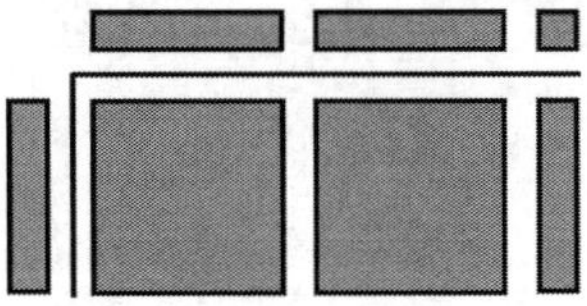

Which of the following products is represented by the algebra-tile model?

F. $1(2x+1)$

G. $2(x+2)$

H. $x(x+2)$

J. $x(2x+1)$

8. A park is to be designed in the shape of a trapezoid as shown.

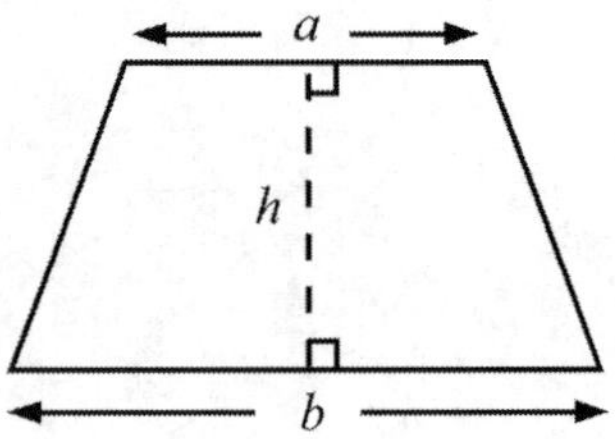

The equation $2A = ha + hb$ relates the area, A, of the trapezoid with respect to its height, h, its top length, a, and its bottom length, b. If the area, A, of the trapezoid is 605 m^2, the top length, a, is 20 m, and its bottom length, b, is 35 m, then what is its height, h?

A. 11 m

B. 22 m

C. 55 m

D. 80 m

OPEN-RESPONSE

9. Garden Border

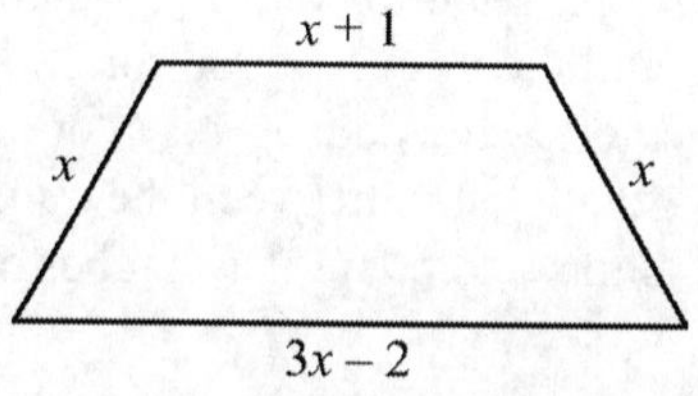

Carla wants to put a border around her garden, which is in the shape of a trapezoid. She uses 17 m of border material to enclose her garden. Determine the dimensions of her garden. Show your work.

10. For her project, Chris collected data for a particular basketball player. She recorded the number of foul shots taken by the player and the points scored for 20 games. She then plotted the data as a scatter plot, showing the relationship between the number of foul shots taken and the number of points scored.

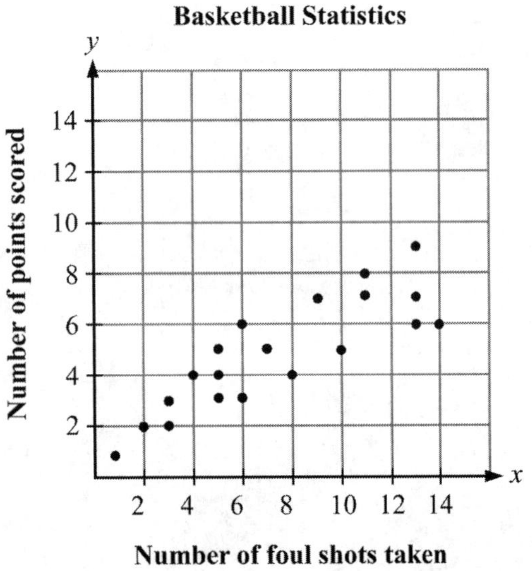

Which point on the graph represents the most points scored by the player in a particular game?

F. (9, 13)

G. (13, 7)

H. (13, 9)

J. (14, 6)

11. Cathy sells six models of DVD players. The table shows the unit cost of each model and the number of DVD players of that model sold in the past month.

Model	Unit Cost ($)	Number Sold
A	120	31
B	145	25
C	165	21
D	175	15
E	195	14
F	225	11

Which statement about the relationship between the unit cost and the number of DVD players sold is **true**?

A. As the unit cost increases, the number sold increases.

B. As the unit cost increases, the number sold decreases.

C. As the unit cost increases, the number sold is constant.

D. There is no relationship between the unit cost and the number sold.

12. Omana entered her data values in lists L_1 and L_2 of her graphing calculator. She then set her window and graphed the data as a scatter plot.

```
WINDOW
  Xmin=-5
  Xmax=13
  Xscl =2
  Ymin=-6
  Ymax=20
  Yscl =1
  Xres=1
```

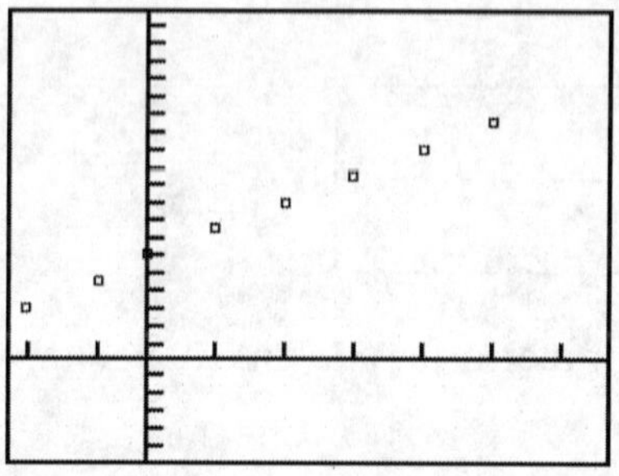

If x is L_1 and y is L_2, which table of values is used to produce the scatter plot?

F.

x	2	1	0	1	2	3	4	5
y	3	6	10	15	21	28	36	45

G.

x	2	1	0	1	2	3	4	5
y	3	4.5	6	7.5	9	10.5	12	13.5

H.

x	−4	−2	0	2	4	6	8	10
y	3	6	10	15	21	28	36	45

J.

x	−4	−2	0	2	4	6	8	10
y	3	4.5	6	7.5	9	10.5	12	13.5

13. The table of values shows the relationship between variables x and y.

x	−2	−1	0	1	2	3	4	5
y	3	6	9	12	15	18	21	24

Which of the following statements correctly describes the relationship between variables x and y?

A. y increases linearly as x increases

B. y decreases linearly as x increases

C. y increases non-linearly as x increases

D. y decreases non-linearly as x increases

OPEN-RESPONSE

14. Cool Coffee

Landon carried out an investigation of the cooling of a cup of coffee. The following data portrays the relationship between the temperature in degrees Celsius and the time, *t*, in minutes.

Time (min)	**Temperature (°C)**
0	65.6
1	62.4
2	59.2
3	56.4
4	53.7
5	51.2
6	48.7

Determine whether the relationship between the temperature of the coffee and time of cooling is linear or non-linear. Justify your answer.

15. The graph below portrays the relationship between the speed of a car, v, in kilometres per hour, and the time, t, in hours.

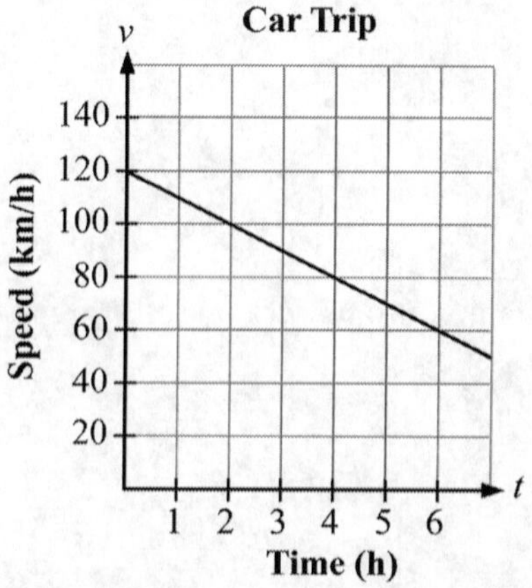

Which of the following equations correctly represents this linear relation?

F. $v = 120 - 6t$

G. $v = 120 - 10t$

H. $v = 120 + 10t$

J. $v = 120 + 2t$

16. Janelle sells 20 pairs of shoes every 5 hours. The number of pairs of shoes Janelle sells, p, over time, t, in hours forms a linear relation. What is the equation representing this relation?

A. $p = 4t$

B. $p = 20t$

C. $p = 20 + 5t$

D. $p = 20 + 4t$

17. Which of the following scenarios can be represented by the equation $y = 20x$?

F. When the time, x, equals 0 hours, the height of a crane above the ground, y, is 20 m.

G. For every DVD, x, purchased, the total cost, y, in dollars increases at a constant rate of \$20.

H. When x is the wage earned in dollars and y is the number of hours worked, the constant change is \$20 per hour.

J. When the initial mass of a porpoise is 20 kg, the constant change of mass in kilograms is y and its age in years is x.

Open Response

18. Repair Rates

Two car service shops advertise the following repair rates:

Cal's Automotive: \$40/h including a flat fee of \$45

Steve's Car Service: \$45/h with no flat fee

Determine the type of variation of each service fee rate. Explain your answers by referring to the concepts of the initial value and the constant rate of change.

19. Gymnasts start with a score of 10.0, and points are deducted for every error made during a routine. At the 1976 Olympic Games in Montreal, Nadia Comaneci of Romania became the first gymnast to score a perfect 10.0 on a routine. By the end of the competition, she had received a perfect score seven different times.

The equation representing the score, *S*, for a performance and the number of mistakes made, *m*, is $S = 10 - 0.1m$. If one performer got a score of 9.2 and the second performer got a score of 8.2, what was the **difference** in the number of mistakes they made?

A. 1

B. 8

C. 10

D. 18

20. The table of values shows a linear relationship between the number of ski rentals, *n*, and the total money, *C*, in dollars collected for the rentals, which includes a fixed deposit for each rental.

Number of rentals	4	10	16	22
Money collected ($)	80	170	260	350

What is the algebraic representation between the money collected, *C*, and the number of ski rentals, *n*?

F. $C = 15n$

G. $C = 20n$

H. $C = 20n + 15$

J. $C = 15n + 20$

21. Two hikers are initially at two different locations from base camp. Each hiker walks away from base camp toward the top of a mountain at a constant rate.

Line A represents the total distance, *d*, in kilometres from base camp with respect to the time, *t*, in hours of Hiker A.

Line B represents the total distance, *d*, in kilometres from base camp with respect to the time, *t*, in hours of Hiker B.

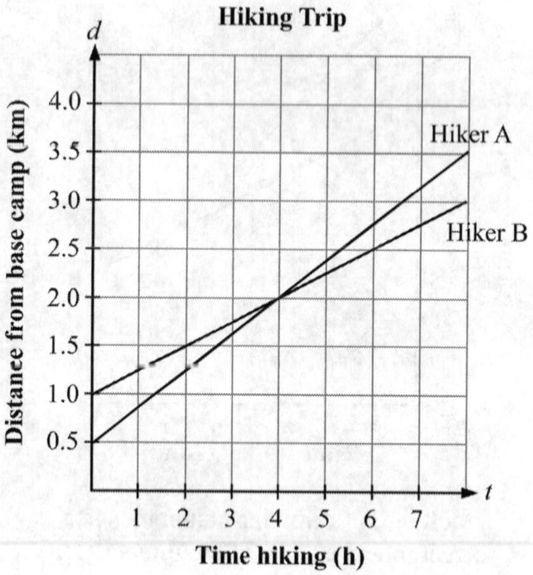

Which of the following statements correctly interprets the graph?

A. Hiker A travels faster then Hiker B and will reach the top of the mountain first.

B. Hiker B travels faster than Hiker A and will reach the top of the mountain first.

C. Hiker A starts farther from the base camp than Hiker B, and he travels faster than Hiker B.

D. Hiker B starts farther from the base camp than Hiker A, and he travels faster than Hiker A.

22. Two brothers left different stores at the same time and headed home at different rates. Boy A started 1 000 m away from home and walked home at a rate of 100 m/min. Boy B started 700 m away from home and walked home at a rate of 25 m/min. The two lines show the relationship between their distance, *d*, from home in metres and their time walked, *t*, in minutes.

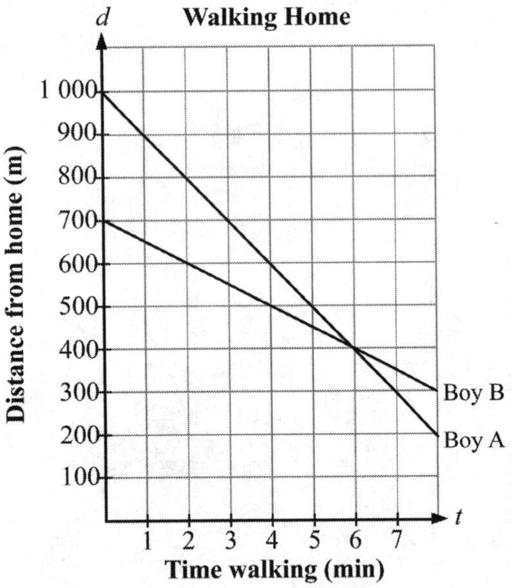

Which of the following statements is a correct interpretation of the intersection point?

F. Boy B and Boy A are walking together when they are 400 m from home.

G. Boy B and Boy A are walking together when they are 200 m from home.

H. After 6 minutes, the two boys have walked a distance of 400 m.

J. After 6 minutes, the two boys arrive at home together.

Open-Response

23. Fencing Fee

The cost, C, in dollars for a fencing company to build a fence with a length, l, in metres is given by the equation: $C = 200 + 15l$

If Mr. Gladwin's fence costs $800 and Mrs. Chadwick's fence costs $980, then determine how much longer Mrs. Chadwick's fence is compared to Mr. Gladwin's. Show your work.

24. If the area of a rectangle is 900 m^2, what is its smallest possible perimeter?

A. 30 m

B. 60 m

C. 120 m

D. 450 m

25. A right triangle with squares *A*, *B*, and *C* attached to its sides is shown.

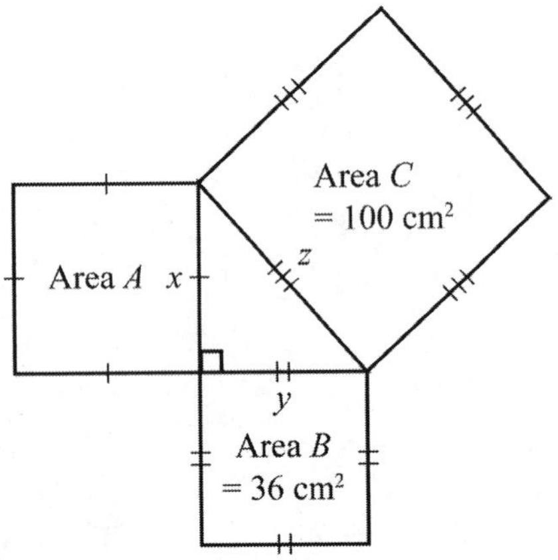

What is the length of side *x*?

F. 4 cm

G. 8 cm

H. 16 cm

J. 64 cm

26. To the nearest square metre, what is the area of the composite shape?

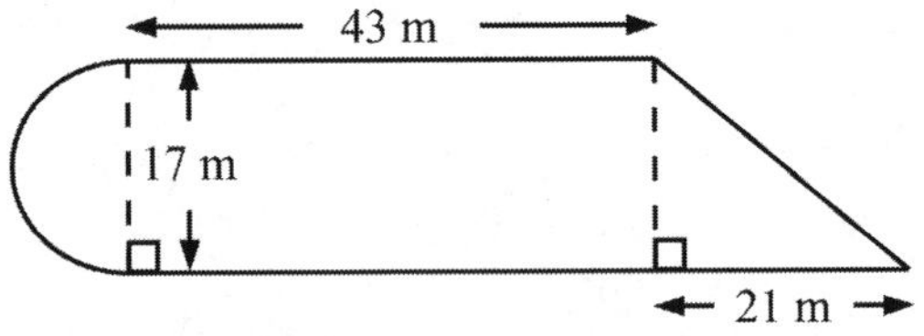

A. 1 023 m^2

B. 1 136 m^2

C. 1 315 m^2

D. 1 996 m^2

27. The manager of a theatre is considering two containers for peanuts, one which is a rectangular prism and the other which is a cylinder.

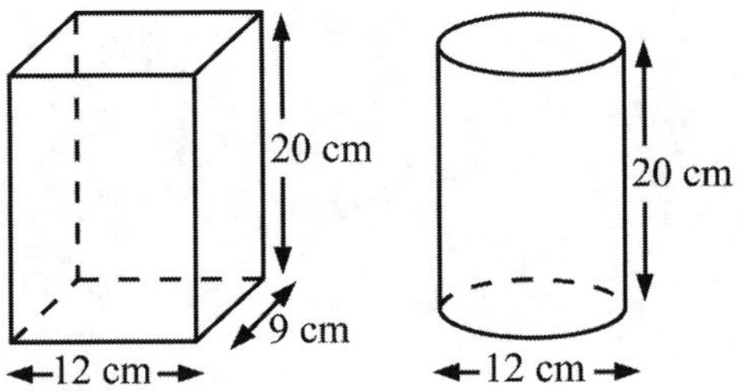

What is the volume of the container that holds more peanuts?

F. 2 160 cm^3

G. 2 262 cm^3

H. 3 770 cm^3

J. 9 048 cm^3

OPEN-RESPONSE

28. Waterworks

A conical container and a cylindrical container are shown.

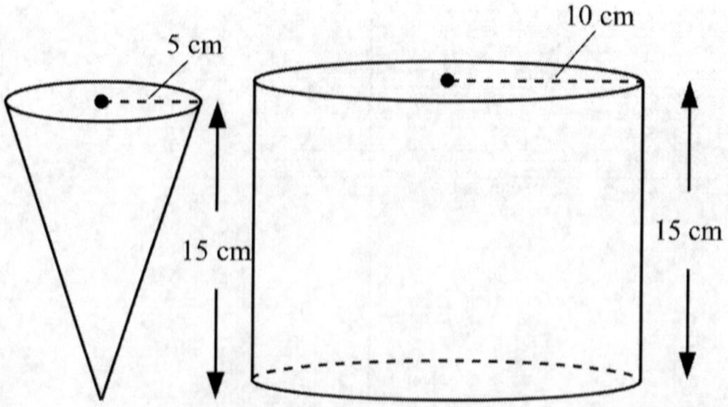

Jessie examined both containers and stated that it would take 6 conical containers of water to fill the cylindrical container. Carrie Ann also examined both containers and stated that it would take 12 conical containers of water to fill the cylindrical container.

Which person made the correct statement? Justify your answer.

29. *ABCD* is a quadrilateral.

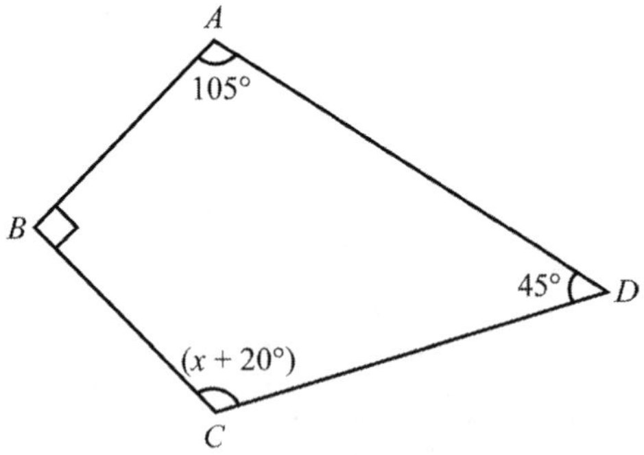

What is the value of x?

A. 100°

B. 120°

C. 130°

D. 140°

30 Robert was designing a piece of metal *ABCDEF* for his project. On his design, he had three parallel lines as shown.

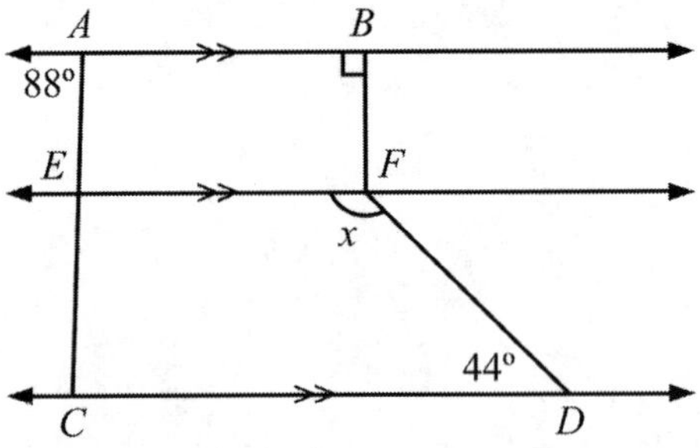

What is the value of x?

F. 88°

G. 92°

H. 136°

J. 180°

OPEN-RESPONSE

31. Bridge Building

A portion of a bridge truss is shown, where the top and bottom girders AB and CD are parallel.

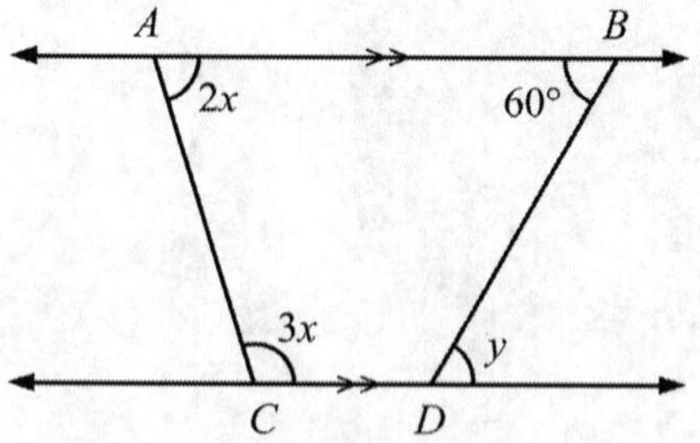

Determine the values of x and y. Show your work.

ANSWERS AND SOLUTIONS—PRACTICE TEST 2

1. B	9. OR	17. G	25. G
2. H	10. H	18. OR	26. A
3. B	11. B	19. C	27. G
4. H	12. J	20. J	28. OR
5. OR	13. A	21. A	29. A
6. C	14. OR	22. F	30. H
7. J	15. G	23. OR	31. OR
8. B	16. A	24. C	

1. B

The ratio of cupcakes to sugar in Rachel's recipe is 16:132, and the ratio of cupcakes to sugar, n, in Tina's recipe is 24:n. The correct representation of this relationship as a proportion is $\frac{16}{132}=\frac{24}{n}$.

2. H

Using the process of equivalent ratios or the cross-product rule enables you to find the number of pages, n, in the cookbook.

Equivalent Ratios	
$\frac{2}{15}=\frac{n}{420}$	Multiply by a number(s) to make the denominators equal.
$\frac{2\times 28}{15\times 28}=\frac{n}{420}$	Multiply each term in the left ratio by 28.
$\frac{56}{420}=\frac{n}{420}$ $n=56$	The denominators are equal, so the numerators must also be equal.
Cross-Product Rule	
$\frac{2}{15}=\frac{n}{420}$	
$(2)(420)=(15)(n)$	Use the cross-product rule.
$\frac{(2)(420)}{15}=\frac{(15)(n)}{15}$	Divide both sides by 15.
$56=n$	
$n=56$	Realign the equation.

There are 56 pages in the cookbook.

3. B

The height of the CN Tower in the photograph is 2.77 cm.
The scale is 1:20 000, so you must multiply 2.77 by 20 000 to get the actual height of the CN Tower.
Let x be the actual height of the tower.
$x = 2.77 \times 20\ 000$
$x = 55\ 400$ cm
Since 100 cm = 1 m, convert 55 400 cm to metres by dividing by 100.
$55\ 400 \div 100 = 554$ m.
The actual height of the CN Tower is 554 m.

4. H

Calculate the number of people who agreed that the Federal Government should do more about global warming in each year, n.

$$2006:\ n = 50\% \times 1\ 000 = \left(\frac{50}{100}\right)(1\ 000)$$
$$= \frac{50\ 000}{100} = 500$$
$$2008:\ n = 56\% \times 1\ 000 = \left(\frac{56}{100}\right)(1\ 000)$$
$$= \frac{56\ 000}{100} = 560$$

Now, subtract the two values to get the difference.
$560 - 500 = 60$
In 2008, 60 more people agreed that the Federal Government should do more about global warming than in 2006.

OR 5.

Calculate the earnings, E, for 35 h at a rate of \$15/h.

$$\begin{aligned} E &= 35\times 15 \\ &= \$525 \end{aligned}$$

Now, calculate the commission, C, earned on Chantelle's total sales of \$12 500 at a rate of 4%.

$$\begin{aligned} C &= 4\% \times 12\ 500 \\ &= \frac{4}{100}\times 12\ 500 \\ &= \frac{50\ 000}{100} \\ &= \$500 \end{aligned}$$

Chantelle's total earnings for the week are \$525 + \$500 = \$1 025.

6. C

The first two steps show correct processes.

$$-3\left(\frac{3}{4}\right)^3 - 2\left(\frac{3}{4}\right)^2$$

$$-3\left(\frac{3}{4}\right)\left(\frac{3}{4}\right)\left(\frac{3}{4}\right) - 2\left(\frac{3}{4}\right)\left(\frac{3}{4}\right)$$

In step 3, Tristan should have multiplied by –3 and 2 to each set of powers to get

$$\begin{aligned} &\left(\frac{-3\times 3}{4}\right)\left(\frac{3}{4}\right)\left(\frac{3}{4}\right) - \left(\frac{2\times 3}{4}\right)\left(\frac{3}{4}\right) \\ &= \left(\frac{-9}{4}\right)\left(\frac{3}{4}\right)\left(\frac{3}{4}\right) - \left(\frac{6}{4}\right)\left(\frac{3}{4}\right) \\ &= \frac{-81}{64} - \frac{18}{16}. \end{aligned}$$

Tristan's first error occurred in step 3.

7. J

In the diagram, the top row has two shaded x-tiles representing $2x$ plus a shaded 1-tile representing 1, resulting in the expression $2x + 1$. The left column has one shaded x-tile representing x. The product of these two expressions is represented by $x(2x+1)$.

8. B

Substitute the values of 605 for A, 20 for a, and 35 for b, then solve for h.

$$\begin{aligned} 2A &= ha + bh \\ 2(605) &= h(20) + h(35) \\ 1\ 210 &= 20h + 35h \quad \text{Collect like terms.} \\ 1\ 210 &= 55h \\ \frac{1\ 210}{55} &= \frac{55h}{55} \quad \text{Divide both sides by 55.} \\ 22 &= h \end{aligned}$$

The height, h, is 22 m.

OR 9.

The border of Carla's garden represents the perimeter, P, which is the sum of all sides.

$P = x + x + 1 + x + 3x - 2$

Collect like terms

$P - (x + x + x + 3x) + (1 - 2)$

$P = (1+1+1+3)x + (-1)$

$P = 6x - 1$

Now, substitute 17 m for P, and solve for x.

$17 = 6x - 1$

Add 1 to both sides

$17 + 1 = 6x - 1 + 1$

$18 = 6x$

Divide both sides by 6

$\frac{18}{6} = \frac{6x}{6}$

$3 = x$

Finally, determine all four dimensions by substituting 3 for x.

Two sides: $x = 3$

op length: $x + 1 = 3 + 1 = 4$

Bottom length:

$$\begin{aligned} &3x - 2 \\ &= 3(3) - 2 \\ &= 9 - 2 \\ &= 7 \end{aligned}$$

The dimensions of Carla's garden are 3 m, 4 m, 3 m, and 7 m.

10. H

The point on the graph representing the most points scored by the player is the point with the highest y-value, namely 9. This point occurs when the x-value is 13, which represents the number of foul shots taken.

The point is (13, 9).

11. B

As illustrated in the table, as the unit cost increases from 120 to 225, the number sold decreases from 31 to 11.

12. J

Based on the window settings for the graph, the first point has an x-value of -4 and a y-value of 3. These values are represented in tables H and J. For every increase of 2 units for the value of x, the values of y increase by a constant amount of 1.5. The point on the y-axis has an x-value of 0 and a y-value of 6.
These points are correctly represented in the table in alternative **J**.

13. A

For every increase of 1 unit for the values of x, the values of y increase by a constant amount of 3. This represents a linear relationship, where y increases by a constant amount as x increases.

OR 14.

To determine whether the relationship between the cooling time in minutes and the temperature in degrees Celsius is linear, you must find the first differences.

Time (min)	**Temperature (°C)**	**First Differences**
0	65.6	—
1	62.4	$62.4-65.6=-3.2$
2	59.2	$59.2-62.4=-3.2$
3	56.4	$56.4-59.2=-2.8$
4	53.7	$53.7-56.4=-2.7$
5	51.2	$51.2-53.7=-2.5$
6	48.7	$48.7-51.2=-2.5$

In a linear relationship, the first differences are the same. Since the first differences are not the same, this relationship is non-linear.

15. G

The constant rate of change on the graph is -10. For every increase in 2 hours, there is a decrease in 20 km/h or -20 km/h.

The rate of change $= \dfrac{\text{rise}}{\text{run}} = \dfrac{-20}{2} = -10$.

The initial value of the graph is 120. Therefore, the equation representing this change is $v = 120 - 10t$, where -10 represents the constant rate of change and 120 represents the initial value of the graph.

16. A

The constant rate of change is 20 pairs of shoes every 5 hours, or $\dfrac{20}{5} = 4$ pairs of shoes every hour. The constant rate of change is 4.
The equation relating the number of pairs of shoes sold, p, and the time in hours, t, is $p = 4t$.

17. G

The equation $y = 20x$ represents a constant rate of change of 20. If x represents the number of DVDs purchased, then \$20 represents the constant rate of change relative to the total cost, y, in dollars.
For every DVD, x, purchased, the total cost, y, in dollars increases at a constant rate of \$20.

OR 18.

In direct variation, the linear relation has a constant rate of change and the relation has an initial value of 0. The rate at Steve's Car Service is a direct variation, since the constant rate of change is \$45/h. For every increase of 1 h of service, the fee goes up \$45. The initial value is 0, since there is no fixed rate for 0 h of service.
In a partial variation, the linear relation has a constant rate of change and the relation has an initial value other than 0. The rate at Cal's Automotive Service is a partial variation, since the constant rate of change is \$40/h. For every increase of 1 h of service, the fee goes up by \$40/h. The initial value is \$45, since the fixed rate for 0 h service is \$45.

19. C

Substitute 9.2 for S into the equation and solve for m, the number of mistakes made by the first gymnast.

$$S = 10 - 0.1m$$
$$9.2 = 10 - 0.1m$$
Subtract 10 from both sides
$$9.2 - 10 = 10 - 10 - 0.1m$$
$$-0.8 = -0.1m$$
Divide both sides by -0.1
$$\frac{-0.8}{-0.1} = \frac{-0.1m}{-0.1}$$
$$8 = m$$

The first gymnast made eight mistakes.
Now, substitute 8.2 for S into the equation, and solve for the number of mistakes made by the second gymnast.

$$S = 10 - 0.1m$$
$$8.2 = 10 - 0.1m$$
Subtract 10 from both sides
$$8.2 - 10 = 10 - 10 - 0.1m$$
$$-1.8 = -0.1m$$
Divide both sides by -0.1
$$\frac{-1.8}{-0.1} = \frac{-0.1m}{-0.1}$$
$$18 = m$$

The second gymnast made 18 mistakes.
The difference in the number of mistakes made by the two gymnasts is $18 - 8 = 10$.

20. J

The rate at which the money collected increases with respect to the number of rentals is \$15/rental. This is determined by taking two pairs of values to find the rise and the run.
Rise = 90, since 170 – 80 = 90.
Run = 6, since 10 – 4 = 6.

The constant rate of change $= \frac{\text{rise}}{\text{run}} = \frac{90}{6} = 15$.

The constant rate of change can then be entered as the coefficient of n, including the unknown initial value of b. $C = 15n + b$.

Substitute any pair of data values to determine the initial value (fixed deposit).
For example, $n = 22$ and $C = 350$

$$C = 15n + b$$
$$350 = 15(22) + b$$
$$350 = 330 + b$$
$$350 - 330 = 330 - 330 + b$$
$$20 = b$$
$$b = 20$$

The fixed deposit is \$20, and the rental rate is \$15/ski rental, resulting in the equation $C = 15n + 20$.

21. A

Hiker A travels up the mountain at a faster rate than Hiker B. This is visible on the graph as the steeper line representing Hiker A compared to the line representing Hiker B.
Also, after hiking for 7 h, Hiker A is farther away (3.2 km) from the base camp than Hiker B (2.8 km).

22. F

On the graph, the lines intersect at the point (6, 400). This point represents a walking time of six minutes and a distance from home of 400 m. Since the point represents both lines, boys A and B are walking together when they are 400 m from home.

OR 23.

Determine the length, l, in metres of fencing for each person's fence, costing $C = \$800$ and $C = \$980$, respectively.

Mr. Gladwin	**Process**
$C = 200 + 15l$ $800 = 200 + 15l$	Substitute values for C.
$800 - 200 = 200 - 200 + 15l$	Subtract 200 from both sides.
$600 = 15l$ $\frac{600}{15} = \frac{15l}{15}$	Divide both sides by 15.
$40 = l$ $l = 40$	Realign equation.

Mrs. Chadwick	**Process**
$C = 200 + 15l$ $980 = 200 + 15l$	Substitute values for C.
$980 - 200 = 200 - 200 + 15l$	Subtract 200 from both sides.
$780 = 15l$ $\frac{780}{15} = \frac{15l}{15}$	Divide both sides by 15.
$52 = l$ $l = 52$	Realign equation.

Mr. Gladwin's fence is 40 m long, and
Mrs. Chadwick's fence is 52 m long.
52 – 40 = 12 m
Mrs. Chadwick's fence is 12 m longer than Mr. Gladwin's fence.

24. C

The smallest possible perimeter, *P*, for a given area, *A*, occurs when the length, *l*, is equal to the width, $w(l = w)$.

$$A = (l)(w)$$
$$A = (w)(w) \quad \text{Replace } l \text{ with } w.$$
$$A = w^2$$
$$\sqrt{A} = w$$
$$w = \sqrt{A} \quad \text{Substitute 900 for } A.$$
$$w = \sqrt{900}$$
$$w = l = 30 \text{ m}$$
$$P = 2(l + w)$$
$$= 2(30 + 30)$$
$$= 2(60)$$
$$= 120 \text{ m}$$

The smallest possible perimeter of this rectangle is 120 m.

25. G

According to the Pythagorean Theorem,
Area C = Area A + Area B.
Since the area of a square is $A = s^2$,

$$z^2 = x^2 + y^2$$
$$100 = x^2 + 36$$
$$x^2 = 100 - 36$$
$$x^2 = 64$$
$$x = \sqrt{64}$$
$$x = 8 \text{ cm}$$

The length of side *x* is 8 cm.

26. A

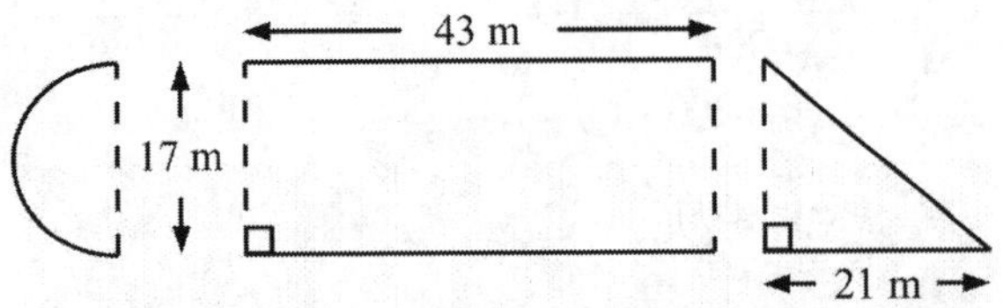

Find the area of this figure by finding the areas of each of the individual shapes.

$$A_{\text{total}} = A_{\text{semicircle}} + A_{\text{rectangle}} + A_{\text{triangle}}$$

Step 1: Find $A_{\text{semicircle}}$

The radius of the circle is $\frac{1}{2}$ the diameter; therefore, $(r) = \frac{17}{2} = 8.5$ m.

$$A_{\text{semicircle}} = \frac{A_{\text{circle}}}{2}$$
$$= \frac{\pi r^2}{2}$$
$$= \frac{\pi(8.5)^2}{2}$$
$$= \frac{\pi(72.25)}{2}$$
$$\approx 113.49 \text{ m}^2$$

Step 2: Find $A_{\text{rectangle}}$

$$A_{\text{rectangle}} = (l)(w)$$
$$= (17)(43)$$
$$= 731 \text{ m}^2$$

Step 3: Find A_{triangle}

$$A_{\text{triangle}} = \frac{1}{2}bh$$
$$= \frac{1}{2}(21)(17)$$
$$= 178.5 \text{ m}^2$$

Step 4: Find A_{total}

$$A_{\text{total}} = A_{\text{semicircle}} + A_{\text{rectangle}} + A_{\text{triangle}}$$
$$= 113.49 + 731 + 178.5$$
$$A_{\text{total}} = 1\,022.99 \text{ m}^2$$

To the nearest square metre, the area of the entire figure is 1 023 m^2.

27. G

The volume of the prism container is

$$V_{\text{prism}} = lwh$$
$$= (12)(9)(20)$$
$$= 2\,160 \text{ cm}^3$$

The volume of the cylinder container is

$$V_{\text{cylinder}} = \pi r^2 h, \text{ where } r = \frac{d}{2} = \frac{12}{2} = 6 \text{ cm}$$
$$= \pi(6)^2(20)$$
$$= \pi(36)(20)$$
$$= 2\,262 \text{ cm}^3$$

The cylindrical container holds more peanuts, since it has a greater volume of 2 262 cm^3.

OR 28.

Determine the volume of each container. To find the volume, V, of the conical container, substitute 5 cm for r and 15 cm for h into the following formula:

$$\begin{aligned} V_{\text{cone}} &= \frac{1}{3}\pi r^2 h \\ &= \frac{1}{3}\pi(5)^2(15) \\ &= \frac{1}{3}\pi(5)(5)(15) \\ &\approx 392.699\text{ cm}^3 \end{aligned}$$

Now, find the volume, V, of the cylindrical container by substituting 10 cm for r and 15 cm for h.

$$\begin{aligned} V_{\text{cylinder}} &= \pi r^2 h \\ &= \pi(10)^2(15) \\ &= \pi(10)(10)(15) \\ &\approx 4\ 712.389\text{ cm}^3 \end{aligned}$$

Finally, determine the number, n, of conical containers of water that would fill the cylindrical container by dividing their volumes.

$$n = \frac{V_{\text{cylinder}}}{V_{\text{cone}}} = \frac{4\ 712.389}{392.699}$$

$$n = 12.0000$$

Carrie Ann is correct. It takes 12 conical containers of water to fill the cylindrical container.

29. A

The sum of the measures of the interior angles of an n-sided polygon is

$$\begin{aligned} S &= 180°(n-2) \\ &= 180°(4-2) \\ &= 180°(2) \\ &= 360° \end{aligned}$$

The sum of the measures of the interior angles of a quadrilateral is 360°. Now, equate the angle expressions to 360°, and solve for the value of x.

$$\begin{aligned} (x+20°)+45°+105°+90° &= 360° \\ x+20°+240° &= 360° \\ x+260° &= 360° \end{aligned}$$

Subtract 260° from both sides:

$$\begin{aligned} x+260°-260° &= 360°-260° \\ x &= 100° \end{aligned}$$

The value of x is 100°.

30. H

$\angle AEF$ is an alternate interior angle of 88°. Alternate interior angles are equal.

$\angle AEF = 88°$

$\angle FEC$ and $\angle AEF$ form a straight line, so

$\angle FEC + \angle AEF = 180°$

$\angle FEC + 88° = 180°$

Subtract 88° from both sides:

$\angle FEC + 88° - 88° = 180° - 88°$

$\angle FEC = 92°$

$\angle AEF$ is a corresponding angle to $\angle ECD$, and since corresponding angles are equal, $\angle ECD = 88°$.

ECDF is a quadrilateral, so the sum of the measures of the interior angles is equal to 360°.

$$\begin{aligned} \angle x + 44° + 88° + 92° &= 360° \\ \angle x + 224° &= 360° \end{aligned}$$

Subtract 224° from both sides:

$$\begin{aligned} \angle x + 224° - 224° &= 360° - 224° \\ \angle x &= 136° \end{aligned}$$

The value of x is 136°.

OR 31.

Angle B (60°) and $\angle y$ are alternate interior angles. Alternate interior angles are equal; therefore, $\angle y = 60°$, $\angle 2x$, and $\angle 3x$ form co-interior angles.

Co-interior angles are supplementary.

$$\begin{aligned} 2x+3x &= 180° \\ 5x &= 180° \\ \frac{5x}{5} &= \frac{180°}{5} \quad \text{Divide both sides by 5} \\ x &= 36° \end{aligned}$$

The value of $\angle x = 36°$, and the value of $\angle y = 60°$.

NOTES

Appendices

GLOSSARY OF TERMS

algebra tiles: Manipulatives used to assist students in their understanding of algebraic expressions and equations.

alternate interior angles: Angles diagonal to one another about the transversal. These angles have the same measure.

altitude: A perpendicular line segment from the base of a figure to the opposite side or vertex.

area: The space within a region measured in square units.

axis: Either of the number lines on a graph that intersect at the origin.

base: The side or face of a polygon or solid from which an altitude rises.

base of a power: The number in a power used as a factor for multiplication (see exponent). In the power 9^3, the base is 9.

BEDMAS or PEDMAS: An acronym for Brackets or Parenthesis, Exponents, Division, Multiplication, Addition, Subtraction that designates the order of operations.

capacity: The greatest amount a container can hold.

circumference: The measure of the distance around a circle $C = \pi d$ or $C = 2\pi r$.

coefficient (numerical): The numerical part of a term that determines the factor by which the variable is multiplied. In $13x$, the numerical coefficient is 13.

coefficient (variable): The variable part of a term that determines the factor by which the numerical portion is multiplied. In $13x$, the variable coefficient is x.

co-interior angles: The two angles between the parallel lines on each side of the transversal. The measures of these angles are supplementary. The sum of their measures is equal to 180°.

common denominator: A number that is a multiple of all the denominators of a set of fractions.

common multiple: A number that is the multiple of two or more numbers.

complementary angles: Two angles that have a sum of exactly 90°.

composite two-dimensional shape: Any number of two-dimensional shapes connected with each other in some way.

cone: A solid formed by the convergence of points from a circular base.

constant rate of change: The amount that the y-variable changes with respect to a change in the x-variable of the relation.

coordinate plane: a two-dimensional surface across which a number line extends horizontally (x-axis) and is intersected by a number line extending vertically (y-axis).

coordinates: The numbers on a coordinate plane that signify the value of x and the value of y for a given point on the plane.

corresponding angles: Angles connected to the parallel lines on each side of the transversal. These angles have the same measure.

cube: A solid with six square faces.

curve of best fit: A curve that passes as close as possible to points plotted on a non-linear graph.

cylinder: A solid with two parallel congruent circular bases.

data: Facts, statistics, or bits of information.

database: An organized collection of data.

degree of a term: The sum of the exponents of its variables. If there is no exponent, the exponent is one.

denominator: The term below the line in a fraction by which the numerator is divided (see numerator).

diagonal: A line connecting two non-adjacent vertices of a figure.

diameter: The longest distance connecting two points on a circle and passing through the origin.

direct proportion: The relation between two quantities whose ratio remains constant and the graph passes through the origin.

direct variation: A linear relation that has a constant rate of change between the variables x and y, and the graph of this relation passes through the origin.

distributive property: The product of a number and a sum is equal to the sum of the individual products of addends and the number.
$a(b + c) = ab + cd$

equation: An algebraic statement equating two or more related variables.

equivalent ratios: Ratios that mean the same thing, but with different numbers for terms.

evaluate: To find the value of an expression by substituting values for variables.

exponent: A notation indicating the number of times a quantity is multiplied by itself. For example, 2 is the exponent in 6^2 (see base of a power.)

exterior angles of a triangle: The sum of the measures of the exterior angles of a triangle is 360°.

exterior angles of a polygon: The sum of the measures of the exterior angles of any polygon is 360°.

extrapolation: Used to find values outside of the given data points or line. Extend the line and read up from the x-axis to the line and read across to the y-axis.

face: Any surface of a solid.

factor: Numbers or expressions that are multiplied to form another number or expression.

first differences: The difference between consecutive y-values, with evenly spaced x-values.

first-degree equations: Mathematical statements containing an equal sign between two polynomials, where each term cannot have a degree greater than 1.

fixed value: The initial value in a variation.

fraction: An indicated quotient of two quantities that represent part of a whole or a group.

greatest common factor (GCF): The largest factor common to two or more numbers.

GST (Goods and Services Tax): In Canada, it is 5%.

hypotenuse: The side of a right triangle that is opposite the right angle.

hypothesis: An educated guess or statement about the relationship between two variables.

inference: A conclusion reached by reasoning, based on the information given.

initial value: See vertical intercept.

interior angles of a polygon: For any polygon with n sides, the sum, S, of the measures of its interior angles is $S = 180°(n - 2)$.

interior angles of a triangle: The sum of the measures of the interior angles of a triangle is 180°.

interpolation: Used to find values within the given data points or line.
Read up from the x-axis to the line and across to the y-axis.

intersecting lines: Lines with one point in common (the point of intersection).

like terms: Terms that have the exact same variables with identical exponents.

line of best fit: A line that passes as close as possible to points plotted on a graph.

linear relation: A relation that has a constant rate of change and can be represented by a straight line.

lowest common denominator (LCD): The lowest of all multiples shared by two or more numbers.

monomial: A polynomial with only one term.

multiplying monomials: Multiply the numerical coefficients together, and combine like variables by adding their respective exponents

$$(6x)\left(3x^2\right) = (6\times3)(x)\left(x^2\right) = 18x^3.$$

numerator: The term above the line in a fraction into which the denominator is divided.

one-dimensional: The length of a line segment is a one-dimensional quantity and a first-degree term.

operation: Any mathematical process or action such as addition, subtraction, multiplication, or division.

ordered pair: A pair of numbers, (x, y), showing the coordinates of a point on a graph.

origin: The point of intersection of the horizontal and vertical axes on a graph; defined as (0, 0).

parallel lines: Lines in the same plane that are equal distance apart.

partial relation: A relationship between two variables wherein their ratio remains constant, but the line does not pass through the origin

partial variation: A linear relation that has a constant rate of change between the variables x and y; however, the line does not pass through the origin.

percent (%): A fraction or ratio with a denominator of 100.

perimeter: The measure of the distance around a closed figure.

perpendicular: Intersecting at a 90° angle.

pi (π): The ratio of the circumference of a circle to its diameter.

point of intersection: Where two lines representing two different conditions for the same real-life context intersect. At this point, the x-variable and the y-variables for both lines are equal.

polygon: A closed two-dimensional figure of three or more line segments.

polynomial: An algebraic expression that consists of one or more terms connected with addition or subtraction signs.

power: Notation of a number with a base and an exponent (see base and exponent) such as *an*, where *a* is called the base and *n* is called the exponent.

predict: To state, tell about, or make known in advance.

prism: A solid formed by two congruent and parallel sides and other faces that are parallelograms (see face).

proportional relationship: Relationships between two equal ratios.
When one set of data increases or decreases in a linear pattern and the other set of data increases or decreases in a similar pattern.

proportion: Two equal ratios.

PST (Provincial Sales Tax): In Ontario, it is 8%.

pyramid: A solid that has one face that is a polygon (the base) and triangular faces that have a vertex.

Pythagorean theorem: For any right triangle, the area of the square formed on the longest side is equal to the sum of the areas of the squares formed on the other two sides ($a^2 + b^2 = c^2$).

quadrilateral: Any polygon with four sides.

radicand: The number whose square root is being taken.

radius (plural: radii): The distance from the centre of a circle to any point lying on the circumference of the circle (see diameter).

rate: A certain quantity or amount relative to a different quantity or amount.

rate of change of linear relations:

$$\text{rate of change} = \frac{\text{rise}}{\text{run}}$$

ratio: A comparison of two or more numbers with the same units.

reciprocals: Two numbers that have a product of 1.

regular polygon: A polygon with equal sides and angles.

relation: Any set of ordered pairs.

rise: The vertical change between two points.

run: The horizontal change between two points.

scatter plot: A graph of points displaying the data of two variables.
The points are plotted as ordered pairs on a coordinate plane.

scenario: A sequence of possible events.

slope of a line: The rate at which the y-values of a point of a line on a coordinate plane change with respect to a change in the x-values. $\text{slope} = \frac{\text{rise}}{\text{run}}$

square of a number: Any number multiplied by itself.

square root: For any product, the factor that is multiplied by itself to get the product. For the product 16, the one factor that is multiplied by itself is +4 or –4, so ±4 are the square roots of 16.

stat edit: A feature on a graphing calculator that allows you to access and make lists. On your calculator: stat→enter→edit

substitution: When a specific value is used in place of a variable in an algebraic expression.

supplementary angles: Two angles whose sum is exactly 180°.

term: Each individual expression in a polynomial or expression. Terms are separated by addition or subtraction signs within an algebraic expression.

three-dimensional (3D): Volume is a three-dimensional quantity and a third-degree term (cm^3) having length, width, and depth or height.

transversal: A line that intersects two or more parallel lines.

two-dimensional (2D): Area is a two-dimensional quantity and a second-degree term (cm^2) having length and width.

unit rate: The rate for a single unit or item.

unlike terms: Terms that have either different variables or different exponents.

variable: A letter or symbol that represents a changing quantity.

vertex (plural: vertices): The point of convergence of two or more lines or sides in a figure or solid.

vertical intercept: The value of the dependent variable y when the value of the independent variable x is zero.

vertically-opposite angles: Angles across two intersecting lines. These angles have the same measure.

volume: The amount of space occupied by an object measured in cubic units.

***x*-axis:** The horizontal number line on a coordinate plane.

***y*-axis:** The vertical number line on a coordinate plane.

FORMULA SHEET

Two-Dimensional Shape	Diagram	Perimeter Formula	Area Formula
Quadrilateral	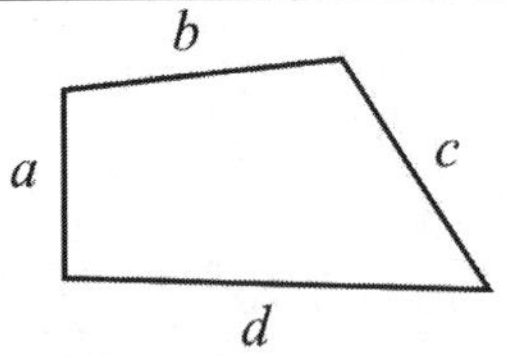	$P = a + b + c + d$	——
Trapezoid	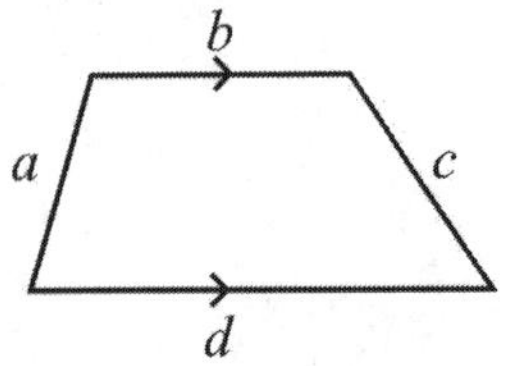	$P = a + b + c + d$	$A = \left(\frac{b+d}{2}\right)(h)$
Isosceles trapezoid	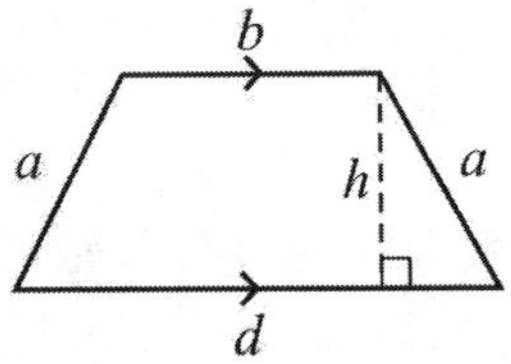	$P = a + a + b + d$	$A = \left(\frac{b+d}{2}\right)(h)$
Parallelogram	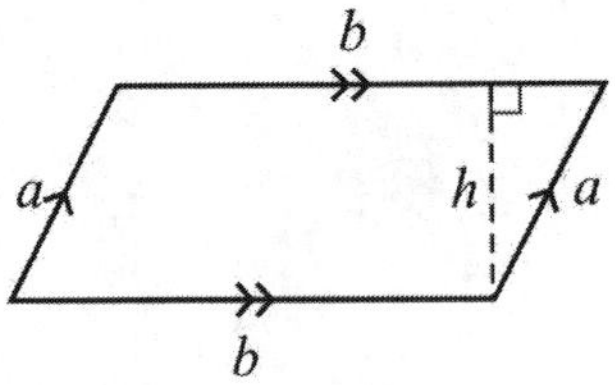	$P = 2a + 2b$	$A = (b)(h)$
Rhombus	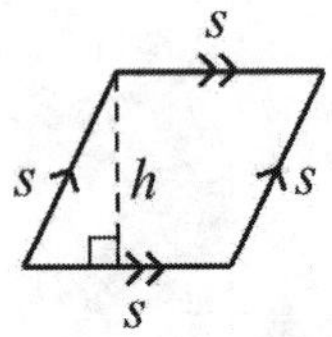	$P = 4s$	$A = (s)(h)$
Rectangle	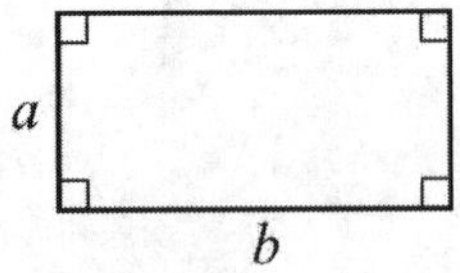	$P = 2l + 2w$ $P = 2(a + b)$	$A = (l)(w)$ $A = (a)(b)$
Square	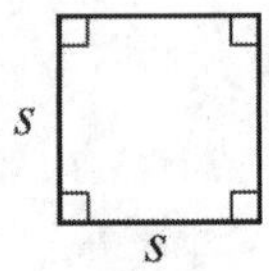	$P = 4s$	$A = s^2$
Scalene triangle	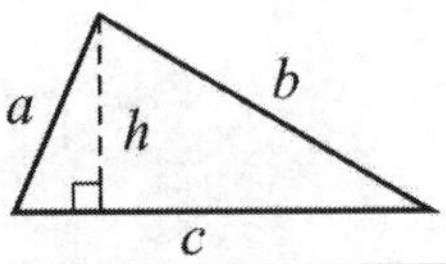	$P = a + b + c$	$A = \frac{(c)(h)}{2}$

Two-Dimensional Shape	Diagram	Perimeter Formula	Area Formula
Isosceles triangle	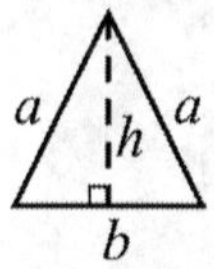	$P = 2a + b$	$A = \frac{(b)(h)}{2}$
Equilateral triangle	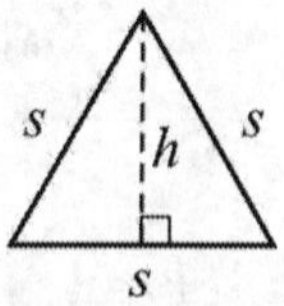	$P = 3s$	$A = \frac{(s)(h)}{2}$
Right triangle	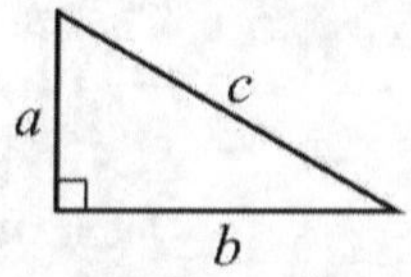	$P = a + b + c$	$A = \frac{(a)(b)}{2}$
Isosceles right triangle	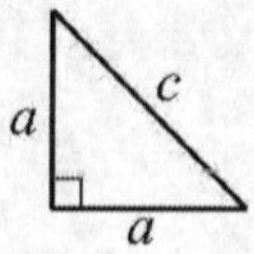	$P = 2a + c$	$A = \frac{a^2}{2}$
Circle	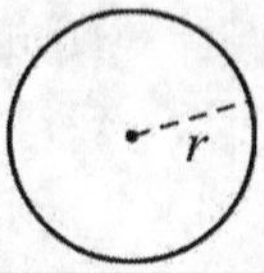	P(circumference) = $2\pi r$	$A = \pi r^2$

Three-Dimensional Shape	Diagram	Volume Formula
Rectangular prism	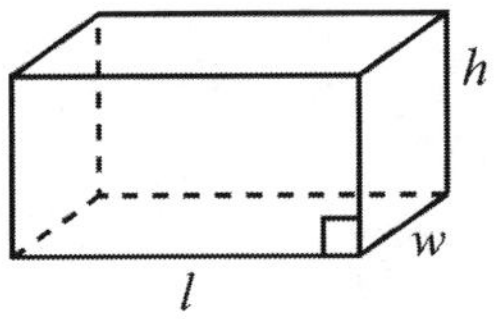	$V_{\text{prism}} = (\text{area of base})(\text{height})$ $V_{\text{prism}} = lwh$
Triangular prism	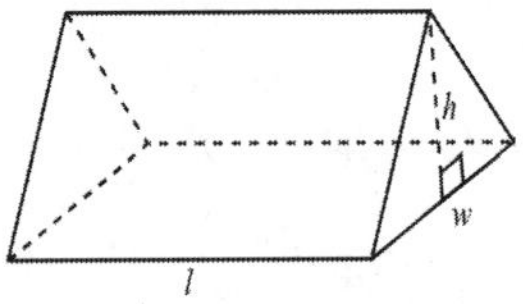	$V_{\text{triangular prism}} = \frac{(\text{area of base})(\text{height})}{2}$ $V_{\text{triangular prism}} = \frac{1}{2}lwh$ or $\frac{lwh}{2}$
Square-based pyramid	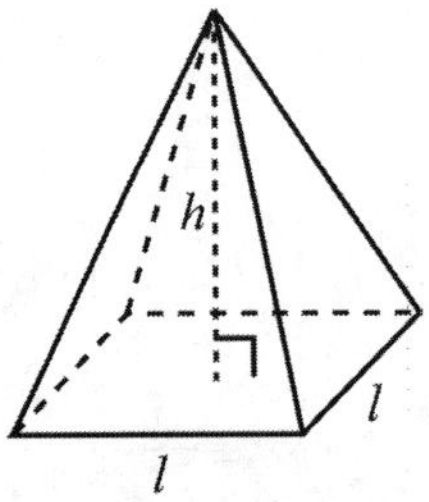	$V_{\text{pyramid}} = \frac{(\text{area of base})(\text{height})}{3}$ $V_{\text{pyramid}} = \frac{1}{3}l^2h$ or $\frac{l^2h}{3}$
Cylinder	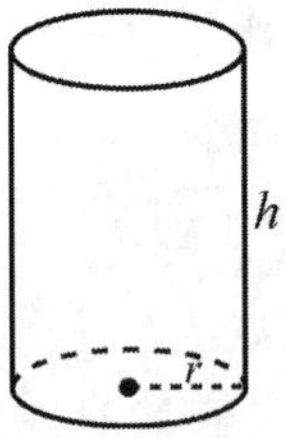	$V_{\text{cylinder}} = (\text{area of base})(\text{height})$ $V_{\text{cylinder}} = \pi r^2 h$
Cone	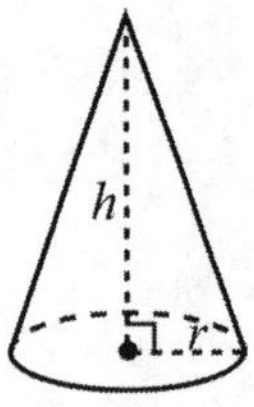	$V_{\text{cone}} = \frac{(\text{area of base})(\text{height})}{3}$ $V_{\text{cone}} = \frac{1}{3}\pi r^2 h$ or $\frac{\pi r^2 h}{3}$
Sphere	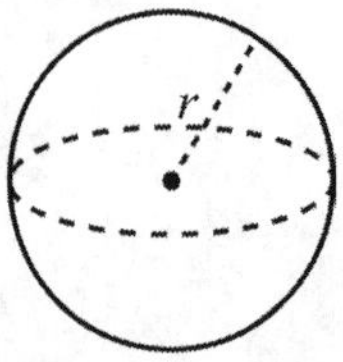	$V_{\text{sphere}} = \frac{4}{3}\pi r^3$ or $\frac{4\pi r^3}{3}$

CREDITS

Every effort has been made to provide proper acknowledgement of the original source and to comply with copyright law. However, some attempts to establish original copyright ownership may have been unsuccessful. If copyright ownership can be identified, please notify Castle Rock Research Corp so that appropriate corrective action can be taken.

Some images in this document are from www.clipart.com, © 2013 Clipart.com, a division of Getty Images.

NOTES

NOTES

NOTES

Student Notes and Problems
Workbook
Ordering Information

Student Notes and Problems (SNAP) Workbooks contain complete explanations of curriculum concepts, including examples and practice exercises

SNAP Workbook—$29.95 each plus applicable sales tax

Ontario SNAP Titles
Physics 12, University Preparation (SPH4U)
Physics 11, University Preparation (SPH3U)
Math 10, Academic, Principles of Mathematics (MPM2D)
Math 9, Academic, Principles of Mathematics (MPM1D)
Math 9, Applied, Foundations of Mathematics (MFM1P)

Total Cost

SOLARO Study Guides Ordered ________

SNAP Books Ordered ________

Cost Subtotal ________

Shipping and Handling
Please call for current rates ________

GST ________

Order Total ________

Payment and Shipping Information

Name ________

School ________

Telephone ________

SHIP TO:

School Code ________

School Name ________

Address ________

City: ________

Postal Code: ________

PAYMENT OPTIONS:

☐ By Credit Care VISA/MC

Name on Card: ________

Number: ________

Expirely Date: ________

☐ By Enclosed Cheque

☐ Invoice School

PO Number: ________

To order books, please visit
www.castlerockresearch.com

Volume pricing is available. Contact us at
orders@castlerockresearch.com